Ethics
&
Politics
By Aristotle

Devoted Publishing
Woodstock, Ontario, 2017

ETHICS & POLITICS
By Aristotle
Edited By Anthony Uyl

Ethics Translated and Originally Published By an Unknown Person and Publisher
Politics Translated From The Greek Of Aristotle By William Ellis, A.M.
Politics Originally Published By: London & Toronto Published By J M Dent & Sons Ltd. & In New York By E. P. Dutton &. Co. First Issue Of This Edition 1912 Reprinted 1919, 1923, 1928

The text of Ethics and Politics is all in the Public Domain. This edition is published by Devoted Publishing a division of 2165467 Ontario Inc.

What kind of philosophies do you have?
Let us know!

Contact us at: devotedpub@hotmail.com
Visit us on Facebook: @DevotedPublishing
Visit our webpage: www.devotedpublishing.com
Published in Woodstock, Ontario, Canada 2017.

ISBN: 978-1-77356-131-8

Table of Contents

Ethics

INTRODUCTION

The Ethics of Aristotle is one half of a single treatise of which his Politics is the other half. Both deal with one and the same subject. This subject is what Aristotle calls in one place the "philosophy of human affairs;" but more frequently Political or Social Science. In the two works taken together we have their author's whole theory of human conduct or practical activity, that is, of all human activity which is not directed merely to knowledge or truth. The two parts of this treatise are mutually complementary, but in a literary sense each is independent and self-contained. The proem to the Ethics is an introduction to the whole subject, not merely to the first part; the last chapter of the Ethics points forward to the Politics, and sketches for that part of the treatise the order of enquiry to be pursued (an order which in the actual treatise is not adhered to).

The principle of distribution of the subject-matter between the two works is far from obvious, and has been much debated. Not much can be gathered from their titles, which in any case were not given to them by their author. Nor do these titles suggest any very compact unity in the works to which they are applied: the plural forms, which survive so oddly in English (Ethics, Politics), were intended to indicate the treatment within a single work of a group of connected questions. The unity of the first group arises from their centring round the topic of character, that of the second from their connection with the existence and life of the city or state. We have thus to regard the Ethics as dealing with one group of problems and the Politics with a second, both falling within the wide compass of Political Science. Each of these groups falls into sub-groups which roughly correspond to the several books in each work. The tendency to take up one by one the various problems which had suggested themselves in the wide field obscures both the unity of the subject-matter and its proper articulation. But it is to be remembered that what is offered us is avowedly rather an enquiry than an exposition of hard and fast doctrine.

Nevertheless each work aims at a relative completeness, and it is important to observe the relation of each to the other. The distinction is not that the one treats of Moral and the other of Political Philosophy, nor again that the one deals with the moral activity of the individual and the other with that of the State, nor once more that the one gives us the theory of human conduct, while the other discusses its application in practice, though not all of these misinterpretations are equally erroneous. The clue to the right interpretation is given by Aristotle himself, where in the last chapter of the Ethics he is paving the way for the Politics. In the Ethics he has not confined himself to the abstract or isolated individual, but has always thought of him, or we might say, in his social and political context, with a given nature due to race and heredity and in certain surroundings. So viewing him he has studied the nature and formation of his character--all that he can make himself or be made by others to be. Especially he has investigated the various admirable forms of human character and the mode of their production. But all this, though it brings more clearly before us what goodness or virtue is, and how it is to be reached, remains mere theory or talk. By itself it does not enable us to become, or to help others to become, good. For this it is necessary to bring into play the great force of the Political Community or State, of which the main instrument is Law. Hence arises the demand for the necessary complement to the Ethics, i.e., a treatise devoted to the questions which centre round the enquiry; by what organisation of social or political forces, by what laws or institutions can we best secure the greatest amount of good character?

We must, however, remember that the production of good character is not the end of either individual or state action: that is the aim of the one and the other because good character is the indispensable condition and chief determinant of happiness, itself the goal of all human doing. The end of all action, individual or collective, is the greatest happiness of the greatest number. There is, Aristotle insists, no difference of kind between the good of one and the good of many or all. The sole difference is one of amount or scale. This does not mean simply that the State exists to secure in larger measure the objects of degree which the isolated individual attempts, but is too feeble, to secure without it. On the contrary, it rather insists that whatever goods society alone enables a man to secure have always had to the individual--whether he realised it or not--the value which, when so secured, he recognises them to possess. The best and happiest life for the individual is that which the State renders possible, and this it does mainly by revealing to him the value of new objects of desire and educating him to appreciate them. To Aristotle or to Plato the State is, above all, a large and powerful educative agency which gives the individual increased opportunities of self-development and greater capacities for the enjoyment of life.

Looking forward, then, to the life of the State as that which aids support, and combines the efforts of the individual to obtain happiness, Aristotle draws no hard and fast distinction between the spheres of action of Man as individual and Man as citizen. Nor does the division of his discussion into the Ethics and the Politics rest upon any such distinction. The distinction implied is rather between two stages in the life of the civilised man--the stage of preparation for the full life of the adult citizen, and the stage of the actual exercise or enjoyment of citizenship. Hence the Ethics, where his attention is directed upon the formation of character, is largely and centrally a treatise on Moral Education. It discusses especially those admirable human qualities which fit a man for life in an organised civic community, which makes him "a good citizen," and considers how they can be fostered or created and their opposites prevented.

This is the kernel of the Ethics, and all the rest is subordinate to this main interest and purpose. Yet "the rest" is not irrelevant; the whole situation in which character grows and operates is concretely conceived. There is a basis of what we should call Psychology, sketched in firm outlines, the deeper presuppositions and the wider issues of human character and conduct are not ignored, and there is no little of what we should call Metaphysics. But neither the Psychology nor the Metaphysics is elaborated, and only so much is brought forward as appears necessary to put the main facts in their proper perspective and setting. It is this combination of width of outlook with close observation of the concrete facts of conduct which gives its abiding value to the work, and justifies the view of it as containing Aristotle's Moral Philosophy. Nor is it Important merely as summing up the moral judgments and speculations of an age now long past. It seizes and dwells upon those elements and features in human practice which are most essential and permanent, and it is small wonder that so much in it survives in our own ways of regarding conduct and speaking of it. Thus it still remains one of the classics of Moral Philosophy, nor is its value likely soon to be exhausted.

As was pointed out above, the proem (Book I., cc. i-iii.) is a prelude to the treatment of the whole subject covered by the Ethics and the Politics together. It sets forth the purpose of the enquiry, describes the spirit in which it is to be undertaken and what ought to be the expectation of the reader, and lastly states the necessary conditions of studying it with profit. The aim of it is the acquisition and propagation of a certain kind of knowledge (science), but this knowledge and the thinking which brings it about are subsidiary to a practical end. The knowledge aimed at is of what is best for man and of the conditions of its realisation. Such knowledge is that which in its consumate form we find in great statesmen, enabling them to organise and administer their states and regulate by law the life of the citizens to their advantage and happiness, but it is the same kind of knowledge which on a smaller scale secures success in the management of the family or of private life.

It is characteristic of such knowledge that it should be deficient in "exactness," in precision of statement, and closeness of logical concatenation. We must not look for a mathematics of conduct. The subject-matter of Human Conduct is not governed by necessary and uniform laws. But this does not mean that it is subject to no laws. There are general principles at work in it, and these can be formulated in "rules," which rules can be systematised or unified. It is all-important to remember that practical or moral rules are only general and always admit of exceptions, and that they arise not from the mere complexity of the facts, but from the liability of the facts to a certain unpredictable variation. At their very best, practical rules state probabilities, not certainties; a relative constancy of connection is all that exists, but it is enough to serve as a guide in life. Aristotle here holds the balance between a misleading hope of reducing the subject-matter of conduct to a few simple rigorous abstract principles, with conclusions necessarily issuing from them, and the view that it is the field of operation of inscrutable forces acting without predictable regularity. He does not pretend to find in it absolute uniformities, or to deduce the details from his principles. Hence, too, he insists on the necessity of experience as the source or test of all that he has to say. Moral experience--the actual possession and exercise of good character-- is necessary truly to understand moral principles and profitably to apply them. The mere intellectual apprehension of them is not possible, or if possible, profitless.

The Ethics is addressed to students who are presumed both to have enough general education to appreciate these points, and also to have a solid foundation of good habits. More than that is not required for the profitable study of it.

If the discussion of the nature and formation of character be regarded as the central topic of the Ethics, the contents of Book I., cc. iv.-xii. may be considered as still belonging to the introduction and setting, but these chapters contain matter of profound importance and have exercised an enormous influence upon subsequent thought. They lay down a principle which governs all Greek thought about human life, viz. that it is only intelligible when viewed as directed towards some end or good. This is the Greek way of expressing that all human life involves an ideal element--something which it is not yet and which under certain conditions it is to be. In that sense Greek Moral Philosophy is essentially idealistic. Further it is always assumed that all human practical activity is directed or "oriented" to a single end, and that that end is knowable or definable in advance of its realisation. To know it is not merely a matter of speculative interest, it is of the highest practical moment for only in the light of it can life be duly guided, and particularly only so can the state be properly organised and administered. This explains the stress laid throughout by Greek Moral Philosophy upon the necessity of knowledge as a condition of the best life. This knowledge is not, though it includes knowledge of the nature of man and his circumstances, it is knowledge of what is best--of man's supreme end or good.

But this end is not conceived as presented to him by a superior power nor even as something which ought to be. The presentation of the Moral Ideal as Duty is almost absent. From the outset it is identified with the object of desire, of what we not merely judge desirable but actually do desire, or that which would, if realised, satisfy human desire. In fact it is what we all, wise and simple, agree in naming "Happiness" (Welfare or Well-being)

In what then does happiness consist? Aristotle summarily sets aside the more or less popular identifications of it with abundance of physical pleasures, with political power and honour, with the mere possession of such superior gifts or attainments as normally entitle men to these, with wealth. None of these can constitute the end or good of man as such. On the other hand, he rejects his master Plato's conception of a good which is the end of the whole universe, or at least dismisses it as irrelevant to his present enquiry. The good towards which all human desires and practical activities are directed must be one conformable to man's special nature and circumstances and attainable by his efforts. There is in Aristotle's theory of human conduct no trace of Plato's "other worldliness", he brings the moral ideal in Bacon's phrase down to "right earth"--and so closer to the facts and problems of actual human living. Turning from criticism of others he states his own positive view of Happiness, and, though he avowedly states it merely in outline his account is pregnant with significance. Human Happiness lies in activity or energising, and that in a way peculiar to man with his given nature and his given circumstances, it is not theoretical, but practical: it is the activity not of reason but still of a being who possesses reason and applies it, and it presupposes in that being the development, and not merely the natural possession, of certain relevant powers and capacities. The last is the prime condition of successful living and therefore of satisfaction, but Aristotle does not ignore other conditions, such as length of life, wealth and good luck, the absence or diminution of which render happiness not impossible, but difficult of attainment.

It is interesting to compare this account of Happiness with Mill's in Utilitarianism. Mill's is much the less consistent: at times he distinguishes and at times he identifies, happiness, pleasure, contentment, and satisfaction. He wavers between belief in its general attainability and an absence of hopefulness. He mixes up in an arbitrary way such ingredients as "not expecting more from life than it is capable of bestowing," "mental cultivation," "improved laws," etc., and in fact leaves the whole conception vague, blurred, and uncertain. Aristotle draws the outline with a firmer hand and presents a more definite ideal. He allows for the influence on happiness of conditions only partly, if at all, within the control of man, but he clearly makes the man positive determinant of man's happiness he in himself, and more particularly in what he makes directly of his own nature, and so indirectly of his circumstances. "'Tis in ourselves that we are thus or thus" But once more this does not involve an artificial or abstract isolation of the individual moral agent from his relation to other persons or things from his context in society and nature, nor ignore the relative dependence of his life upon a favourable environment.

The main factor which determines success or failure in human life is the acquisition of certain powers, for Happiness is just the exercise or putting forth of these in actual living, everything else is secondary and subordinate. These powers arise from the due development of certain natural aptitudes which belong (in various degrees) to human nature as such and therefore to all normal human beings. In their developed form they are known as virtues (the Greek means simply "goodnesses," "perfections," "excellences," or "fitnesses"), some of them are physical, but others are psychical, and among the latter some, and these distinctively or peculiarly human, are "rational," i e, presuppose the possession and exercise of mind or intelligence. These last fall into two groups, which Aristotle distinguishes as Goodnesses of Intellect and Goodnesses of Character. They have in common that they all excite in us admiration and praise of their possessors, and that they are not natural endowments, but acquired characteristics But they differ in important ways. (1) the former are excellences or developed powers of the reason as such--of that in us which sees and formulates laws, rules, regularities systems, and is content in the vision of them, while the latter involve a submission or obedience to such rules of something in us which is in itself capricious and irregular, but capable of regulation, viz our instincts and feelings, (2) the former are acquired by study and instruction, the latter by discipline. The latter constitute "character," each of them as a "moral virtue" (literally "a goodness of character"), and upon

9

them primarily depends the realisation of happiness. This is the case at least for the great majority of men, and for all men their possession is an indispensable basis of the best, i e, the most desirable life. They form the chief or central subject-matter of the Ethics.

Perhaps the truest way of conceiving Aristotle's meaning here is to regard a moral virtue as a form of obedience to a maxim or rule of conduct accepted by the agent as valid for a class of recurrent situations in human life. Such obedience requires knowledge of the rule and acceptance of it as the rule of the agent's own actions, but not necessarily knowledge of its ground or of its systematic connexion with other similarly known and similarly accepted rules (It may be remarked that the Greek word usually translated "reason," means in almost all cases in the Ethics such a rule, and not the faculty which apprehends, formulates, considers them).

The "moral virtues and vices" make up what we call character, and the important questions arise: (1) What is character? and (2) How is it formed? (for character in this sense is not a natural endowment; it is formed or produced). Aristotle deals with these questions in the reverse order. His answers are peculiar and distinctive--not that they are absolutely novel (for they are anticipated in Plato), but that by him they are for the first time distinctly and clearly formulated.

(1.) Character, good or bad, is produced by what Aristotle calls "habituation," that is, it is the result of the repeated doing of acts which have a similar or common quality. Such repetition acting upon natural aptitudes or propensities gradually fixes them in one or other of two opposite directions, giving them a bias towards good or evil. Hence the several acts which determine goodness or badness of character must be done in a certain way, and thus the formation of good character requires discipline and direction from without. Not that the agent himself contributes nothing to the formation of his character, but that at first he needs guidance. The point is not so much that the process cannot be safely left to Nature, but that it cannot be entrusted to merely intellectual instruction. The process is one of assimilation, largely by imitation and under direction and control. The result is a growing understanding of what is done, a choice of it for its own sake, a fixity and steadiness of purpose. Right acts and feelings become, through habit, easier and more pleasant, and the doing of them a "second nature." The agent acquires the power of doing them freely, willingly, more and more "of himself."

But what are "right" acts? In the first place, they are those that conform to a rule--to the right rule, and ultimately to reason. The Greeks never waver from the conviction that in the end moral conduct is essentially reasonable conduct. But there is a more significant way of describing their "rightness," and here for the first time Aristotle introduces his famous "Doctrine of the Mean." Reasoning from the analogy of "right" physical acts, he pronounces that rightness always means adaptation or adjustment to the special requirements of a situation. To this adjustment he gives a quantitative interpretation. To do (or to feel) what is right in a given situation is to do or to feel just the amount required--neither more nor less: to do wrong is to do or to feel too much or too little--to fall short of or over-shoot, "a mean" determined by the situation. The repetition of acts which lie in the mean is the cause of the formation of each and every "goodness of character," and for this "rules" can be given.

(2) What then is a "moral virtue," the result of such a process duly directed? It is no mere mood of feeling, no mere liability to emotion, no mere natural aptitude or endowment, it is a permanent state of the agent's self, or, as we might in modern phrase put it, of his will, it consists in a steady self-imposed obedience to a rule of action in certain situations which frequently recur in human life. The rule prescribes the control and regulation within limits of the agent's natural impulses to act and feel thus and thus. The situations fall into groups which constitute the "fields" of the several "moral virtues", for each there is a rule, conformity to which secures rightness in the individual acts. Thus the moral ideal appears as a code of rules, accepted by the agent, but as yet to him without rational justification and without system or unity. But the rules prescribe no mechanical uniformity: each within its limits permits variety, and the exactly right amount adopted to the requirements of the individual situation (and every actual situation is individual) must be determined by the intuition of the moment. There is no attempt to reduce the rich possibilities of right action to a single monotonous type. On the contrary, there are acknowledged to be many forms of moral virtue, and there is a long list of them, with their correlative vices enumerated.

The Doctrine of the Mean here takes a form in which it has impressed subsequent thinkers, but which has less importance than is usually ascribed to it. In the "Table of the Virtues and Vices," each of the virtues is flanked by two opposite vices, which are respectively the excess and defect of that which in due measure constitutes the virtue. Aristotle tries to show that this is the case in regard to every virtue named and recognised as such, but his treatment is often forced and the endeavour is not very successful. Except as a convenient principle of arrangement of the various forms of praiseworthy or blameworthy characters, generally acknowledged as such by Greek opinion, this form of the doctrine is of no great significance.

Books III-V are occupied with a survey of the moral virtues and vices. These seem to have been undertaken in order to verify in detail the general account, but this aim is not kept steadily in view. Nor is there any well-considered principle of classification. What we find is a sort of portrait-gallery of the various types of moral excellence which the Greeks of the author's age admired and strove to encourage. The discussion is full of acute, interesting and sometimes profound observations. Some of the types are those which are and will be admired at all times, but others are connected with peculiar features of Greek life which have now passed away. The most important is that of Justice or the Just Man, to which we may later return. But the discussion is preceded by an attempt to elucidate some difficult and obscure points in the general account of moral virtue and action (Book III, cc i-v). This section is concerned with the notion of Responsibility. The discussion designedly excludes what we may call the metaphysical issues of the problem, which here present themselves, it moves on the level of thought of the practical man, the statesman, and the legislator. Coercion and ignorance of relevant circumstances render acts involuntary and exempt their doer from responsibility, otherwise the act is voluntary and the agent responsible, choice or preference of what is done, and inner consent to the deed, are to be presumed. Neither passion nor ignorance of the right rule can extenuate responsibility. But there is a difference between acts done voluntarily and acts done of set choice or purpose. The latter imply Deliberation. Deliberation involves thinking, thinking out means to ends: in deliberate acts the whole nature of the agent consents to and enters into the act, and in a peculiar sense they are his, they are him in action, and the most significant evidence of what he is. Aristotle is unable wholly to avoid allusion to the metaphysical difficulties and what he does here say upon them is obscure and unsatisfactory. But he insists upon the importance in moral action of the agent's inner consent, and on the reality of his individual responsibility. For his present purpose the metaphysical difficulties are irrelevant.

The treatment of Justice in Book V has always been a source of great difficulty to students of the Ethics. Almost more than any other part of the work it has exercised influence upon mediaeval and modern thought upon the subject. The distinctions and divisions have become part of the stock-in-trade of would be philosophic jurists. And yet, oddly enough, most of these distinctions have been misunderstood and the whole purport of the discussion misconceived. Aristotle is here dealing with justice in a restricted sense viz as that special goodness of character which is required of every adult citizen and which can be produced by early discipline or habituation. It is the temper or habitual attitude demanded of the citizen for the due exercise of his functions as taking part in the administration of the civic community--as a member of the judicature and executive. The Greek citizen was only exceptionally, and at rare intervals if ever, a law-maker while at any moment he might be called upon to act as a judge (juryman or arbitrator) or as an administrator. For the work of a legislator far more than the moral virtue of justice or fairmindedness was necessary, these were requisite to the rarer and higher "intellectual virtue" of practical wisdom. Then here, too, the discussion moves on a low level, and the raising of fundamental problems is excluded. Hence "distributive justice" is concerned not with the large question of the distribution of political power and privileges among the constituent members or classes of the state but with the smaller questions of the distribution among those of casual gains and even with the division among private claimants of a common fund or inheritance, while "corrective justice" is concerned solely with the management of legal redress. The whole treatment is confused by the unhappy attempt to give a precise mathematical form to the principles of justice in the various fields distinguished. Still it remains an interesting first endeavour to give greater exactness to some of the leading conceptions of jurisprudence.

Book VI appears to have in view two aims: (1) to describe goodness of intellect and discover its highest form or forms; (2) to show how this is related to goodness of character, and so to conduct generally. As all thinking is either theoretical or practical, goodness of intellect has two supreme forms-- Theoretical and Practical Wisdom. The first, which apprehends the eternal laws of the universe, has no direct relation to human conduct: the second is identical with that master science of human life of which the whole treatise, consisting of the Ethics and the Politics, is an exposition. It is this science which supplies the right rules of conduct Taking them as they emerge in and from practical experience, it formulates them more precisely and organises them into a system where they are all seen to converge upon happiness. The mode in which such knowledge manifests itself is in the power to show that such and such rules of action follow from the very nature of the end or good for man. It presupposes and starts from a clear conception of the end and the wish for it as conceived, and it proceeds by a deduction which is deliberation writ large. In the man of practical wisdom this process has reached its perfect result, and the code of right rules is apprehended as a system with a single principle and so as something wholly rational or reasonable He has not on each occasion to seek and find the right rule applicable to the situation, he produces it at once from within himself, and can at need justify it by exhibiting its rationale, i.e., its connection with the end. This is the consummate form of reason applied to conduct, but there are minor forms of it, less independent or original, but nevertheless of great value, such as the power to think out the proper cause of policy in novel circumstances or the power to see the proper line of treatment to follow in a court of law.

The form of the thinking which enters into conduct is that which terminates in the production of a rule which declares some means to the end of life. The process presupposes (a) a clear and just apprehension of the nature of that end--such as the Ethics itself endeavours to supply; (b) a correct perception of the conditions of action, (a) at least is impossible except to a man whose character has been duly formed by discipline; it arises only in a man who has acquired moral virtue. For such action and feeling as forms bad character, blinds the eye of the soul and corrupts the moral principle, and the place of practical wisdom is taken by that parody of itself which Aristotle calls "cleverness"--the "wisdom" of the unscrupulous man of the world. Thus true practical wisdom and true goodness of character are interdependent; neither is genuinely possible or "completely" present without the other. This is Aristotle's contribution to the discussion of the question, so central in Greek Moral Philosophy, of the relation of the intellectual and the passionate factors in conduct.

Aristotle is not an intuitionist, but he recognises the implication in conduct of a direct and immediate apprehension both of the end and of the character of his circumstances under which it is from moment to moment realised. The directness of such apprehension makes it analogous to sensation or sense-perception; but it is on his view in the end due to the existence or activity in man of that power in him which is the highest thing in his nature, and akin to or identical with the divine nature--mind, or intelligence. It is this which reveals to us what is best for us--the ideal of a happiness which is the object of our real wish and the goal of all our efforts. But beyond and above the practical ideal of what is best for man begins to show itself another and still higher ideal--that of a life not distinctively human or in a narrow sense practical, yet capable of being participated in by man even under the actual circumstances of this world. For a time, however, this further and higher ideal is ignored.

The next book (Book VII.), is concerned partly with moral conditions, in which the agent seems to rise above the level of moral virtue or fall below that of moral vice, but partly and more largely with conditions in which the agent occupies a middle position between the two. Aristotle's attention is here directed chiefly towards the phenomena of "Incontinence," weakness of will or imperfect self-control. This condition was to the Greeks a matter of only too frequent experience, but it appeared to them peculiarly difficult to understand. How can a man know what is good or best for him, and yet chronically fail to act upon his knowledge? Socrates was driven to the paradox of denying the possibility, but the facts are too strong for him. Knowledge of the right rule may be present, nay the rightfulness of its authority may be acknowledged, and yet time after time it may be disobeyed; the will may be good and yet overmastered by the force of desire, so that the act done is contrary to the agent's will. Nevertheless the act may be the agent's, and the will therefore divided against itself. Aristotle is aware of the seriousness and difficulty of the problem, but in spite of the vividness with which he pictures, and the acuteness with which he analyses, the situation in which such action occurs, it cannot be said that he solves the problem. It is time that he rises above the abstract view of it as a conflict between reason and passion, recognising that passion is involved in the knowledge which in conduct prevails or is overborne, and that the force which leads to the wrong act is not blind or ignorant passion, but always has some reason in it. But he tends to lapse back into the abstraction, and his final account is perplexed and obscure. He finds the source of the phenomenon in the nature of the desire for bodily pleasures, which is not irrational but has something rational in it. Such pleasures are not necessarily or inherently bad, as has sometimes been maintained; on the contrary, they are good, but only in certain amounts or under certain conditions, so that the will is often misled, hesitates, and is lost.

Books VIII. and IX. (on Friendship) are almost an interruption of the argument. The subject-matter of them was a favourite topic of ancient writers, and the treatment is smoother and more orderly than elsewhere in the Ethics. The argument is clear, and may be left without comment to the readers. These books contain a necessary and attractive complement to the somewhat dry account of Greek morality in the preceding books, and there are in them profound reflections on what may be called the metaphysics of friendship or love.

At the beginning of Book X. we return to the topic of Pleasure, which is now regarded from a different point of view. In Book VII. the antagonists were those who over-emphasised the irrationality or badness of Pleasure: here it is rather those who so exaggerate its value as to confuse or identify it with the good or Happiness. But there is offered us in this section much more than criticism of the errors of others. Answers are given both to the psychological question, "What is Pleasure?" and to the ethical question, "What is its value?" Pleasure, we are told, is the natural concomitant and index of perfect activity, distinguishable but inseparable from it--"the activity of a subject at its best acting upon an object at its best." It is therefore always and in itself a good, but its value rises and falls with that of the activity with which it is conjoined, and which it intensifies and perfects. Hence it follows that the highest and best pleasures are those which accompany the highest and best activity.

Pleasure is, therefore, a necessary element in the best life, but it is not the whole of it nor the principal ingredient. The value of a life depends upon the nature and worth of the activity which it involves; given the maximum of full free action, the maximum of pleasure necessary follows. But on what sort of life is such activity possible? This leads us back to the question, What is happiness? In what life can man find the fullest satisfaction for his desires? To this question Aristotle gives an answer which cannot but surprise us after what has preceded. True Happiness, great satisfaction, cannot be found by man in any form of "practical" life, no, not in the fullest and freest exercise possible of the "moral virtues," not in the life of the citizen or of the great soldier or statesman. To seek it there is to court failure and disappointment. It is to be found in the life of the onlooker, the disinterested spectator; or, to put it more distinctly, "in the life of the philosopher, the life of scientific and philosophic contemplation." The highest and most satisfying form of life possible to man is "the contemplative life"; it is only in a secondary sense and for those incapable of their life, that the practical or moral ideal is the best. It is time that such a life is not distinctively human, but it is the privilege of man to partake in it, and such participation, at however rare intervals and for however short a period, is the highest Happiness which human life can offer. All other activities have value only because and in so far as they render this life possible.

But it must not be forgotten that Aristotle conceives of this life as one of intense activity or energising: it is just this which gives it its supremacy. In spite of the almost religious fervour with which he speaks of it ("the most orthodox of his disciples" paraphrases his meaning by describing its content as "the service and vision of God"), it is clear that he identified it with the life of the philosopher, as he understood it, a life of ceaseless Intellectual activity in which at least at times all the distractions and disturbances inseparable from practical life seemed to disappear and become as nothing. This ideal was partly an inheritance from the more ardent idealism of his master Plato, but partly it was the expression of personal experience.

The nobility of this ideal cannot be questioned; the conception of the end of man or a life lived for truth--of a life blissfully absorbed in the vision of truth--is a lofty and inspiring one. But we cannot resist certain criticisms upon its presentation by Aristotle: (1) the relation of it to the lower ideal of practice is left somewhat obscure; (2) it is described in such a way as renders its realisation possible only to a gifted few, and under exceptional circumstances; (3) it seems in various ways, as regards its content, to be unnecessarily and unjustifiably limited. But it must be borne in mind that this is a first endeavour to determine its principle, and that similar failures have attended the attempts to describe the "religious" or the "spiritual" ideals of life, which have continually been suggested by the apparently inherent limitations of the "practical" or "moral" life, which is the subject of Moral Philosophy.

The Moral Ideal to those who have most deeply reflected on it leads to the thought of an Ideal beyond and above it, which alone gives it meaning, but which seems to escape from definite conception by man. The richness and variety of this Ideal ceaselessly invite, but as ceaselessly defy, our attempts to imprison it in a definite formula or portray it in detailed imagination. Yet the thought of it is and remains inexpungable from our minds.

This conception of the best life is not forgotten in the Politics The end of life in the state is itself well-living and well-doing--a life which helps to produce the best life The great agency in the production of such life is the State operating through Law, which is Reason backed by Force. For its greatest efficiency there is required the development of a science of legislation. The main drift of what he says here is that the most desirable thing would be that the best reason of the community should be embodied in its laws. But so far as that is not possible, it still is true that anyone who would make himself and others better must become a miniature legislator--must study the general principles of law, morality, and education. The conception of [Grek: politikae] with which he opened the Ethics would serve as a guide to a father educating his children as well as to the legislator legislating for the state. Finding in his predecessors no developed doctrine on this subject, Aristotle proposes himself to undertake the construction of it, and sketches in advance the programme of the Politics in the concluding sentence of the Ethics His ultimate object is to answer the questions, What is the best form of Polity, how should each be constituted, and what laws and customs should it adopt and employ? Not till this answer is given will "the philosophy of human affairs" be complete.

On looking back it will be seen that the discussion of the central topic of the nature and formation of character has expanded into a Philosophy of Human Conduct, merging at its beginning and end into metaphysics The result is a Moral Philosophy set against a background of Political Theory and general Philosophy. The most characteristic features of this Moral Philosophy are due to the fact of its essentially teleological view of human life and action: (1) Every human activity, but especially every human practical activity, is directed towards a simple End discoverable by reflection, and this End is conceived of as the object of universal human desire, as something to be enjoyed, not as something which ought to be done or enacted. Anstotle's Moral Philosophy is not hedonistic but it is eudæmomstic, the end is the enjoyment of Happiness, not the fulfilment of Duty. (2) Every human practical activity derives its value from its efficiency as a means to that end, it is good or bad, right or wrong, as it conduces or fails to conduce to Happiness Thus his Moral Philosophy is essentially utilitarian or prudential Right action presupposes Thought or Thinking, partly on the development of a clearer and distincter conception of the end of desire, partly as the deduction from that of rules which state the normally effective conditions of its realisation. The thinking involved in right conduct is calculation-- calculation of means to an end fixed by nature and foreknowable Action itself is at its best just the realisation of a scheme preconceived and thought out beforehand, commending itself by its inherent attractiveness or promise of enjoyment.

This view has the great advantage of exhibiting morality as essentially reasonable, but the accompanying disadvantage of lowering it into a somewhat prosaic and unideal Prudentialism, nor is it saved from this by the tacking on to it, by a sort of after-thought, of the second and higher Ideal--an addition which ruins the coherence of the account without really transmuting its substance The source of our dissatisfaction with the whole theory lies deeper than in its tendency to identify the end with the maximum of enjoyment or satisfaction, or to regard the goodness or badness of acts and feelings as lying solely in their efficacy to produce such a result It arises from the application to morality of the distinction of means and end For this distinction, for all its plausibility and usefulness in ordinary thought and speech, cannot finally be maintained In morality--and this is vital to its character-- everything is both means and end, and so neither in distinction or separation, and all thinking about it which presupposes the finality of this distinction wanders into misconception and error. The thinking which really matters in conduct is not a thinking which imaginatively forecasts ideals which promise to fulfil desire, or calculates means to their attainment--that is sometimes useful, sometimes harmful, and always subordinate, but thinking which reveals to the agent the situation in which he is to act, both, that is, the universal situation on which as man he always and everywhere stands, and the ever-varying and ever-novel situation in which he as this individual, here and now, finds himself. In such knowledge of given or historic fact lie the natural determinants of his conduct, in such knowledge alone lies the condition of his freedom and his good.

But this does not mean that Moral Philosophy has not still much to learn from Aristotle's Ethics. The work still remains one of the best introductions to a study of its important subject-matter, it spreads before us a view of the relevant facts, it reduces them to manageable compass and order, it raises some of the central problems, and makes acute and valuable suggestions towards their solution. Above all, it perpetually incites to renewed and independent reflection upon them.

J. A. SMITH

BOOK I

I

Every art, and every science reduced to a teachable form, and in like manner every action and moral choice, aims, it is thought, at some good: for which reason a common and by no means a bad description of the Chief Good is, "that which all things aim at."

Now there plainly is a difference in the Ends proposed: for in some cases they are acts of working, and in others certain works or tangible results beyond and beside the acts of working: and where there are certain Ends beyond and beside the actions, the works are in their nature better than the acts of working. Again, since actions and arts and sciences are many, the Ends likewise come to be many: of the healing art, for instance, health; of the ship-building art, a vessel; of the military art, victory; and of domestic management, wealth; are respectively the Ends.

And whatever of such actions, arts, or sciences range under some one faculty (as under that of horsemanship the art of making bridles, and all that are connected with the manufacture of horse-furniture in general; this itself again, and every action connected with war, under the military art; and in the same way others under others), in all such, the Ends of the master-arts are more choice-worthy than those ranging under them, because it is with a view to the former that the latter are pursued.

(And in this comparison it makes no difference whether the acts of working are themselves the Ends of the actions, or something further beside them, as is the case in the arts and sciences we have been just speaking of.)

II

Since then of all things which may be done there is some one End which we desire for its own sake, and with a view to which we desire everything else; and since we do not choose in all instances with a further End in view (for then men would go on without limit, and so the desire would be unsatisfied and fruitless), this plainly must be the Chief Good, i.e. the best thing of all.

Surely then, even with reference to actual life and conduct, the knowledge of it must have great weight; and like archers, with a mark in view, we shall be more likely to hit upon what is right: and if so, we ought to try to describe, in outline at least, what it is and of which of the sciences and faculties it is the End.

Now one would naturally suppose it to be the End of that which is most commanding and most inclusive: and to this description, [Greek: politikae] plainly answers: for this it is that determines which of the sciences should be in the communities, and which kind individuals are to learn, and what degree of proficiency is to be required. Again; we see also ranging under this the most highly esteemed faculties, such as the art military, and that of domestic management, and Rhetoric. Well then, since this uses all the other practical sciences, and moreover lays down rules as to what men are to do, and from what to abstain, the End of this must include the Ends of the rest, and so must be The Good of Man. And grant that this is the same to the individual and to the community, yet surely that of the latter is plainly greater and more perfect to discover and preserve: for to do this even for a single individual were a matter for contentment; but to do it for a whole nation, and for communities generally, were more noble and godlike.

III

Such then are the objects proposed by our treatise, which is of the nature of [Greek: politikae]: and I conceive I shall have spoken on them satisfactorily, if they be made as distinctly clear as the nature of the subject-matter will admit: for exactness must not be looked for in all discussions alike, any more than in all works of handicraft. Now the notions of nobleness and justice, with the examination of which politikea is concerned, admit of variation and error to such a degree, that they are supposed by some to exist conventionally only, and not in the nature of things: but then, again, the things which are allowed to be goods admit of a similar error, because harm comes to many from them: for before now some have perished through wealth, and others through valour.

We must be content then, in speaking of such things and from such data, to set forth the truth roughly and in outline; in other words, since we are speaking of general matter and from general data, to draw also conclusions merely general. And in the same spirit should each person receive what we say: for the man of education will seek exactness so far in each subject as the nature of the thing admits, it being plainly much the same absurdity to put up with a mathematician who tries to persuade instead of proving, and to demand strict demonstrative reasoning of a Rhetorician.

Now each man judges well what he knows, and of these things he is a good judge: on each particular matter then he is a good judge who has been instructed in it, and in a general way the man of general mental cultivation.

Hence the young man is not a fit student of Moral Philosophy, for he has no experience in the actions of life, while all that is said presupposes and is concerned with these: and in the next place, since he is apt to follow the impulses of his passions, he will hear as though he heard not, and to no profit, the end in view being practice and not mere knowledge.

And I draw no distinction between young in years, and youthful in temper and disposition: the defect to which I allude being no direct result of the time, but of living at the beck and call of passion, and following each object as it rises. For to them that are such the knowledge comes to be unprofitable, as to those of imperfect self-control: but, to those who form their desires and act in accordance with reason, to have knowledge on these points must be very profitable.

Let thus much suffice by way of preface on these three points, the student, the spirit in which our observations should be received, and the object which we propose.

IV

And now, resuming the statement with which we commenced, since all knowledge and moral choice grasps at good of some kind or another, what good is that which we say [Greek: politikai] aims at? or, in other words, what is the highest of all the goods which are the objects of action?

So far as name goes, there is a pretty general agreement: for HAPPINESS both the multitude and the refined few call it, and "living well" and "doing well" they conceive to be the same with "being happy;" but about the Nature of this Happiness, men dispute, and the multitude do not in their account of it agree with the wise. For some say it is some one of those things which are palpable and apparent, as pleasure or wealth or honour; in fact, some one thing, some another; nay, oftentimes the same man gives a different account of it; for when ill, he calls it health; when poor, wealth: and conscious of their own ignorance, men admire those who talk grandly and above their comprehension. Some again held it to be something by itself, other than and beside these many good things, which is in fact to all these the cause of their being good.

Now to sift all the opinions would be perhaps rather a fruitless task; so it shall suffice to sift those which are most generally current, or are thought to have some reason in them.

And here we must not forget the difference between reasoning from principles, and reasoning to principles: for with good cause did Plato too doubt about this, and inquire whether the right road is from principles or to principles, just as in the racecourse from the judges to the further end, or vice versâ.

Of course, we must begin with what is known; but then this is of two kinds, what we do know, and what we may know: perhaps then as individuals we must begin with what we do know. Hence the necessity that he should have been well trained in habits, who is to study, with any tolerable chance of profit, the principles of nobleness and justice and moral philosophy generally. For a principle is a matter of fact, and if the fact is sufficiently clear to a man there will be no need in addition of the reason for the fact. And he that has been thus trained either has principles already, or can receive them easily: as for him who neither has nor can receive them, let him hear his sentence from Hesiod:

He is best of all who of himself conceiveth all things;
Good again is he too who can adopt a good suggestion;
But whoso neither of himself conceiveth nor hearing from another
Layeth it to heart;--he is a useless man.

V

But to return from this digression.

Now of the Chief Good (i.e. of Happiness) men seem to form their notions from the different modes of life, as we might naturally expect: the many and most low conceive it to be pleasure, and hence they are content with the life of sensual enjoyment. For there are three lines of life which stand out prominently to view: that just mentioned, and the life in society, and, thirdly, the life of contemplation.

Now the many are plainly quite slavish, choosing a life like that of brute animals: yet they obtain some consideration, because many of the great share the tastes of Sardanapalus. The refined and active again conceive it to be honour: for this may be said to be the end of the life in society: yet it is plainly too superficial for the object of our search, because it is thought to rest with those who pay rather than with him who receives it, whereas the Chief Good we feel instinctively must be something which is our own, and not easily to be taken from us.

And besides, men seem to pursue honour, that they may believe themselves to be good: for instance, they seek to be honoured by the wise, and by those among whom they are known, and for virtue: clearly then, in the opinion at least of these men, virtue is higher than honour. In truth, one would be much more inclined to think this to be the end of the life in society; yet this itself is plainly not sufficiently final: for it is conceived possible, that a man possessed of virtue might sleep or be inactive all through his life, or, as a third case, suffer the greatest evils and misfortunes: and the man who should live thus no one would call happy, except for mere disputation's sake.

And for these let thus much suffice, for they have been treated of at sufficient length in my Encyclia.

A third line of life is that of contemplation, concerning which we shall make our examination in the sequel.

As for the life of money-making, it is one of constraint, and wealth manifestly is not the good we are seeking, because it is for use, that is, for the sake of something further: and hence one would rather conceive the forementioned ends to be the right ones, for men rest content with them for their own sakes. Yet, clearly, they are not the objects of our search either, though many words have been wasted on them. So much then for these.

VI

Again, the notion of one Universal Good (the same, that is, in all things), it is better perhaps we should examine, and discuss the meaning of it, though such an inquiry is unpleasant, because they are friends of ours who have introduced these [Greek: eidae]. Still perhaps it may appear better, nay to be our duty where the safety of the truth is concerned, to upset if need be even our own theories, specially as we are lovers of wisdom: for since both are dear to us, we are bound to prefer the truth. Now they who invented this doctrine of [Greek: eidae], did not apply it to those things in which they spoke of priority and posteriority, and so they never made any [Greek: idea] of numbers; but good is predicated in the categories of Substance, Quality, and Relation; now that which exists of itself, i.e. Substance, is prior in the nature of things to that which is relative, because this latter is an off-shoot, as it were, and result of that which is; on their own principle then there cannot be a common [Greek: idea] in the case of these.

In the next place, since good is predicated in as many ways as there are modes of existence [for it is predicated in the category of Substance, as God, Intellect--and in that of Quality, as The Virtues--and in that of Quantity, as The Mean--and in that of Relation, as The Useful--and in that of Time, as Opportunity--and in that of Place, as Abode; and other such like things], it manifestly cannot be something common and universal and one in all: else it would not have been predicated in all the categories, but in one only.

Thirdly, since those things which range under one [Greek: idea] are also under the cognisance of one science, there would have been, on their theory, only one science taking cognisance of all goods collectively: but in fact there are many even for those which range under one category: for instance, of Opportunity or Seasonableness (which I have before mentioned as being in the category of Time), the science is, in war, generalship; in disease, medical science; and of the Mean (which I quoted before as being in the category of Quantity), in food, the medical science; and in labour or exercise, the gymnastic science. A person might fairly doubt also what in the world they mean by very-this that or the other, since, as they would themselves allow, the account of the humanity is one and the same in the very-Man, and in any individual Man: for so far as the individual and the very-Man are both Man, they will not differ at all: and if so, then very-good and any particular good will not differ, in so far as both are good. Nor will it do to say, that the eternity of the very-good makes it to be more good; for what has lasted white ever so long, is no whiter than what lasts but for a day.

No. The Pythagoreans do seem to give a more credible account of the matter, who place "One" among the goods in their double list of goods and bads: which philosophers, in fact, Speusippus seems to have followed.

But of these matters let us speak at some other time. Now there is plainly a loophole to object to what has been advanced, on the plea that the theory I have attacked is not by its advocates applied to all good: but those goods only are spoken of as being under one [Greek: idea], which are pursued, and with which men rest content simply for their own sakes: whereas those things which have a tendency to produce or preserve them in any way, or to hinder their contraries, are called good because of these other goods, and after another fashion. It is manifest then that the goods may be so called in two senses, the one class for their own sakes, the other because of these.

Very well then, let us separate the independent goods from the instrumental, and see whether they are spoken of as under one [Greek: idea]. But the question next arises, what kind of goods are we to call independent? All such as are pursued even when separated from other goods, as, for instance, being wise, seeing, and certain pleasures and honours (for these, though we do pursue them with some further end in view, one would still place among the independent goods)? or does it come in fact to this, that we can call nothing independent good except the [Greek: idea], and so the concrete of it will be nought?

If, on the other hand, these are independent goods, then we shall require that the account of the goodness be the same clearly in all, just as that of the whiteness is in snow and white lead. But how stands the fact? Why of honour and wisdom and pleasure the accounts are distinct and different in so far as they are good. The Chief Good then is not something common, and after one [Greek: idea].

But then, how does the name come to be common (for it is not seemingly a case of fortuitous equivocation)? Are different individual things called good by virtue of being from one source, or all conducing to one end, or rather by way of analogy, for that intellect is to the soul as sight to the body, and so on? However, perhaps we ought to leave these questions now, for an accurate investigation of them is more properly the business of a different philosophy. And likewise respecting the [Greek: idea]: for even if there is some one good predicated in common of all things that are good, or separable and capable of existing independently, manifestly it cannot be the object of human action or attainable by Man; but we are in search now of something that is so.

It may readily occur to any one, that it would be better to attain a knowledge of it with a view to such concrete goods as are attainable and practical, because, with this as a kind of model in our hands, we shall the better know what things are good for us individually, and when we know them, we shall attain them.

Some plausibility, it is true, this argument possesses, but it is contradicted by the facts of the Arts and Sciences; for all these, though aiming at some good, and seeking that which is deficient, yet pretermit the knowledge of it: now it is not exactly probable that all artisans without exception should be ignorant of so great a help as this would be, and not even look after it; neither is it easy to see wherein a weaver or a carpenter will be profited in respect of his craft by knowing the very-good, or how a man will be the more apt to effect cures or to command an army for having seen the [Greek: idea] itself. For manifestly it is not health after this general and abstract fashion which is the subject of the physician's investigation, but the health of Man, or rather perhaps of this or that man; for he has to heal individuals.--Thus much on these points.

VII

And now let us revert to the Good of which we are in search: what can it be? for manifestly it is different in different actions and arts: for it is different in the healing art and in the art military, and similarly in the rest. What then is the Chief Good in each? Is it not "that for the sake of which the other things are done?" and this in the healing art is health, and in the art military victory, and in that of house-building a house, and in any other thing something else; in short, in every action and moral choice the End, because in all cases men do everything else with a view to this. So that if there is some one End of all things which are and may be done, this must be the Good proposed by doing, or if more than one, then these.

Thus our discussion after some traversing about has come to the same point which we reached before. And this we must try yet more to clear up.

Now since the ends are plainly many, and of these we choose some with a view to others (wealth, for instance, musical instruments, and, in general, all instruments), it is clear that all are not final: but the Chief Good is manifestly something final; and so, if there is some one only which is final, this must be the object of our search: but if several, then the most final of them will be it.

Now that which is an object of pursuit in itself we call more final than that which is so with a view to something else; that again which is never an object of choice with a view to something else than those which are so both in themselves and with a view to this ulterior object: and so by the term "absolutely final," we denote that which is an object of choice always in itself, and never with a view to any other.

And of this nature Happiness is mostly thought to be, for this we choose always for its own sake, and never with a view to anything further: whereas honour, pleasure, intellect, in fact every excellence we choose for their own sakes, it is true (because we would choose each of these even if no result were to follow), but we choose them also with a view to happiness, conceiving that through their instrumentality we shall be happy: but no man chooses happiness with a view to them, nor in fact with a view to any other thing whatsoever.

The same result is seen to follow also from the notion of self-sufficiency, a quality thought to belong to the final good. Now by sufficient for Self, we mean not for a single individual living a solitary life, but for his parents also and children and wife, and, in general, friends and countrymen; for man is by nature adapted to a social existence. But of these, of course, some limit must be fixed: for if one extends it to parents and descendants and friends' friends, there is no end to it. This point, however, must be left for future investigation: for the present we define that to be self-sufficient "which taken alone makes life choice-worthy, and to be in want of nothing;" now of such kind we think Happiness to be: and further, to be most choice-worthy of all things; not being reckoned with any other thing, for if it were so reckoned, it is plain we must then allow it, with the addition of ever so small a good, to be more choice-worthy than it was before: because what is put to it becomes an addition of so much more good, and of goods the greater is ever the more choice-worthy.

So then Happiness is manifestly something final and self-sufficient, being the end of all things which are and may be done.

But, it may be, to call Happiness the Chief Good is a mere truism, and what is wanted is some clearer account of its real nature. Now this object may be easily attained, when we have discovered what is the work of man; for as in the case of flute-player, statuary, or artisan of any kind, or, more generally, all who have any work or course of action, their Chief Good and Excellence is thought to reside in their work, so it would seem to be with man, if there is any work belonging to him.

Are we then to suppose, that while carpenter and cobbler have certain works and courses of action, Man as Man has none, but is left by Nature without a work? or would not one rather hold, that as eye, hand, and foot, and generally each of his members, has manifestly some special work; so too the whole Man, as distinct from all these, has some work of his own?

What then can this be? not mere life, because that plainly is shared with him even by vegetables, and we want what is peculiar to him. We must separate off then the life of mere nourishment and growth, and next will come the life of sensation: but this again manifestly is common to horses, oxen, and every animal. There remains then a kind of life of the Rational Nature apt to act: and of this Nature there are two parts denominated Rational, the one as being obedient to Reason, the other as having and exerting it. Again, as this life is also spoken of in two ways, we must take that which is in the way of actual working, because this is thought to be most properly entitled to the name. If then the work of Man is a working of the soul in accordance with reason, or at least not independently of reason, and we say that the work of any given subject, and of that subject good of its kind, are the same in kind (as, for instance, of a harp-player and a good harp-player, and so on in every case, adding to the work eminence in the way of excellence; I mean, the work of a harp-player is to play the harp, and of a good harp-player to play it well); if, I say, this is so, and we assume the work of Man to be life of a certain kind, that is to say a working of the soul, and actions with reason, and of a good man to do these things well and nobly, and in fact everything is finished off well in the way of the excellence which peculiarly belongs to it: if all this is so, then the Good of Man comes to be "a working of the Soul in the way of Excellence," or, if Excellence admits of degrees, in the way of the best and most perfect Excellence.

And we must add, in a complete life; for as it is not one swallow or one fine day that makes a spring, so it is not one day or a short time that makes a man blessed and happy.

Let this then be taken for a rough sketch of the Chief Good: since it is probably the right way to give first the outline, and fill it in afterwards. And it would seem that any man may improve and connect what is good in the sketch, and that time is a good discoverer and co-operator in such matters: it is thus in fact that all improvements in the various arts have been brought about, for any man may fill up a deficiency.

You must remember also what has been already stated, and not seek for exactness in all matters alike, but in each according to the subject-matter, and so far as properly belongs to the system. The carpenter and geometrician, for instance, inquire into the right line in different fashion: the former so far as he wants it for his work, the latter inquires into its nature and properties, because he is concerned with the truth.

So then should one do in other matters, that the incidental matters may not exceed the direct ones.

And again, you must not demand the reason either in all things alike, because in some it is sufficient that the fact has been well demonstrated, which is the case with first principles; and the fact is the first step, i.e. starting-point or principle.

And of these first principles some are obtained by induction, some by perception, some by a course of habituation, others in other different ways. And we must try to trace up each in their own nature, and take pains to secure their being well defined, because they have great influence on what follows: it is thought, I mean, that the starting-point or principle is more than half the whole matter, and that many of the points of inquiry come simultaneously into view thereby.

VIII

We must now inquire concerning Happiness, not only from our conclusion and the data on which our reasoning proceeds, but likewise from what is commonly said about it: because with what is true all things which really are are in harmony, but with that which is false the true very soon jars.

Now there is a common division of goods into three classes; one being called external, the other two those of the soul and body respectively, and those belonging to the soul we call most properly and specially good. Well, in our definition we assume that the actions and workings of the soul constitute Happiness, and these of course belong to the soul. And so our account is a good one, at least according to this opinion, which is of ancient date, and accepted by those who profess philosophy. Rightly too are certain actions and workings said to be the end, for thus it is brought into the number of the goods of the soul instead of the external. Agreeing also with our definition is the common notion, that the happy man lives well and does well, for it has been stated by us to be pretty much a kind of living well and doing well.

But further, the points required in Happiness are found in combination in our account of it.

For some think it is virtue, others practical wisdom, others a kind of scientific philosophy; others that it is these, or else some one of them, in combination with pleasure, or at least not independently of it; while others again take in external prosperity.

Of these opinions, some rest on the authority of numbers or antiquity, others on that of few, and those men of note: and it is not likely that either of these classes should be wrong in all points, but be right at least in some one, or even in most.

Now with those who assert it to be Virtue (Excellence), or some kind of Virtue, our account agrees: for working in the way of Excellence surely belongs to Excellence.

And there is perhaps no unimportant difference between conceiving of the Chief Good as in possession or as in use, in other words, as a mere state or as a working. For the state or habit may possibly exist in a subject without effecting any good, as, for instance, in him who is asleep, or in any other way inactive; but the working cannot so, for it will of necessity act, and act well. And as at the Olympic games it is not the finest and strongest men who are crowned, but they who enter the lists, for out of these the prize-men are selected; so too in life, of the honourable and the good, it is they who act who rightly win the prizes.

Their life too is in itself pleasant: for the feeling of pleasure is a mental sensation, and that is to each pleasant of which he is said to be fond: a horse, for instance, to him who is fond of horses, and a sight to him who is fond of sights: and so in like manner just acts to him who is fond of justice, and more generally the things in accordance with virtue to him who is fond of virtue. Now in the case of the multitude of men the things which they individually esteem pleasant clash, because they are not such by nature, whereas to the lovers of nobleness those things are pleasant which are such by nature: but the actions in accordance with virtue are of this kind, so that they are pleasant both to the individuals and also in themselves.

So then their life has no need of pleasure as a kind of additional appendage, but involves pleasure in itself. For, besides what I have just mentioned, a man is not a good man at all who feels no pleasure in noble actions, just as no one would call that man just who does not feel pleasure in acting justly, or liberal who does not in liberal actions, and similarly in the case of the other virtues which might be enumerated: and if this be so, then the actions in accordance with virtue must be in themselves pleasurable. Then again they are certainly good and noble, and each of these in the highest degree; if we are to take as right the judgment of the good man, for he judges as we have said.

Thus then Happiness is most excellent, most noble, and most pleasant, and these attributes are not separated as in the well-known Delian inscription--

"Most noble is that which is most just, but best is health; And naturally most pleasant is the obtaining one's desires."

For all these co-exist in the best acts of working: and we say that Happiness is these, or one, that is, the best of them.

Still it is quite plain that it does require the addition of external goods, as we have said: because without appliances it is impossible, or at all events not easy, to do noble actions: for friends, money, and political influence are in a manner instruments whereby many things are done: some things there are again a deficiency in which mars blessedness; good birth, for instance, or fine offspring, or even personal beauty: for he is not at all capable of Happiness who is very ugly, or is ill-born, or solitary and childless; and still less perhaps supposing him to have very bad children or friends, or to have lost good ones by death. As we have said already, the addition of prosperity of this kind does seem necessary to complete the idea of Happiness; hence some rank good fortune, and others virtue, with Happiness.

And hence too a question is raised, whether it is a thing that can be learned, or acquired by habituation or discipline of some other kind, or whether it comes in the way of divine dispensation, or even in the way of chance.

Now to be sure, if anything else is a gift of the Gods to men, it is probable that Happiness is a gift of theirs too, and specially because of all human goods it is the highest. But this, it may be, is a question belonging more properly to an investigation different from ours: and it is quite clear, that on the supposition of its not being sent from the Gods direct, but coming to us by reason of virtue and learning of a certain kind, or discipline, it is yet one of the most Godlike things; because the prize and End of virtue is manifestly somewhat most excellent, nay divine and blessed.

It will also on this supposition be widely participated, for it may through learning and diligence of a certain kind exist in all who have not been maimed for virtue.

And if it is better we should be happy thus than as a result of chance, this is in itself an argument that the case is so; because those things which are in the way of nature, and in like manner of art, and of every cause, and specially the best cause, are by nature in the best way possible: to leave them to chance what is greatest and most noble would be very much out of harmony with all these facts.

The question may be determined also by a reference to our definition of Happiness, that it is a working of the soul in the way of excellence or virtue of a certain kind: and of the other goods, some we must have to begin with, and those which are co-operative and useful are given by nature as instruments.

These considerations will harmonise also with what we said at the commencement: for we assumed the End of [Greek Text: poletikae] to be most excellent: now this bestows most care on making the members of the community of a certain character; good that is and apt to do what is honourable.

With good reason then neither ox nor horse nor any other brute animal do we call happy, for none of them can partake in such working: and for this same reason a child is not happy either, because by reason of his tender age he cannot yet perform such actions: if the term is applied, it is by way of anticipation.

For to constitute Happiness, there must be, as we have said, complete virtue and a complete life: for many changes and chances of all kinds arise during a life, and he who is most prosperous may become involved in great misfortunes in his old age, as in the heroic poems the tale is told of Priam: but the man who has experienced such fortune and died in wretchedness, no man calls happy.

Are we then to call no man happy while he lives, and, as Solon would have us, look to the end? And again, if we are to maintain this position, is a man then happy when he is dead? or is not this a complete absurdity, specially in us who say Happiness is a working of a certain kind?

If on the other hand we do not assert that the dead man is happy, and Solon does not mean this, but only that one would then be safe in pronouncing a man happy, as being thenceforward out of the reach of evils and misfortunes, this too admits of some dispute, since it is thought that the dead has somewhat both of good and evil (if, as we must allow, a man may have when alive but not aware of the circumstances), as honour and dishonour, and good and bad fortune of children and descendants generally.

Nor is this view again without its difficulties: for, after a man has lived in blessedness to old age and died accordingly, many changes may befall him in right of his descendants; some of them may be good and obtain positions in life accordant to their merits, others again quite the contrary: it is plain too that the descendants may at different intervals or grades stand in all manner of relations to the ancestors. Absurd indeed would be the position that even the dead man is to change about with them and become at one time happy and at another miserable. Absurd however it is on the other hand that the affairs of the descendants should in no degree and during no time affect the ancestors.

But we must revert to the point first raised, since the present question will be easily determined from that.

If then we are to look to the end and then pronounce the man blessed, not as being so but as having been so at some previous time, surely it is absurd that when he is happy the truth is not to be asserted of him, because we are unwilling to pronounce the living happy by reason of their liability to changes, and because, whereas we have conceived of happiness as something stable and no way easily changeable, the fact is that good and bad fortune are constantly circling about the same people: for it is quite plain, that if we are to depend upon the fortunes of men, we shall often have to call the same man happy, and a little while after miserable, thus representing our happy man

"Chameleon-like, and based on rottenness."

Is not this the solution? that to make our sentence dependent on the changes of fortune, is no way right: for not in them stands the well, or the ill, but though human life needs these as accessories (which we have allowed already), the workings in the way of virtue are what determine Happiness, and the contrary the contrary.

And, by the way, the question which has been here discussed, testifies incidentally to the truth of our account of Happiness. For to nothing does a stability of human results attach so much as it does to the workings in the way of virtue, since these are held to be more abiding even than the sciences: and of these last again the most precious are the most abiding, because the blessed live in them most and most continuously, which seems to be the reason why they are not forgotten. So then this stability which is sought will be in the happy man, and he will be such through life, since always, or most of all, he will be doing and contemplating the things which are in the way of virtue: and the various chances of life he will bear most nobly, and at all times and in all ways harmoniously, since he is the truly good man, or in the terms of our proverb "a faultless cube."

And whereas the incidents of chance are many, and differ in greatness and smallness, the small pieces of good or ill fortune evidently do not affect the balance of life, but the great and numerous, if happening for good, will make life more blessed (for it is their nature to contribute to ornament, and the using of them comes to be noble and excellent), but if for ill, they bruise as it were and maim the blessedness: for they bring in positive pain, and hinder many acts of working. But still, even in these, nobleness shines through when a man bears contentedly many and great mischances not from insensibility to pain but because he is noble and high-spirited.

And if, as we have said, the acts of working are what determine the character of the life, no one of the blessed can ever become wretched, because he will never do those things which are hateful and mean. For the man who is truly good and sensible bears all fortunes, we presume, becomingly, and always does what is noblest under the circumstances, just as a good general employs to the best advantage the force he has with him; or a good shoemaker makes the handsomest shoe he can out of the leather which has been given him; and all other good artisans likewise. And if this be so, wretched never can the happy man come to be: I do not mean to say he will be blessed should he fall into fortunes like those of Priam.

Nor, in truth, is he shifting and easily changeable, for on the one hand from his happiness he will not be shaken easily nor by ordinary mischances, but, if at all, by those which are great and numerous; and, on the other, after such mischances he cannot regain his happiness in a little time; but, if at all, in a long and complete period, during which he has made himself master of great and noble things.

Why then should we not call happy the man who works in the way of perfect virtue, and is furnished with external goods sufficient for acting his part in the drama of life: and this during no ordinary period but such as constitutes a complete life as we have been describing it.

Or we must add, that not only is he to live so, but his death must be in keeping with such life, since the future is dark to us, and Happiness we assume to be in every way an end and complete. And, if this be so, we shall call them among the living blessed who have and will have the things specified, but blessed as Men.

On these points then let it suffice to have denned thus much.

IX

Now that the fortunes of their descendants, and friends generally, contribute nothing towards forming the condition of the dead, is plainly a very heartless notion, and contrary to the current opinions.

But since things which befall are many, and differ in all kinds of ways, and some touch more nearly, others less, to go into minute particular distinctions would evidently be a long and endless task: and so it may suffice to speak generally and in outline.

If then, as of the misfortunes which happen to one's self, some have a certain weight and turn the balance of life, while others are, so to speak, lighter; so it is likewise with those which befall all our friends alike; if further, whether they whom each suffering befalls be alive or dead makes much more difference than in a tragedy the presupposing or actual perpetration of the various crimes and horrors, we must take into our account this difference also, and still more perhaps the doubt concerning the dead whether they really partake of any good or evil; it seems to result from all these considerations, that if anything does pierce the veil and reach them, be the same good or bad, it must be something trivial and small, either in itself or to them; or at least of such a magnitude or such a kind as neither to make happy them that are not so otherwise, nor to deprive of their blessedness them that are.

It is plain then that the good or ill fortunes of their friends do affect the dead somewhat: but in such kind and degree as neither to make the happy unhappy nor produce any other such effect.

X

Having determined these points, let us examine with respect to Happiness, whether it belongs to the class of things praiseworthy or things precious; for to that of faculties it evidently does not.

Now it is plain that everything which is a subject of praise is praised for being of a certain kind and bearing a certain relation to something else: for instance, the just, and the valiant, and generally the good man, and virtue itself, we praise because of the actions and the results: and the strong man, and the quick runner, and so forth, we praise for being of a certain nature and bearing a certain relation to something good and excellent (and this is illustrated by attempts to praise the gods; for they are presented in a ludicrous aspect by being referred to our standard, and this results from the fact, that all praise does, as we have said, imply reference to a standard). Now if it is to such objects that praise belongs, it is evident that what is applicable to the best objects is not praise, but something higher and better: which is plain matter of fact, for not only do we call the gods blessed and happy, but of men also we pronounce those blessed who most nearly resemble the gods. And in like manner in respect of goods; no man thinks of praising Happiness as he does the principle of justice, but calls it blessed, as being somewhat more godlike and more excellent.

Eudoxus too is thought to have advanced a sound argument in support of the claim of pleasure to the highest prize: for the fact that, though it is one of the good things, it is not praised, he took for an indication of its superiority to those which are subjects of praise: a superiority he attributed also to a god and the Chief Good, on the ground that they form the standard to which everything besides is referred. For praise applies to virtue, because it makes men apt to do what is noble; but encomia to definite works of body or mind.

However, it is perhaps more suitable to a regular treatise on encomia to pursue this topic with exactness: it is enough for our purpose that from what has been said it is evident that Happiness belongs to the class of things precious and final. And it seems to be so also because of its being a starting-point; which it is, in that with a view to it we all do everything else that is done; now the starting-point and cause of good things we assume to be something precious and divine.

XI

Moreover, since Happiness is a kind of working of the soul in the way of perfect Excellence, we must inquire concerning Excellence: for so probably shall we have a clearer view concerning Happiness; and again, he who is really a statesman is generally thought to have spent most pains on this, for he wishes to make the citizens good and obedient to the laws. (For examples of this class we have the lawgivers of the Cretans and Lacedaemonians and whatever other such there have been.) But if this investigation belongs properly to [Greek: politikae], then clearly the inquiry will be in accordance with our original design.

Well, we are to inquire concerning Excellence, i.e. Human Excellence of course, because it was the Chief Good of Man and the Happiness of Man that we were inquiring of just now. By Human Excellence we mean not that of man's body but that of his soul; for we call Happiness a working of the Soul.

And if this is so, it is plain that some knowledge of the nature of the Soul is necessary for the statesman, just as for the Oculist a knowledge of the whole body, and the more so in proportion as [Greek: politikae] is more precious and higher than the healing art: and in fact physicians of the higher class do busy themselves much with the knowledge of the body.

So then the statesman is to consider the nature of the Soul: but he must do so with these objects in view, and so far only as may suffice for the objects of his special inquiry: for to carry his speculations to a greater exactness is perhaps a task more laborious than falls within his province.

In fact, the few statements made on the subject in my popular treatises are quite enough, and accordingly we will adopt them here: as, that the Soul consists of two parts, the Irrational and the Rational (as to whether these are actually divided, as are the parts of the body, and everything that is capable of division; or are only metaphysically speaking two, being by nature inseparable, as are convex and concave circumferences, matters not in respect of our present purpose). And of the Irrational, the one part seems common to other objects, and in fact vegetative; I mean the cause of nourishment and growth (for such a faculty of the Soul one would assume to exist in all things that receive nourishment, even in embryos, and this the same as in the perfect creatures; for this is more likely than that it should be a different one).

Now the Excellence of this manifestly is not peculiar to the human species but common to others: for this part and this faculty is thought to work most in time of sleep, and the good and bad man are least distinguishable while asleep; whence it is a common saying that during one half of life there is no difference between the happy and the wretched; and this accords with our anticipations, for sleep is an inactivity of the soul, in so far as it is denominated good or bad, except that in some wise some of its movements find their way through the veil and so the good come to have better dreams than ordinary men. But enough of this: we must forego any further mention of the nutritive part, since it is not naturally capable of the Excellence which is peculiarly human.

And there seems to be another Irrational Nature of the Soul, which yet in a way partakes of Reason. For in the man who controls his appetites, and in him who resolves to do so and fails, we praise the Reason or Rational part of the Soul, because it exhorts aright and to the best course: but clearly there is in them, beside the Reason, some other natural principle which fights with and strains against the Reason. (For in plain terms, just as paralysed limbs of the body when their owners would move them to the right are borne aside in a contrary direction to the left, so is it in the case of the Soul, for the impulses of men who cannot control their appetites are to contrary points: the difference is that in the case of the body we do see what is borne aside but in the case of the soul we do not. But, it may be, not the less on that account are we to suppose that there is in the Soul also somewhat besides the Reason, which is opposed to this and goes against it; as to how it is different, that is irrelevant.)

But of Reason this too does evidently partake, as we have said: for instance, in the man of self-control it obeys Reason: and perhaps in the man of perfected self-mastery, or the brave man, it is yet more obedient; in them it agrees entirely with the Reason.

So then the Irrational is plainly twofold: the one part, the merely vegetative, has no share of Reason, but that of desire, or appetition generally, does partake of it in a sense, in so far as it is obedient to it and capable of submitting to its rule. (So too in common phrase we say we have [Greek: logos] of our father or friends, and this in a different sense from that in which we say we have [Greek: logos] of mathematics.)

Now that the Irrational is in some way persuaded by the Reason, admonition, and every act of rebuke and exhortation indicate. If then we are to say that this also has Reason, then the Rational, as well as the Irrational, will be twofold, the one supremely and in itself, the other paying it a kind of filial regard.

The Excellence of Man then is divided in accordance with this difference: we make two classes, calling the one Intellectual, and the other Moral; pure science, intelligence, and practical wisdom--Intellectual: liberality, and perfected self-mastery--Moral: in speaking of a man's Moral character, we do not say he is a scientific or intelligent but a meek man, or one of perfected self-mastery: and we praise the man of science in right of his mental state; and of these such as are praiseworthy we call Excellences.

BOOK II

I

Well: human Excellence is of two kinds, Intellectual and Moral: now the Intellectual springs originally, and is increased subsequently, from teaching (for the most part that is), and needs therefore experience and time; whereas the Moral comes from custom, and so the Greek term denoting it is but a slight deflection from the term denoting custom in that language.

From this fact it is plain that not one of the Moral Virtues comes to be in us merely by nature: because of such things as exist by nature, none can be changed by custom: a stone, for instance, by nature gravitating downwards, could never by custom be brought to ascend, not even if one were to try and accustom it by throwing it up ten thousand times; nor could file again be brought to descend, nor in fact could anything whose nature is in one way be brought by custom to be in another. The Virtues then come to be in us neither by nature, nor in despite of nature, but we are furnished by nature with a capacity for receiving themu and are perfected in them through custom.

Again, in whatever cases we get things by nature, we get the faculties first and perform the acts of working afterwards; an illustration of which is afforded by the case of our bodily senses, for it was not from having often seen or heard that we got these senses, but just the reverse: we had them and so exercised them, but did not have them because we had exercised them. But the Virtues we get by first performing single acts of working, which, again, is the case of other things, as the arts for instance; for what we have to make when we have learned how, these we learn how to make by making: men come to be builders, for instance, by building; harp-players, by playing on the harp: exactly so, by doing just actions we come to be just; by doing the actions of self-mastery we come to be perfected in self-mastery; and by doing brave actions brave.

And to the truth of this testimony is borne by what takes place in communities: because the law-givers make the individual members good men by habituation, and this is the intention certainly of every law-giver, and all who do not effect it well fail of their intent; and herein consists the difference between a good Constitution and a bad.

Again, every Virtue is either produced or destroyed from and by the very same circumstances: art too in like manner; I mean it is by playing the harp that both the good and the bad harp-players are formed: and similarly builders and all the rest; by building well men will become good builders; by doing it badly bad ones: in fact, if this had not been so, there would have been no need of instructors, but all men would have been at once good or bad in their several arts without them.

So too then is it with the Virtues: for by acting in the various relations in which we are thrown with our fellow men, we come to be, some just, some unjust: and by acting in dangerous positions and being habituated to feel fear or confidence, we come to be, some brave, others cowards.

Similarly is it also with respect to the occasions of lust and anger: for some men come to be perfected in self-mastery and mild, others destitute of all self-control and passionate; the one class by behaving in one way under them, the other by behaving in another. Or, in one word, the habits are produced from the acts of working like to them: and so what we have to do is to give a certain character to these particular acts, because the habits formed correspond to the differences of these.

So then, whether we are accustomed this way or that straight from childhood, makes not a small but an important difference, or rather I would say it makes all the difference.

II

Since then the object of the present treatise is not mere speculation, as it is of some others (for we are inquiring not merely that we may know what virtue is but that we may become virtuous, else it would have been useless), we must consider as to the particular actions how we are to do them, because, as we have just said, the quality of the habits that shall be formed depends on these.

Now, that we are to act in accordance with Right Reason is a general maxim, and may for the present be taken for granted: we will speak of it hereafter, and say both what Right Reason is, and what are its relations to the other virtues.

But let this point be first thoroughly understood between us, that all which can be said on moral action must be said in outline, as it were, and not exactly: for as we remarked at the commencement, such reasoning only must be required as the nature of the subject-matter admits of, and matters of moral action and expediency have no fixedness any more than matters of health. And if the subject in its general maxims is such, still less in its application to particular cases is exactness attainable: because these fall not under any art or system of rules, but it must be left in each instance to the individual agents to look to the exigencies of the particular case, as it is in the art of healing, or that of navigating a ship. Still, though the present subject is confessedly such, we must try and do what we can for it.

First then this must be noted, that it is the nature of such things to be spoiled by defect and excess; as we see in the case of health and strength (since for the illustration of things which cannot be seen we must use those that can), for excessive training impairs the strength as well as deficient: meat and drink, in like manner, in too great or too small quantities, impair the health: while in due proportion they cause, increase, and preserve it.

Thus it is therefore with the habits of perfected Self-Mastery and Courage and the rest of the Virtues: for the man who flies from and fears all things, and never stands up against anything, comes to be a coward; and he who fears nothing, but goes at everything, comes to be rash. In like manner too, he that tastes of every pleasure and abstains from none comes to lose all self-control; while he who avoids all, as do the dull and clownish, comes as it were to lose his faculties of perception: that is to say, the habits of perfected Self-Mastery and Courage are spoiled by the excess and defect, but by the mean state are preserved.

Furthermore, not only do the origination, growth, and marring of the habits come from and by the same circumstances, but also the acts of working after the habits are formed will be exercised on the same: for so it is also with those other things which are more directly matters of sight, strength for instance: for this comes by taking plenty of food and doing plenty of work, and the man who has attained strength is best able to do these: and so it is with the Virtues, for not only do we by abstaining from pleasures come to be perfected in Self-Mastery, but when we have come to be so we can best abstain from them: similarly too with Courage: for it is by accustoming ourselves to despise objects of fear and stand up against them that we come to be brave; and after we have come to be so we shall be best able to stand up against such objects.

III

And for a test of the formation of the habits we must take the pleasure or pain which succeeds the acts; for he is perfected in Self-Mastery who not only abstains from the bodily pleasures but is glad to do so; whereas he who abstains but is sorry to do it has not Self-Mastery: he again is brave who stands up against danger, either with positive pleasure or at least without any pain; whereas he who does it with pain is not brave.

For Moral Virtue has for its object-matter pleasures and pains, because by reason of pleasure we do what is bad, and by reason of pain decline doing what is right (for which cause, as Plato observes, men should have been trained straight from their childhood to receive pleasure and pain from proper objects, for this is the right education). Again: since Virtues have to do with actions and feelings, and on every feeling and every action pleasure and pain follow, here again is another proof that Virtue has for its object-matter pleasure and pain. The same is shown also by the fact that punishments are effected through the instrumentality of these; because they are of the nature of remedies, and it is the nature of remedies to be the contraries of the ills they cure. Again, to quote what we said before: every habit of the Soul by its very nature has relation to, and exerts itself upon, things of the same kind as those by which it is naturally deteriorated or improved: now such habits do come to be vicious by reason of pleasures and pains, that is, by men pursuing or avoiding respectively, either such as they ought not, or at wrong times, or in wrong manner, and so forth (for which reason, by the way, some people define the Virtues as certain states of impassibility and utter quietude, but they are wrong because they speak without modification, instead of adding "as they ought," "as they ought not," and "when," and so on). Virtue then is assumed to be that habit which is such, in relation to pleasures and pains, as to effect the best results, and Vice the contrary.

The following considerations may also serve to set this in a clear light. There are principally three things moving us to choice and three to avoidance, the honourable, the expedient, the pleasant; and their three contraries, the dishonourable, the hurtful, and the painful: now the good man is apt to go right, and the bad man wrong, with respect to all these of course, but most specially with respect to pleasure: because not only is this common to him with all animals but also it is a concomitant of all those things which move to choice, since both the honourable and the expedient give an impression of pleasure.

Again, it grows up with us all from infancy, and so it is a hard matter to remove from ourselves this feeling, engrained as it is into our very life.

Again, we adopt pleasure and pain (some of us more, and some less) as the measure even of actions: for this cause then our whole business must be with them, since to receive right or wrong impressions of pleasure and pain is a thing of no little importance in respect of the actions. Once more; it is harder, as Heraclitus says, to fight against pleasure than against anger: now it is about that which is more than commonly difficult that art comes into being, and virtue too, because in that which is difficult the good is of a higher order: and so for this reason too both virtue and moral philosophy generally must wholly busy themselves respecting pleasures and pains, because he that uses these well will be good, he that does so ill will be bad.

Let us then be understood to have stated, that Virtue has for its object-matter pleasures and pains, and that it is either increased or marred by the same circumstances (differently used) by which it is originally generated, and that it exerts itself on the same circumstances out of which it was generated.

Now I can conceive a person perplexed as to the meaning of our statement, that men must do just actions to become just, and those of self-mastery to acquire the habit of self-mastery; "for," he would say, "if men are doing the actions they have the respective virtues already, just as men are grammarians or musicians when they do the actions of either art." May we not reply by saying that it is not so even in the case of the arts referred to: because a man may produce something grammatical either by chance or the suggestion of another; but then only will he be a grammarian when he not only produces something grammatical but does so grammarian-wise, i.e. in virtue of the grammatical knowledge he himself possesses.

Again, the cases of the arts and the virtues are not parallel: because those things which are produced by the arts have their excellence in themselves, and it is sufficient therefore that these when produced should be in a certain state: but those which are produced in the way of the virtues, are, strictly speaking, actions of a certain kind (say of Justice or perfected Self-Mastery), not merely if in themselves they are in a certain state but if also he who does them does them being himself in a certain state, first if knowing what he is doing, next if with deliberate preference, and with such preference for the things' own sake; and thirdly if being himself stable and unapt to change. Now to constitute possession of the arts these requisites are not reckoned in, excepting the one point of knowledge: whereas for possession of the virtues knowledge avails little or nothing, but the other requisites avail not a little, but, in fact, are all in all, and these requisites as a matter of fact do come from oftentimes doing the actions of Justice and perfected Self-Mastery.

The facts, it is true, are called by the names of these habits when they are such as the just or perfectly self-mastering man would do; but he is not in possession of the virtues who merely does these facts, but he who also so does them as the just and self-mastering do them.

We are right then in saying, that these virtues are formed in a man by his doing the actions; but no one, if he should leave them undone, would be even in the way to become a good man. Yet people in general do not perform these actions, but taking refuge in talk they flatter themselves they are philosophising, and that they will so be good men: acting in truth very like those sick people who listen to the doctor with great attention but do nothing that he tells them: just as these then cannot be well bodily under such a course of treatment, so neither can those be mentally by such philosophising.

IV

Next, we must examine what Virtue is. Well, since the things which come to be in the mind are, in all, of three kinds, Feelings, Capacities, States, Virtue of course must belong to one of the three classes.

By Feelings, I mean such as lust, anger, fear, confidence, envy, joy, friendship, hatred, longing, emulation, compassion, in short all such as are followed by pleasure or pain: by Capacities, those in right of which we are said to be capable of these feelings; as by virtue of which we are able to have been made angry, or grieved, or to have compassionated; by States, those in right of which we are in a certain relation good or bad to the aforementioned feelings; to having been made angry, for instance, we are in a wrong relation if in our anger we were too violent or too slack, but if we were in the happy medium we are in a right relation to the feeling. And so on of the rest.

Now Feelings neither the virtues nor vices are, because in right of the Feelings we are not denominated either good or bad, but in right of the virtues and vices we are.

Again, in right of the Feelings we are neither praised nor blamed (for a man is not commended for being afraid or being angry, nor blamed for being angry merely but for being so in a particular way), but in right of the virtues and vices we are.

Again, both anger and fear we feel without moral choice, whereas the virtues are acts of moral choice, or at least certainly not independent of it.

Moreover, in right of the Feelings we are said to be moved, but in right of the virtues and vices not to be moved, but disposed, in a certain way.

And for these same reasons they are not Capacities, for we are not called good or bad merely because we are able to feel, nor are we praised or blamed.

And again, Capacities we have by nature, but we do not come to be good or bad by nature, as we have said before.

Since then the virtues are neither Feelings nor Capacities, it remains that they must be States.

V

Now what the genus of Virtue is has been said; but we must not merely speak of it thus, that it is a state but say also what kind of a state it is. We must observe then that all excellence makes that whereof it is the excellence both to be itself in a good state and to perform its work well. The excellence of the eye, for instance, makes both the eye good and its work also: for by the excellence of the eye we see well. So too the excellence of the horse makes a horse good, and good in speed, and in carrying his rider, and standing up against the enemy. If then this is universally the case, the excellence of Man, i.e. Virtue, must be a state whereby Man comes to be good and whereby he will perform well his proper work. Now how this shall be it is true we have said already, but still perhaps it may throw light on the subject to see what is its characteristic nature.

In all quantity then, whether continuous or discrete, one may take the greater part, the less, or the exactly equal, and these either with reference to the thing itself, or relatively to us: and the exactly equal is a mean between excess and defect. Now by the mean of the thing, i.e. absolute mean, I denote that which is equidistant from either extreme (which of course is one and the same to all), and by the mean relatively to ourselves, that which is neither too much nor too little for the particular individual. This of course is not one nor the same to all: for instance, suppose ten is too much and two too little, people take six for the absolute mean; because it exceeds the smaller sum by exactly as much as it is itself exceeded by the larger, and this mean is according to arithmetical proportion.

But the mean relatively to ourselves must not be so found ; for it does not follow, supposing ten minæ is too large a quantity to eat and two too small, that the trainer will order his man six; because for the person who is to take it this also may be too much or too little: for Milo it would be too little, but for a man just commencing his athletic exercises too much: similarly too of the exercises themselves, as running or wrestling.

So then it seems every one possessed of skill avoids excess and defect, but seeks for and chooses the mean, not the absolute but the relative.

Now if all skill thus accomplishes well its work by keeping an eye on the mean, and bringing the works to this point (whence it is common enough to say of such works as are in a good state, "one cannot add to or take ought from them," under the notion of excess or defect destroying goodness but the mean state preserving it), and good artisans, as we say, work with their eye on this, and excellence, like nature, is more exact and better than any art in the world, it must have an aptitude to aim at the mean.

It is moral excellence, i.e. Virtue, of course which I mean, because this it is which is concerned with feelings and actions, and in these there can be excess and defect and the mean: it is possible, for instance, to feel the emotions of fear, confidence, lust, anger, compassion, and pleasure and pain generally, too much or too little, and in either case wrongly; but to feel them when we ought, on what occasions, towards whom, why, and as, we should do, is the mean, or in other words the best state, and this is the property of Virtue.

In like manner too with respect to the actions, there may be excess and defect and the mean. Now Virtue is concerned with feelings and actions, in which the excess is wrong and the defect is blamed but the mean is praised and goes right; and both these circumstances belong to Virtue. Virtue then is in a sense a mean state, since it certainly has an aptitude for aiming at the mean.

Again, one may go wrong in many different ways (because, as the Pythagoreans expressed it, evil is of the class of the infinite, good of the finite), but right only in one; and so the former is easy, the latter difficult; easy to miss the mark, but hard to hit it: and for these reasons, therefore, both the excess and defect belong to Vice, and the mean state to Virtue; for, as the poet has it,

"Men may be bad in many ways,
But good in one alone."

Virtue then is "a state apt to exercise deliberate choice, being in the relative mean, determined by reason, and as the man of practical wisdom would determine."

It is a middle state between too faulty ones, in the way of excess on one side and of defect on the other: and it is so moreover, because the faulty states on one side fall short of, and those on the other exceed, what is right, both in the case of the feelings and the actions; but Virtue finds, and when found adopts, the mean.

And so, viewing it in respect of its essence and definition, Virtue is a mean state; but in reference to the chief good and to excellence it is the highest state possible.

But it must not be supposed that every action or every feeling is capable of subsisting in this mean state, because some there are which are so named as immediately to convey the notion of badness, as malevolence, shamelessness, envy; or, to instance in actions, adultery, theft, homicide; for all these and suchlike are blamed because they are in themselves bad, not the having too much or too little of them.

In these then you never can go right, but must always be wrong: nor in such does the right or wrong depend on the selection of a proper person, time, or manner (take adultery for instance), but simply doing any one soever of those things is being wrong.

You might as well require that there should be determined a mean state, an excess and a defect in respect of acting unjustly, being cowardly, or giving up all control of the passions: for at this rate there will be of excess and defect a mean state; of excess, excess; and of defect, defect.

But just as of perfected self-mastery and courage there is no excess and defect, because the mean is in one point of view the highest possible state, so neither of those faulty states can you have a mean state, excess, or defect, but howsoever done they are wrong: you cannot, in short, have of excess and defect a mean state, nor of a mean state excess and defect.

VI

It is not enough, however, to state this in general terms, we must also apply it to particular instances, because in treatises on moral conduct general statements have an air of vagueness, but those which go into detail one of greater reality: for the actions after all must be in detail, and the general statements, to be worth anything, must hold good here.

We must take these details then from the Table.

I. In respect of fears and confidence or boldness:

The Mean state is Courage: men may exceed, of course, either in absence of fear or in positive confidence: the former has no name (which is a common case), the latter is called rash: again, the man who has too much fear and too little confidence is called a coward.

II. In respect of pleasures and pains (but not all, and perhaps fewer pains than pleasures):

The Mean state here is perfected Self-Mastery, the defect total absence of Self-control. As for defect in respect of pleasure, there are really no people who are chargeable with it, so, of course, there is really no name for such characters, but, as they are conceivable, we will give them one and call them insensible.

III. In respect of giving and taking wealth (a):

The mean state is Liberality, the excess Prodigality, the defect Stinginess: here each of the extremes involves really an excess and defect contrary to each other: I mean, the prodigal gives out too much and takes in too little, while the stingy man takes in too much and gives out too little. (It must be understood that we are now giving merely an outline and summary, intentionally: and we will, in a later part of the treatise, draw out the distinctions with greater exactness.)

IV. In respect of wealth (b):

There are other dispositions besides these just mentioned; a mean state called Munificence (for the munificent man differs from the liberal, the former having necessarily to do with great wealth, the latter with but small); the excess called by the names either of Want of taste or Vulgar Profusion, and the defect Paltriness (these also differ from the extremes connected with liberality, and the manner of their difference shall also be spoken of later).

V. In respect of honour and dishonour (a):

The mean state Greatness of Soul, the excess which may be called braggadocio, and the defect Littleness of Soul.

VI. In respect of honour and dishonour (b):

Now there is a state bearing the same relation to Greatness of Soul as we said just now Liberality does to Munificence, with the difference that is of being about a small amount of the same thing: this state having reference to small honour, as Greatness of Soul to great honour; a man may, of course, grasp at honour either more than he should or less; now he that exceeds in his grasping at it is called ambitious, he that falls short unambitious, he that is just as he should be has no proper name: nor in fact have the states, except that the disposition of the ambitious man is called ambition. For this reason those who are in either extreme lay claim to the mean as a debateable land, and we call the virtuous character sometimes by the name ambitious, sometimes by that of unambitious, and we commend sometimes the one and sometimes the other. Why we do it shall be said in the subsequent part of the treatise; but now we will go on with the rest of the virtues after the plan we have laid down.

VII. In respect of anger:

Here too there is excess, defect, and a mean state; but since they may be said to have really no proper names, as we call the virtuous character Meek, we will call the mean state Meekness, and of the extremes, let the man who is excessive be denominated Passionate, and the faulty state Passionateness, and him who is deficient Angerless, and the defect Angerlessness.

There are also three other mean states, having some mutual resemblance, but still with differences; they are alike in that they all have for their object-matter intercourse of words and deeds, and they differ in that one has respect to truth herein, the other two to what is pleasant; and this in two ways, the one in relaxation and amusement, the other in all things which occur in daily life. We must say a word or two about these also, that we may the better see that in all matters the mean is praiseworthy, while the extremes are neither right nor worthy of praise but of blame.

Now of these, it is true, the majority have really no proper names, but still we must try, as in the other cases, to coin some for them for the sake of clearness and intelligibleness.

I. In respect of truth: The man who is in the mean state we will call Truthful, and his state Truthfulness, and as to the disguise of truth, if it be on the side of exaggeration, Braggadocia, and him that has it a Braggadocio; if on that of diminution, Reserve and Reserved shall be the terms.

II. In respect of what is pleasant in the way of relaxation or amusement: The mean state shall be called Easy-pleasantry, and the character accordingly a man of Easy-pleasantry; the excess Buffoonery, and the man a Buffoon; the man deficient herein a Clown, and his state Clownishness.

III. In respect of what is pleasant in daily life: He that is as he should be may be called Friendly, and his mean state Friendliness: he that exceeds, if it be without any interested motive, somewhat too Complaisant, if with such motive, a Flatterer: he that is deficient and in all instances unpleasant, Quarrelsome and Cross.

There are mean states likewise in feelings and matters concerning them. Shamefacedness, for instance, is no virtue, still a man is praised for being shamefaced: for in these too the one is denominated the man in the mean state, the other in the excess; the Dumbfoundered, for instance, who is overwhelmed with shame on all and any occasions: the man who is in the defect, i.e. who has no shame at all in his composition, is called Shameless: but the right character Shamefaced.

Indignation against successful vice, again, is a state in the mean between Envy and Malevolence: they all three have respect to pleasure and pain produced by what happens to one's neighbour: for the man who has this right feeling is annoyed at undeserved success of others, while the envious man goes beyond him and is annoyed at all success of others, and the malevolent falls so far short of feeling annoyance that he even rejoices [at misfortune of others].

But for the discussion of these also there will be another opportunity, as of Justice too, because the term is used in more senses than one. So after this we will go accurately into each and say how they are mean states: and in like manner also with respect to the Intellectual Excellences.

Now as there are three states in each case, two faulty either in the way of excess or defect, and one right, which is the mean state, of course all are in a way opposed to one another; the extremes, for instance, not only to the mean but also to one another, and the mean to the extremes: for just as the half is greater if compared with the less portion, and less if compared with the greater, so the mean states, compared with the defects, exceed, whether in feelings or actions, and vice versa. The brave man, for instance, shows as rash when compared with the coward, and cowardly when compared with the rash;

similarly too the man of perfected self-mastery, viewed in comparison with the man destitute of all perception, shows like a man of no self-control, but in comparison with the man who really has no self-control, he looks like one destitute of all perception: and the liberal man compared with the stingy seems prodigal, and by the side of the prodigal, stingy.

And so the extreme characters push away, so to speak, towards each other the man in the mean state; the brave man is called a rash man by the coward, and a coward by the rash man, and in the other cases accordingly. And there being this mutual opposition, the contrariety between the extremes is greater than between either and the mean, because they are further from one another than from the mean, just as the greater or less portion differ more from each other than either from the exact half.

Again, in some cases an extreme will bear a resemblance to the mean; rashness, for instance, to courage, and prodigality to liberality; but between the extremes there is the greatest dissimilarity. Now things which are furthest from one another are defined to be contrary, and so the further off the more contrary will they be.

Further: of the extremes in some cases the excess, and in others the defect, is most opposed to the mean: to courage, for instance, not rashness which is the excess, but cowardice which is the defect; whereas to perfected self-mastery not insensibility which is the defect but absence of all self-control which is the excess.

And for this there are two reasons to be given; one from the nature of the thing itself, because from the one extreme being nearer and more like the mean, we do not put this against it, but the other; as, for instance, since rashness is thought to be nearer to courage than cowardice is, and to resemble it more, we put cowardice against courage rather than rashness, because those things which are further from the mean are thought to be more contrary to it. This then is one reason arising from the thing itself; there is another arising from our own constitution and make: for in each man's own case those things give the impression of being more contrary to the mean to which we individually have a natural bias. Thus we have a natural bias towards pleasures, for which reason we are much more inclined to the rejection of all self-control, than to self-discipline.

These things then to which the bias is, we call more contrary, and so total want of self-control (the excess) is more contrary than the defect is to perfected self-mastery.

VII

Now that Moral Virtue is a mean state, and how it is so, and that it lies between two faulty states, one in the way of excess and another in the way of defect, and that it is so because it has an aptitude to aim at the mean both in feelings and actions, all this has been set forth fully and sufficiently.

And so it is hard to be good: for surely hard it is in each instance to find the mean, just as to find the mean point or centre of a circle is not what any man can do, but only he who knows how: just so to be angry, to give money, and be expensive, is what any man can do, and easy: but to do these to the right person, in due proportion, at the right time, with a right object, and in the right manner, this is not as before what any man can do, nor is it easy; and for this cause goodness is rare, and praiseworthy, and noble.

Therefore he who aims at the mean should make it his first care to keep away from that extreme which is more contrary than the other to the mean; just as Calypso in Homer advises Ulysses,

"Clear of this smoke and surge thy barque direct;"

because of the two extremes the one is always more, and the other less, erroneous; and, therefore, since to hit exactly on the mean is difficult, one must take the least of the evils as the safest plan; and this a man will be doing, if he follows this method.

We ought also to take into consideration our own natural bias; which varies in each man's case, and will be ascertained from the pleasure and pain arising in us. Furthermore, we should force ourselves off in the contrary direction, because we shall find ourselves in the mean after we have removed ourselves far from the wrong side, exactly as men do in straightening bent timber.

But in all cases we must guard most carefully against what is pleasant, and pleasure itself, because we are not impartial judges of it.

We ought to feel in fact towards pleasure as did the old counsellors towards Helen, and in all cases pronounce a similar sentence; for so by sending it away from us, we shall err the less.

Well, to speak very briefly, these are the precautions by adopting which we shall be best able to attain the mean.

Still, perhaps, after all it is a matter of difficulty, and specially in the particular instances: it is not easy, for instance, to determine exactly in what manner, with what persons, for what causes, and for what length of time, one ought to feel anger: for we ourselves sometimes praise those who are defective in this feeling, and we call them meek; at another, we term the hot-tempered manly and spirited.

Then, again, he who makes a small deflection from what is right, be it on the side of too much or too little, is not blamed, only he who makes a considerable one; for he cannot escape observation. But to what point or degree a man must err in order to incur blame, it is not easy to determine exactly in words: nor in fact any of those points which are matter of perception by the Moral Sense: such questions are matters of detail, and the decision of them rests with the Moral Sense.

At all events thus much is plain, that the mean state is in all things praiseworthy, and that practically we must deflect sometimes towards excess sometimes towards defect, because this will be the easiest method of hitting on the mean, that is, on what is right.

BOOK III

I

Now since Virtue is concerned with the regulation of feelings and actions, and praise and blame arise upon such as are voluntary, while for the involuntary allowance is made, and sometimes compassion is excited, it is perhaps a necessary task for those who are investigating the nature of Virtue to draw out the distinction between what is voluntary and what involuntary; and it is certainly useful for legislators, with respect to the assigning of honours and punishments.

Involuntary actions then are thought to be of two kinds, being done either on compulsion, or by reason of ignorance. An action is, properly speaking, compulsory, when the origination is external to the agent, being such that in it the agent (perhaps we may more properly say the patient) contributes nothing; as if a wind were to convey you anywhere, or men having power over your person.

But when actions are done, either from fear of greater evils, or from some honourable motive, as, for instance, if you were ordered to commit some base act by a despot who had your parents or children in his power, and they were to be saved upon your compliance or die upon your refusal, in such cases there is room for a question whether the actions are voluntary or involuntary.

A similar question arises with respect to cases of throwing goods overboard in a storm: abstractedly no man throws away his property willingly, but with a view to his own and his shipmates' safety any one would who had any sense.

The truth is, such actions are of a mixed kind, but are most like voluntary actions; for they are choiceworthy at the time when they are being done, and the end or object of the action must be taken with reference to the actual occasion. Further, we must denominate an action voluntary or involuntary at the time of doing it: now in the given case the man acts voluntarily, because the originating of the motion of his limbs in such actions rests with himself; and where the origination is in himself it rests with himself to do or not to do.

Such actions then are voluntary, though in the abstract perhaps involuntary because no one would choose any of such things in and by itself.

But for such actions men sometimes are even praised, as when they endure any disgrace or pain to secure great and honourable equivalents; if vice versâ, then they are blamed, because it shows a base mind to endure things very disgraceful for no honourable object, or for a trifling one.

For some again no praise is given, but allowance is made; as where a man does what he should not by reason of such things as overstrain the powers of human nature, or pass the limits of human endurance.

Some acts perhaps there are for which compulsion cannot be pleaded, but a man should rather suffer the worst and die; how absurd, for instance, are the pleas of compulsion with which Alcmaeon in Euripides' play excuses his matricide!

But it is difficult sometimes to decide what kind of thing should be chosen instead of what, or what endured in preference to what, and much moreso to abide by one's decisions: for in general the alternatives are painful, and the actions required are base, and so praise or blame is awarded according as persons have been compelled or no.

What kind of actions then are to be called compulsory? may we say, simply and abstractedly whenever the cause is external and the agent contributes nothing; and that where the acts are in themselves such as one would not wish but choiceworthy at the present time and in preference to such and such things, and where the origination rests with the agent, the actions are in themselves involuntary but at the given time and in preference to such and such things voluntary; and they are more like voluntary than involuntary, because the actions consist of little details, and these are voluntary.

But what kind of things one ought to choose instead of what, it is not easy to settle, for there are many differences in particular instances.

But suppose a person should say, things pleasant and honourable exert a compulsive force (for that they are external and do compel); at that rate every action is on compulsion, because these are universal motives of action.

Again, they who act on compulsion and against their will do so with pain; but they who act by reason of what is pleasant or honourable act with pleasure.

It is truly absurd for a man to attribute his actions to external things instead of to his own capacity for being easily caught by them; or, again, to ascribe the honourable to himself, and the base ones to pleasure.

So then that seems to be compulsory "whose origination is from without, the party compelled contributing nothing." Now every action of which ignorance is the cause is not-voluntary, but that only is involuntary which is attended with pain and remorse; for clearly the man who has done anything by reason of ignorance, but is not annoyed at his own action, cannot be said to have done it with his will because he did not know he was doing it, nor again against his will because he is not sorry for it.

So then of the class "acting by reason of ignorance," he who feels regret afterwards is thought to be an involuntary agent, and him that has no such feeling, since he certainly is different from the other, we will call a not-voluntary agent; for as there is a real difference it is better to have a proper name.

Again, there seems to be a difference between acting because of ignorance and acting with ignorance: for instance, we do not usually assign ignorance as the cause of the actions of the drunken or angry man, but either the drunkenness or the anger, yet they act not knowingly but with ignorance.

Again, every bad man is ignorant what he ought to do and what to leave undone, and by reason of such error men become unjust and wholly evil.

Again, we do not usually apply the term involuntary when a man is ignorant of his own true interest; because ignorance which affects moral choice constitutes depravity but not involuntariness: nor does any ignorance of principle (because for this men are blamed) but ignorance in particular details, wherein consists the action and wherewith it is concerned, for in these there is both compassion and allowance, because he who acts in ignorance of any of them acts in a proper sense involuntarily.

It may be as well, therefore, to define these particular details; what they are, and how many; viz. who acts, what he is doing, with respect to what or in what, sometimes with what, as with what instrument, and with what result (as that of preservation, for instance), and how, as whether softly or violently.

All these particulars, in one and the same case, no man in his senses could be ignorant of; plainly not of the agent, being himself. But what he is doing a man may be ignorant, as men in speaking say a thing escaped them unawares; or as Aeschylus did with respect to the Mysteries, that he was not aware that it was unlawful to speak of them; or as in the case of that catapult accident the other day the man said he discharged it merely to display its operation. Or a person might suppose a son to be an enemy, as Merope did; or that the spear really pointed was rounded off; or that the stone was a pumice; or in striking with a view to save might kill; or might strike when merely wishing to show another, as people do in sham-fighting.

Now since ignorance is possible in respect to all these details in which the action consists, he that acted in ignorance of any of them is thought to have acted involuntarily, and he most so who was in ignorance as regards the most important, which are thought to be those in which the action consists, and the result.

Further, not only must the ignorance be of this kind, to constitute an action involuntary, but it must be also understood that the action is followed by pain and regret.

Now since all involuntary action is either upon compulsion or by reason of ignorance, Voluntary Action would seem to be "that whose origination is in the agent, he being aware of the particular details in which the action consists."

For, it may be, men are not justified by calling those actions involuntary, which are done by reason of Anger or Lust.

Because, in the first place, if this be so no other animal but man, and not even children, can be said to act voluntarily. Next, is it meant that we never act voluntarily when we act from Lust or Anger, or that we act voluntarily in doing what is right and involuntarily in doing what is discreditable? The latter supposition is absurd, since the cause is one and the same. Then as to the former, it is a strange thing to maintain actions to be involuntary which we are bound to grasp at: now there are occasions on which anger is a duty, and there are things which we are bound to lust after, health, for instance, and learning.

Again, whereas actions strictly involuntary are thought to be attended with pain, those which are done to gratify lust are thought to be pleasant.

Again: how does the involuntariness make any difference between wrong actions done from deliberate calculation, and those done by reason of anger? for both ought to be avoided, and the irrational feelings are thought to be just as natural to man as reason, and so of course must be such actions of the individual as are done from Anger and Lust. It is absurd then to class these actions among the involuntary.

II

Having thus drawn out the distinction between voluntary and involuntary action our next step is to examine into the nature of Moral Choice, because this seems most intimately connected with Virtue and to be a more decisive test of moral character than a man's acts are.

Now Moral Choice is plainly voluntary, but the two are not co-extensive, voluntary being the more comprehensive term; for first, children and all other animals share in voluntary action but not in Moral Choice; and next, sudden actions we call voluntary but do not ascribe them to Moral Choice.

Nor do they appear to be right who say it is lust or anger, or wish, or opinion of a certain kind; because, in the first place, Moral Choice is not shared by the irrational animals while Lust and Anger are. Next; the man who fails of self-control acts from Lust but not from Moral Choice; the man of self-control, on the contrary, from Moral Choice, not from Lust. Again: whereas Lust is frequently opposed to Moral Choice, Lust is not to Lust.

Lastly: the object-matter of Lust is the pleasant and the painful, but of Moral Choice neither the one nor the other. Still less can it be Anger, because actions done from Anger are thought generally to be least of all consequent on Moral Choice.

Nor is it Wish either, though appearing closely connected with it; because, in the first place, Moral Choice has not for its objects impossibilities, and if a man were to say he chose them he would be thought to be a fool; but Wish may have impossible things for its objects, immortality for instance.

Wish again may be exercised on things in the accomplishment of which one's self could have nothing to do, as the success of any particular actor or athlete; but no man chooses things of this nature, only such as he believes he may himself be instrumental in procuring.

Further: Wish has for its object the End rather, but Moral Choice the means to the End; for instance, we wish to be healthy but we choose the means which will make us so; or happiness again we wish for, and commonly say so, but to say we choose is not an appropriate term, because, in short, the province of Moral Choice seems to be those things which are in our own power.

Neither can it be Opinion; for Opinion is thought to be unlimited in its range of objects, and to be exercised as well upon things eternal and impossible as on those which are in our own power: again, Opinion is logically divided into true and false, not into good and bad as Moral Choice is.

However, nobody perhaps maintains its identity with Opinion simply; but it is not the same with opinion of any kind, because by choosing good and bad things we are constituted of a certain character, but by having opinions on them we are not.

Again, we choose to take or avoid, and so on, but we opine what a thing is, or for what it is serviceable, or how; but we do not opine to take or avoid.

Further, Moral Choice is commended rather for having a right object than for being judicious, but Opinion for being formed in accordance with truth.

Again, we choose such things as we pretty well know to be good, but we form opinions respecting such as we do not know at all.

And it is not thought that choosing and opining best always go together, but that some opine the better course and yet by reason of viciousness choose not the things which they should.

It may be urged, that Opinion always precedes or accompanies Moral Choice; be it so, this makes no difference, for this is not the point in question, but whether Moral Choice is the same as Opinion of a certain kind.

Since then it is none of the aforementioned things, what is it, or how is it characterised? Voluntary it plainly is, but not all voluntary action is an object of Moral Choice. May we not say then, it is "that voluntary which has passed through a stage of previous deliberation?" because Moral Choice is attended with reasoning and intellectual process. The etymology of its Greek name seems to give a hint of it, being when analysed "chosen in preference to somewhat else."

III

Well then; do men deliberate about everything, and is anything soever the object of Deliberation, or are there some matters with respect to which there is none? (It may be as well perhaps to say, that by "object of Deliberation" is meant such matter as a sensible man would deliberate upon, not what any fool or madman might.)

Well: about eternal things no one deliberates; as, for instance, the universe, or the incommensurability of the diameter and side of a square.

Nor again about things which are in motion but which always happen in the same way either necessarily, or naturally, or from some other cause, as the solstices or the sunrise.

Nor about those which are variable, as drought and rains; nor fortuitous matters, as finding of treasure.

Nor in fact even about all human affairs; no Lacedæmonian, for instance, deliberates as to the best course for the Scythian government to adopt; because in such cases we have no power over the result.

But we do deliberate respecting such practical matters as are in our own power (which are what are left after all our exclusions).

I have adopted this division because causes seem to be divisible into nature, necessity, chance, and moreover intellect, and all human powers.

And as man in general deliberates about what man in general can effect, so individuals do about such practical things as can be effected through their own instrumentality.

Again, we do not deliberate respecting such arts or sciences as are exact and independent: as, for instance, about written characters, because we have no doubt how they should be formed; but we do deliberate on all such things as are usually done through our own instrumentality, but not invariably in the same way; as, for instance, about matters connected with the healing art, or with money-making; and, again, more about piloting ships than gymnastic exercises, because the former has been less exactly determined, and so forth; and more about arts than sciences, because we more frequently doubt respecting the former.

So then Deliberation takes place in such matters as are under general laws, but still uncertain how in any given case they will issue, i.e. in which there is some indefiniteness; and for great matters we associate coadjutors in counsel, distrusting our ability to settle them alone.

Further, we deliberate not about Ends, but Means to Ends. No physician, for instance, deliberates whether he will cure, nor orator whether he will persuade, nor statesman whether he will produce a good constitution, nor in fact any man in any other function about his particular End; but having set before them a certain End they look how and through what means it may be accomplished: if there is a choice of means, they examine further which are easiest and most creditable; or, if there is but one means of accomplishing the object, then how it may be through this, this again through what, till they come to the first cause; and this will be the last found; for a man engaged in a process of deliberation seems to seek and analyse, as a man, to solve a problem, analyses the figure given him. And plainly not every search is Deliberation, those in mathematics to wit, but every Deliberation is a search, and the last step in the analysis is the first in the constructive process. And if in the course of their search men come upon an impossibility, they give it up; if money, for instance, be necessary, but cannot be got: but if the thing appears possible they then attempt to do it.

And by possible I mean what may be done through our own instrumentality (of course what may be done through our friends is through our own instrumentality in a certain sense, because the origination in such cases rests with us). And the object of search is sometimes the necessary instruments, sometimes the method of using them; and similarly in the rest sometimes through what, and sometimes how or through what.

So it seems, as has been said, that Man is the originator of his actions; and Deliberation has for its object whatever may be done through one's own instrumentality, and the actions are with a view to other things; and so it is, not the End, but the Means to Ends on which Deliberation is employed.

Nor, again, is it employed on matters of detail, as whether the substance before me is bread, or has been properly cooked; for these come under the province of sense, and if a man is to be always deliberating, he may go on ad infinitum.

Further, exactly the same matter is the object both of Deliberation and Moral Choice; but that which is the object of Moral Choice is thenceforward separated off and definite, because by object of Moral Choice is denoted that which after Deliberation has been preferred to something else: for each man leaves off searching how he shall do a thing when he has brought the origination up to himself, i.e. to the governing principle in himself, because it is this which makes the choice. A good illustration of this is furnished by the old regal constitutions which Homer drew from, in which the Kings would announce to the commonalty what they had determined before.

Now since that which is the object of Moral Choice is something in our own power, which is the object of deliberation and the grasping of the Will, Moral Choice must be "a grasping after something in our own power consequent upon Deliberation:" because after having deliberated we decide, and then grasp by our Will in accordance with the result of our deliberation.

Let this be accepted as a sketch of the nature and object of Moral Choice, that object being "Means to Ends."

IV

That Wish has for its object-matter the End, has been already stated; but there are two opinions respecting it; some thinking that its object is real good, others whatever impresses the mind with a notion of good.

Now those who maintain that the object of Wish is real good are beset by this difficulty, that what is wished for by him who chooses wrongly is not really an object of Wish (because, on their theory, if it is an object of wish, it must be good, but it is, in the case supposed, evil). Those who maintain, on the contrary, that that which impresses the mind with a notion of good is properly the object of Wish, have to meet this difficulty, that there is nothing naturally an object of Wish but to each individual whatever seems good to him; now different people have different notions, and it may chance contrary ones.

But, if these opinions do not satisfy us, may we not say that, abstractedly and as a matter of objective truth, the really good is the object of Wish, but to each individual whatever impresses his mind with the notion of good. And so to the good man that is an object of Wish which is really and truly so, but to the bad man anything may be; just as physically those things are wholesome to the healthy which are really so, but other things to the sick. And so too of bitter and sweet, and hot and heavy, and so on. For the good man judges in every instance correctly, and in every instance the notion conveyed to his mind is the true one.

For there are fair and pleasant things peculiar to, and so varying with, each state; and perhaps the most distinguishing characteristic of the good man is his seeing the truth in every instance, he being, in fact, the rule and measure of these matters.

The multitude of men seem to be deceived by reason of pleasure, because though it is not really a good it impresses their minds with the notion of goodness, so they choose what is pleasant as good and avoid pain as an evil.

Now since the End is the object of Wish, and the means to the End of Deliberation and Moral Choice, the actions regarding these matters must be in the way of Moral Choice, i.e. voluntary: but the acts of working out the virtues are such actions, and therefore Virtue is in our power.

And so too is Vice: because wherever it is in our power to do it is also in our power to forbear doing, and vice versâ: therefore if the doing (being in a given case creditable) is in our power, so too is the forbearing (which is in the same case discreditable), and vice versâ.

But if it is in our power to do and to forbear doing what is creditable or the contrary, and these respectively constitute the being good or bad, then the being good or vicious characters is in our power.

As for the well-known saying, "No man voluntarily is wicked or involuntarily happy," it is partly true, partly false; for no man is happy against his will, of course, but wickedness is voluntary. Or must we dispute the statements lately made, and not say that Man is the originator or generator of his actions as much as of his children?

But if this is matter of plain manifest fact, and we cannot refer our actions to any other originations beside those in our own power, those things must be in our own power, and so voluntary, the originations of which are in ourselves.

Moreover, testimony seems to be borne to these positions both privately by individuals, and by law-givers too, in that they chastise and punish those who do wrong (unless they do so on compulsion, or by reason of ignorance which is not self-caused), while they honour those who act rightly, under the notion of being likely to encourage the latter and restrain the former. But such things as are not in our own power, i.e. not voluntary, no one thinks of encouraging us to do, knowing it to be of no avail for one to have been persuaded not to be hot (for instance), or feel pain, or be hungry, and so forth, because we shall have those sensations all the same.

And what makes the case stronger is this: that they chastise for the very fact of ignorance, when it is thought to be self-caused; to the drunken, for instance, penalties are double, because the origination in such case lies in a man's own self: for he might have helped getting drunk, and this is the cause of his ignorance.

Again, those also who are ignorant of legal regulations which they are bound to know, and which are not hard to know, they chastise; and similarly in all other cases where neglect is thought to be the cause of the ignorance, under the notion that it was in their power to prevent their ignorance, because they might have paid attention.

But perhaps a man is of such a character that he cannot attend to such things: still men are themselves the causes of having become such characters by living carelessly, and also of being unjust or destitute of self-control, the former by doing evil actions, the latter by spending their time in drinking and such-like; because the particular acts of working form corresponding characters, as is shown by those who are practising for any contest or particular course of action, for such men persevere in the acts of working.

As for the plea, that a man did not know that habits are produced from separate acts of working, we reply, such ignorance is a mark of excessive stupidity.

Furthermore, it is wholly irrelevant to say that the man who acts unjustly or dissolutely does not wish to attain the habits of these vices: for if a man wittingly does those things whereby he must become unjust he is to all intents and purposes unjust voluntarily; but he cannot with a wish cease to be unjust and become just. For, to take the analogous case, the sick man cannot with a wish be well again, yet in a supposable case he is voluntarily ill because he has produced his sickness by living intemperately and disregarding his physicians. There was a time then when he might have helped being ill, but now he has let himself go he cannot any longer; just as he who has let a stone out of his hand cannot recall it, and yet it rested with him to aim and throw it, because the origination was in his power. Just so the unjust man, and he who has lost all self-control, might originally have helped being what they are, and so they are voluntarily what they are; but now that they are become so they no longer have the power of being otherwise.

And not only are mental diseases voluntary, but the bodily are so in some men, whom we accordingly blame: for such as are naturally deformed no one blames, only such as are so by reason of want of exercise, and neglect: and so too of weakness and maiming: no one would think of upbraiding, but would rather compassionate, a man who is blind by nature, or from disease, or from an accident; but every one would blame him who was so from excess of wine, or any other kind of intemperance. It seems, then, that in respect of bodily diseases, those which depend on ourselves are censured, those which do not are not censured; and if so, then in the case of the mental disorders, those which are censured must depend upon ourselves.

But suppose a man to say, "that (by our own admission) all men aim at that which conveys to their minds an impression of good, and that men have no control over this impression, but that the End impresses each with a notion correspondent to his own individual character; that to be sure if each man is in a way the cause of his own moral state, so he will be also of the kind of impression he receives: whereas, if this is not so, no one is the cause to himself of doing evil actions, but he does them by reason of ignorance of the true End, supposing that through their means he will secure the chief good. Further, that this aiming at the End is no matter of one's own choice, but one must be born with a power of mental vision, so to speak, whereby to judge fairly and choose that which is really good; and he is blessed by nature who has this naturally well: because it is the most important thing and the fairest, and what a man cannot get or learn from another but will have such as nature has given it; and for this to be so given well and fairly would be excellence of nature in the highest and truest sense."

If all this be true, how will Virtue be a whit more voluntary than Vice? Alike to the good man and the bad, the End gives its impression and is fixed by nature or howsoever you like to say, and they act so and so, referring everything else to this End.

Whether then we suppose that the End impresses each man's mind with certain notions not merely by nature, but that there is somewhat also dependent on himself; or that the End is given by nature, and yet Virtue is voluntary because the good man does all the rest voluntarily, Vice must be equally so; because his own agency equally attaches to the bad man in the actions, even if not in the selection of the End.

If then, as is commonly said, the Virtues are voluntary (because we at least co-operate in producing our moral states, and we assume the End to be of a certain kind according as we are ourselves of certain characters), the Vices must be voluntary also, because the cases are exactly similar.

Well now, we have stated generally respecting the Moral Virtues, the genus (in outline), that they are mean states, and that they are habits, and how they are formed, and that they are of themselves calculated to act upon the circumstances out of which they were formed, and that they are in our own power and voluntary, and are to be done so as right Reason may direct.

But the particular actions and the habits are not voluntary in the same sense; for of the actions we are masters from beginning to end (supposing of course a knowledge of the particular details), but only of the origination of the habits, the addition by small particular accessions not being cognisiable (as is the case with sicknesses): still they are voluntary because it rested with us to use our circumstances this way or that.

Here we will resume the particular discussion of the Moral Virtues, and say what they are, what is their object-matter, and how they stand respectively related to it: of course their number will be thereby shown. First, then, of Courage. Now that it is a mean state, in respect of fear and boldness, has been already said: further, the objects of our fears are obviously things fearful or, in a general way of statement, evils; which accounts for the common definition of fear, viz. "expectation of evil."

Of course we fear evils of all kinds: disgrace, for instance, poverty, disease, desolateness, death; but not all these seem to be the object-matter of the Brave man, because there are things which to fear is right and noble, and not to fear is base; disgrace, for example, since he who fears this is a good man and has a sense of honour, and he who does not fear it is shameless (though there are those who call him Brave by analogy, because he somewhat resembles the Brave man who agrees with him in being free from fear); but poverty, perhaps, or disease, and in fact whatever does not proceed from viciousness, nor is attributable to his own fault, a man ought not to fear: still, being fearless in respect of these would not constitute a man Brave in the proper sense of the term.

Yet we do apply the term in right of the similarity of the cases; for there are men who, though timid in the dangers of war, are liberal men and are stout enough to face loss of wealth.

And, again, a man is not a coward for fearing insult to his wife or children, or envy, or any such thing; nor is he a Brave man for being bold when going to be scourged.

What kind of fearful things then do constitute the object-matter of the Brave man? first of all, must they not be the greatest, since no man is more apt to withstand what is dreadful. Now the object of the greatest dread is death, because it is the end of all things, and the dead man is thought to be capable neither of good nor evil. Still it would seem that the Brave man has not for his object-matter even death in every circumstance; on the sea, for example, or in sickness: in what circumstances then? must it not be in the most honourable? now such is death in war, because it is death in the greatest and most honourable danger; and this is confirmed by the honours awarded in communities, and by monarchs.

He then may be most properly denominated Brave who is fearless in respect of honourable death and such sudden emergencies as threaten death; now such specially are those which arise in the course of war.

It is not meant but that the Brave man will be fearless also on the sea (and in sickness), but not in the same way as sea-faring men; for these are light-hearted and hopeful by reason of their experience, while landsmen though Brave are apt to give themselves up for lost and shudder at the notion of such a death: to which it should be added that Courage is exerted in circumstances which admit of doing something to help one's self, or in which death would be honourable; now neither of these requisites attach to destruction by drowning or sickness.

V

Again, fearful is a term of relation, the same thing not being so to all, and there is according to common parlance somewhat so fearful as to be beyond human endurance: this of course would be fearful to every man of sense, but those objects which are level to the capacity of man differ in magnitude and admit of degrees, so too the objects of confidence or boldness.

Now the Brave man cannot be frighted from his propriety (but of course only so far as he is man); fear such things indeed he will, but he will stand up against them as he ought and as right reason may direct, with a view to what is honourable, because this is the end of the virtue.

Now it is possible to fear these things too much, or too little, or again to fear what is not really fearful as if it were such. So the errors come to be either that a man fears when he ought not to fear at all, or that he fears in an improper way, or at a wrong time, and so forth; and so too in respect of things inspiring confidence. He is Brave then who withstands, and fears, and is bold, in respect of right objects, from a right motive, in right manner, and at right times: since the Brave man suffers or acts as he ought and as right reason may direct.

Now the end of every separate act of working is that which accords with the habit, and so to the Brave man Courage; which is honourable; therefore such is also the End, since the character of each is determined by the End.

So honour is the motive from which the Brave man withstands things fearful and performs the acts which accord with Courage.

Of the characters on the side of Excess, he who exceeds in utter absence of fear has no appropriate name (I observed before that many states have none), but he would be a madman or inaccessible to pain if he feared nothing, neither earthquake, nor the billows, as they tell of the Celts.

He again who exceeds in confidence in respect of things fearful is rash. He is thought moreover to be a braggart, and to advance unfounded claims to the character of Brave: the relation which the Brave man really bears to objects of fear this man wishes to appear to bear, and so imitates him in whatever points he can; for this reason most of them exhibit a curious mixture of rashness and cowardice; because, affecting rashness in these circumstances, they do not withstand what is truly fearful.

The man moreover who exceeds in feeling fear is a coward, since there attach to him the circumstances of fearing wrong objects, in wrong ways, and so forth. He is deficient also in feeling confidence, but he is most clearly seen as exceeding in the case of pains; he is a fainthearted kind of man, for he fears all things: the Brave man is just the contrary, for boldness is the property of the light-hearted and hopeful.

So the coward, the rash, and the Brave man have exactly the same object-matter, but stand differently related to it: the two first-mentioned respectively exceed and are deficient, the last is in a mean state and as he ought to be. The rash again are precipitate, and, being eager before danger, when actually in it fall away, while the Brave are quick and sharp in action, but before are quiet and composed.

Well then, as has been said, Courage is a mean state in respect of objects inspiring boldness or fear, in the circumstances which have been stated, and the Brave man chooses his line and withstands danger either because to do so is honourable, or because not to do so is base. But dying to escape from poverty, or the pangs of love, or anything that is simply painful, is the act not of a Brave man but of a coward; because it is mere softness to fly from what is toilsome, and the suicide braves the terrors of death not because it is honourable but to get out of the reach of evil.

VI

Courage proper is somewhat of the kind I have described, but there are dispositions, differing in five ways, which also bear in common parlance the name of Courage.

We will take first that which bears most resemblance to the true, the Courage of Citizenship, so named because the motives which are thought to actuate the members of a community in braving danger are the penalties and disgrace held out by the laws to cowardice, and the dignities conferred on the Brave; which is thought to be the reason why those are the bravest people among whom cowards are visited with disgrace and the Brave held in honour.

Such is the kind of Courage Homer exhibits in his characters; Diomed and Hector for example. The latter says,

"Polydamas will be the first to fix
Disgrace upon me."

Diomed again,

"For Hector surely will hereafter say,
Speaking in Troy, Tydides by my hand"--

This I say most nearly resembles the Courage before spoken of, because it arises from virtue, from a feeling of shame, and a desire of what is noble (that is, of honour), and avoidance of disgrace which is base. In the same rank one would be inclined to place those also who act under compulsion from their commanders; yet are they really lower, because not a sense of honour but fear is the motive from which they act, and what they seek to avoid is not that which is base but that which is simply painful: commanders do in fact compel their men sometimes, as Hector says (to quote Homer again),

"But whomsoever I shall find cowering afar from the fight,
The teeth of dogs he shall by no means escape."

Those commanders who station staunch troops by doubtful ones, or who beat their men if they flinch, or who draw their troops up in line with the trenches, or other similar obstacles, in their rear, do in effect the same as Hector, for they all use compulsion.

But a man is to be Brave, not on compulsion, but from a sense of honour.

In the next place, Experience and Skill in the various particulars is thought to be a species of Courage: whence Socrates also thought that Courage was knowledge.

This quality is exhibited of course by different men under different circumstances, but in warlike matters, with which we are now concerned, it is exhibited by the soldiers ("the regulars"): for there are, it would seem, many things in war of no real importance which these have been constantly used to see; so they have a show of Courage because other people are not aware of the real nature of these things. Then again by reason of their skill they are better able than any others to inflict without suffering themselves, because they are able to use their arms and have such as are most serviceable both with a view to offence and defence: so that their case is parallel to that of armed men fighting with unarmed or trained athletes with amateurs, since in contests of this kind those are the best fighters, not who are the bravest men, but who are the strongest and are in the best condition.

In fact, the regular troops come to be cowards whenever the danger is greater than their means of meeting it; supposing, for example, that they are inferior in numbers and resources: then they are the first to fly, but the mere militia stand and fall on the ground (which as you know really happened at the Hermæum), for in the eyes of these flight was disgraceful and death preferable to safety bought at such a price: while "the regulars" originally went into the danger under a notion of their own superiority, but on discovering their error they took to flight, having greater fear of death than of disgrace; but this is not the feeling of the Brave man.

Thirdly, mere Animal Spirit is sometimes brought under the term Courage: they are thought to be

Brave who are carried on by mere Animal Spirit, as are wild beasts against those who have wounded them, because in fact the really Brave have much Spirit, there being nothing like it for going at danger of any kind; whence those frequent expressions in Homer, "infused strength into his spirit," "roused his strength and spirit," or again, "and keen strength in his nostrils," "his blood boiled:" for all these seem to denote the arousing and impetuosity of the Animal Spirit.

Now they that are truly Brave act from a sense of honour, and this Animal Spirit co-operates with them; but wild beasts from pain, that is because they have been wounded, or are frightened; since if they are quietly in their own haunts, forest or marsh, they do not attack men. Surely they are not Brave because they rush into danger when goaded on by pain and mere Spirit, without any view of the danger: else would asses be Brave when they are hungry, for though beaten they will not then leave their pasture: profligate men besides do many bold actions by reason of their lust. We may conclude then that they are not Brave who are goaded on to meet danger by pain and mere Spirit; but still this temper which arises from Animal Spirit appears to be most natural, and would be Courage of the true kind if it could have added to it moral choice and the proper motive. So men also are pained by a feeling of anger, and take pleasure in revenge; but they who fight from these causes may be good fighters, but they are not truly Brave (in that they do not act from a sense of honour, nor as reason directs, but merely from the present feeling), still they bear some resemblance to that character.

Nor, again, are the Sanguine and Hopeful therefore Brave: since their boldness in dangers arises from their frequent victories over numerous foes. The two characters are alike, however, in that both are confident; but then the Brave are so from the afore-mentioned causes, whereas these are so from a settled conviction of their being superior and not likely to suffer anything in return (they who are intoxicated do much the same, for they become hopeful when in that state); but when the event disappoints their expectations they run away: now it was said to be the character of a Brave man to withstand things which are fearful to man or produce that impression, because it is honourable so to do and the contrary is dishonourable.

For this reason it is thought to be a greater proof of Courage to be fearless and undisturbed under the pressure of sudden fear than under that which may be anticipated, because Courage then comes rather from a fixed habit, or less from preparation: since as to foreseen dangers a man might take his line even from calculation and reasoning, but in those which are sudden he will do so according to his fixed habit of mind.

Fifthly and lastly, those who are acting under Ignorance have a show of Courage and are not very far from the Hopeful; but still they are inferior inasmuch as they have no opinion of themselves; which the others have, and therefore stay and contest a field for some little time; but they who have been deceived fly the moment they know things to be otherwise than they supposed, which the Argives experienced when they fell on the Lacedæmonians, taking them for the men of Sicyon. We have described then what kind of men the Brave are, and what they who are thought to be, but are not really, Brave.

VII

It must be remarked, however, that though Courage has for its object-matter boldness and fear it has not both equally so, but objects of fear much more than the former; for he that under pressure of these is undisturbed and stands related to them as he ought is better entitled to the name of Brave than he who is properly affected towards objects of confidence. So then men are termed Brave for withstanding painful things.

It follows that Courage involves pain and is justly praised, since it is a harder matter to withstand things that are painful than to abstain from such as are pleasant.

It must not be thought but that the End and object of Courage is pleasant, but it is obscured by the surrounding circumstances: which happens also in the gymnastic games; to the boxers the End is pleasant with a view to which they act, I mean the crown and the honours; but the receiving the blows they do is painful and annoying to flesh and blood, and so is all the labour they have to undergo; and, as these drawbacks are many, the object in view being small appears to have no pleasantness in it.

If then we may say the same of Courage, of course death and wounds must be painful to the Brave man and against his will: still he endures these because it is honourable so to do or because it is dishonourable not to do so. And the more complete his virtue and his happiness so much the more will he be pained at the notion of death: since to such a man as he is it is best worth while to live, and he with full consciousness is deprived of the greatest goods by death, and this is a painful idea. But he is not the less Brave for feeling it to be so, nay rather it may be he is shown to be more so because he chooses the honour that may be reaped in war in preference to retaining safe possession of these other goods. The fact is that to act with pleasure does not belong to all the virtues, except so far as a man realises the End of his actions.

But there is perhaps no reason why not such men should make the best soldiers, but those who are less truly Brave but have no other good to care for: these being ready to meet danger and bartering their lives against small gain.

Let thus much be accepted as sufficient on the subject of Courage; the true nature of which it is not difficult to gather, in outline at least, from what has been said.

VIII

Next let us speak of Perfected Self-Mastery, which seems to claim the next place to Courage, since these two are the Excellences of the Irrational part of the Soul.

That it is a mean state, having for its object-matter Pleasures, we have already said (Pains being in fact its object-matter in a less degree and dissimilar manner), the state of utter absence of self-control has plainly the same object-matter; the next thing then is to determine what kind of Pleasures.

Let Pleasures then be understood to be divided into mental and bodily: instances of the former being love of honour or of learning: it being plain that each man takes pleasure in that of these two objects which he has a tendency to like, his body being no way affected but rather his intellect. Now men are not called perfectly self-mastering or wholly destitute of self-control in respect of pleasures of this class: nor in fact in respect of any which are not bodily; those for example who love to tell long stories, and are prosy, and spend their days about mere chance matters, we call gossips but not wholly destitute of self-control, nor again those who are pained at the loss of money or friends.

It is bodily Pleasures then which are the object-matter of Perfected Self-Mastery, but not even all these indifferently: I mean, that they who take pleasure in objects perceived by the Sight, as colours, and forms, and painting, are not denominated men of Perfected Self-Mastery, or wholly destitute of self-control; and yet it would seem that one may take pleasure even in such objects, as one ought to do, or excessively, or too little.

So too of objects perceived by the sense of Hearing; no one applies the terms before quoted respectively to those who are excessively pleased with musical tunes or acting, or to those who take such pleasure as they ought.

Nor again to those persons whose pleasure arises from the sense of Smell, except incidentally: I mean, we do not say men have no self-control because they take pleasure in the scent of fruit, or flowers, or incense, but rather when they do so in the smells of unguents and sauces: since men destitute of self-control take pleasure herein, because hereby the objects of their lusts are recalled to their imagination (you may also see other men take pleasure in the smell of food when they are hungry): but to take pleasure in such is a mark of the character before named since these are objects of desire to him.

Now not even brutes receive pleasure in right of these senses, except incidentally. I mean, it is not the scent of hares' flesh but the eating it which dogs take pleasure in, perception of which pleasure is caused by the sense of Smell. Or again, it is not the lowing of the ox but eating him which the lion likes; but of the fact of his nearness the lion is made sensible by the lowing, and so he appears to take pleasure in this. In like manner, he has no pleasure in merely seeing or finding a stag or wild goat, but in the prospect of a meal.

The habits of Perfect Self-Mastery and entire absence of self-control have then for their object-matter such pleasures as brutes also share in, for which reason they are plainly servile and brutish: they are Touch and Taste.

But even Taste men seem to make little or no use of; for to the sense of Taste belongs the distinguishing of flavours; what men do, in fact, who are testing the quality of wines or seasoning "made dishes."

But men scarcely take pleasure at all in these things, at least those whom we call destitute of self-control do not, but only in the actual enjoyment which arises entirely from the sense of Touch, whether in eating or in drinking, or in grosser lusts. This accounts for the wish said to have been expressed once by a great glutton, "that his throat had been formed longer than a crane's neck," implying that his pleasure was derived from the Touch.

The sense then with which is connected the habit of absence of self-control is the most common of all the senses, and this habit would seem to be justly a matter of reproach, since it attaches to us not in so far as we are men but in so far as we are animals. Indeed it is brutish to take pleasure in such things and to like them best of all; for the most respectable of the pleasures arising from the touch have been set aside; those, for instance, which occur in the course of gymnastic training from the rubbing and the warm bath: because the touch of the man destitute of self-control is not indifferently of any part of the body but only of particular parts.

IX

Now of lusts or desires some are thought to be universal, others peculiar and acquired; thus desire for food is natural since every one who really needs desires also food, whether solid or liquid, or both (and, as Homer says, the man in the prime of youth needs and desires intercourse with the other sex); but when we come to this or that particular kind, then neither is the desire universal nor in all men is it directed to the same objects. And therefore the conceiving of such desires plainly attaches to us as individuals. It must be admitted, however, that there is something natural in it: because different things are pleasant to different men and a preference of some particular objects to chance ones is universal. Well then, in the case of the desires which are strictly and properly natural few men go wrong and all in one direction, that is, on the side of too much: I mean, to eat and drink of such food as happens to be on the table till one is overfilled is exceeding in quantity the natural limit, since the natural desire is simply a supply of a real deficiency. For this reason these men are called belly-mad, as filling it beyond what they ought, and it is the slavish who become of this character.

But in respect of the peculiar pleasures many men go wrong and in many different ways; for whereas the term "fond of so and so" implies either taking pleasure in wrong objects, or taking pleasure excessively, or as the mass of men do, or in a wrong way, they who are destitute of all self-control exceed in all these ways; that is to say, they take pleasure in some things in which they ought not to do so (because they are properly objects of detestation), and in such as it is right to take pleasure in they do so more than they ought and as the mass of men do.

Well then, that excess with respect to pleasures is absence of self-control, and blameworthy, is plain. But viewing these habits on the side of pains, we find that a man is not said to have the virtue for withstanding them (as in the case of Courage), nor the vice for not withstanding them; but the man destitute of self-control is such, because he is pained more than he ought to be at not obtaining things which are pleasant (and thus his pleasure produces pain to him), and the man of Perfected Self-Mastery is such in virtue of not being pained by their absence, that is, by having to abstain from what is pleasant.

Now the man destitute of self-control desires either all pleasant things indiscriminately or those which are specially pleasant, and he is impelled by his desire to choose these things in preference to all others; and this involves pain, not only when he misses the attainment of his objects but, in the very desiring them, since all desire is accompanied by pain. Surely it is a strange case this, being pained by reason of pleasure.

As for men who are defective on the side of pleasure, who take less pleasure in things than they ought, they are almost imaginary characters, because such absence of sensual perception is not natural to man: for even the other animals distinguish between different kinds of food, and like some kinds and dislike others. In fact, could a man be found who takes no pleasure in anything and to whom all things are alike, he would be far from being human at all: there is no name for such a character because it is simply imaginary.

But the man of Perfected Self-Mastery is in the mean with respect to these objects: that is to say, he neither takes pleasure in the things which delight the vicious man, and in fact rather dislikes them, nor at all in improper objects; nor to any great degree in any object of the class; nor is he pained at their absence; nor does he desire them; or, if he does, only in moderation, and neither more than he ought, nor at improper times, and so forth; but such things as are conducive to health and good condition of body, being also pleasant, these he will grasp at in moderation and as he ought to do, and also such other pleasant things as do not hinder these objects, and are not unseemly or disproportionate to his means; because he that should grasp at such would be liking such pleasures more than is proper; but the man of Perfected Self-Mastery is not of this character, but regulates his desires by the dictates of right reason.

X

Now the vice of being destitute of all Self-Control seems to be more truly voluntary than Cowardice, because pleasure is the cause of the former and pain of the latter, and pleasure is an object of choice, pain of avoidance. And again, pain deranges and spoils the natural disposition of its victim, whereas pleasure has no such effect and is more voluntary and therefore more justly open to reproach.

It is so also for the following reason; that it is easier to be inured by habit to resist the objects of pleasure, there being many things of this kind in life and the process of habituation being unaccompanied by danger; whereas the case is the reverse as regards the objects of fear.

Again, Cowardice as a confirmed habit would seem to be voluntary in a different way from the particular instances which form the habit; because it is painless, but these derange the man by reason of pain so that he throws away his arms and otherwise behaves himself unseemly, for which reason they are even thought by some to exercise a power of compulsion.

But to the man destitute of Self-Control the particular instances are on the contrary quite voluntary, being done with desire and direct exertion of the will, but the general result is less voluntary: since no man desires to form the habit.

The name of this vice (which signifies etymologically unchastened-ness) we apply also to the faults of children, there being a certain resemblance between the cases: to which the name is primarily applied, and to which secondarily or derivatively, is not relevant to the present subject, but it is evident that the later in point of time must get the name from the earlier. And the metaphor seems to be a very good one; for whatever grasps after base things, and is liable to great increase, ought to be chastened; and to this description desire and the child answer most truly, in that children also live under the direction of desire and the grasping after what is pleasant is most prominently seen in these.

Unless then the appetite be obedient and subjected to the governing principle it will become very great: for in the fool the grasping after what is pleasant is insatiable and undiscriminating; and every acting out of the desire increases the kindred habit, and if the desires are great and violent in degree they even expel Reason entirely; therefore they ought to be moderate and few, and in no respect to be opposed to Reason. Now when the appetite is in such a state we denominate it obedient and chastened.

In short, as the child ought to live with constant regard to the orders of its educator, so should the appetitive principle with regard to those of Reason.

So then in the man of Perfected Self-Mastery, the appetitive principle must be accordant with Reason: for what is right is the mark at which both principles aim: that is to say, the man of perfected self-mastery desires what he ought in right manner and at right times, which is exactly what Reason directs. Let this be taken for our account of Perfected Self-Mastery.

BOOK IV

I

We will next speak of Liberality. Now this is thought to be the mean state, having for its object-matter Wealth: I mean, the Liberal man is praised not in the circumstances of war, nor in those which constitute the character of perfected self-mastery, nor again in judicial decisions, but in respect of giving and receiving Wealth, chiefly the former. By the term Wealth I mean "all those things whose worth is measured by money."

Now the states of excess and defect in regard of Wealth are respectively Prodigality and Stinginess: the latter of these terms we attach invariably to those who are over careful about Wealth, but the former we apply sometimes with a complex notion; that is to say, we give the name to those who fail of self-control and spend money on the unrestrained gratification of their passions; and this is why they are thought to be most base, because they have many vices at once.

It must be noted, however, that this is not a strict and proper use of the term, since its natural etymological meaning is to denote him who has one particular evil, viz. the wasting his substance: he is unsaved (as the term literally denotes) who is wasting away by his own fault; and this he really may be said to be; the destruction of his substance is thought to be a kind of wasting of himself, since these things are the means of living. Well, this is our acceptation of the term Prodigality.

Again. Whatever things are for use may be used well or ill, and Wealth belongs to this class. He uses each particular thing best who has the virtue to whose province it belongs: so that he will use Wealth best who has the virtue respecting Wealth, that is to say, the Liberal man. Expenditure and giving are thought to be the using of money, but receiving and keeping one would rather call the possessing of it. And so the giving to proper persons is more characteristic of the Liberal man, than the receiving from proper quarters and forbearing to receive from the contrary. In fact generally, doing well by others is more characteristic of virtue than being done well by, and doing things positively honourable than forbearing to do things dishonourable; and any one may see that the doing well by others and doing things positively honourable attaches to the act of giving, but to that of receiving only the being done well by or forbearing to do what is dishonourable.

Besides, thanks are given to him who gives, not to him who merely forbears to receive, and praise even more. Again, forbearing to receive is easier than giving, the case of being too little freehanded with one's own being commoner than taking that which is not one's own.

And again, it is they who give that are denominated Liberal, while they who forbear to receive are commended, not on the score of Liberality but of just dealing, while for receiving men are not, in fact, praised at all.

And the Liberal are liked almost best of all virtuous characters, because they are profitable to others, and this their profitableness consists in their giving.

Furthermore: all the actions done in accordance with virtue are honourable, and done from the motive of honour: and the Liberal man, therefore, will give from a motive of honour, and will give rightly; I mean, to proper persons, in right proportion, at right times, and whatever is included in the term "right giving:" and this too with positive pleasure, or at least without pain, since whatever is done in accordance with virtue is pleasant or at least not unpleasant, most certainly not attended with positive pain.

But the man who gives to improper people, or not from a motive of honour but from some other cause, shall be called not Liberal but something else. Neither shall he be so denominated who does it with pain: this being a sign that he would prefer his wealth to the honourable action, and this is no part of the Liberal man's character; neither will such an one receive from improper sources, because the so receiving is not characteristic of one who values not wealth: nor again will he be apt to ask, because one who does kindnesses to others does not usually receive them willingly; but from proper sources (his own property, for instance) he will receive, doing this not as honourable but as necessary, that he may have somewhat to give: neither will he be careless of his own, since it is his wish through these to help others in need: nor will he give to chance people, that he may have wherewith to give to those to whom he ought, at right times, and on occasions when it is honourable so to do.

Again, it is a trait in the Liberal man's character even to exceed very much in giving so as to leave too little for himself, it being characteristic of such an one not to have a thought of self.

Now Liberality is a term of relation to a man's means, for the Liberal-ness depends not on the amount of what is given but on the moral state of the giver which gives in proportion to his means. There is then no reason why he should not be the more Liberal man who gives the less amount, if he has less to give out of.

Again, they are thought to be more Liberal who have inherited, not acquired for themselves, their means; because, in the first place, they have never experienced want, and next, all people love most their own works, just as parents do and poets.

It is not easy for the Liberal man to be rich, since he is neither apt to receive nor to keep but to lavish, and values not wealth for its own sake but with a view to giving it away. Hence it is commonly charged upon fortune that they who most deserve to be rich are least so. Yet this happens reasonably enough; it is impossible he should have wealth who does not take any care to have it, just as in any similar case.

Yet he will not give to improper people, nor at wrong times, and so on: because he would not then be acting in accordance with Liberality, and if he spent upon such objects, would have nothing to spend on those on which he ought: for, as I have said before, he is Liberal who spends in proportion to his means, and on proper objects, while he who does so in excess is prodigal (this is the reason why we never call despots prodigal, because it does not seem to be easy for them by their gifts and expenditure to go beyond their immense possessions).

To sum up then. Since Liberality is a mean state in respect of the giving and receiving of wealth, the Liberal man will give and spend on proper objects, and in proper proportion, in great things and in small alike, and all this with pleasure to himself; also he will receive from right sources, and in right proportion: because, as the virtue is a mean state in respect of both, he will do both as he ought, and, in fact, upon proper giving follows the correspondent receiving, while that which is not such is contrary to it. (Now those which follow one another come to co-exist in the same person, those which are contraries plainly do not.)

Again, should it happen to him to spend money beyond what is needful, or otherwise than is well, he will be vexed, but only moderately and as he ought; for feeling pleasure and pain at right objects, and in right manner, is a property of Virtue.

The Liberal man is also a good man to have for a partner in respect of wealth: for he can easily be wronged, since he values not wealth, and is more vexed at not spending where he ought to have done so than at spending where he ought not, and he relishes not the maxim of Simonides.

But the Prodigal man goes wrong also in these points, for he is neither pleased nor pained at proper objects or in proper manner, which will become more plain as we proceed. We have said already that Prodigality and Stinginess are respectively states of excess and defect, and this in two things, giving and receiving (expenditure of course we class under giving). Well now, Prodigality exceeds in giving and forbearing to receive and is deficient in receiving, while Stinginess is deficient in giving and exceeds in receiving, but it is in small things.

The two parts of Prodigality, to be sure, do not commonly go together; it is not easy, I mean, to give to all if you receive from none, because private individuals thus giving will soon find their means run short, and such are in fact thought to be prodigal. He that should combine both would seem to be no little superior to the Stingy man: for he may be easily cured, both by advancing in years, and also by the want of means, and he may come thus to the mean: he has, you see, already the facts of the Liberal man, he gives and forbears to receive, only he does neither in right manner or well. So if he could be wrought upon by habituation in this respect, or change in any other way, he would be a real Liberal man, for he will give to those to whom he should, and will forbear to receive whence he ought not. This is the reason too why he is thought not to be low in moral character, because to exceed in giving and in forbearing to receive is no sign of badness or meanness, but only of folly.

Well then, he who is Prodigal in this fashion is thought far superior to the Stingy man for the aforementioned reasons, and also because he does good to many, but the Stingy man to no one, not even to himself. But most Prodigals, as has been said, combine with their other faults that of receiving from improper sources, and on this point are Stingy: and they become grasping, because they wish to spend and cannot do this easily, since their means soon run short and they are necessitated to get from some other quarter; and then again, because they care not for what is honourable, they receive recklessly, and from all sources indifferently, because they desire to give but care not how or whence. And for this reason their givings are not Liberal, inasmuch as they are not honourable, nor purely disinterested, nor done in right fashion; but they oftentimes make those rich who should be poor, and to those who are quiet respectable kind of people they will give nothing, but to flatterers, or those who subserve their pleasures in any way, they will give much. And therefore most of them are utterly devoid of self-restraint; for as they are open-handed they are liberal in expenditure upon the unrestrained gratification of their passions, and turn off to their pleasures because they do not live with reference to what is honourable.

Thus then the Prodigal, if unguided, slides into these faults; but if he could get care bestowed on him he might come to the mean and to what is right.

Stinginess, on the contrary, is incurable: old age, for instance, and incapacity of any kind, is thought to make people Stingy; and it is more congenial to human nature than Prodigality, the mass of men being fond of money rather than apt to give: moreover it extends far and has many phases, the modes of stinginess being thought to be many. For as it consists of two things, defect of giving and excess of receiving, everybody does not have it entire, but it is sometimes divided, and one class of persons exceed in receiving, the other are deficient in giving. I mean those who are designated by such appellations as sparing, close-fisted, niggards, are all deficient in giving; but other men's property they neither desire nor are willing to receive, in some instances from a real moderation and shrinking from what is base.

There are some people whose motive, either supposed or alleged, for keeping their property is this, that they may never be driven to do anything dishonourable: to this class belongs the skinflint, and every one of similar character, so named from the excess of not-giving. Others again decline to receive their neighbour's goods from a motive of fear; their notion being that it is not easy to take other people's things yourself without their taking yours: so they are content neither to receive nor give.

The other class again who are Stingy in respect of receiving exceed in that they receive anything from any source; such as they who work at illiberal employments, brothel keepers, and such-like, and usurers who lend small sums at large interest: for all these receive from improper sources, and improper amounts. Their common characteristic is base-gaining, since they all submit to disgrace for the sake of gain and that small; because those who receive great things neither whence they ought, nor what they ought (as for instance despots who sack cities and plunder temples), we denominate wicked, impious, and unjust, but not Stingy.

Now the dicer and bath-plunderer and the robber belong to the class of the Stingy, for they are given to base gain: both busy themselves and submit to disgrace for the sake of gain, and the one class incur the greatest dangers for the sake of their booty, while the others make gain of their friends to whom they ought to be giving.

So both classes, as wishing to make gain from improper sources, are given to base gain, and all such receivings are Stingy. And with good reason is Stinginess called the contrary of Liberality: both because it is a greater evil than Prodigality, and because men err rather in this direction than in that of the Prodigality which we have spoken of as properly and completely such.

Let this be considered as what we have to say respecting Liberality and the contrary vices.

II

Next in order would seem to come a dissertation on Magnificence, this being thought to be, like liberality, a virtue having for its object-matter Wealth; but it does not, like that, extend to all transactions in respect of Wealth, but only applies to such as are expensive, and in these circumstances it exceeds liberality in respect of magnitude, because it is (what the very name in Greek hints at) fitting expense on a large scale: this term is of course relative: I mean, the expenditure of equipping and commanding a trireme is not the same as that of giving a public spectacle: "fitting" of course also is relative to the individual, and the matter wherein and upon which he has to spend. And a man is not denominated Magnificent for spending as he should do in small or ordinary things, as, for instance,

"Oft to the wandering beggar did I give,"

but for doing so in great matters: that is to say, the Magnificent man is liberal, but the liberal is not thereby Magnificent. The falling short of such a state is called Meanness, the exceeding it Vulgar Profusion, Want of Taste, and so on; which are faulty, not because they are on an excessive scale in respect of right objects but, because they show off in improper objects, and in improper manner: of these we will speak presently. The Magnificent man is like a man of skill, because he can see what is fitting, and can spend largely in good taste; for, as we said at the commencement, the confirmed habit is determined by the separate acts of working, and by its object-matter.

Well, the expenses of the Magnificent man are great and fitting: such also are his works (because this secures the expenditure being not great merely, but befitting the work). So then the work is to be proportionate to the expense, and this again to the work, or even above it: and the Magnificent man will incur such expenses from the motive of honour, this being common to all the virtues, and besides he will do it with pleasure and lavishly; excessive accuracy in calculation being Mean. He will consider also how a thing may be done most beautifully and fittingly, rather, than for how much it may be done, and how at the least expense.

So the Magnificent man must be also a liberal man, because the liberal man will also spend what he ought, and in right manner: but it is the Great, that is to say tke large scale, which is distinctive of the Magnificent man, the object-matter of liberality being the same, and without spending more money than another man he will make the work more magnificent. I mean, the excellence of a possession and of a work is not the same: as a piece of property that thing which is most valuable is worth most, gold for instance; but as a work that which is great and beautiful, because the contemplation of such an object is admirable, and so is that which is Magnificent. So the excellence of a work is Magnificence on a large scale. There are cases of expenditure which we call honourable, such as are dedicatory offerings to the gods, and the furnishing their temples, and sacrifices, and in like manner everything that has reference to the Deity, and all such public matters as are objects of honourable ambition, as when men think in any case that it is their duty to furnish a chorus for the stage splendidly, or fit out and maintain a trireme, or give a grand public feast.

Now in all these, as has been already stated, respect is had also to the rank and the means of the man who is doing them: because they should be proportionate to these, and befit not the work only but also the doer of the work. For this reason a poor man cannot be a Magnificent man, since he has not means wherewith to spend largely and yet becomingly; and if he attempts it he is a fool, inasmuch as it is out of proportion and contrary to propriety, whereas to be in accordance with virtue a thing must be done rightly.

Such expenditure is fitting moreover for those to whom such things previously belong, either through themselves or their ancestors or people with whom they are connected, and to the high-born or people of high repute, and so on: because all these things imply greatness and reputation.

So then the Magnificent man is pretty much as I have described him, and Magnificence consists in such expenditures: because they are the greatest and most honourable: and of private ones such as come but once for all, marriage to wit, and things of that kind; and any occasion which engages the interest of the community in general, or of those who are in power; and what concerns receiving and despatching strangers; and gifts, and repaying gifts: because the Magnificent man is not apt to spend upon himself but on the public good, and gifts are pretty much in the same case as dedicatory offerings.

It is characteristic also of the Magnificent man to furnish his house suitably to his wealth, for this also in a way reflects credit; and again, to spend rather upon such works as are of long duration, these being most honourable. And again, propriety in each case, because the same things are not suitable to gods and men, nor in a temple and a tomb. And again, in the case of expenditures, each must be great of its kind, and great expense on a great object is most magnificent, that is in any case what is great in these particular things.

There is a difference too between greatness of a work and greatness of expenditure: for instance, a very beautiful ball or cup is magnificent as a present to a child, while the price of it is small and almost mean. Therefore it is characteristic of the Magnificent man to do magnificently whatever he is about: for whatever is of this kind cannot be easily surpassed, and bears a proper proportion to the expenditure.

Such then is the Magnificent man.

The man who is in the state of excess, called one of Vulgar Profusion, is in excess because he spends improperly, as has been said. I mean in cases requiring small expenditure he lavishes much and shows off out of taste; giving his club a feast fit for a wedding-party, or if he has to furnish a chorus for a comedy, giving the actors purple to wear in the first scene, as did the Megarians. And all such things he will do, not with a view to that which is really honourable, but to display his wealth, and because he thinks he shall be admired for these things; and he will spend little where he ought to spend much, and much where he should spend little.

The Mean man will be deficient in every case, and even where he has spent the most he will spoil the whole effect for want of some trifle; he is procrastinating in all he does, and contrives how he may spend the least, and does even that with lamentations about the expense, and thinking that he does all things on a greater scale than he ought.

Of course, both these states are faulty, but they do not involve disgrace because they are neither hurtful to others nor very unseemly.

III

The very name of Great-mindedness implies, that great things are its object-matter; and we will first settle what kind of things. It makes no difference, of course, whether we regard the moral state in the abstract or as exemplified in an individual.

Well then, he is thought to be Great-minded who values himself highly and at the same time justly, because he that does so without grounds is foolish, and no virtuous character is foolish or senseless. Well, the character I have described is Great-minded. The man who estimates himself lowly, and at the same time justly, is modest; but not Great-minded, since this latter quality implies greatness, just as beauty implies a large bodily conformation while small people are neat and well made but not beautiful.

Again, he who values himself highly without just grounds is a Vain man: though the name must not be applied to every case of unduly high self-estimation. He that values himself below his real worth is Small-minded, and whether that worth is great, moderate, or small, his own estimate falls below it. And he is the strongest case of this error who is really a man of great worth, for what would he have done had his worth been less?

The Great-minded man is then, as far as greatness is concerned, at the summit, but in respect of propriety he is in the mean, because he estimates himself at his real value (the other characters respectively are in excess and defect). Since then he justly estimates himself at a high, or rather at the highest possible rate, his character will have respect specially to one thing: this term "rate" has reference of course to external goods: and of these we should assume that to be the greatest which we attribute to the gods, and which is the special object of desire to those who are in power, and which is the prize proposed to the most honourable actions: now honour answers to these descriptions, being the greatest of external goods. So the Great-minded man bears himself as he ought in respect of honour and dishonour. In fact, without need of words, the Great-minded plainly have honour for their object-matter: since honour is what the great consider themselves specially worthy of, and according to a certain rate.

The Small-minded man is deficient, both as regards himself, and also as regards the estimation of the Great-minded: while the Vain man is in excess as regards himself, but does not get beyond the Great-minded man. Now the Great-minded man, being by the hypothesis worthy of the greatest things, must be of the highest excellence, since the better a man is the more is he worth, and he who is best is worth the most: it follows then, that to be truly Great-minded a man must be good, and whatever is great in each virtue would seem to belong to the Great-minded. It would no way correspond with the character of the Great-minded to flee spreading his hands all abroad; nor to injure any one; for with what object in view will he do what is base, in whose eyes nothing is great? in short, if one were to go into particulars, the Great-minded man would show quite ludicrously unless he were a good man: he would not be in fact deserving of honour if he were a bad man, honour being the prize of virtue and given to the good.

This virtue, then, of Great-mindedness seems to be a kind of ornament of all the other virtues, in that it makes them better and cannot be without them; and for this reason it is a hard matter to be really and truly Great-minded; for it cannot be without thorough goodness and nobleness of character.

Honour then and dishonour are specially the object-matter of the Great-minded man: and at such as is great, and given by good men, he will be pleased moderately as getting his own, or perhaps somewhat less for no honour can be quite adequate to perfect virtue: but still he will accept this because they have nothing higher to give him. But such as is given by ordinary people and on trifling grounds he will entirely despise, because these do not come up to his deserts: and dishonour likewise, because in his case there cannot be just ground for it.

Now though, as I have said, honour is specially the object-matter of the Great-minded man, I do not mean but that likewise in respect of wealth and power, and good or bad fortune of every kind, he will bear himself with moderation, fall out how they may, and neither in prosperity will he be overjoyed nor in adversity will he be unduly pained. For not even in respect of honour does he so bear himself; and yet it is the greatest of all such objects, since it is the cause of power and wealth being choiceworthy, for certainly they who have them desire to receive honour through them. So to whom honour even is a small thing to him will all other things also be so; and this is why such men are thought to be supercilious.

It seems too that pieces of good fortune contribute to form this character of Great-mindedness: I mean, the nobly born, or men of influence, or the wealthy, are considered to be entitled to honour, for they are in a position of eminence and whatever is eminent by good is more entitled to honour: and this is why such circumstances dispose men rather to Great-mindedness, because they receive honour at the hands of some men.

Now really and truly the good man alone is entitled to honour; only if a man unites in himself goodness with these external advantages he is thought to be more entitled to honour: but they who have them without also having virtue are not justified in their high estimate of themselves, nor are they rightly denominated Great-minded; since perfect virtue is one of the indispensable conditions to such & character.

Further, such men become supercilious and insolent, it not being easy to bear prosperity well without goodness; and not being able to bear it, and possessed with an idea of their own superiority to others, they despise them, and do just whatever their fancy prompts; for they mimic the Great-minded man, though they are not like him, and they do this in such points as they can, so without doing the actions which can only flow from real goodness they despise others. Whereas the Great-minded man despises on good grounds (for he forms his opinions truly), but the mass of men do it at random.

Moreover, he is not a man to incur little risks, nor does he court danger, because there are but few things he has a value for; but he will incur great dangers, and when he does venture he is prodigal of his life as knowing that there are terms on which it is not worth his while to live. He is the sort of man to do kindnesses, but he is ashamed to receive them; the former putting a man in the position of superiority, the latter in that of inferiority; accordingly he will greatly overpay any kindness done to him, because the original actor will thus be laid under obligation and be in the position of the party benefited. Such men seem likewise to remember those they have done kindnesses to, but not those from whom they have received them: because he who has received is inferior to him who has done the kindness and our friend wishes to be superior; accordingly he is pleased to hear of his own kind acts but not of those done to himself (and this is why, in Homer, Thetis does not mention to Jupiter the kindnesses she had done him, nor did the Lacedæmonians to the Athenians but only the benefits they had received).

Further, it is characteristic of the Great-minded man to ask favours not at all, or very reluctantly, but to do a service very readily; and to bear himself loftily towards the great or fortunate, but towards people of middle station affably; because to be above the former is difficult and so a grand thing, but to be above the latter is easy; and to be high and mighty towards the former is not ignoble, but to do it towards those of humble station would be low and vulgar; it would be like parading strength against the weak.

And again, not to put himself in the way of honour, nor to go where others are the chief men; and to be remiss and dilatory, except in the case of some great honour or work; and to be concerned in few things, and those great and famous. It is a property of him also to be open, both in his dislikes and his likings, because concealment is a consequent of fear. Likewise to be careful for reality rather than appearance, and talk and act openly (for his contempt for others makes him a bold man, for which same reason he is apt to speak the truth, except where the principle of reserve comes in), but to be reserved towards the generality of men.

And to be unable to live with reference to any other but a friend; because doing so is servile, as may be seen in that all flatterers are low and men in low estate are flatterers. Neither is his admiration easily excited, because nothing is great in his eyes; nor does he bear malice, since remembering anything, and specially wrongs, is no part of Great-mindedness, but rather overlooking them; nor does he talk of other men; in fact, he will not speak either of himself or of any other; he neither cares to be praised himself nor to have others blamed; nor again does he praise freely, and for this reason he is not apt to speak ill even of his enemies except to show contempt and insolence.

And he is by no means apt to make laments about things which cannot be helped, or requests about those which are trivial; because to be thus disposed with respect to these things is consequent only upon real anxiety about them. Again, he is the kind of man to acquire what is beautiful and unproductive rather than what is productive and profitable: this being rather the part of an independent man. Also slow motion, deep-toned voice, and deliberate style of speech, are thought to be characteristic of the Great-minded man: for he who is earnest about few things is not likely to be in a hurry, nor he who esteems nothing great to be very intent: and sharp tones and quickness are the result of these.

This then is my idea of the Great-minded man; and he who is in the defect is a Small-minded man, he who is in the excess a Vain man. However, as we observed in respect of the last character we discussed, these extremes are not thought to be vicious exactly, but only mistaken, for they do no harm.

The Small-minded man, for instance, being really worthy of good deprives himself of his deserts, and seems to have somewhat faulty from not having a sufficiently high estimate of his own desert, in fact from self-ignorance: because, but for this, he would have grasped after what he really is entitled to, and that is good. Still such characters are not thought to be foolish, but rather laggards. But the having such an opinion of themselves seems to have a deteriorating effect on the character: because in all cases men's aims are regulated by their supposed desert, and thus these men, under a notion of their own want of desert, stand aloof from honourable actions and courses, and similarly from external goods.

But the Vain are foolish and self-ignorant, and that palpably: because they attempt honourable things, as though they were worthy, and then they are detected. They also set themselves off, by dress, and carriage, and such-like things, and desire that their good circumstances may be seen, and they talk of them under the notion of receiving honour thereby. Small-mindedness rather than Vanity is opposed to Great-mindedness, because it is more commonly met with and is worse.

Well, the virtue of Great-mindedness has for its object great Honour, as we have said: and there seems to be a virtue having Honour also for its object (as we stated in the former book), which may seem to bear to Great-mindedness the same relation that Liberality does to Magnificence: that is, both these virtues stand aloof from what is great but dispose us as we ought to be disposed towards moderate and small matters. Further: as in giving and receiving of wealth there is a mean state, an excess, and a defect, so likewise in grasping after Honour there is the more or less than is right, and also the doing so from right sources and in right manner.

For we blame the lover of Honour as aiming at Honour more than he ought, and from wrong sources; and him who is destitute of a love of Honour as not choosing to be honoured even for what is noble. Sometimes again we praise the lover of Honour as manly and having a love for what is noble, and him who has no love for it as being moderate and modest (as we noticed also in the former discussion of these virtues).

It is clear then that since "Lover of so and so" is a term capable of several meanings, we do not always denote the same quality by the term "Lover of Honour;" but when we use it as a term of commendation we denote more than the mass of men are; when for blame more than a man should be.

And the mean state having no proper name the extremes seem to dispute for it as unoccupied ground: but of course where there is excess and defect there must be also the mean. And in point of fact, men do grasp at Honour more than they should, and less, and sometimes just as they ought; for instance, this state is praised, being a mean state in regard of Honour, but without any appropriate name. Compared with what is called Ambition it shows like a want of love for Honour, and compared with this it shows like Ambition, or compared with both, like both faults: nor is this a singular case among the virtues. Here the extreme characters appear to be opposed, because the mean has no name appropriated to it.

IV

Meekness is a mean state, having for its object-matter Anger: and as the character in the mean has no name, and we may almost say the same of the extremes, we give the name of Meekness (leaning rather to the defect, which has no name either) to the character in the mean.

The excess may be called an over-aptness to Anger: for the passion is Anger, and the producing causes many and various. Now he who is angry at what and with whom he ought, and further, in right manner and time, and for proper length of time, is praised, so this Man will be Meek since Meekness is praised. For the notion represented by the term Meek man is the being imperturbable, and not being led away by passion, but being angry in that manner, and at those things, and for that length of time, which Reason may direct. This character however is thought to err rather on the side of defect, inasmuch as he is not apt to take revenge but rather to make allowances and forgive. And the defect, call it Angerlessness or what you will, is blamed: I mean, they who are not angry at things at which they ought to be angry are thought to be foolish, and they who are angry not in right manner, nor in right time, nor with those with whom they ought; for a man who labours under this defect is thought to have no perception, nor to be pained, and to have no tendency to avenge himself, inasmuch as he feels no anger: now to bear with scurrility in one's own person, and patiently see one's own friends suffer it, is a slavish thing.

As for the excess, it occurs in all forms; men are angry with those with whom, and at things with which, they ought not to be, and more than they ought, and too hastily, and for too great a length of time. I do not mean, however, that these are combined in any one person: that would in fact be impossible, because the evil destroys itself, and if it is developed in its full force it becomes unbearable.

Now those whom we term the Passionate are soon angry, and with people with whom and at things at which they ought not, and in an excessive degree, but they soon cool again, which is the best point about them. And this results from their not repressing their anger, but repaying their enemies (in that they show their feeings by reason of their vehemence), and then they have done with it.

The Choleric again are excessively vehement, and are angry at everything, and on every occasion; whence comes their Greek name signifying that their choler lies high.

The Bitter-tempered are hard to reconcile and keep their anger for a long while, because they repress the feeling: but when they have revenged themselves then comes a lull; for the vengeance destroys their anger by producing pleasure in lieu of pain. But if this does not happen they keep the weight on their minds: because, as it does not show itself, no one attempts to reason it away, and digesting anger within one's self takes time. Such men are very great nuisances to themselves and to their best friends.

Again, we call those Cross-grained who are angry at wrong objects, and in excessive degree, and for too long a time, and who are not appeased without vengeance or at least punishing the offender.

To Meekness we oppose the excess rather than the defect, because it is of more common occurrence: for human nature is more disposed to take than to forgo revenge. And the Cross-grained are worse to live with [than they who are too phlegmatic].

Now, from what has been here said, that is also plain which was said before. I mean, it is no easy matter to define how, and with what persons, and at what kind of things, and how long one ought to be angry, and up to what point a person is right or is wrong. For he that transgresses the strict rule only a little, whether on the side of too much or too little, is not blamed: sometimes we praise those who are deficient in the feeling and call them Meek, sometimes we call the irritable Spirited as being well qualified for government. So it is not easy to lay down, in so many words, for what degree or kind of transgression a man is blameable: because the decision is in particulars, and rests therefore with the Moral Sense. Thus much, however, is plain, that the mean state is praiseworthy, in virtue of which we are angry with those with whom, and at those things with which, we ought to be angry, and in right manner, and so on; while the excesses and defects are blameable, slightly so if only slight, more so if greater, and when considerable very blameable.

It is clear, therefore, that the mean state is what we are to hold to.

This then is to be taken as our account of the various moral states which have Anger for their object-matter.

V

Next, as regards social intercourse and interchange of words and acts, some men are thought to be Over-Complaisant who, with a view solely to giving pleasure, agree to everything and never oppose, but think their line is to give no pain to those they are thrown amongst: they, on the other hand, are called Cross and Contentious who take exactly the contrary line to these, and oppose in everything, and have no care at all whether they give pain or not.

Now it is quite clear of course, that the states I have named are blameable, and that the mean between them is praiseworthy, in virtue of which a man will let pass what he ought as he ought, and also will object in like manner. However, this state has no name appropriated, but it is most like Friendship; since the man who exhibits it is just the kind of man whom we would call the amiable friend, with the addition of strong earnest affection; but then this is the very point in which it differs from Friendship, that it is quite independent of any feeling or strong affection for those among whom the man mixes: I mean, that he takes everything as he ought, not from any feeling of love or hatred, but simply because his natural disposition leads him to do so; he will do it alike to those whom he does know and those whom he does not, and those with whom he is intimate and those with whom he is not; only in each case as propriety requires, because it is not fitting to care alike for intimates and strangers, nor again to pain them alike.

It has been stated in a general way that his social intercourse will be regulated by propriety, and his aim will be to avoid giving pain and to contribute to pleasure, but with a constant reference to what is noble and expedient.

His proper object-matter seems to be the pleasures and pains which arise out of social intercourse, but whenever it is not honourable or even hurtful to him to contribute to pleasure, in these instances he will run counter and prefer to give pain.

Or if the things in question involve unseemliness to the doer, and this not inconsiderable, or any harm, whereas his opposition will cause some little pain, here he will not agree but will run counter.

Again, he will regulate differently his intercourse with great men and with ordinary men, and with all people according to the knowledge he has of them; and in like manner, taking in any other differences which may exist, giving to each his due, and in itself preferring to give pleasure and cautious not to give pain, but still guided by the results, I mean by what is noble and expedient according as they preponderate.

Again, he will inflict trifling pain with a view to consequent pleasure.

Well, the man bearing the mean character is pretty well such as I have described him, but he has no name appropriated to him: of those who try to give pleasure, the man who simply and disinterestedly tries to be agreeable is called Over-Complaisant, he who does it with a view to secure some profit in the way of wealth, or those things which wealth may procure, is a Flatterer: I have said before, that the man who is "always non-content" is Cross and Contentious. Here the extremes have the appearance of being opposed to one another, because the mean has no appropriate name.

VI

The mean state which steers clear of Exaggeration has pretty much the same object-matter as the last we described, and likewise has no name appropriated to it. Still it may be as well to go over these states: because, in the first place, by a particular discussion of each we shall be better acquainted with the general subject of moral character, and next we shall be the more convinced that the virtues are mean states by seeing that this is universally the case.

In respect then of living in society, those who carry on this intercourse with a view to pleasure and pain have been already spoken of; we will now go on to speak of those who are True or False, alike in their words and deeds and in the claims which they advance.

Now the Exaggerator is thought to have a tendency to lay claim to things reflecting credit on him, both when they do not belong to him at all and also in greater degree than that in which they really do: whereas the Reserved man, on the contrary, denies those which really belong to him or else depreciates them, while the mean character being a Plain-matter-of-fact person is Truthful in life and word, admitting the existence of what does really belong to him and making it neither greater nor less than the truth.

It is possible of course to take any of these lines either with or without some further view: but in general men speak, and act, and live, each according to his particular character and disposition, unless indeed a man is acting from any special motive.

Now since falsehood is in itself low and blameable, while truth is noble and praiseworthy, it follows that the Truthful man (who is also in the mean) is praiseworthy, and the two who depart from strict truth are both blameable, but especially the Exaggerator.

We will now speak of each, and first of the Truthful man: I call him Truthful, because we are not now meaning the man who is true in his agreements nor in such matters as amount to justice or injustice (this would come within the province of a different virtue), but, in such as do not involve any such serious difference as this, the man we are describing is true in life and word simply because he is in a certain moral state.

And he that is such must be judged to be a good man: for he that has a love for Truth as such, and is guided by it in matters indifferent, will be so likewise even more in such as are not indifferent; for surely he will have a dread of falsehood as base, since he shunned it even in itself: and he that is of such a character is praiseworthy, yet he leans rather to that which is below the truth, this having an appearance of being in better taste because exaggerations are so annoying.

As for the man who lays claim to things above what really belongs to him without any special motive, he is like a base man because he would not otherwise have taken pleasure in falsehood, but he shows as a fool rather than as a knave. But if a man does this with a special motive, suppose for honour or glory, as the Braggart does, then he is not so very blameworthy, but if, directly or indirectly, for pecuniary considerations, he is more unseemly.

Now the Braggart is such not by his power but by his purpose, that is to say, in virtue of his moral state, and because he is a man of a certain kind; just as there are liars who take pleasure in falsehood for its own sake while others lie from a desire of glory or gain. They who exaggerate with a view to glory pretend to such qualities as are followed by praise or highest congratulation; they who do it with a view to gain assume those which their neighbours can avail themselves of, and the absence of which can be concealed, as a man's being a skilful soothsayer or physician; and accordingly most men pretend to such things and exaggerate in this direction, because the faults I have mentioned are in them.

The Reserved, who depreciate their own qualities, have the appearance of being more refined in their characters, because they are not thought to speak with a view to gain but to avoid grandeur: one very common trait in such characters is their denying common current opinions, as Socrates used to do. There are people who lay claim falsely to small things and things the falsity of their pretensions to which is obvious; these are called Factotums and are very despicable.

This very Reserve sometimes shows like Exaggeration; take, for instance, the excessive plainness of dress affected by the Lacedaemonians: in fact, both excess and the extreme of deficiency partake of the nature of Exaggeration. But they who practise Reserve in moderation, and in cases in which the truth is not very obvious and plain, give an impression of refinement. Here it is the Exaggerator (as being the worst character) who appears to be opposed to the Truthful Man.

VII

Next, as life has its pauses and in them admits of pastime combined with Jocularity, it is thought that in this respect also there is a kind of fitting intercourse, and that rules may be prescribed as to the kind of things one should say and the manner of saying them; and in respect of hearing likewise (and there will be a difference between the saying and hearing such and such things). It is plain that in regard to these things also there will be an excess and defect and a mean.

Now they who exceed in the ridiculous are judged to be Buffoons and Vulgar, catching at it in any and every way and at any cost, and aiming rather at raising laughter than at saying what is seemly and at avoiding to pain the object of their wit. They, on the other hand, who would not for the world make a joke themselves and are displeased with such as do are thought to be Clownish and Stern. But they who are Jocular in good taste are denominated by a Greek term expressing properly ease of movement, because such are thought to be, as one may say, motions of the moral character; and as bodies are judged of by their motions so too are moral characters.

Now as the ridiculous lies on the surface, and the majority of men take more pleasure than they ought in Jocularity and Jesting, the Buffoons too get this name of Easy Pleasantry, as if refined and gentlemanlike; but that they differ from these, and considerably too, is plain from what has been said.

One quality which belongs to the mean state is Tact: it is characteristic of a man of Tact to say and listen to such things as are fit for a good man and a gentleman to say and listen to: for there are things which are becoming for such a one to say and listen to in the way of Jocularity, and there is a difference between the Jocularity of the Gentleman and that of the Vulgarian; and again, between that of the educated and uneducated man. This you may see from a comparison of the Old and New Comedy: in the former obscene talk made the fun; in the latter it is rather innuendo: and this is no slight difference as regards decency.

Well then, are we to characterise him who jests well by his saying what is becoming a gentleman, or by his avoiding to pain the object of his wit, or even by his giving him pleasure? or will not such a definition be vague, since different things are hateful and pleasant to different men?

Be this as it may, whatever he says such things will he also listen to, since it is commonly held that a man will do what he will bear to hear: this must, however, be limited; a man will not do quite all that he will hear: because jesting is a species of scurrility and there are some points of scurrility forbidden by law; it may be certain points of jesting should have been also so forbidden. So then the refined and gentlemanlike man will bear himself thus as being a law to himself. Such is the mean character, whether denominated the man of Tact or of Easy Pleasantry.

But the Buffoon cannot resist the ridiculous, sparing neither himself nor any one else so that he can but raise his laugh, saying things of such kind as no man of refinement would say and some which he would not even tolerate if said by others in his hearing. The Clownish man is for such intercourse wholly useless: inasmuch as contributing nothing jocose of his own he is savage with all who do.

Yet some pause and amusement in life are generally judged to be indispensable.

The three mean states which have been described do occur in life, and the object-matter of all is interchange of words and deeds. They differ, in that one of them is concerned with truth, and the other two with the pleasurable: and of these two again, the one is conversant with the jocosities of life, the other with all other points of social intercourse.

VIII

To speak of Shame as a Virtue is incorrect, because it is much more like a feeling than a moral state. It is defined, we know, to be "a kind of fear of disgrace," and its effects are similar to those of the fear of danger, for they who feel Shame grow red and they who fear death turn pale. So both are evidently in a way physical, which is thought to be a mark of a feeling rather than a moral state.

Moreover, it is a feeling not suitable to every age, but only to youth: we do think that the young should be Shamefaced, because since they live at the beck and call of passion they do much that is wrong and Shame acts on them as a check. In fact, we praise such young men as are Shamefaced, but no one would ever praise an old man for being given to it, inasmuch as we hold that he ought not to do things which cause Shame; for Shame, since it arises at low bad actions, does not at all belong to the good man, because such ought not to be done at all: nor does it make any difference to allege that some things are disgraceful really, others only because they are thought so; for neither should be done, so that a man ought not to be in the position of feeling Shame. In truth, to be such a man as to do anything disgraceful is the part of a faulty character. And for a man to be such that he would feel Shame if he should do anything disgraceful, and to think that this constitutes him a good man, is absurd: because Shame is felt at voluntary actions only, and a good man will never voluntarily do what is base.

True it is, that Shame may be good on a certain supposition, as "if a man should do such things, he would feel Shame:" but then the Virtues are good in themselves, and not merely in supposed cases. And, granted that impudence and the not being ashamed to do what is disgraceful is base, it does not the more follow that it is good for a man to do such things and feel Shame.

Nor is Self-Control properly a Virtue, but a kind of mixed state: however, all about this shall be set forth in a future Book.

BOOK V

I

Now the points for our inquiry in respect of Justice and Injustice are, what kind of actions are their object-matter, and what kind of a mean state Justice is, and between what points the abstract principle of it, i.e. the Just, is a mean. And our inquiry shall be, if you please, conducted in the same method as we have observed in the foregoing parts of this treatise.

We see then that all men mean by the term Justice a moral state such that in consequence of it men have the capacity of doing what is just, and actually do it, and wish it: similarly also with respect to Injustice, a moral state such that in consequence of it men do unjustly and wish what is unjust: let us also be content then with these as a ground-work sketched out.

I mention the two, because the same does not hold with regard to States whether of mind or body as with regard to Sciences or Faculties: I mean that whereas it is thought that the same Faculty or Science embraces contraries, a State will not: from health, for instance, not the contrary acts are done but the healthy ones only; we say a man walks healthily when he walks as the healthy man would.

However, of the two contrary states the one may be frequently known from the other, and oftentimes the states from their subject-matter: if it be seen clearly what a good state of body is, then is it also seen what a bad state is, and from the things which belong to a good state of body the good state itself is seen, and vice versa. If, for instance, the good state is firmness of flesh it follows that the bad state is flabbiness of flesh; and whatever causes firmness of flesh is connected with the good state. It follows moreover in general, that if of two contrary terms the one is used in many senses so also will the other be; as, for instance, if "the Just," then also "the Unjust." Now Justice and Injustice do seem to be used respectively in many senses, but, because the line of demarcation between these is very fine and minute, it commonly escapes notice that they are thus used, and it is not plain and manifest as where the various significations of terms are widely different for in these last the visible difference is great, for instance, the word [Greek: klehis] is used equivocally to denote the bone which is under the neck of animals and the instrument with which people close doors.

Let it be ascertained then in how many senses the term "Unjust man" is used. Well, he who violates the law, and he who is a grasping man, and the unequal man, are all thought to be Unjust and so manifestly the Just man will be, the man who acts according to law, and the equal man "The Just" then will be the lawful and the equal, and "the Unjust" the unlawful and the unequal.

Well, since the Unjust man is also a grasping man, he will be so, of course, with respect to good things, but not of every kind, only those which are the subject-matter of good and bad fortune and which are in themselves always good but not always to the individual. Yet men pray for and pursue these things: this they should not do but pray that things which are in the abstract good may be so also to them, and choose what is good for themselves.

But the Unjust man does not always choose actually the greater part, but even sometimes the less; as in the case of things which are simply evil: still, since the less evil is thought to be in a manner a good and the grasping is after good, therefore even in this case he is thought to be a grasping man, i.e. one who strives for more good than fairly falls to his share: of course he is also an unequal man, this being an inclusive and common term.

We said that the violator of Law is Unjust, and the keeper of the Law Just: further, it is plain that all Lawful things are in a manner Just, because by Lawful we understand what have been defined by the legislative power and each of these we say is Just. The Laws too give directions on all points, aiming either at the common good of all, or that of the best, or that of those in power (taking for the standard real goodness or adopting some other estimate); in one way we mean by Just, those things which are apt to produce and preserve happiness and its ingredients for the social community.

Further, the Law commands the doing the deeds not only of the brave man (as not leaving the ranks, nor flying, nor throwing away one's arms), but those also of the perfectly self-mastering man, as abstinence from adultery and wantonness; and those of the meek man, as refraining from striking others or using abusive language: and in like manner in respect of the other virtues and vices commanding some things and forbidding others, rightly if it is a good law, in a way somewhat inferior if it is one extemporised.

Now this Justice is in fact perfect Virtue, yet not simply so but as exercised towards one's neighbour: and for this reason Justice is thought oftentimes to be the best of the Virtues, and

"neither Hesper nor the Morning-star
So worthy of our admiration:"

and in a proverbial saying we express the same;

"All virtue is in Justice comprehended."

And it is in a special sense perfect Virtue because it is the practice of perfect Virtue. And perfect it is because he that has it is able to practise his virtue towards his neighbour and not merely on himself; I mean, there are many who can practise virtue in the regulation of their own personal conduct who are wholly unable to do it in transactions with their neighbour. And for this reason that saying of Bias is thought to be a good one,

"Rule will show what a man is;"

for he who bears Rule is necessarily in contact with others, i.e. in a community. And for this same reason Justice alone of all the Virtues is thought to be a good to others, because it has immediate relation to some other person, inasmuch as the Just man does what is advantageous to another, either to his ruler or fellow-subject. Now he is the basest of men who practises vice not only in his own person but towards his friends also; but he the best who practises virtue not merely in his own person but towards his neighbour, for this is a matter of some difficulty.

However, Justice in this sense is not a part of Virtue but is co-extensive with Virtue; nor is the Injustice which answers to it a part of Vice but co-extensive with Vice. Now wherein Justice in this sense differs from Virtue appears from what has been said: it is the same really, but the point of view is not the same: in so far as it has respect to one's neighbour it is Justice, in so far as it is such and such a moral state it is simply Virtue.

II

But the object of our inquiry is Justice, in the sense in which it is a part of Virtue (for there is such a thing, as we commonly say), and likewise with respect to particular Injustice. And of the existence of this last the following consideration is a proof: there are many vices by practising which a man acts unjustly, of course, but does not grasp at more than his share of good; if, for instance, by reason of cowardice he throws away his shield, or by reason of ill-temper he uses abusive language, or by reason of stinginess does not give a friend pecuniary assistance; but whenever he does a grasping action, it is often in the way of none of these vices, certainly not in all of them, still in the way of some vice or other (for we blame him), and in the way of Injustice. There is then some kind of Injustice distinct from that co-extensive with Vice and related to it as a part to a whole, and some "Unjust" related to that which is co-extensive with violation of the law as a part to a whole.

Again, suppose one man seduces a man's wife with a view to gain and actually gets some advantage by it, and another does the same from impulse of lust, at an expense of money and damage; this latter will be thought to be rather destitute of self-mastery than a grasping man, and the former Unjust but not destitute of self-mastery: now why? plainly because of his gaining.

Again, all other acts of Injustice we refer to some particular depravity, as, if a man commits adultery, to abandonment to his passions; if he deserts his comrade, to cowardice; if he strikes another, to anger: but if he gains by the act to no other vice than to Injustice.

Thus it is clear that there is a kind of Injustice different from and besides that which includes all Vice, having the same name because the definition is in the same genus; for both have their force in dealings with others, but the one acts upon honour, or wealth, or safety, or by whatever one name we can include all these things, and is actuated by pleasure attendant on gain, while the other acts upon all things which constitute the sphere of the good man's action.

Now that there is more than one kind of Justice, and that there is one which is distinct from and besides that which is co-extensive with, Virtue, is plain: we must next ascertain what it is, and what are its characteristics.

Well, the Unjust has been divided into the unlawful and the unequal, and the Just accordingly into the lawful and the equal: the aforementioned Injustice is in the way of the unlawful. And as the unequal and the more are not the same, but differing as part to whole (because all more is unequal, but not all unequal more), so the Unjust and the Injustice we are now in search of are not the same with, but other than, those before mentioned, the one being the parts, the other the wholes; for this particular Injustice is a part of the Injustice co-extensive with Vice, and likewise this Justice of the Justice co-extensive with Virtue. So that what we have now to speak of is the particular Justice and Injustice, and likewise the particular Just and Unjust.

Here then let us dismiss any further consideration of the Justice ranking as co-extensive with Virtue (being the practice of Virtue in all its bearings towards others), and of the co-relative Injustice (being similarly the practice of Vice). It is clear too, that we must separate off the Just and the Unjust involved in these: because one may pretty well say that most lawful things are those which naturally result in action from Virtue in its fullest sense, because the law enjoins the living in accordance with each Virtue and forbids living in accordance with each Vice. And the producing causes of Virtue in all its bearings are those enactments which have been made respecting education for society.

By the way, as to individual education, in respect of which a man is simply good without reference to others, whether it is the province of [Greek: politikhae] or some other science we must determine at a future time: for it may be it is not the same thing to be a good man and a good citizen in every case.

Now of the Particular Justice, and the Just involved in it, one species is that which is concerned in the distributions of honour, or wealth, or such other things as are to be shared among the members of the social community (because in these one man as compared with another may have either an equal or an unequal share), and the other is that which is Corrective in the various transactions between man and man.

And of this latter there are two parts: because of transactions some are voluntary and some involuntary; voluntary, such as follow; selling, buying, use, bail, borrowing, deposit, hiring: and this class is called voluntary because the origination of these transactions is voluntary.

The involuntary again are either such as effect secrecy; as theft, adultery, poisoning, pimping, kidnapping of slaves, assassination, false witness; or accompanied with open violence; as insult, bonds, death, plundering, maiming, foul language, slanderous abuse.

III

Well, the unjust man we have said is unequal, and the abstract "Unjust" unequal: further, it is plain that there is some mean of the unequal, that is to say, the equal or exact half (because in whatever action there is the greater and the less there is also the equal, i.e. the exact half). If then the Unjust is unequal the Just is equal, which all must allow without further proof: and as the equal is a mean the Just must be also a mean. Now the equal implies two terms at least: it follows then that the Just is both a mean and equal, and these to certain persons; and, in so far as it is a mean, between certain things (that is, the greater and the less), and, so far as it is equal, between two, and in so far as it is just it is so to certain persons. The Just then must imply four terms at least, for those to which it is just are two, and the terms representing the things are two.

And there will be the same equality between the terms representing the persons, as between those representing the things: because as the latter are to one another so are the former: for if the persons are not equal they must not have equal shares; in fact this is the very source of all the quarrelling and wrangling in the world, when either they who are equal have and get awarded to them things not equal, or being not equal those things which are equal. Again, the necessity of this equality of ratios is shown by the common phrase "according to rate," for all agree that the Just in distributions ought to be according to some rate: but what that rate is to be, all do not agree; the democrats are for freedom, oligarchs for wealth, others for nobleness of birth, and the aristocratic party for virtue.

The Just, then, is a certain proportionable thing. For proportion does not apply merely to number in the abstract, but to number generally, since it is equality of ratios, and implies four terms at least (that this is the case in what may be called discrete proportion is plain and obvious, but it is true also in continual proportion, for this uses the one term as two, and mentions it twice; thus A:B:C may be expressed A:B::B:C. In the first, B is named twice; and so, if, as in the second, B is actually written twice, the proportionals will be four): and the Just likewise implies four terms at the least, and the ratio between the two pair of terms is the same, because the persons and the things are divided similarly. It will stand then thus, A:B::C:D, and then permutando A:C::B:D, and then (supposing C and D to represent the things) A+C:B+D::A:B. The distribution in fact consisting in putting together these terms thus: and if they are put together so as to preserve this same ratio, the distribution puts them together justly. So then the joining together of the first and third and second and fourth proportionals is the Just in the distribution, and this Just is the mean relatively to that which violates the proportionate, for the proportionate is a mean and the Just is proportionate. Now mathematicians call this kind of proportion geometrical: for in geometrical proportion the whole is to the whole as each part to each part.

Furthermore this proportion is not continual, because the person and thing do not make up one term.

The Just then is this proportionate, and the Unjust that which violates the proportionate; and so there comes to be the greater and the less: which in fact is the case in actual transactions, because he who acts unjustly has the greater share and he who is treated unjustly has the less of what is good: but in the case of what is bad this is reversed: for the less evil compared with the greater comes to be reckoned for good, because the less evil is more choiceworthy than the greater, and what is choiceworthy is good, and the more so the greater good.

This then is the one species of the Just.

IV

And the remaining one is the Corrective, which arises in voluntary as well as involuntary transactions. Now this just has a different form from the aforementioned; for that which is concerned in distribution of common property is always according to the aforementioned proportion: I mean that, if the division is made out of common property, the shares will bear the same proportion to one another as the original contributions did: and the Unjust which is opposite to this Just is that which violates the proportionate.

But the Just which arises in transactions between men is an equal in a certain sense, and the Unjust an unequal, only not in the way of that proportion but of arithmetical. Because it makes no difference whether a robbery, for instance, is committed by a good man on a bad or by a bad man on a good, nor whether a good or a bad man has committed adultery: the law looks only to the difference created by the injury and treats the men as previously equal, where the one does and the other suffers injury, or the one has done and the other suffered harm. And so this Unjust, being unequal, the judge endeavours to reduce to equality again, because really when the one party has been wounded and the other has struck him, or the one kills and the other dies, the suffering and the doing are divided into unequal shares; well, the judge tries to restore equality by penalty, thereby taking from the gain.

For these terms gain and loss are applied to these cases, though perhaps the term in some particular instance may not be strictly proper, as gain, for instance, to the man who has given a blow, and loss to him who has received it: still, when the suffering has been estimated, the one is called loss and the other gain.

And so the equal is a mean between the more and the less, which represent gain and loss in contrary ways (I mean, that the more of good and the less of evil is gain, the less of good and the more of evil is loss): between which the equal was stated to be a mean, which equal we say is Just: and so the Corrective Just must be the mean between loss and gain. And this is the reason why, upon a dispute arising, men have recourse to the judge: going to the judge is in fact going to the Just, for the judge is meant to be the personification of the Just. And men seek a judge as one in the mean, which is expressed in a name given by some to judges ([Greek: mesidioi], or middle-men) under the notion that if they can hit on the mean they shall hit on the Just. The Just is then surely a mean since the judge is also.

So it is the office of a judge to make things equal, and the line, as it were, having been unequally divided, he takes from the greater part that by which it exceeds the half, and adds this on to the less. And when the whole is divided into two exactly equal portions then men say they have their own, when they have gotten the equal; and the equal is a mean between the greater and the less according to arithmetical equality.

This, by the way, accounts for the etymology of the term by which we in Greek express the ideas of Just and Judge; ([Greek: dikaion] quasi [Greek: dichaion], that is in two parts, and [Greek: dikastaes] quasi [Greek: dichastaes], he who divides into two parts). For when from one of two equal magnitudes somewhat has been taken and added to the other, this latter exceeds the former by twice that portion: if it had been merely taken from the former and not added to the latter, then the latter would have exceeded the former only by that one portion; but in the other case, the greater exceeds the mean by one, and the mean exceeds also by one that magnitude from which the portion was taken. By this illustration, then, we obtain a rule to determine what one ought to take from him who has the greater, and what to add to him who has the less. The excess of the mean over the less must be added to the less, and the excess of the greater over the mean be taken from the greater.

Thus let there be three straight lines equal to one another. From one of them cut off a portion, and add as much to another of them. The whole line thus made will exceed the remainder of the first-named line, by twice the portion added, and will exceed the untouched line by that portion. And these terms loss and gain are derived from voluntary exchange: that is to say, the having more than what was one's own is called gaining, and the having less than one's original stock is called losing; for instance, in buying or selling, or any other transactions which are guaranteed by law: but when the result is neither more nor less, but exactly the same as there was originally, people say they have their own, and neither lose nor gain.

So then the Just we have been speaking of is a mean between loss and gain arising in involuntary transactions; that is, it is the having the same after the transaction as one had before it took place.

V

There are people who have a notion that Reciprocation is simply just, as the Pythagoreans said: for they defined the Just simply and without qualification as "That which reciprocates with another." But this simple Reciprocation will not fit on either to the Distributive Just, or the Corrective (and yet this is the interpretation they put on the Rhadamanthian rule of Just, If a man should suffer what he hath done, then there would be straightforward justice"), for in many cases differences arise: as, for instance, suppose one in authority has struck a man, he is not to be struck in turn; or if a man has struck one in authority, he must not only be struck but punished also. And again, the voluntariness or involuntariness of actions makes a great difference.

But in dealings of exchange such a principle of Justice as this Reciprocation forms the bond of union, but then it must be Reciprocation according to proportion and not exact equality, because by proportionate reciprocity of action the social community is held together, For either Reciprocation of evil is meant, and if this be not allowed it is thought to be a servile condition of things: or else Reciprocation of good, and if this be not effected then there is no admission to participation which is the very bond of their union.

And this is the moral of placing the Temple of the Graces ([Greek: charites]) in the public streets; to impress the notion that there may be requital, this being peculiar to [Greek: charis] because a man ought to requite with a good turn the man who has done him a favour and then to become himself the originator of another [Greek: charis], by doing him a favour.

Now the acts of mutual giving in due proportion may be represented by the diameters of a parallelogram, at the four angles of which the parties and their wares are so placed that the side connecting the parties be opposite to that connecting the wares, and each party be connected by one side with his own ware, as in the accompanying diagram.

The builder is to receive from the shoemaker of his ware, and to give him of his own: if then there be first proportionate equality, and then the Reciprocation takes place, there will be the just result which we are speaking of: if not, there is not the equal, nor will the connection stand: for there is no reason why the ware of the one may not be better than that of the other, and therefore before the exchange is made they must have been equalised. And this is so also in the other arts: for they would have been destroyed entirely if there were not a correspondence in point of quantity and quality between the producer and the consumer. For, we must remember, no dealing arises between two of the same kind, two physicians, for instance; but say between a physician and agriculturist, or, to state it generally, between those who are different and not equal, but these of course must have been equalised before the exchange can take place.

It is therefore indispensable that all things which can be exchanged should be capable of comparison, and for this purpose money has come in, and comes to be a kind of medium, for it measures all things and so likewise the excess and defect; for instance, how many shoes are equal to a house or a given quantity of food. As then the builder to the shoemaker, so many shoes must be to the house (or food, if instead of a builder an agriculturist be the exchanging party); for unless there is this proportion there cannot be exchange or dealing, and this proportion cannot be unless the terms are in some way equal; hence the need, as was stated above, of some one measure of all things. Now this is really and truly the Demand for them, which is the common bond of all such dealings. For if the parties were not in want at all or not similarly of one another's wares, there would either not be any exchange, or at least not the same.

And money has come to be, by general agreement, a representative of Demand: and the account of its Greek name [Greek: nomisma] is this, that it is what it is not naturally but by custom or law ([Greek: nomos]), and it rests with us to change its value, or make it wholly useless.

Very well then, there will be Reciprocation when the terms have been equalised so as to stand in this proportion; Agriculturist : Shoemaker : : wares of Shoemaker : wares of Agriculturist; but you must bring them to this form of proportion when they exchange, otherwise the one extreme will combine both exceedings of the mean: but when they have exactly their own then they are equal and have dealings, because the same equality can come to be in their case. Let A represent an agriculturist, C food, B a shoemaker, D his wares equalised with A's. Then the proportion will be correct, $A:B::C:D$; now Reciprocation will be practicable, if it were not, there would have been no dealing.

Now that what connects men in such transactions is Demand, as being some one thing, is shown by the fact that, when either one does not want the other or neither want one another, they do not exchange at all: whereas they do when one wants what the other man has, wine for instance, giving in return corn for exportation.

And further, money is a kind of security to us in respect of exchange at some future time (supposing that one wants nothing now that we shall have it when we do): the theory of money being that whenever one brings it one can receive commodities in exchange: of course this too is liable to depreciation, for its purchasing power is not always the same, but still it is of a more permanent nature than the commodities it represents. And this is the reason why all things should have a price set upon them, because thus there may be exchange at any time, and if exchange then dealing. So money, like a measure, making all things commensurable equalises them: for if there was not exchange there would not have been dealing, nor exchange if there were not equality, nor equality if there were not the capacity of being commensurate: it is impossible that things so greatly different should be really commensurate, but we can approximate sufficiently for all practical purposes in reference to Demand. The common measure must be some one thing, and also from agreement (for which reason it is called [Greek: nomisma]), for this makes all things commensurable: in fact, all things are measured by money. Let B represent ten minæ, A a house worth five minæ, or in other words half B, C a bed worth 1/10th of B: it is clear then how many beds are equal to one house, namely, five.

It is obvious also that exchange was thus conducted before the existence of money: for it makes no difference whether you give for a house five beds or the price of five beds. We have now said then what the abstract Just and Unjust are, and these having been defined it is plain that just acting is a mean between acting unjustly and being acted unjustly towards: the former being equivalent to having more, and the latter to having less.

But Justice, it must be observed, is a mean state not after the same manner as the forementioned virtues, but because it aims at producing the mean, while Injustice occupies both the extremes.

And Justice is the moral state in virtue of which the just man is said to have the aptitude for practising the Just in the way of moral choice, and for making division between , himself and another, or between two other men, not so as to give to himself the greater and to his neighbour the less share of what is choiceworthy and contrariwise of what is hurtful, but what is proportionably equal, and in like manner when adjudging the rights of two other men.

Injustice is all this with respect to the Unjust: and since the Unjust is excess or defect of what is good or hurtful respectively, in violation of the proportionate, therefore Injustice is both excess and defect because it aims at producing excess and defect; excess, that is, in a man's own case of what is simply advantageous, and defect of what is hurtful: and in the case of other men in like manner generally speaking, only that the proportionate is violated not always in one direction as before but whichever way it happens in the given case. And of the Unjust act the less is being acted unjustly towards, and the greater the acting unjustly towards others.

Let this way of describing the nature of Justice and Injustice, and likewise the Just and the Unjust generally, be accepted as sufficient.

VI

Again, since a man may do unjust acts and not yet have formed a character of injustice, the question arises whether a man is unjust in each particular form of injustice, say a thief, or adulterer, or robber, by doing acts of a given character.

We may say, I think, that this will not of itself make any difference; a man may, for instance, have had connection with another's wife, knowing well with whom he was sinning, but he may have done it not of deliberate choice but from the impulse of passion: of course he acts unjustly, but he has not necessarily formed an unjust character: that is, he may have stolen yet not be a thief; or committed an act of adultery but still not be an adulterer, and so on in other cases which might be enumerated.

Of the relation which Reciprocation bears to the Just we have already spoken: and here it should be noticed that the Just which we are investigating is both the Just in the abstract and also as exhibited in Social Relations, which latter arises in the case of those who live in communion with a view to independence and who are free and equal either proportionately or numerically.

It follows then that those who are not in this position have not among themselves the Social Just, but still Just of some kind and resembling that other. For Just implies mutually acknowledged law, and law the possibility of injustice, for adjudication is the act of distinguishing between the Just and the Unjust.

And among whomsoever there is the possibility of injustice among these there is that of acting unjustly; but it does not hold conversely that injustice attaches to all among whom there is the possibility of acting unjustly, since by the former we mean giving one's self the larger share of what is abstractedly good and the less of what is abstractedly evil.

This, by the way, is the reason why we do not allow a man to govern, but Principle, because a man governs for himself and comes to be a despot: but the office of a ruler is to be guardian of the Just and therefore of the Equal. Well then, since he seems to have no peculiar personal advantage, supposing him a Just man, for in this case he does not allot to himself the larger share of what is abstractedly good unless it falls to his share proportionately (for which reason he really governs for others, and so Justice, men say, is a good not to one's self so much as to others, as was mentioned before), therefore some compensation must be given him, as there actually is in the shape of honour and privilege; and wherever these are not adequate there rulers turn into despots.

But the Just which arises in the relations of Master and Father, is not identical with, but similar to, these; because there is no possibility of injustice towards those things which are absolutely one's own; and a slave or child (so long as this last is of a certain age and not separated into an independent being), is, as it were, part of a man's self, and no man chooses to hurt himself, for which reason there cannot be injustice towards one's own self: therefore neither is there the social Unjust or Just, which was stated to be in accordance with law and to exist between those among whom law naturally exists, and these were said to be they to whom belongs equality of ruling and being ruled.

Hence also there is Just rather between a man and his wife than between a man and his children or slaves; this is in fact the Just arising in domestic relations: and this too is different from the Social Just.

VII

Further, this last-mentioned Just is of two kinds, natural and conventional; the former being that which has everywhere the same force and does not depend upon being received or not; the latter being that which originally may be this way or that indifferently but not after enactment: for instance, the price of ransom being fixed at a mina, or the sacrificing a goat instead of two sheep; and again, all cases of special enactment, as the sacrificing to Brasidas as a hero; in short, all matters of special decree.

But there are some men who think that all the Justs are of this latter kind, and on this ground: whatever exists by nature, they say, is unchangeable and has everywhere the same force; fire, for instance, burns not here only but in Persia as well, but the Justs they see changed in various places.

Now this is not really so, and yet it is in a way (though among the gods perhaps by no means): still even amongst ourselves there is somewhat existing by nature: allowing that everything is subject to change, still there is that which does exist by nature, and that which does not.

Nay, we may go further, and say that it is practically plain what among things which can be otherwise does exist by nature, and what does not but is dependent upon enactment and conventional, even granting that both are alike subject to be changed: and the same distinctive illustration will apply to this and other cases; the right hand is naturally the stronger, still some men may become equally strong in both.

A parallel may be drawn between the Justs which depend upon convention and expedience, and measures; for wine and corn measures are not equal in all places, but where men buy they are large, and where these same sell again they are smaller: well, in like manner the Justs which are not natural, but of human invention, are not everywhere the same, for not even the forms of government are, and yet there is one only which by nature would be best in all places.

Now of Justs and Lawfuls each bears to the acts which embody and exemplify it the relation of an universal to a particular; the acts being many, but each of the principles only singular because each is an universal. And so there is a difference between an unjust act and the abstract Unjust, and the just act and the abstract Just: I mean, a thing is unjust in itself, by nature or by ordinance; well, when this has been embodied in act, there is an unjust act, but not till then, only some unjust thing. And similarly of a just act. (Perhaps [Greek: dikaiopragaema] is more correctly the common or generic term for just act, the word [Greek: dikaioma], which I have here used, meaning generally and properly the act corrective of the unjust act.) Now as to each of them, what kinds there are, and how many, and what is their object-matter, we must examine afterwards.

VIII

For the present we proceed to say that, the Justs and the Unjusts being what have been mentioned, a man is said to act unjustly or justly when he embodies these abstracts in voluntary actions, but when in involuntary, then he neither acts unjustly or justly except accidentally; I mean that the being just or unjust is really only accidental to the agents in such cases.

So both unjust and just actions are limited by the being voluntary or the contrary: for when an embodying of the Unjust is voluntary, then it is blamed and is at the same time also an unjust action: but, if voluntariness does not attach, there will be a thing which is in itself unjust but not yet an unjust action.

By voluntary, I mean, as we stated before, whatsoever of things in his own power a man does with knowledge, and the absence of ignorance as to the person to whom, or the instrument with which, or the result with which he does; as, for instance, whom he strikes, what he strikes him with, and with what probable result; and each of these points again, not accidentally nor by compulsion; as supposing another man were to seize his hand and strike a third person with it, here, of course, the owner of the hand acts not voluntarily, because it did not rest with him to do or leave undone: or again, it is conceivable that the person struck may be his father, and he may know that it is a man, or even one of the present company, whom he is striking, but not know that it is his father. And let these same distinctions be supposed to be carried into the case of the result and in fact the whole of any given action. In fine then, that is involuntary which is done through ignorance, or which, not resulting from ignorance, is not in the agent's control or is done on compulsion.

I mention these cases, because there are many natural things which we do and suffer knowingly but still no one of which is either voluntary or involuntary, growing old, or dying, for instance.

Again, accidentality may attach to the unjust in like manner as to the just acts. For instance, a man may have restored what was deposited with him, but against his will and from fear of the consequences of a refusal: we must not say that he either does what is just, or does justly, except accidentally: and in like manner the man who through compulsion and against his will fails to restore a deposit, must be said to do unjustly, or to do what is unjust, accidentally only.

Again, voluntary actions we do either from deliberate choice or without it; from it, when we act from previous deliberation; without it, when without any previous deliberation. Since then hurts which may be done in transactions between man and man are threefold, those mistakes which are attended with ignorance are, when a man either does a thing not to the man to whom he meant to do it, or not the thing he meant to do, or not with the instrument, or not with the result which he intended: either he did not think he should hit him at all, or not with this, or this is not the man he thought he should hit, or he did not think this would be the result of the blow but a result has followed which he did not anticipate; as, for instance, he did it not to wound but merely to prick him; or it is not the man whom, or the way in which, he meant.

Now when the hurt has come about contrary to all reasonable expectation, it is a Misadventure; when though not contrary to expectation yet without any viciousness, it is a Mistake; for a man makes a mistake when the origination of the cause rests with himself, he has a misadventure when it is external to himself. When again he acts with knowledge, but not from previous deliberation, it is an unjust action; for instance, whatever happens to men from anger or other passions which are necessary or natural: for when doing these hurts or making these mistakes they act unjustly of course and their actions are unjust, still they are not yet confirmed unjust or wicked persons by reason of these, because the hurt did not arise from depravity in the doer of it: but when it does arise from deliberate choice, then the doer is a confirmed unjust and depraved man.

And on this principle acts done from anger are fairly judged not to be from malice prepense, because it is not the man who acts in wrath who is the originator really but he who caused his wrath. And again, the question at issue in such cases is not respecting the fact but respecting the justice of the case, the occasion of anger being a notion of injury. I mean, that the parties do not dispute about the fact, as in questions of contract (where one of the two must be a rogue, unless real forgetfulness can be pleaded), but, admitting the fact, they dispute on which side the justice of the case lies (the one who plotted against the other, i.e. the real aggressor, of course, cannot be ignorant), so that the one thinks there is injustice committed while the other does not.

Well then, a man acts unjustly if he has hurt another of deliberate purpose, and he who commits such acts of injustice is ipso facto an unjust character when they are in violation of the proportionate or the equal; and in like manner also a man is a just character when he acts justly of deliberate purpose, and he does act justly if he acts voluntarily.

Then as for involuntary acts of harm, they are either such as are excusable or such as are not: under the former head come all errors done not merely in ignorance but from ignorance; under the latter all that are done not from ignorance but in ignorance caused by some passion which is neither natural nor fairly attributable to human infirmity.

IX

Now a question may be raised whether we have spoken with sufficient distinctness as to being unjustly dealt with, and dealing unjustly towards others. First, whether the case is possible which Euripides has put, saying somewhat strangely,

"My mother he hath slain; the tale is short,
Either he willingly did slay her willing,
Or else with her will but against his own."

ent dealing is voluntary?

And next, are cases of being unjustly dealt with to be ruled all one way as every act of unjust dealing is voluntary? or may we say that some cases are voluntary and some involuntary?

Similarly also as regards being justly dealt with: all just acting is voluntary, so that it is fair to suppose that the being dealt with unjustly or justly must be similarly opposed, as to being either voluntary or involuntary.

Now as for being justly dealt with, the position that every case of this is voluntary is a strange one, for some are certainly justly dealt with without their will. The fact is a man may also fairly raise this question, whether in every case he who has suffered what is unjust is therefore unjustly dealt with, or rather that the case is the same with suffering as it is with acting; namely that in both it is possible to participate in what is just, but only accidentally. Clearly the case of what is unjust is similar: for doing things in themselves unjust is not identical with acting unjustly, nor is suffering them the same as being unjustly dealt with. So too of acting justly and being justly dealt with, since it is impossible to be unjustly dealt with unless some one else acts unjustly or to be justly dealt with unless some one else acts justly.

Now if acting unjustly is simply "hurting another voluntarily" (by which I mean, knowing whom you are hurting, and wherewith, and how you are hurting him), and the man who fails of self-control voluntarily hurts himself, then this will be a case of being voluntarily dealt unjustly with, and it will be possible for a man to deal unjustly with himself. (This by the way is one of the questions raised, whether it is possible for a man to deal unjustly with himself.) Or again, a man may, by reason of failing of self-control, receive hurt from another man acting voluntarily, and so here will be another case of being unjustly dealt with voluntarily.

The solution, I take it, is this: the definition of being unjustly dealt with is not correct, but we must add, to the hurting with the knowledge of the person hurt and the instrument and the manner of hurting him, the fact of its being against the wish of the man who is hurt.

So then a man may be hurt and suffer what is in itself unjust voluntarily, but unjustly dealt with voluntarily no man can be: since no man wishes to be hurt, not even he who fails of self-control, who really acts contrary to his wish: for no man wishes for that which he does not think to be good, and the man who fails of self-control does not what he thinks he ought to do.

And again, he that gives away his own property (as Homer says Glaucus gave to Diomed, "armour of gold for brass, armour worth a hundred oxen for that which was worth but nine") is not unjustly dealt with, because the giving rests entirely with himself; but being unjustly dealt with does not, there must be some other person who is dealing unjustly towards him.

With respect to being unjustly dealt with then, it is clear that it is not voluntary.

There remain yet two points on which we purposed to speak: first, is he chargeable with an unjust act who in distribution has given the larger share to one party contrary to the proper rate, or he that has the larger share? next, can a man deal unjustly by himself?

In the first question, if the first-named alternative is possible and it is the distributor who acts unjustly and not he who has the larger share, then supposing that a person knowingly and willingly gives more to another than to himself here is a case of a man dealing unjustly by himself; which, in fact, moderate men are thought to do, for it is a characteristic of the equitable man to take less than his due.

Is not this the answer? that the case is not quite fairly stated, because of some other good, such as credit or the abstract honourable, in the supposed case the man did get the larger share. And again, the difficulty is solved by reference to the definition of unjust dealing: for the man suffers nothing contrary to his own wish, so that, on this score at least, he is not unjustly dealt with, but, if anything, he is hurt only.

It is evident also that it is the distributor who acts unjustly and not the man who has the greater share: because the mere fact of the abstract Unjust attaching to what a man does, does not constitute unjust action, but the doing this voluntarily: and voluntariness attaches to that quarter whence is the origination of the action, which clearly is in the distributor not in the receiver. And again the term doing is used in several senses; in one sense inanimate objects kill, or the hand, or the slave by his master's bidding; so the man in question does not act unjustly but does things which are in themselves unjust.

Again, suppose that a man has made a wrongful award in ignorance; in the eye of the law he does not act unjustly nor is his awarding unjust, but yet he is in a certain sense: for the Just according to law and primary or natural Just are not coincident: but, if he knowingly decided unjustly, then he himself as well as the receiver got the larger share, that is, either of favour from the receiver or private revenge against the other party: and so the man who decided unjustly from these motives gets a larger share, in exactly the same sense as a man would who received part of the actual matter of the unjust action: because in this case the man who wrongly adjudged, say a field, did not actually get land but money by his unjust decision.

Now men suppose that acting Unjustly rests entirely with themselves, and conclude that acting Justly is therefore also easy. But this is not really so; to have connection with a neighbour's wife, or strike one's neighbour, or give the money with one's hand, is of course easy and rests with one's self: but the doing these acts with certain inward dispositions neither is easy nor rests entirely with one's self. And in like way, the knowing what is Just and what Unjust men think no great instance of wisdom because it is not hard to comprehend those things of which the laws speak. They forget that these are not Just actions, except accidentally: to be Just they must be done and distributed in a certain manner: and this is a more difficult task than knowing what things are wholesome; for in this branch of knowledge it is an easy matter to know honey, wine, hellebore, cautery, or the use of the knife, but the knowing how one should administer these with a view to health, and to whom and at what time, amounts in fact to being a physician.

From this very same mistake they suppose also, that acting Unjustly is equally in the power of the Just man, for the Just man no less, nay even more, than the Unjust, may be able to do the particular acts; he may be able to have intercourse with a woman or strike a man; or the brave man to throw away his shield and turn his back and run this way or that. True: but then it is not the mere doing these things which constitutes acts of cowardice or injustice (except accidentally), but the doing them with certain inward dispositions: just as it is not the mere using or not using the knife, administering or not administering certain drugs, which constitutes medical treatment or curing, but doing these things in a certain particular way.

Again the abstract principles of Justice have their province among those who partake of what is abstractedly good, and can have too much or too little of these. Now there are beings who cannot have too much of them, as perhaps the gods; there are others, again, to whom no particle of them is of use, those who are incurably wicked to whom all things are hurtful; others to whom they are useful to a certain degree: for this reason then the province of Justice is among Men.

We have next to speak of Equity and the Equitable, that is to say, of the relations of Equity to Justice and the Equitable to the Just; for when we look into the matter the two do not appear identical nor yet different in kind; and we sometimes commend the Equitable and the man who embodies it in his actions, so that by way of praise we commonly transfer the term also to other acts instead of the term good, thus showing that the more Equitable a thing is the better it is: at other times following a certain train of reasoning we arrive at a difficulty, in that the Equitable though distinct from the Just is yet praiseworthy; it seems to follow either that the Just is not good or the Equitable not Just, since they are by hypothesis different; or if both are good then they are identical.

This is a tolerably fair statement of the difficulty which on these grounds arises in respect of the Equitable; but, in fact, all these may be reconciled and really involve no contradiction: for the Equitable is Just, being also better than one form of Just, but is not better than the Just as though it were different from it in kind: Just and Equitable then are identical, and, both being good, the Equitable is the better of the two.

What causes the difficulty is this; the Equitable is Just, but not the Just which is in accordance with written law, being in fact a correction of that kind of Just. And the account of this is, that every law is necessarily universal while there are some things which it is not possible to speak of rightly in any universal or general statement. Where then there is a necessity for general statement, while a general statement cannot apply rightly to all cases, the law takes the generality of cases, being fully aware of the error thus involved; and rightly too notwithstanding, because the fault is not in the law, or in the framer of the law, but is inherent in the nature of the thing, because the matter of all action is necessarily such.

When then the law has spoken in general terms, and there arises a case of exception to the general rule, it is proper, in so far as the lawgiver omits the case and by reason of his universality of statement is wrong, to set right the omission by ruling it as the lawgiver himself would rule were he there present, and would have provided by law had he foreseen the case would arise. And so the Equitable is Just but better than one form of Just; I do not mean the abstract Just but the error which arises out of the universality of statement: and this is the nature of the Equitable, "a correction of Law, where Law is defective by reason of its universality."

This is the reason why not all things are according to law, because there are things about which it is simply impossible to lay down a law, and so we want special enactments for particular cases. For to speak generally, the rule of the undefined must be itself undefined also, just as the rule to measure Lesbian building is made of lead: for this rule shifts according to the form of each stone and the special enactment according to the facts of the case in question.

It is clear then what the Equitable is; namely that it is Just but better than one form of Just: and hence it appears too who the Equitable man is: he is one who has a tendency to choose and carry out these principles, and who is not apt to press the letter of the law on the worse side but content to waive his strict claims though backed by the law: and this moral state is Equity, being a species of Justice, not a different moral state from Justice.

X

The answer to the second of the two questions indicated above, "whether it is possible for a man to deal unjustly by himself," is obvious from what has been already stated. In the first place, one class of Justs is those which are enforced by law in accordance with Virtue in the most extensive sense of the term: for instance, the law does not bid a man kill himself; and whatever it does not bid it forbids: well, whenever a man does hurt contrary to the law (unless by way of requital of hurt), voluntarily, i.e. knowing to whom he does it and wherewith, he acts Unjustly. Now he that from rage kills himself, voluntarily, does this in contravention of Right Reason, which the law does not permit. He therefore acts Unjustly: but towards whom? towards the Community, not towards himself (because he suffers with his own consent, and no man can be Unjustly dealt with with his own consent), and on this principle the Community punishes him; that is a certain infamy is attached to the suicide as to one who acts Unjustly towards the Community.

Next, a man cannot deal Unjustly by himself in the sense in which a man is Unjust who only does Unjust acts without being entirely bad (for the two things are different, because the Unjust man is in a way bad, as the coward is, not as though he were chargeable with badness in the full extent of the term, and so he does not act Unjustly in this sense), because if it were so then it would be possible for the same thing to have been taken away from and added to the same person: but this is really not possible, the Just and the Unjust always implying a plurality of persons.

Again, an Unjust action must be voluntary, done of deliberate purpose, and aggressive (for the man who hurts because he has first suffered and is merely requiting the same is not thought to act Unjustly), but here the man does to himself and suffers the same things at the same time.
Again, it would imply the possibility of being Unjustly dealt with with one's own consent.

And, besides all this, a man cannot act Unjustly without his act falling under some particular crime; now a man cannot seduce his own wife, commit a burglary on his own premises, or steal his own property. After all, the general answer to the question is to allege what was settled respecting being Unjustly dealt with with one's own consent.

It is obvious, moreover, that being Unjustly dealt by and dealing Unjustly by others are both wrong; because the one is having less, the other having more, than the mean, and the case is parallel to that of the healthy in the healing art, and that of good condition in the art of training: but still the dealing Unjustly by others is the worst of the two, because this involves wickedness and is blameworthy; wickedness, I mean, either wholly, or nearly so (for not all voluntary wrong implies injustice), but the being Unjustly dealt by does not involve wickedness or injustice.

In itself then, the being Unjustly dealt by is the least bad, but accidentally it may be the greater evil of the two. However, scientific statement cannot take in such considerations; a pleurisy, for instance, is called a greater physical evil than a bruise: and yet this last may be the greater accidentally; it may chance that a bruise received in a fall may cause one to be captured by the enemy and slain.

Further: Just, in the way of metaphor and similitude, there may be I do not say between a man and himself exactly but between certain parts of his nature; but not Just of every kind, only such as belongs to the relation of master and slave, or to that of the head of a family. For all through this treatise the rational part of the Soul has been viewed as distinct from the irrational.

Now, taking these into consideration, there is thought to be a possibility of injustice towards one's self, because herein it is possible for men to suffer somewhat in contradiction of impulses really their own; and so it is thought that there is Just of a certain kind between these parts mutually, as between ruler and ruled.

Let this then be accepted as an account of the distinctions which we recognise respecting Justice and the rest of the moral virtues.

BOOK VI

I

I having stated in a former part of this treatise that men should choose the mean instead of either the excess or defect, and that the mean is according to the dictates of Right Reason; we will now proceed to explain this term.

For in all the habits which we have expressly mentioned, as likewise in all the others, there is, so to speak, a mark with his eye fixed on which the man who has Reason tightens or slacks his rope; and there is a certain limit of those mean states which we say are in accordance with Right Reason, and lie between excess on the one hand and defect on the other.

Now to speak thus is true enough but conveys no very definite meaning: as, in fact, in all other pursuits requiring attention and diligence on which skill and science are brought to bear; it is quite true of course to say that men are neither to labour nor relax too much or too little, but in moderation, and as Right Reason directs; yet if this were all a man had he would not be greatly the wiser; as, for instance, if in answer to the question, what are proper applications to the body, he were to be told, "Oh! of course, whatever the science of medicine, and in such manner as the physician, directs."

And so in respect of the mental states it is requisite not merely that this should be true which has been already stated, but further that it should be expressly laid down what Right Reason is, and what is the definition of it.

Now in our division of the Excellences of the Soul, we said there were two classes, the Moral and the Intellectual: the former we have already gone through; and we will now proceed to speak of the others, premising a few words respecting the Soul itself. It was stated before, you will remember, that the Soul consists of two parts, the Rational, and Irrational: we must now make a similar division of the Rational.

Let it be understood then that there are two parts of the Soul possessed of Reason; one whereby we realise those existences whose causes cannot be otherwise than they are, and one whereby we realise those which can be otherwise than they are (for there must be, answering to things generically different, generically different parts of the soul naturally adapted to each, since these parts of the soul possess their knowledge in virtue of a certain resemblance and appropriateness in themselves to the objects of which they are percipients); and let us name the former, "that which is apt to know," the latter, "that which is apt to calculate" (because deliberating and calculating are the same, and no one ever deliberates about things which cannot be otherwise than they are: and so the Calculative will be one part of the Rational faculty of the soul).

We must discover, then, which is the best state of each of these, because that will be the Excellence of each; and this again is relative to the work each has to do.

II

There are in the Soul three functions on which depend moral action and truth; Sense, Intellect, Appetition, whether vague Desire or definite Will. Now of these Sense is the originating cause of no moral action, as is seen from the fact that brutes have Sense but are in no way partakers of moral action.

[Intellect and Will are thus connected,] what in the Intellectual operation is Affirmation and Negation that in the Will is Pursuit and Avoidance, And so, since Moral Virtue is a State apt to exercise Moral Choice and Moral Choice is Will consequent on deliberation, the Reason must be true and the Will right, to constitute good Moral Choice, and what the Reason affirms the Will must pursue. Now this Intellectual operation and this Truth is what bears upon Moral Action; of course truth and falsehood than the conclusion such knowledge as he has will be merely accidental.

III

Let thus much be accepted as a definition of Knowledge. Matter which may exist otherwise than it actually does in any given case (commonly called Contingent) is of two kinds, that which is the object of Making, and that which is the object of Doing; now Making and Doing are two different things (as we show in the exoteric treatise), and so that state of mind, conjoined with Reason, which is apt to Do, is distinct from that also conjoined with Reason, which is apt to Make: and for this reason they are not included one by the other, that is, Doing is not Making, nor Making Doing. Now as Architecture is an Art, and is the same as "a certain state of mind, conjoined with Reason, which is apt to Make," and as there is no Art which is not such a state, nor any such state which is not an Art, Art, in its strict and proper sense, must be "a state of mind, conjoined with true Reason, apt to Make."

Now all Art has to do with production, and contrivance, and seeing how any of those things may be produced which may either be or not be, and the origination of which rests with the maker and not with the thing made.

And, so neither things which exist or come into being necessarily, nor things in the way of nature, come under the province of Art, because these are self-originating. And since Making and Doing are distinct, Art must be concerned with the former and not the latter. And in a certain sense Art and Fortune are concerned with the same things, as, Agathon says by the way,

"Art Fortune loves, and is of her beloved."

So Art, as has been stated, is "a certain state of mind, apt to Make, conjoined with true Reason;" its absence, on the contrary, is the same state conjoined with false Reason, and both are employed upon Contingent matter.

IV

As for Practical Wisdom, we shall ascertain its nature by examining to what kind of persons we in common language ascribe it.

It is thought then to be the property of the Practically Wise man to be able to deliberate well respecting what is good and expedient for himself, not in any definite line, as what is conducive to health or strength, but what to living well. A proof of this is that we call men Wise in this or that, when they calculate well with a view to some good end in a case where there is no definite rule. And so, in a general way of speaking, the man who is good at deliberation will be Practically Wise. Now no man deliberates respecting things which cannot be otherwise than they are, nor such as lie not within the range of his own action: and so, since Knowledge requires strict demonstrative reasoning, of which Contingent matter does not admit (I say Contingent matter, because all matters of deliberation must be Contingent and deliberation cannot take place with respect to things which are Necessarily), Practical Wisdom cannot be Knowledge nor Art; nor the former, because what falls under the province of Doing must be Contingent; not the latter, because Doing and Making are different in kind.

It remains then that it must be "a state of mind true, conjoined with Reason, and apt to Do, having for its object those things which are good or bad for Man:" because of Making something beyond itself is always the object, but cannot be of Doing because the very well-doing is in itself an End.

For this reason we think Pericles and men of that stamp to be Practically Wise, because they can see what is good for themselves and for men in general, and we also think those to be such who are skilled in domestic management or civil government. In fact, this is the reason why we call the habit of perfected self-mastery by the name which in Greek it bears, etymologically signifying "that which preserves the Practical Wisdom:" for what it does preserve is the Notion I have mentioned, i.e. of one's own true interest, For it is not every kind of Notion which the pleasant and the painful corrupt and pervert, as, for instance, that "the three angles of every rectilineal triangle are equal to two right angles," but only those bearing on moral action.

For the Principles of the matters of moral action are the final cause of them: now to the man who has been corrupted by reason of pleasure or pain the Principle immediately becomes obscured, nor does he see that it is his duty to choose and act in each instance with a view to this final cause and by reason of it: for viciousness has a tendency to destroy the moral Principle: and so Practical Wisdom must be "a state conjoined with reason, true, having human good for its object, and apt to do."

Then again Art admits of degrees of excellence, but Practical Wisdom does not: and in Art he who goes wrong purposely is preferable to him who does so unwittingly, but not so in respect of Practical Wisdom or the other Virtues. It plainly is then an Excellence of a certain kind, and not an Art.

Now as there are two parts of the Soul which have Reason, it must be the Excellence of the Opinionative [which we called before calculative or deliberative], because both Opinion and Practical

Wisdom are exercised upon Contingent matter. And further, it is not simply a state conjoined with Reason, as is proved by the fact that such a state may be forgotten and so lost while Practical Wisdom cannot.

V

Now Knowledge is a conception concerning universals and Necessary matter, and there are of course certain First Principles in all trains of demonstrative reasoning (that is of all Knowledge because this is connected with reasoning): that faculty, then, which takes in the first principles of that which comes under the range of Knowledge, cannot be either Knowledge, or Art, or Practical Wisdom: not Knowledge, because what is the object of Knowledge must be derived from demonstrative reasoning; not either of the other two, because they are exercised upon Contingent matter only. Nor can it be Science which takes in these, because the Scientific Man must in some cases depend on demonstrative Reasoning.

It comes then to this: since the faculties whereby we always attain truth and are never deceived when dealing with matter Necessary or even Contingent are Knowledge, Practical Wisdom, Science, and Intuition, and the faculty which takes in First Principles cannot be any of the three first; the last, namely Intuition, must be it which performs this function.

VI

Science is a term we use principally in two meanings: in the first place, in the Arts we ascribe it to those who carry their arts to the highest accuracy; Phidias, for instance, we call a Scientific or cunning sculptor; Polycleitus a Scientific or cunning statuary; meaning, in this instance, nothing else by Science than an excellence of art: in the other sense, we think some to be Scientific in a general way, not in any particular line or in any particular thing, just as Homer says of a man in his Margites; "Him the Gods made neither a digger of the ground, nor ploughman, nor in any other way Scientific."

So it is plain that Science must mean the most accurate of all Knowledge; but if so, then the Scientific man must not merely know the deductions from the First Principles but be in possession of truth respecting the First Principles. So that Science must be equivalent to Intuition and Knowledge; it is, so to speak, Knowledge of the most precious objects, with a head on.

I say of the most precious things, because it is absurd to suppose [Greek: politikae], or Practical Wisdom, to be the highest, unless it can be shown that Man is the most excellent of all that exists in the Universe. Now if "healthy" and "good" are relative terms, differing when applied to men or to fish, but "white" and "straight" are the same always, men must allow that the Scientific is the same always, but the Practically Wise varies: for whatever provides all things well for itself, to this they would apply the term Practically Wise, and commit these matters to it; which is the reason, by the way, that they call some brutes Practically Wise, such that is as plainly have a faculty of forethought respecting their own subsistence.

And it is quite plain that Science and [Greek: politikae] cannot be identical: because if men give the name of Science to that faculty which is employed upon what is expedient for themselves, there will be many instead of one, because there is not one and the same faculty employed on the good of all animals collectively, unless in the same sense as you may say there is one art of healing with respect to all living beings.

If it is urged that man is superior to all other animals, that makes no difference: for there are many other things more Godlike in their nature than Man, as, most obviously, the elements of which the Universe is composed.

It is plain then that Science is the union of Knowledge and Intuition, and has for its objects those things which are most precious in their nature. Accordingly, Anexagoras, Thales, and men of that stamp, people call Scientific, but not Practically Wise because they see them ignorant of what concerns themselves; and they say that what they know is quite out of the common run certainly, and wonderful, and hard, and very fine no doubt, but still useless because they do not seek after what is good for them as men.

But Practical Wisdom is employed upon human matters, and such as are objects of deliberation (for we say, that to deliberate well is most peculiarly the work of the man who possesses this Wisdom), and no man deliberates about things which cannot be otherwise than they are, nor about any save those that have some definite End and this End good resulting from Moral Action; and the man to whom we should give the name of Good in Counsel, simply and without modification, is he who in the way of calculation has a capacity for attaining that of practical goods which is the best for Man. Nor again does Practical Wisdom consist in a knowledge of general principles only, but it is necessary that one should know also the particular details, because it is apt to act, and action is concerned with details: for which reason sometimes men who have not much knowledge are more practical than others who have; among others, they who derive all they know from actual experience: suppose a man to know, for instance, that light meats are easy of digestion and wholesome, but not what kinds of meat are light, he will not produce a healthy state; that man will have a much better chance of doing so, who knows that the flesh of birds is light and wholesome. Since then Practical Wisdom is apt to act, one ought to have both kinds of knowledge, or, if only one, the knowledge of details rather than of Principles. So there will be in respect of Practical Wisdom the distinction of supreme and subordinate.

VII

Further: [Greek: politikhae] and Practical Wisdom are the same mental state, but the point of view is not the same.

Of Practical Wisdom exerted upon a community that which I would call the Supreme is the faculty of Legislation; the subordinate, which is concerned with the details, generally has the common name [Greek: politikhae], and its functions are Action and Deliberation (for the particular enactment is a matter of action, being the ultimate issue of this branch of Practical Wisdom, and therefore people commonly say, that these men alone are really engaged in government, because they alone act, filling the same place relatively to legislators, that workmen do to a master).

Again, that is thought to be Practical Wisdom in the most proper sense which has for its object the interest of the Individual: and this usually appropriates the common name: the others are called respectively Domestic Management, Legislation, Executive Government divided into two branches, Deliberative and Judicial. Now of course, knowledge for one's self is one kind of knowledge, but it admits of many shades of difference: and it is a common notion that the man who knows and busies himself about his own concerns merely is the man of Practical Wisdom, while they who extend their solicitude to society at large are considered meddlesome.

Euripides has thus embodied this sentiment; "How," says one of his Characters, "How foolish am I, who whereas I might have shared equally, idly numbered among the multitude of the army ... for them that are busy and meddlesome [Jove hates]," because the generality of mankind seek their own good and hold that this is their proper business. It is then from this opinion that the notion has arisen that such men are the Practically-Wise. And yet it is just possible that the good of the individual cannot be secured independently of connection with a family or a community. And again, how a man should manage his own affairs is sometimes not quite plain, and must be made a matter of inquiry.

A corroboration of what I have said is the fact, that the young come to be geometricians, and mathematicians, and Scientific in such matters, but it is not thought that a young man can come to be possessed of Practical Wisdom: now the reason is, that this Wisdom has for its object particular facts, which come to be known from experience, which a young man has not because it is produced only by length of time.

By the way, a person might also inquire why a boy may be made a mathematician but not Scientific or a natural philosopher. Is not this the reason? that mathematics are taken in by the process of abstraction, but the principles of Science and natural philosophy must be gained by experiment; and the latter young men talk of but do not realise, while the nature of the former is plain and clear.

Again, in matter of practice, error attaches either to the general rule, in the process of deliberation, or to the particular fact: for instance, this would be a general rule, "All water of a certain gravity is bad;" the particular fact, "this water is of that gravity."

And that Practical Wisdom is not knowledge is plain, for it has to do with the ultimate issue, as has been said, because every object of action is of this nature.

To Intuition it is opposed, for this takes in those principles which cannot be proved by reasoning, while Practical Wisdom is concerned with the ultimate particular fact which cannot be realised by Knowledge but by Sense; I do not mean one of the five senses, but the same by which we take in the mathematical fact, that no rectilineal figure can be contained by less than three lines, i.e. that a triangle is the ultimate figure, because here also is a stopping point.

This however is Sense rather than Practical Wisdom, which is of another kind.

VIII

Now the acts of inquiring and deliberating differ, though deliberating is a kind of inquiring. We ought to ascertain about Good Counsel likewise what it is, whether a kind of Knowledge, or Opinion, or Happy Conjecture, or some other kind of faculty. Knowledge it obviously is not, because men do not inquire about what they know, and Good Counsel is a kind of deliberation, and the man who is deliberating is inquiring and calculating.

Neither is it Happy Conjecture; because this is independent of reasoning, and a rapid operation;

but men deliberate a long time, and it is a common saying that one should execute speedily what has been resolved upon in deliberation, but deliberate slowly.

Quick perception of causes again is a different faculty from good counsel, for it is a species of Happy Conjecture. Nor is Good Counsel Opinion of any kind.

Well then, since he who deliberates ill goes wrong, and he who deliberates well does so rightly, it is clear that Good Counsel is rightness of some kind, but not of Knowledge nor of Opinion: for Knowledge cannot be called right because it cannot be wrong, and Rightness of Opinion is Truth: and again, all which is the object of opinion is definitely marked out.

Still, however, Good Counsel is not independent of Reason, Does it remain then that it is a rightness of Intellectual Operation simply, because this does not amount to an assertion; and the objection to Opinion was that it is not a process of inquiry but already a definite assertion; whereas whosoever deliberates, whether well or ill, is engaged in inquiry and calculation.

Well, Good Counsel is a Rightness of deliberation, and so the first question must regard the nature and objects of deliberation. Now remember Rightness is an equivocal term; we plainly do not mean Rightness of any kind whatever; the [Greek: akrataes], for instance, or the bad man, will obtain by his calculation what he sets before him as an object, and so he may be said to have deliberated rightly in one sense, but will have attained a great evil. Whereas to have deliberated well is thought to be a good, because Good Counsel is Rightness of deliberation of such a nature as is apt to attain good.

But even this again you may get by false reasoning, and hit upon the right effect though not through right means, your middle term being fallacious: and so neither will this be yet Good Counsel in consequence of which you get what you ought but not through proper means.

Again, one man may hit on a thing after long deliberation, another quickly. And so that before described will not be yet Good Counsel, but the Rightness must be with reference to what is expedient; and you must have a proper end in view, pursue it in a right manner and right time.

Once more. One may deliberate well either generally or towards some particular End. Good counsel in the general then is that which goes right towards that which is the End in a general way of consideration; in particular, that which does so towards some particular End.

IX

Since then deliberating well is a quality of men possessed of Practical Wisdom, Good Counsel must be "Rightness in respect of what conduces to a given End, of which Practical Wisdom is the true conception." There is too the faculty of Judiciousness, and also its absence, in virtue of which we call men Judicious or the contrary.

Now Judiciousness is neither entirely identical with Knowledge or Opinion (for then all would have been Judicious), nor is it any one specific science, as medical science whose object matter is things wholesome; or geometry whose object matter is magnitude: for it has not for its object things which always exist and are immutable, nor of those things which come into being just any which may chance; but those in respect of which a man might doubt and deliberate.

And so it has the same object matter as Practical Wisdom; yet the two faculties are not identical, because Practical Wisdom has the capacity for commanding and taking the initiative, for its End is "what one should do or not do:" but Judiciousness is only apt to decide upon suggestions (though we do in Greek put "well" on to the faculty and its concrete noun, these really mean exactly the same as the plain words), and Judiciousness is neither the having Practical Wisdom, nor attaining it: but just as learning is termed [Greek: sunievai] when a man uses his knowledge, so judiciousness consists in employing the Opinionative faculty in judging concerning those things which come within the province of Practical Wisdom, when another enunciates them; and not judging merely, but judging well (for [Greek: eu] and [Greek: kalos] mean exactly the same thing). And the Greek name of this faculty is derived from the use of the term [Greek: suvievai] in learning: [Greek: mavthaveiv] and [Greek: suvievai] being often used as synonymous.

X

The faculty called [Greek: gvomh], in right of which we call men [Greek: euyvomoves], or say they have [Greek: gvomh], is "the right judgment of the equitable man." A proof of which is that we most commonly say that the equitable man has a tendency to make allowance, and the making allowance in certain cases is equitable. And [Greek: sungvomae] (the word denoting allowance) is right [Greek: gvomh] having a capacity of making equitable decisions, By "right" I mean that which attains the True. Now all these mental states tend to the same object, as indeed common language leads us to expect: I mean, we speak of [Greek: gnomae], Judiciousness, Practical Wisdom, and Practical Intuition, attributing the possession of [Greek: gnomae] and Practical Intuition to the same Individuals whom we denominate Practically-Wise and Judicious: because all these faculties are employed upon the extremes, i.e. on particular details; and in right of his aptitude for deciding on the matters which come within the province of the Practically-Wise, a man is Judicious and possessed of good [Greek: gnomae]; i.e. he is disposed to make allowance, for considerations of equity are entertained by all good men alike in transactions with their fellows.

And all matters of Moral Action belong to the class of particulars, otherwise called extremes: for the man of Practical Wisdom must know them, and Judiciousness and [Greek: gnomae] are concerned with matters of Moral Actions, which are extremes.

Intuition, moreover, takes in the extremes at both ends: I mean, the first and last terms must be taken in not by reasoning but by Intuition [so that Intuition comes to be of two kinds], and that which belongs to strict demonstrative reasonings takes in immutable, i.e. Necessary, first terms; while that which is employed in practical matters takes in the extreme, the Contingent, and the minor Premiss: for the minor Premisses are the source of the Final Cause, Universals being made up out of Particulars. To take in these, of course, we must have Sense, i.e. in other words Practical Intuition. And for this reason these are thought to be simply gifts of nature; and whereas no man is thought to be Scientific by nature, men are thought to have [Greek: gnomae], and Judiciousness, and Practical Intuition: a proof of which is that we think these faculties are a consequence even of particular ages, and this given age has Practical Intuition and [Greek: gnomae], we say, as if under the notion that nature is the cause. And thus Intuition is both the beginning and end, because the proofs are based upon the one kind of extremes and concern the other.

And so one should attend to the undemonstrable dicta and opinions of the skilful, the old and the Practically-Wise, no less than to those which are based on strict reasoning, because they see aright, having gained their power of moral vision from experience.

XI

Well, we have now stated the nature and objects of Practical Wisdom and Science respectively, and that they belong each to a different part of the Soul. But I can conceive a person questioning their utility. "Science," he would say, "concerns itself with none of the causes of human happiness (for it has nothing to do with producing anything): Practical Wisdom has this recommendation, I grant, but where is the need of it, since its province is those things which are just and honourable, and good for man, and these are the things which the good man as such does; but we are not a bit the more apt to do them because we know them, since the Moral Virtues are Habits; just as we are not more apt to be healthy or in good condition from mere knowledge of what relates to these (I mean, of course, things so called not from their producing health, etc., but from their evidencing it in a particular subject), for we are not more apt to be healthy and in good condition merely from knowing the art of medicine or training.

"If it be urged that knowing what is good does not by itself make a Practically-Wise man but becoming good; still this Wisdom will be no use either to those that are good, and so have it already, or to those who have it not; because it will make no difference to them whether they have it themselves or put themselves under the guidance of others who have; and we might be contented to be in respect of this as in respect of health: for though we wish to be healthy still we do not set about learning the art of healing.

"Furthermore, it would seem to be strange that, though lower in the scale than Science, it is to be its master; which it is, because whatever produces results takes the rule and directs in each matter."

This then is what we are to talk about, for these are the only points now raised.

Now first we say that being respectively Excellences of different parts of the Soul they must be choiceworthy, even on the supposition that they neither of them produce results.

In the next place we say that they do produce results; that Science makes Happiness, not as the medical art but as healthiness makes health: because, being a part of Virtue in its most extensive sense, it makes a man happy by being possessed and by working.

Next, Man's work as Man is accomplished by virtue of Practical Wisdom and Moral Virtue, the latter giving the right aim and direction, the former the right means to its attainment; but of the fourth part of the Soul, the mere nutritive principle, there is no such Excellence, because nothing is in its power to do or leave undone.

As to our not being more apt to do what is noble and just by reason of possessing Practical Wisdom, we must begin a little higher up, taking this for our starting-point. As we say that men may do things in themselves just and yet not be just men; for instance, when men do what the laws require of them, either against their will, or by reason of ignorance or something else, at all events not for the sake of the things themselves; and yet they do what they ought and all that the good man should do; so it seems that to be a good man one must do each act in a particular frame of mind, I mean from Moral Choice and for the sake of the things themselves which are done. Now it is Virtue which makes the Moral Choice right, but whatever is naturally required to carry out that Choice comes under the province not of Virtue but of a different faculty. We must halt, as it were, awhile, and speak more clearly on these points.

There is then a certain faculty, commonly named Cleverness, of such a nature as to be able to do and attain whatever conduces to any given purpose: now if that purpose be a good one the faculty is praiseworthy; if otherwise, it goes by a name which, denoting strictly the ability, implies the willingness to do anything; we accordingly call the Practically-Wise Clever, and also those who can and will do anything.

Now Practical Wisdom is not identical with Cleverness, nor is it without this power of adapting means to ends: but this Eye of the Soul (as we may call it) does not attain its proper state without goodness, as we have said before and as is quite plain, because the syllogisms into which Moral Action may be analysed have for their Major Premiss, "since----------is the End and the Chief Good" (fill up the blank with just anything you please, for we merely want to exhibit the Form, so that anything will do), but how this blank should be filled is seen only by the good man: because Vice distorts the moral vision and causes men to be deceived in respect of practical principles.

It is clear, therefore, that a man cannot be a Practically-Wise, without being a good, man.

XII

We must inquire again also about Virtue: for it may be divided into Natural Virtue and Matured, which two bear to each other a relation similar to that which Practical Wisdom bears to Cleverness, one not of identity but resemblance. I speak of Natural Virtue, because men hold that each of the moral dispositions attach to us all somehow by nature: we have dispositions towards justice, self-mastery and courage, for instance, immediately from our birth: but still we seek Goodness in its highest sense as something distinct from these, and that these dispositions should attach to us in a somewhat different fashion. Children and brutes have these natural states, but then they are plainly hurtful unless combined with an intellectual element: at least thus much is matter of actual experience and observation, that as a strong body destitute of sight must, if set in motion, fall violently because it has not sight, so it is also in the case we are considering: but if it can get the intellectual element it then excels in acting. Just so the Natural State of Virtue, being like this strong body, will then be Virtue in the highest sense when it too is combined with the intellectual element.

So that, as in the case of the Opinionative faculty, there are two forms, Cleverness and Practical Wisdom; so also in the case of the Moral there are two, Natural Virtue and Matured; and of these the latter cannot be formed without Practical Wisdom.

This leads some to say that all the Virtues are merely intellectual Practical Wisdom, and Socrates was partly right in his inquiry and partly wrong: wrong in that he thought all the Virtues were merely intellectual Practical Wisdom, right in saying they were not independent of that faculty.

A proof of which is that now all, in defining Virtue, add on the "state" [mentioning also to what standard it has reference, namely that] "which is accordant with Right Reason:" now "right" means in accordance with Practical Wisdom. So then all seem to have an instinctive notion that that state which is in accordance with Practical Wisdom is Virtue; however, we must make a slight change in their statement, because that state is Virtue, not merely which is in accordance with but which implies the possession of Right Reason; which, upon such matters, is Practical Wisdom. The difference between us and Socrates is this: he thought the Virtues were reasoning processes (i.e. that they were all instances of Knowledge in its strict sense), but we say they imply the possession of Reason.

From what has been said then it is clear that one cannot be, strictly speaking, good without Practical Wisdom nor Practically-Wise without moral goodness.

And by the distinction between Natural and Matured Virtue one can meet the reasoning by which it might be argued "that the Virtues are separable because the same man is not by nature most inclined to all at once so that he will have acquired this one before he has that other:" we would reply that this is possible with respect to the Natural Virtues but not with respect to those in right of which a man is denominated simply good: because they will all belong to him together with the one faculty of Practical Wisdom.

It is plain too that even had it not been apt to act we should have needed it, because it is the Excellence of a part of the Soul; and that the moral choice cannot be right independently of Practical Wisdom and Moral Goodness; because this gives the right End, that causes the doing these things which conduce to the End.

Then again, it is not Master of Science (i.e. of the superior part of the Soul), just as neither is the healing art Master of health; for it does not make use of it, but looks how it may come to be: so it commands for the sake of it but does not command it.

The objection is, in fact, about as valid as if a man should say [Greek: politikae] governs the gods because it gives orders about all things in the communty.

APPENDIX

On [Greek: epistaemae], from I. Post. Analyt. chap. i. and ii.
(Such parts only are translated as throw light on the Ethics.)

All teaching, and all intellectual learning, proceeds on the basis of previous knowledge, as will appear on an examination of all. The Mathematical Sciences, and every other system, draw their conclusions in this method. So too of reasonings, whether by syllogism, or induction: for both teach through what is previously known, the former assuming the premisses as from wise men, the latter proving universals from the evidentness of the particulars. In like manner too rhetoricians persuade, either through examples (which amounts to induction), or through enthymemes (which amounts to syllogism).

Well, we suppose that we know things (in the strict and proper sense of the word) when we suppose ourselves to know the cause by reason of which the thing is to be the cause of it; and that this cannot be otherwise. It is plain that the idea intended to be conveyed by the term knowing is something of this kind; because they who do not really know suppose themselves thus related to the matter in hand and they who do know really are so that of whatsoever there is properly speaking Knowledge this cannot be otherwise than it is Whether or no there is another way of knowing we will say afterwards, but we do say that we know through demonstration, by which I mean a syllogism apt to produce Knowledge, i.e. in right of which through having it, we know.

If Knowledge then is such as we have described it, the Knowledge produced by demonstrative reasoning must be drawn from premisses true and first, and incapable of syllogistic proof, and better known, and prior in order of time, and causes of the conclusion, for so the principles will be akin to the conclusion demonstrated.

(Syllogism, of course there may be without such premisses, but it will not be demonstration because it will not produce knowledge).

True, they must be, because it is impossible to know that which is not.

First, that is indemonstrable, because, if demonstrable, he cannot be said to know them who has no demonstration of them for knowing such things as are demonstrable is the same as having demonstration of them.

Causes they must be, and better known, and prior in time, causes, because we then know when we are acquainted with the cause, and prior, if causes, and known beforehand, not merely comprehended in idea but known to exist (The terms prior, and better known, bear two senses for prior by nature and prior relatively to ourselves are not the same, nor better known by nature, and better known to us I mean, by prior and better known relatively to ourselves, such things as are nearer to sensation, but abstractedly so such as are further Those are furthest which are most universal those nearest which are particulars, and these are mutually opposed) And by first, I mean principles akin to the conclusion, for principle means the same as first And the principle or first step in demonstration is a proposition incapable of syllogistic proof, i. e. one to which there is none prior. Now of such syllogistic principles I call that a [Greek: thxsis] which you cannot demonstrate, and which is unnecessary with a view to learning something else. That which is necessary in order to learn something else is an Axiom.

Further, since one is to believe and know the thing by having a syllogism of the kind called demonstration, and what constitutes it to be such is the nature of the premisses, it is necessary not merely to know before, but to know better than the conclusion, either all or at least some of, the principles, because that which is the cause of a quality inhering in something else always inheres itself more as the cause of our loving is itself more lovable. So, since the principles are the cause of our knowing and behoving we know and believe them more, because by reason of them we know also the conclusion following.

Further: the man who is to have the Knowledge which comes through demonstration must not merely know and believe his principles better than he does his conclusion, but he must believe nothing more firmly than the contradictories of those principles out of which the contrary fallacy may be constructed: since he who knows, is to be simply and absolutely infallible.

BOOK VII

I

Next we must take a different point to start from, and observe that of what is to be avoided in respect of moral character there are three forms; Vice, Imperfect Self-Control, and Brutishness. Of the two former it is plain what the contraries are, for we call the one Virtue, the other Self-Control; and as answering to Brutishness it will be most suitable to assign Superhuman, i.e. heroical and godlike Virtue, as, in Homer, Priam says of Hector "that he was very excellent, nor was he like the offspring of mortal man, but of a god." and so, if, as is commonly said, men are raised to the position of gods by reason of very high excellence in Virtue, the state opposed to the Brutish will plainly be of this nature: because as brutes are not virtuous or vicious so neither are gods; but the state of these is something more precious than Virtue, of the former something different in kind from Vice.

And as, on the one hand, it is a rare thing for a man to be godlike (a term the Lacedaemonians are accustomed to use when they admire a man exceedingly; [Greek:seios anhæp] they call him), so the brutish man is rare; the character is found most among barbarians, and some cases of it are caused by disease or maiming; also such men as exceed in vice all ordinary measures we therefore designate by this opprobrious term. Well, we must in a subsequent place make some mention of this disposition, and Vice has been spoken of before: for the present we must speak of Imperfect Self-Control and its kindred faults of Softness and Luxury, on the one hand, and of Self-Control and Endurance on the other; since we are to conceive of them, not as being the same states exactly as Virtue and Vice respectively, nor again as differing in kind. And we should adopt the same course as before, i.e. state the phenomena, and, after raising and discussing difficulties which suggest themselves, then exhibit, if possible, all the opinions afloat respecting these affections of the moral character; or, if not all, the greater part and the most important: for we may consider we have illustrated the matter sufficiently when the difficulties have been solved, and such theories as are most approved are left as a residuum.

The chief points may be thus enumerated. It is thought,

I. That Self-Control and Endurance belong to the class of things good and praiseworthy, while Imperfect Self-Control and Softness belong to that of things low and blameworthy.

II. That the man of Self-Control is identical with the man who is apt to abide by his resolution, and the man of Imperfect Self-Control with him who is apt to depart from his resolution.

III. That the man of Imperfect Self-Control does things at the instigation of his passions, knowing them to be wrong, while the man of Self-Control, knowing his lusts to be wrong, refuses, by the influence of reason, to follow their suggestions.

IV. That the man of Perfected Self-Mastery unites the qualities of Self-Control and Endurance, and some say that every one who unites these is a man of Perfect Self-Mastery, others do not.

V. Some confound the two characters of the man who has no Self-Control, and the man of Imperfect Self-Control, while others distinguish between them.

VI. It is sometimes said that the man of Practical Wisdom cannot be a man of Imperfect Self-Control, sometimes that men who are Practically Wise and Clever are of Imperfect Self-Control.

VII. Again, men are said to be of Imperfect Self-Control, not simply but with the addition of the thing wherein, as in respect of anger, of honour, and gain.

These then are pretty well the common statements.

II

Now a man may raise a question as to the nature of the right conception in violation of which a man fails of Self-Control.

That he can so fail when knowing in the strict sense what is right some say is impossible: for it is a strange thing, as Socrates thought, that while Knowledge is present in his mind something else should master him and drag him about like a slave. Socrates in fact contended generally against the theory, maintaining there is no such state as that of Imperfect Self-Control, for that no one acts contrary to what is best conceiving it to be best but by reason of ignorance what is best.

With all due respect to Socrates, his account of the matter is at variance with plain facts, and we must inquire with respect to the affection, if it be caused by ignorance what is the nature of the ignorance: for that the man so failing does not suppose his acts to be right before he is under the influence of passion is quite plain.

There are people who partly agree with Socrates and partly not: that nothing can be stronger than Knowledge they agree, but that no man acts in contravention of his conviction of what is better they do not agree; and so they say that it is not Knowledge, but only Opinion, which the man in question has and yet yields to the instigation of his pleasures.

But then, if it is Opinion and not Knowledge, that is it the opposing conception be not strong but only mild (as in the case of real doubt), the not abiding by it in the face of strong lusts would be excusable: but wickedness is not excusable, nor is anything which deserves blame.

Well then, is it Practical Wisdom which in this case offers opposition: for that is the strongest principle? The supposition is absurd, for we shall have the same man uniting Practical Wisdom and Imperfect Self-Control, and surely no single person would maintain that it is consistent with the character of Practical Wisdom to do voluntarily what is very wrong; and besides we have shown before that the very mark of a man of this character is aptitude to act, as distinguished from mere knowledge of what is right; because he is a man conversant with particular details, and possessed of all the other virtues.

Again, if the having strong and bad lusts is necessary to the idea of the man of Self-Control, this character cannot be identical with the man of Perfected Self-Mastery, because the having strong desires or bad ones does not enter into the idea of this latter character: and yet the man of Self-Control must have such: for suppose them good; then the moral state which should hinder a man from following their suggestions must be bad, and so Self-Control would not be in all cases good: suppose them on the other hand to be weak and not wrong, it would be nothing grand; nor anything great, supposing them to be wrong and weak.

Again, if Self-Control makes a man apt to abide by all opinions without exception, it may be bad, as suppose the case of a false opinion: and if Imperfect Self-Control makes a man apt to depart from all without exception, we shall have cases where it will be good; take that of Neoptolemus in the Philoctetes of Sophocles, for instance: he is to be praised for not abiding by what he was persuaded to by Ulysses, because he was pained at being guilty of falsehood.

Or again, false sophistical reasoning presents a difficulty: for because men wish to prove paradoxes that they may be counted clever when they succeed, the reasoning that has been used becomes a difficulty: for the intellect is fettered; a man being unwilling to abide by the conclusion because it does not please his judgment, but unable to advance because he cannot disentangle the web of sophistical reasoning.

Or again, it is conceivable on this supposition that folly joined with Imperfect Self-Control may turn out, in a given case, goodness: for by reason of his imperfection of self-control a man acts in a way which contradicts his notions; now his notion is that what is really good is bad and ought not to be done; and so he will eventually do what is good and not what is bad.

Again, on the same supposition, the man who acting on conviction pursues and chooses things because they are pleasant must be thought a better man than he who does so not by reason of a quasi-rational conviction but of Imperfect Self-Control: because he is more open to cure by reason of the possibility of his receiving a contrary conviction. But to the man of Imperfect Self-Control would apply the proverb, "when water chokes, what should a man drink then?" for had he never been convinced at all in respect of what he does, then by a conviction in a contrary direction he might have stopped in his course; but now though he has had convictions he notwithstanding acts against them.

Again, if any and every thing is the object-matter of Imperfect and Perfect Self-Control, who is the man of Imperfect Self-Control simply? because no one unites all cases of it, and we commonly say that some men are so simply, not adding any particular thing in which they are so.

Well, the difficulties raised are pretty near such as I have described them, and of these theories we must remove some and leave others as established; because the solving of a difficulty is a positive act of establishing something as true.

III

Now we must examine first whether men of Imperfect Self-Control act with a knowledge of what is right or not: next, if with such knowledge, in what sense; and next what are we to assume is the object-matter of the man of Imperfect Self-Control, and of the man of Self-Control; I mean, whether pleasure and pain of all kinds or certain definite ones; and as to Self-Control and Endurance, whether these are designations of the same character or different. And in like manner we must go into all questions which are connected with the present.

But the real starting point of the inquiry is, whether the two characters of Self-Control and Imperfect Self-Control are distinguished by their object-matter, or their respective relations to it. I mean, whether the man of Imperfect Self-Control is such simply by virtue of having such and such object-matter; or not, but by virtue of his being related to it in such and such a way, or by virtue of both: next, whether Self-Control and Imperfect Self-Control are unlimited in their object-matter: because he who is designated without any addition a man of Imperfect Self-Control is not unlimited in his object-matter, but has exactly the same as the man who has lost all Self-Control: nor is he so designated because of his relation to this object-matter merely (for then his character would be identical with that just mentioned, loss of all Self-Control), but because of his relation to it being such and such. For the man who has lost all Self-Control is led on with deliberate moral choice, holding that it is his line to pursue pleasure as it rises: while the man of Imperfect Self-Control does not think that he ought to pursue it, but does pursue it all the same.

Now as to the notion that it is True Opinion and not Knowledge in contravention of which men fail in Self-Control, it makes no difference to the point in question, because some of those who hold Opinions have no doubt about them but suppose themselves to have accurate Knowledge; if then it is urged that men holding Opinions will be more likely than men who have Knowledge to act in contravention of their conceptions, as having but a moderate belief in them; we reply, Knowledge will not differ in this respect from Opinion: because some men believe their own Opinions no less firmly than others do their positive Knowledge: Heraclitus is a case in point.

Rather the following is the account of it: the term knowing has two senses; both the man who does not use his Knowledge, and he who does, are said to know: there will be a difference between a man's acting wrongly, who though possessed of Knowledge does not call it into operation, and his doing so who has it and actually exercises it: the latter is a strange case, but the mere having, if not exercising, presents no anomaly.

Again, as there are two kinds of propositions affecting action, universal and particular, there is no reason why a man may not act against his Knowledge, having both propositions in his mind, using the universal but not the particular, for the particulars are the objects of moral action.

There is a difference also in universal propositions; a universal proposition may relate partly to a man's self and partly to the thing in question: take the following for instance; "dry food is good for every man," this may have the two minor premisses, "this is a man," and "so and so is dry food;" but whether a given substance is so and so a man either has not the Knowledge or does not exert it. According to these different senses there will be an immense difference, so that for a man to know in the one sense, and yet act wrongly, would be nothing strange, but in any of the other senses it would be a matter for wonder.

Again, men may have Knowledge in a way different from any of those which have been now stated: for we constantly see a man's state so differing by having and not using Knowledge, that he has it in a sense and also has not; when a man is asleep, for instance, or mad, or drunk: well, men under the actual operation of passion are in exactly similar conditions; for anger, lust, and some other such-like things, manifestly make changes even in the body, and in some they even cause madness; it is plain then that we must say the men of Imperfect Self-Control are in a state similar to these.

And their saying what embodies Knowledge is no proof of their actually then exercising it, because they who are under the operation of these passions repeat demonstrations; or verses of Empedocles, just as children, when first learning, string words together, but as yet know nothing of their meaning, because they must grow into it, and this is a process requiring time: so that we must suppose these men who fail in Self-Control to say these moral sayings just as actors do. Furthermore, a man may look at the account of the phænomenon in the following way, from an examination of the actual working of the mind: All action may be analysed into a syllogism, in which the one premiss is an universal maxim and the other concerns particulars of which Sense [moral or physical, as the case may be] is cognisant: now when one results from these two, it follows necessarily that, as far as theory goes the mind must assert the conclusion, and in practical propositions the man must act accordingly. For instance, let the universal be, "All that is sweet should be tasted," the particular, "This is sweet;" it follows necessarily that he who is able and is not hindered should not only draw, but put in practice, the conclusion "This is to be tasted." When then there is in the mind one universal proposition forbidding to taste, and the other "All that is sweet is pleasant" with its minor "This is sweet" (which is the one that really works), and desire happens to be in the man, the first universal bids him avoid this but the desire leads him on to taste; for it has the power of moving the various organs: and so it results that he fails in Self-Control, in a certain sense under the influence of Reason and Opinion not contrary in itself to Reason but only accidentally so; because it is the desire that is contrary to Right Reason, but not the Opinion: and so for this reason brutes are not accounted of Imperfect Self-Control, because they have no power of conceiving universals but only of receiving and retaining particular impressions.

As to the manner in which the ignorance is removed and the man of Imperfect Self-Control recovers his Knowledge, the account is the same as with respect to him who is drunk or asleep, and is not peculiar to this affection, so physiologists are the right people to apply to. But whereas the minor premiss of every practical syllogism is an opinion on matter cognisable by Sense and determines the actions; he who is under the influence of passion either has not this, or so has it that his having does not amount to knowing but merely saying, as a man when drunk might repeat Empedocles' verses; and because the minor term is neither universal, nor is thought to have the power of producing Knowledge in like manner as the universal term: and so the result which Socrates was seeking comes out, that is to say, the affection does not take place in the presence of that which is thought to be specially and properly Knowledge, nor is this dragged about by reason of the affection, but in the presence of that Knowledge which is conveyed by Sense.

Let this account then be accepted of the question respecting the failure in Self-Control, whether it is with Knowledge or not; and, if with knowledge, with what kind of knowledge such failure is possible.

IV

The next question to be discussed is whether there is a character to be designated by the term "of Imperfect Self-Control" simply, or whether all who are so are to be accounted such, in respect of some particular thing; and, if there is such a character, what is his object-matter.

Now that pleasures and pains are the object-matter of men of Self-Control and of Endurance, and also of men of Imperfect Self-Control and Softness, is plain.

Further, things which produce pleasure are either necessary, or objects of choice in themselves but yet admitting of excess. All bodily things which produce pleasure are necessary; and I call such those which relate to food and other grosser appetites, in short such bodily things as we assumed were the Object-matter of absence of Self-Control and of Perfected Self-Mastery.

The other class of objects are not necessary, but objects of choice in themselves: I mean, for instance, victory, honour, wealth, and such-like good or pleasant things. And those who are excessive in their liking for such things contrary to the principle of Right Reason which is in their own breasts we do not designate men of Imperfect Self-Control simply, but with the addition of the thing wherein, as in respect of money, or gain, or honour, or anger, and not simply; because we consider them as different characters and only having that title in right of a kind of resemblance (as when we add to a man's name "conqueror in the Olympic games" the account of him as Man differs but little from the account of him as the Man who conquered in the Olympic games, but still it is different). And a proof of the real difference between these so designated with an addition and those simply so called is this, that Imperfect Self-Control is blamed, not as an error merely but also as being a vice, either wholly or partially; but none of these other cases is so blamed.

But of those who have for their object-matter the bodily enjoyments, which we say are also the object-matter of the man of Perfected Self-Mastery and the man who has lost all Self-Control, he that pursues excessive pleasures and too much avoids things which are painful (as hunger and thirst, heat and cold, and everything connected with touch and taste), not from moral choice but in spite of his moral choice and intellectual conviction, is termed "a man of Imperfect Self-Control," not with the addition of any particular object-matter as we do in respect of want of control of anger but simply.

And a proof that the term is thus applied is that the kindred term "Soft" is used in respect of these enjoyments but not in respect of any of those others. And for this reason we put into the same rank the man of Imperfect Self-Control, the man who has lost it entirely, the man who has it, and the man of Perfected Self-Mastery; but not any of those other characters, because the former have for their object-matter the same pleasures and pains: but though they have the same object-matter, they are not related to it in the same way, but two of them act upon moral choice, two without it. And so we should say that man is more entirely given up to his passions who pursues excessive pleasures, and avoids moderate pains, being either not at all, or at least but little, urged by desire, than the man who does so because his desire is very strong: because we think what would the former be likely to do if he had the additional stimulus of youthful lust and violent pain consequent on the want of those pleasures which we have denominated necessary?

Well then, since of desires and pleasures there are some which are in kind honourable and good (because things pleasant are divisible, as we said before, into such as are naturally objects of choice, such as are naturally objects of avoidance, and such as are in themselves indifferent, money, gain, honour, victory, for instance); in respect of all such and those that are indifferent, men are blamed not merely for being affected by or desiring or liking them, but for exceeding in any way in these feelings.

And so they are blamed, whosoever in spite of Reason are mastered by, that is pursue, any object, though in its nature noble and good; they, for instance, who are more earnest than they should be respecting honour, or their children or parents; not but what these are good objects and men are praised for being earnest about them: but still they admit of excess; for instance, if any one, as Niobe did, should fight even against the gods, or feel towards his father as Satyrus, who got therefrom the nickname of [Greek: philophator], because he was thought to be very foolish.

Now depravity there is none in regard of these things, for the reason assigned above, that each of them in itself is a thing naturally choiceworthy, yet the excesses in respect of them are wrong and matter for blame: and similarly there is no Imperfect Self-Control in respect of these things; that being not merely a thing that should be avoided but blameworthy.

But because of the resemblance of the affection to the Imperfection of Self-Control the term is used with the addition in each case of the particular object-matter, just as men call a man a bad physician, or bad actor, whom they would not think of calling simply bad. As then in these cases we do not apply the term simply because each of the states is not a vice, but only like a vice in the way of analogy, so it is plain that in respect of Imperfect Self-Control and Self-Control we must limit the names to those states which have the same object-matter as Perfected Self-Mastery and utter loss of Self-Control, and that we do apply it to the case of anger only in the way of resemblance: for which reason, with an addition, we designate a man of Imperfect Self-Control in respect of anger, as of honour or of gain.

V

As there are some things naturally pleasant, and of these two kinds; those, namely, which are pleasant generally, and those which are so relatively to particular kinds of animals and men; so there are others which are not naturally pleasant but which come to be so in consequence either of maimings, or custom, or depraved natural tastes: and one may observe moral states similar to those we have been speaking of, having respectively these classes of things for their object-matter.

I mean the Brutish, as in the case of the female who, they say, would rip up women with child and eat the foetus; or the tastes which are found among the savage tribes bordering on the Pontus, some liking raw flesh, and some being cannibals, and some lending one another their children to make feasts of; or what is said of Phalaris. These are instances of Brutish states, caused in some by disease or madness; take, for instance, the man who sacrificed and ate his mother, or him who devoured the liver of his fellow-servant. Instances again of those caused by disease or by custom, would be, plucking out of hair, or eating one's nails, or eating coals and earth. ... Now wherever nature is really the cause no one would think of calling men of Imperfect Self-Control, ... nor, in like manner, such as are in a diseased state through custom.

Obviously the having any of these inclinations is something foreign to what is denominated Vice, just as Brutishness is: and when a man has them his mastering them is not properly Self-Control, nor his being mastered by them Imperfection of Self-Control in the proper sense, but only in the way of resemblance; just as we may say a man of ungovernable wrath fails of Self-Control in respect of anger but not simply fails of Self-Control. For all excessive folly, cowardice, absence of Self-Control, or irritability, are either Brutish or morbid. The man, for instance, who is naturally afraid of all things, even if a mouse should stir, is cowardly after a Brutish sort; there was a man again who, by reason of disease, was afraid of a cat: and of the fools, they who are naturally destitute of Reason and live only by Sense are Brutish, as are some tribes of the far-off barbarians, while others who are so by reason of diseases, epileptic or frantic, are in morbid states.

So then, of these inclinations, a man may sometimes merely have one without yielding to it: I mean, suppose that Phalaris had restrained his unnatural desire to eat a child: or he may both have and yield to it. As then Vice when such as belongs to human nature is called Vice simply, while the other is so called with the addition of "brutish" or "morbid," but not simply Vice, so manifestly there is Brutish and Morbid Imperfection of Self-Control, but that alone is entitled to the name without any qualification which is of the nature of utter absence of Self-Control, as it is found in Man.

VI

It is plain then that the object-matter of Imperfect Self-Control and Self-Control is restricted to the same as that of utter absence of Self-Control and that of Perfected Self-Mastery, and that the rest is the object-matter of a different species so named metaphorically and not simply: we will now examine the position, "that Imperfect Self-Control in respect of Anger is less disgraceful than that in respect of Lusts."

In the first place, it seems that Anger does in a way listen to Reason but mishears it; as quick servants who run out before they have heard the whole of what is said and then mistake the order; dogs, again, bark at the slightest stir, before they have seen whether it be friend or foe; just so Anger, by reason of its natural heat and quickness, listening to Reason, but without having heard the command of Reason, rushes to its revenge. That is to say, Reason or some impression on the mind shows there is insolence or contempt in the offender, and then Anger, reasoning as it were that one ought to fight against what is such, fires up immediately: whereas Lust, if Reason or Sense, as the case may be, merely says a thing is sweet, rushes to the enjoyment of it: and so Anger follows Reason in a manner, but Lust does not and is therefore more disgraceful: because he that cannot control his anger yields in a manner to Reason, but the other to his Lust and not to Reason at all.

Again, a man is more excusable for following such desires as are natural, just as he is for following such Lusts as are common to all and to that degree in which they are common. Now Anger and irritability are more natural than Lusts when in excess and for objects not necessary. (This was the ground of the defence the man made who beat his father, "My father," he said, "used to beat his, and his father his again, and this little fellow here," pointing to his child, "will beat me when he is grown a man: it runs in the family." And the father, as he was being dragged along, bid his son leave off beating him at the door, because he had himself been used to drag his father so far and no farther.)

Again, characters are less unjust in proportion as they involve less insidiousness. Now the Angry man is not insidious, nor is Anger, but quite open: but Lust is: as they say of Venus,

"Cyprus-born Goddess, weaver of deceits"

Or Homer of the girdle called the Cestus,

"Persuasiveness cheating e'en the subtlest mind."

And so since this kind of Imperfect Self-Control is more unjust, it is also more disgraceful than that in respect of Anger, and is simply Imperfect Self-Control, and Vice in a certain sense. Again, no man feels pain in being insolent, but every one who acts through Anger does act with pain; and he who acts insolently does it with pleasure. If then those things are most unjust with which we have most right to be angry, then Imperfect Self-Control, arising from Lust, is more so than that arising from Anger: because in Anger there is no insolence.

Well then, it is clear that Imperfect Self-Control in respect of Lusts is more disgraceful than that in respect of Anger, and that the object-matter of Self-Control, and the Imperfection of it, are bodily Lusts and pleasures; but of these last we must take into account the differences; for, as was said at the commencement, some are proper to the human race and natural both in kind and degree, others Brutish, and others caused by maimings and diseases.

Now the first of these only are the object-matter of Perfected Self-Mastery and utter absence of Self-Control; and therefore we never attribute either of these states to Brutes (except metaphorically, and whenever any one kind of animal differs entirely from another in insolence, mischievousness, or voracity), because they have not moral choice or process of deliberation, but are quite different from that kind of creature just as are madmen from other men.

Brutishness is not so low in the scale as Vice, yet it is to be regarded with more fear: because it is not that the highest principle has been corrupted, as in the human creature, but the subject has it not at all.

It is much the same, therefore, as if one should compare an inanimate with an animate being, which were the worse: for the badness of that which has no principle of origination is always less harmful; now Intellect is a principle of origination. A similar case would be the comparing injustice and an unjust man together: for in different ways each is the worst: a bad man would produce ten thousand times as much harm as a bad brute.

VII

Now with respect to the pleasures and pains which come to a man through Touch and Taste, and the desiring or avoiding such (which we determined before to constitute the object-matter of the states of utter absence of Self-Control and Perfected Self-Mastery), one may be so disposed as to yield to temptations to which most men would be superior, or to be superior to those to which most men would yield: in respect of pleasures, these characters will be respectively the man of Imperfect Self-Control, and the man of Self-Control; and, in respect of pains, the man of Softness and the man of Endurance: but the moral state of most men is something between the two, even though they lean somewhat to the worse characters.

Again, since of the pleasures indicated some are necessary and some are not, others are so to a certain degree but not the excess or defect of them, and similarly also of Lusts and pains, the man who pursues the excess of pleasant things, or such as are in themselves excess, or from moral choice, for their own sake, and not for anything else which is to result from them, is a man utterly void of Self-Control: for he must be incapable of remorse, and so incurable, because he that has not remorse is incurable. (He that has too little love of pleasure is the opposite character, and the man of Perfected Self-Mastery the mean character.) He is of a similar character who avoids the bodily pains, not because he cannot, but because he chooses not to, withstand them.

But of the characters who go wrong without choosing so to do, the one is led on by reason of pleasure, the other because he avoids the pain it would cost him to deny his lust; and so they are different the one from the other. Now every one would pronounce a man worse for doing something base without any impulse of desire, or with a very slight one, than for doing the same from the impulse of a very strong desire; for striking a man when not angry than if he did so in wrath: because one naturally says, "What would he have done had he been under the influence of passion?" (and on this ground, by the bye, the man utterly void of Self-Control is worse than he who has it imperfectly). However, of the two characters which have been mentioned [as included in that of utter absence of Self-Control], the one is rather Softness, the other properly the man of no Self-Control.

Furthermore, to the character of Imperfect Self-Control is opposed that of Self-Control, and to that of Softness that of Endurance: because Endurance consists in continued resistance but Self-Control in actual mastery, and continued resistance and actual mastery are as different as not being conquered is from conquering; and so Self-Control is more choiceworthy than Endurance.

Again, he who fails when exposed to those temptations against which the common run of men hold out, and are well able to do so, is Soft and Luxurious (Luxury being a kind of Softness): the kind of man, I mean, to let his robe drag in the dirt to avoid the trouble of lifting it, and who, aping the sick man, does not however suppose himself wretched though he is like a wretched man. So it is too with respect to Self-Control and the Imperfection of it: if a man yields to pleasures or pains which are violent and excessive it is no matter for wonder, but rather for allowance if he made what resistance he could (instances are, Philoctetes in Theodectes' drama when wounded by the viper; or Cercyon in the Alope of Carcinus, or men who in trying to suppress laughter burst into a loud continuous fit of it, as happened, you remember, to Xenophantus), but it is a matter for wonder when a man yields to and cannot contend against those pleasures or pains which the common herd are able to resist; always supposing his failure not to be owing to natural constitution or disease, I mean, as the Scythian kings are constitutionally Soft, or the natural difference between the sexes.

Again, the man who is a slave to amusement is commonly thought to be destitute of Self-Control, but he really is Soft; because amusement is an act of relaxing, being an act of resting, and the character in question is one of those who exceed due bounds in respect of this.

Moreover of Imperfect Self-Control there are two forms, Precipitancy and Weakness: those who have it in the latter form though they have made resolutions do not abide by them by reason of passion; the others are led by passion because they have never formed any resolutions at all: while there are some who, like those who by tickling themselves beforehand get rid of ticklishness, having felt and seen beforehand the approach of temptation, and roused up themselves and their resolution, yield not to passion; whether the temptation be somewhat pleasant or somewhat painful. The Precipitate form of Imperfect Self-Control they are most liable to who are constitutionally of a sharp or melancholy temperament: because the one by reason of the swiftness, the other by reason of the violence, of their passions, do not wait for Reason, because they are disposed to follow whatever notion is impressed upon their minds.

VIII

Again, the man utterly destitute of Self-Control, as was observed before, is not given to remorse: for it is part of his character that he abides by his moral choice: but the man of Imperfect Self-Control is almost made up of remorse: and so the case is not as we determined it before, but the former is incurable and the latter may be cured: for depravity is like chronic diseases, dropsy and consumption for instance, but Imperfect Self-Control is like acute disorders: the former being a continuous evil, the latter not so. And, in fact, Imperfect Self-Control and Confirmed Vice are different in kind: the latter being imperceptible to its victim, the former not so.

But, of the different forms of Imperfect Self-Control, those are better who are carried off their feet by a sudden access of temptation than they who have Reason but do not abide by it; these last being overcome by passion less in degree, and not wholly without premeditation as are the others: for the man of Imperfect Self-Control is like those who are soon intoxicated and by little wine and less than the common run of men. Well then, that Imperfection of Self-Control is not Confirmed Viciousness is plain: and yet perhaps it is such in a way, because in one sense it is contrary to moral choice and in another the result of it: at all events, in respect of the actions, the case is much like what Demodocus said of the Miletians. "The people of Miletus are not fools, but they do just the kind of things that fools do;" and so they of Imperfect Self-Control are not unjust, but they do unjust acts.

But to resume. Since the man of Imperfect Self-Control is of such a character as to follow bodily pleasures in excess and in defiance of Right Reason, without acting on any deliberate conviction, whereas the man utterly destitute of Self-Control does act upon a conviction which rests on his natural inclination to follow after these pleasures; the former may be easily persuaded to a different course, but the latter not: for Virtue and Vice respectively preserve and corrupt the moral principle; now the motive is the principle or starting point in moral actions, just as axioms and postulates are in mathematics: and neither in morals nor mathematics is it Reason which is apt to teach the principle; but Excellence, either natural or acquired by custom, in holding right notions with respect to the principle. He who does this in morals is the man of Perfected Self-Mastery, and the contrary character is the man utterly destitute of Self-Control.

Again, there is a character liable to be taken off his feet in defiance of Right Reason because of passion; whom passion so far masters as to prevent his acting in accordance with Right Reason, but not so far as to make him be convinced that it is his proper line to follow after such pleasures without limit: this character is the man of Imperfect Self-Control, better than he who is utterly destitute of it, and not a bad man simply and without qualification: because in him the highest and best part, i.e. principle, is preserved: and there is another character opposed to him who is apt to abide by his resolutions, and not to depart from them; at all events, not at the instigation of passion. It is evident then from all this, that Self-Control is a good state and the Imperfection of it a bad one.

Next comes the question, whether a man is a man of Self-Control for abiding by his conclusions and moral choice be they of what kind they may, or only by the right one; or again, a man of Imperfect Self-Control for not abiding by his conclusions and moral choice be they of whatever kind; or, to put the case we did before, is he such for not abiding by false conclusions and wrong moral choice?

Is not this the truth, that incidentally it is by conclusions and moral choice of any kind that the one character abides and the other does not, but per se true conclusions and right moral choice: to explain what is meant by incidentally, and per se; suppose a man chooses or pursues this thing for the sake of that, he is said to pursue and choose that per se, but this only incidentally. For the term per se we use commonly the word "simply," and so, in a way, it is opinion of any kind soever by which the two characters respectively abide or not, but he is "simply" entitled to the designations who abides or not by the true opinion.

There are also people, who have a trick of abiding by their own opinions, who are commonly called Positive, as they who are hard to be persuaded, and whose convictions are not easily changed: now these people bear some resemblance to the character of Self-Control, just as the prodigal to the liberal or the rash man to the brave, but they are different in many points. The man of Self-Control does not change by reason of passion and lust, yet when occasion so requires he will be easy of persuasion: but the Positive man changes not at the call of Reason, though many of this class take up certain desires and are led by their pleasures. Among the class of Positive are the Opinionated, the Ignorant, and the Bearish: the first, from the motives of pleasure and pain: I mean, they have the pleasurable feeling of a kind of victory in not having their convictions changed, and they are pained when their decrees, so to speak, are reversed: so that, in fact, they rather resemble the man of Imperfect Self-Control than the man of Self-Control.

Again, there are some who depart from their resolutions not by reason of any Imperfection of Self-Control; take, for instance, Neoptolemus in the Philoctetes of Sophocles. Here certainly pleasure was the motive of his departure from his resolution, but then it was one of a noble sort: for to be truthful was noble in his eyes and he had been persuaded by Ulysses to lie.

So it is not every one who acts from the motive of pleasure who is utterly destitute of Self-Control or base or of Imperfect Self-Control, only he who acts from the impulse of a base pleasure.

Moreover as there is a character who takes less pleasure than he ought in bodily enjoyments, and he also fails to abide by the conclusion of his Reason, the man of Self-Control is the mean between him and the man of Imperfect Self-Control: that is to say, the latter fails to abide by them because of somewhat too much, the former because of somewhat too little; while the man of Self-Control abides by them, and never changes by reason of anything else than such conclusions.

Now of course since Self-Control is good both the contrary States must be bad, as indeed they plainly are: but because the one of them is seen in few persons, and but rarely in them, Self-Control comes to be viewed as if opposed only to the Imperfection of it, just as Perfected Self-Mastery is thought to be opposed only to utter want of Self-Control.

Again, as many terms are used in the way of similitude, so people have come to talk of the Self-Control of the man of Perfected Self-Mastery in the way of similitude: for the man of Self-Control and the man of Perfected Self-Mastery have this in common, that they do nothing against Right Reason on the impulse of bodily pleasures, but then the former has bad desires, the latter not; and the latter is so constituted as not even to feel pleasure contrary to his Reason, the former feels but does not yield to it. Like again are the man of Imperfect Self-Control and he who is utterly destitute of it, though in reality distinct: both follow bodily pleasures, but the latter under a notion that it is the proper line for him to take, his former without any such notion.

IX

And it is not possible for the same man to be at once a man of Practical Wisdom and of Imperfect Self-Control: because the character of Practical Wisdom includes, as we showed before, goodness of moral character. And again, it is not knowledge merely, but aptitude for action, which constitutes Practical Wisdom: and of this aptitude the man of Imperfect Self-Control is destitute. But there is no reason why the Clever man should not be of Imperfect Self-Control: and the reason why some men are occasionally thought to be men of Practical Wisdom, and yet of Imperfect Self-Control, is this, that Cleverness differs from Practical Wisdom in the way I stated in a former book, and is very near it so far as the intellectual element is concerned but differs in respect of the moral choice.

Nor is the man of Imperfect Self-Control like the man who both has and calls into exercise his knowledge, but like the man who, having it, is overpowered by sleep or wine. Again, he acts voluntarily (because he knows, in a certain sense, what he does and the result of it), but he is not a confirmed bad man, for his moral choice is good, so he is at all events only half bad. Nor is he unjust, because he does not act with deliberate intent: for of the two chief forms of the character, the one is not apt to abide by his deliberate resolutions, and the other, the man of constitutional strength of passion, is not apt to deliberate at all.

So in fact the man of Imperfect Self-Control is like a community which makes all proper enactments, and has admirable laws, only does not act on them, verifying the scoff of Anaxandrides,

"That State did will it, which cares nought for laws;"

whereas the bad man is like one which acts upon its laws, but then unfortunately they are bad ones. Imperfection of Self-Control and Self-Control, after all, are above the average state of men; because he of the latter character is more true to his Reason, and the former less so, than is in the power of most men.

Again, of the two forms of Imperfect Self-Control that is more easily cured which they have who are constitutionally of strong passions, than that of those who form resolutions and break them; and they that are so through habituation than they that are so naturally; since of course custom is easier to change than nature, because the very resemblance of custom to nature is what constitutes the difficulty of changing it; as Evenus says,

"Practice, I say, my friend, doth long endure,
And at the last is even very nature."

We have now said then what Self-Control is, what Imperfection of Self-Control, what Endurance, and what Softness, and how these states are mutually related.

X

To consider the subject of Pleasure and Pain falls within the province of the Social-Science Philosopher, since he it is who has to fix the Master-End which is to guide us in dominating any object absolutely evil or good.

But we may say more: an inquiry into their nature is absolutely necessary. First, because we maintained that Moral Virtue and Moral Vice are both concerned with Pains and Pleasures: next, because the greater part of mankind assert that Happiness must include Pleasure (which by the way accounts for the word they use, makarioz; chaireiu being the root of that word).

Now some hold that no one Pleasure is good, either in itself or as a matter of result, because Good and Pleasure are not identical. Others that some Pleasures are good but the greater number bad. There is yet a third view; granting that every Pleasure is good, still the Chief Good cannot possibly be Pleasure.

In support of the first opinion (that Pleasure is utterly not-good) it is urged that:

I. Every Pleasure is a sensible process towards a complete state; but no such process is akin to the end to be attained: e.g. no process of building to the completed house.

II. The man of Perfected Self-Mastery avoids Pleasures.

III. The man of Practical Wisdom aims at avoiding Pain, not at attaining Pleasure.

IV. Pleasures are an impediment to thought, and the more so the more keenly they are felt. An obvious instance will readily occur.

V. Pleasure cannot be referred to any Art: and yet every good is the result of some Art.

VI. Children and brutes pursue Pleasures.

In support of the second (that not all Pleasures are good), That there are some base and matter of reproach, and some even hurtful: because some things that are pleasant produce disease.

In support of the third (that Pleasure is not the Chief Good), That it is not an End but a process towards creating an End.

This is, I think, a fair account of current views on the matter.

XI

But that the reasons alleged do not prove it either to be not-good or the Chief Good is plain from the following considerations.

First. Good being either absolute or relative, of course the natures and states embodying it will be so too; therefore also the movements and the processes of creation. So, of those which are thought to be bad some will be bad absolutely, but relatively not bad, perhaps even choiceworthy; some not even choiceworthy relatively to any particular person, only at certain times or for a short time but not in themselves choiceworthy.

Others again are not even Pleasures at all though they produce that impression on the mind: all such I mean as imply pain and whose purpose is cure; those of sick people, for instance.

Next, since Good may be either an active working or a state, those [Greek: kinaeseis or geneseis] which tend to place us in our natural state are pleasant incidentally because of that tendency: but the active working is really in the desires excited in the remaining (sound) part of our state or nature: for there are Pleasures which have no connection with pain or desire: the acts of contemplative intellect, for instance, in which case there is no deficiency in the nature or state of him who performs the acts.

A proof of this is that the same pleasant thing does not produce the sensation of Pleasure when the natural state is being filled up or completed as when it is already in its normal condition: in this latter case what give the sensation are things pleasant per se, in the former even those things which are contrary. I mean, you find people taking pleasure in sharp or bitter things of which no one is naturally or in itself pleasant; of course not therefore the Pleasures arising from them, because it is obvious that as is the classification of pleasant things such must be that of the Pleasures arising from them.

Next, it does not follow that there must be something else better than any given pleasure because (as some say) the End must be better than the process which creates it. For it is not true that all Pleasures are processes or even attended by any process, but (some are) active workings or even Ends: in fact they result not from our coming to be something but from our using our powers. Again, it is not true that the End is, in every case, distinct from the process: it is true only in the case of such processes as conduce to the perfecting of the natural state.

For which reason it is wrong to say that Pleasure is "a sensible process of production." For "process etc." should be substituted "active working of the natural state," for "sensible" "unimpeded." The reason of its being thought to be a "process etc." is that it is good in the highest sense: people confusing "active working" and "process," whereas they really are distinct.

Next, as to the argument that there are bad Pleasures because some things which are pleasant are also hurtful to health, it is the same as saying that some healthful things are bad for "business." In this sense, of course, both may be said to be bad, but then this does not make them out to be bad simpliciter: the exercise of the pure Intellect sometimes hurts a man's health: but what hinders Practical Wisdom or any state whatever is, not the Pleasure peculiar to, but some Pleasure foreign to it: the Pleasures arising from the exercise of the pure Intellect or from learning only promote each.

Next. "No Pleasure is the work of any Art." What else would you expect? No active working is the work of any Art, only the faculty of so working. Still the perfumer's Art or the cook's are thought to belong to Pleasure.

Next. "The man of Perfected Self-Mastery avoids Pleasures." "The man of Practical Wisdom aims at escaping Pain rather than at attaining Pleasure."

"Children and brutes pursue Pleasures."

One answer will do for all.

We have already said in what sense all Pleasures are good per se and in what sense not all are good: it is the latter class that brutes and children pursue, such as are accompanied by desire and pain, that is the bodily Pleasures (which answer to this description) and the excesses of them: in short, those in respect of which the man utterly destitute of Self-Control is thus utterly destitute. And it is the absence of the pain arising from these Pleasures that the man of Practical Wisdom aims at. It follows that these Pleasures are what the man of Perfected Self-Mastery avoids: for obviously he has Pleasures peculiarly his own.

XII

Then again, it is allowed that Pain is an evil and a thing to be avoided partly as bad per se, partly as being a hindrance in some particular way. Now the contrary of that which is to be avoided, quâ it is to be avoided, i.e. evil, is good. Pleasure then must be a good.

The attempted answer of Speusippus, "that Pleasure may be opposed and yet not contrary to Pain, just as the greater portion of any magnitude is contrary to the less but only opposed to the exact half," will not hold: for he cannot say that Pleasure is identical with evil of any kind. Again. Granting that some Pleasures are low, there is no reason why some particular Pleasure may not be very good, just as some particular Science may be although there are some which are low.

Perhaps it even follows, since each state may have active working unimpeded, whether the active workings of all be Happiness or that of some one of them, that this active working, if it be unimpeded, must be choiceworthy: now Pleasure is exactly this. So that the Chief Good may be Pleasure of some kind, though most Pleasures be (let us assume) low per se.

And for this reason all men think the happy life is pleasant, and interweave Pleasure with Happiness. Reasonably enough: because Happiness is perfect, but no impeded active working is perfect; and therefore the happy man needs as an addition the goods of the body and the goods external and fortune that in these points he may not be fettered. As for those who say that he who is being tortured on the wheel, or falls into great misfortunes is happy provided only he be good, they talk nonsense, whether they mean to do so or not. On the other hand, because fortune is needed as an addition, some hold good fortune to be identical with Happiness: which it is not, for even this in excess is a hindrance, and perhaps then has no right to be called good fortune since it is good only in so far as it contributes to Happiness.

The fact that all animals, brute and human alike, pursue Pleasure, is some presumption of its being in a sense the Chief Good;

("There must be something in what most folks say,") only as one and the same nature or state neither is nor is thought to be the best, so neither do all pursue the same Pleasure, Pleasure nevertheless all do. Nay further, what they pursue is, perhaps, not what they think nor what they would say they pursue, but really one and the same: for in all there is some instinct above themselves. But the bodily Pleasures have received the name exclusively, because theirs is the most frequent form and that which is universally partaken of; and so, because to many these alone are known they believe them to be the only ones which exist.

It is plain too that, unless Pleasure and its active working be good, it will not be true that the happy man's life embodies Pleasure: for why will he want it on the supposition that it is not good and that he can live even with Pain? because, assuming that Pleasure is not good, then Pain is neither evil nor good, and so why should he avoid it?

Besides, the life of the good man is not more pleasurable than any other unless it be granted that his active workings are so too.

XIII

Some inquiry into the bodily Pleasures is also necessary for those who say that some Pleasures, to be sure, are highly choiceworthy (the good ones to wit), but not the bodily Pleasures; that is, those which are the object-matter of the man utterly destitute of Self-Control.

If so, we ask, why are the contrary Pains bad? they cannot be (on their assumption) because the contrary of bad is good.

May we not say that the necessary bodily Pleasures are good in the sense in which that which is not-bad is good? or that they are good only up to a certain point? because such states or movements as cannot have too much of the better cannot have too much of Pleasure, but those which can of the former can also of the latter. Now the bodily Pleasures do admit of excess: in fact the low bad man is such because he pursues the excess of them instead of those which are necessary (meat, drink, and the objects of other animal appetites do give pleasure to all, but not in right manner or degree to all). But his relation to Pain is exactly the contrary: it is not excessive Pain, but Pain at all, that he avoids [which makes him to be in this way too a bad low man], because only in the case of him who pursues excessive Pleasure is Pain contrary to excessive Pleasure.

It is not enough however merely to state the truth, we should also show how the false view arises; because this strengthens conviction. I mean, when we have given a probable reason why that impresses people as true which really is not true, it gives them a stronger conviction of the truth. And so we must now explain why the bodily Pleasures appear to people to be more choiceworthy than any others.

The first obvious reason is, that bodily Pleasure drives out Pain; and because Pain is felt in excess men pursue Pleasure in excess, i.e. generally bodily Pleasure, under the notion of its being a remedy for that Pain. These remedies, moreover, come to be violent ones; which is the very reason they are pursued, since the impression they produce on the mind is owing to their being looked at side by side with their contrary.

And, as has been said before, there are the two following reasons why bodily Pleasure is thought to be not-good.

I. Some Pleasures of this class are actings of a low nature, whether congenital as in brutes, or acquired by custom as in low bad men.

II. Others are in the nature of cures, cures that is of some deficiency; now of course it is better to have [the healthy state] originally than that it should accrue afterwards.

But some Pleasures result when natural states are being perfected: these therefore are good as a matter of result.

Again, the very fact of their being violent causes them to be pursued by such as can relish no others: such men in fact create violent thirsts for themselves (if harmless ones then we find no fault, if harmful then it is bad and low) because they have no other things to take pleasure in, and the neutral state is distasteful to some people constitutionally; for toil of some kind is inseparable from life, as physiologists testify, telling us that the acts of seeing or hearing are painful, only that we are used to the pain and do not find it out.

Similarly in youth the constant growth produces a state much like that of vinous intoxication, and youth is pleasant. Again, men of the melancholic temperament constantly need some remedial process (because the body, from its temperament, is constantly being worried), and they are in a chronic state of violent desire. But Pleasure drives out Pain; not only such Pleasure as is directly contrary to Pain but even any Pleasure provided it be strong: and this is how men come to be utterly destitute of Self-Mastery, i.e. low and bad.

But those Pleasures which are unconnected with Pains do not admit of excess: i.e. such as belong to objects which are naturally pleasant and not merely as a matter of result: by the latter class I mean such as are remedial, and the reason why these are thought to be pleasant is that the cure results from the action in some way of that part of the constitution which remains sound. By "pleasant naturally" I mean such as put into action a nature which is pleasant.

The reason why no one and the same thing is invariably pleasant is that our nature is, not simple, but complex, involving something different from itself (so far as we are corruptible beings). Suppose then that one part of this nature be doing something, this something is, to the other part, unnatural: but, if there be an equilibrium of the two natures, then whatever is being done is indifferent. It is obvious that if there be any whose nature is simple and not complex, to such a being the same course of acting will always be the most pleasurable.

For this reason it is that the Divinity feels Pleasure which is always one, i.e. simple: not motion merely but also motionlessness acts, and Pleasure resides rather in the absence than in the presence of motion.

The reason why the Poet's dictum "change is of all things most pleasant" is true, is "a baseness in our blood;" for as the bad man is easily changeable, bad must be also the nature that craves change, i.e. it is neither simple nor good.

We have now said our say about Self-Control and its opposite; and about Pleasure and Pain. What each is, and how the one set is good the other bad. We have yet to speak of Friendship.

BOOK VIII

I

Next would seem properly to follow a dissertation on Friendship: because, in the first place, it is either itself a virtue or connected with virtue; and next it is a thing most necessary for life, since no one would choose to live without friends though he should have all the other good things in the world: and, in fact, men who are rich or possessed of authority and influence are thought to have special need of friends: for where is the use of such prosperity if there be taken away the doing of kindnesses of which friends are the most usual and most commendable objects? Or how can it be kept or preserved without friends? because the greater it is so much the more slippery and hazardous: in poverty moreover and all other adversities men think friends to be their only refuge.

Furthermore, Friendship helps the young to keep from error: the old, in respect of attention and such deficiencies in action as their weakness makes them liable to; and those who are in their prime, in respect of noble deeds ("They two together going," Homer says, you may remember), because they are thus more able to devise plans and carry them out.

Again, it seems to be implanted in us by Nature: as, for instance, in the parent towards the offspring and the offspring towards the parent (not merely in the human species, but likewise in birds and most animals), and in those of the same tribe towards one another, and specially in men of the same nation; for which reason we commend those men who love their fellows: and one may see in the course of travel how close of kin and how friendly man is to man.

Furthermore, Friendship seems to be the bond of Social Communities, and legislators seem to be more anxious to secure it than Justice even. I mean, Unanimity is somewhat like to Friendship, and this they certainly aim at and specially drive out faction as being inimical.

Again, where people are in Friendship Justice is not required; but, on the other hand, though they are just they need Friendship in addition, and that principle which is most truly just is thought to partake of the nature of Friendship.

Lastly, not only is it a thing necessary but honourable likewise: since we praise those who are fond of friends, and the having numerous friends is thought a matter of credit to a man; some go so far as to hold, that "good man" and "friend" are terms synonymous.

Yet the disputed points respecting it are not few: some men lay down that it is a kind of resemblance, and that men who are like one another are friends: whence come the common sayings, "Like will to like," "Birds of a feather," and so on. Others, on the contrary, say, that all such come under the maxim, "Two of a trade never agree."

Again, some men push their inquiries on these points higher and reason physically: as Euripides, who says,

"The earth by drought consumed doth love the rain,
And the great heaven, overcharged with rain,
Doth love to fall in showers upon the earth."

Heraclitus, again, maintains, that "contrariety is expedient, and that the best agreement arises from things differing, and that all things come into being in the way of the principle of antagonism."

Empedocles, among others, in direct opposition to these, affirms, that "like aims at like."

These physical questions we will take leave to omit, inasmuch as they are foreign to the present inquiry; and we will examine such as are proper to man and concern moral characters and feelings: as, for instance, "Does Friendship arise among all without distinction, or is it impossible for bad men to be friends?" and, "Is there but one species of Friendship, or several?" for they who ground the opinion that there is but one on the fact that Friendship admits of degrees hold that upon insufficient proof; because things which are different in species admit likewise of degrees (on this point we have spoken before).

II

Our view will soon be cleared on these points when we have ascertained what is properly the object-matter of Friendship: for it is thought that not everything indiscriminately, but some peculiar matter alone, is the object of this affection; that is to say, what is good, or pleasurable, or useful. Now it would seem that that is useful through which accrues any good or pleasure, and so the objects of Friendship, as absolute Ends, are the good and the pleasurable.

A question here arises; whether it is good absolutely or that which is good to the individuals, for which men feel Friendship (these two being sometimes distinct): and similarly in respect of the pleasurable. It seems then that each individual feels it towards that which is good to himself, and that abstractedly it is the real good which is the object of Friendship, and to each individual that which is good to each. It comes then to this; that each individual feels Friendship not for what is but for that which conveys to his mind the impression of being good to himself. But this will make no real difference, because that which is truly the object of Friendship will also convey this impression to the mind.

There are then three causes from which men feel Friendship: but the term is not applied to the case of fondness for things inanimate because there is no requital of the affection nor desire for the good of those objects: it certainly savours of the ridiculous to say that a man fond of wine wishes well to it: the only sense in which it is true being that he wishes it to be kept safe and sound for his own use and benefit. But to the friend they say one should wish all good for his sake. And when men do thus wish good to another (he not reciprocating the feeling), people call them Kindly; because Friendship they describe as being "Kindliness between persons who reciprocate it." But must they not add that the feeling must be mutually known? for many men are kindly disposed towards those whom they have never seen but whom they conceive to be amiable or useful: and this notion amounts to the same thing as a real feeling between them.

Well, these are plainly Kindly-disposed towards one another: but how can one call them friends while their mutual feelings are unknown to one another? to complete the idea of Friendship, then, it is requisite that they have kindly feelings towards one another, and wish one another good from one of the aforementioned causes, and that these kindly feelings should be mutually known.

III

As the motives to Friendship differ in kind so do the respective feelings and Friendships. The species then of Friendship are three, in number equal to the objects of it, since in the line of each there may be "mutual affection mutually known."

Now they who have Friendship for one another desire one another's good according to the motive of their Friendship; accordingly they whose motive is utility have no Friendship for one another really, but only in so far as some good arises to them from one another.

And they whose motive is pleasure are in like case: I mean, they have Friendship for men of easy pleasantry, not because they are of a given character but because they are pleasant to themselves. So then they whose motive to Friendship is utility love their friends for what is good to themselves; they whose motive is pleasure do so for what is pleasurable to themselves; that is to say, not in so far as the friend beloved is but in so far as he is useful or pleasurable. These Friendships then are a matter of result: since the object is not beloved in that he is the man he is but in that he furnishes advantage or pleasure as the case may be. Such Friendships are of course very liable to dissolution if the parties do not continue alike: I mean, that the others cease to have any Friendship for them when they are no longer pleasurable or useful. Now it is the nature of utility not to be permanent but constantly varying: so, of course, when the motive which made them friends is vanished, the Friendship likewise dissolves; since it existed only relatively to those circumstances.

Friendship of this kind is thought to exist principally among the old (because men at that time of life pursue not what is pleasurable but what is profitable); and in such, of men in their prime and of the young, as are given to the pursuit of profit. They that are such have no intimate intercourse with one another; for sometimes they are not even pleasurable to one another; nor, in fact, do they desire such intercourse unless their friends are profitable to them, because they are pleasurable only in so far as they have hopes of advantage. With these Friendships is commonly ranked that of hospitality.

But the Friendship of the young is thought to be based on the motive of pleasure: because they live at the beck and call of passion and generally pursue what is pleasurable to themselves and the object of the present moment: and as their age changes so likewise do their pleasures.

This is the reason why they form and dissolve Friendships rapidly: since the Friendship changes with the pleasurable object and such pleasure changes quickly.

The young are also much given up to Love; this passion being, in great measure, a matter of impulse and based on pleasure: for which cause they conceive Friendships and quickly drop them, changing often in the same day: but these wish for society and intimate intercourse with their friends, since they thus attain the object of their Friendship.

That then is perfect Friendship which subsists between those who are good and whose similarity consists in their goodness: for these men wish one another's good in similar ways; in so far as they are good (and good they are in themselves); and those are specially friends who wish good to their friends for their sakes, because they feel thus towards them on their own account and not as a mere matter of result; so the Friendship between these men continues to subsist so long as they are good; and goodness, we know, has in it a principle of permanence.

Moreover, each party is good abstractedly and also relatively to his friend, for all good men are not only abstractedly good but also useful to one another. Such friends are also mutually pleasurable because all good men are so abstractedly, and also relatively to one another, inasmuch as to each individual those actions are pleasurable which correspond to his nature, and all such as are like them. Now when men are good these will be always the same, or at least similar.

Friendship then under these circumstances is permanent, as we should reasonably expect, since it combines in itself all the requisite qualifications of friends. I mean, that Friendship of whatever kind is based upon good or pleasure (either abstractedly or relatively to the person entertaining the sentiment of Friendship), and results from a similarity of some sort; and to this kind belong all the aforementioned requisites in the parties themselves, because in this the parties are similar, and so on: moreover, in it there is the abstractedly good and the abstractedly pleasant, and as these are specially the object-matter of Friendship so the feeling and the state of Friendship is found most intense and most excellent in men thus qualified.

Rare it is probable Friendships of this kind will be, because men of this kind are rare. Besides, all requisite qualifications being presupposed, there is further required time and intimacy: for, as the proverb says, men cannot know one another "till they have eaten the requisite quantity of salt together;" nor can they in fact admit one another to intimacy, much less be friends, till each has appeared to the other and been proved to be a fit object of Friendship. They who speedily commence an interchange of friendly actions may be said to wish to be friends, but they are not so unless they are also proper objects of Friendship and mutually known to be such: that is to say, a desire for Friendship may arise quickly but not Friendship itself.

IV

Well, this Friendship is perfect both in respect of the time and in all other points; and exactly the same and similar results accrue to each party from the other; which ought to be the case between friends.

The friendship based upon the pleasurable is, so to say, a copy of this, since the good are sources of pleasure to one another: and that based on utility likewise, the good being also useful to one another. Between men thus connected Friendships are most permanent when the same result accrues to both from one another, pleasure, for instance; and not merely so but from the same source, as in the case of two men of easy pleasantry; and not as it is in that of a lover and the object of his affection, these not deriving their pleasure from the same causes, but the former from seeing the latter and the latter from receiving the attentions of the former: and when the bloom of youth fades the Friendship sometimes ceases also, because then the lover derives no pleasure from seeing and the object of his affection ceases to receive the attentions which were paid before: in many cases, however, people so connected continue friends, if being of similar tempers they have come from custom to like one another's disposition.

Where people do not interchange pleasure but profit in matters of Love, the Friendship is both less intense in degree and also less permanent: in fact, they who are friends because of advantage commonly part when the advantage ceases; for, in reality, they never were friends of one another but of the advantage.

So then it appears that from motives of pleasure or profit bad men may be friends to one another, or good men to bad men or men of neutral character to one of any character whatever: but disinterestedly, for the sake of one another, plainly the good alone can be friends; because bad men have no pleasure even in themselves unless in so far as some advantage arises.

And further, the Friendship of the good is alone superior to calumny; it not being easy for men to believe a third person respecting one whom they have long tried and proved: there is between good men mutual confidence, and the feeling that one's friend would never have done one wrong, and all other such things as are expected in Friendship really worthy the name; but in the other kinds there is nothing to prevent all such suspicions.

I call them Friendships, because since men commonly give the name of friends to those who are connected from motives of profit (which is justified by political language, for alliances between states are thought to be contracted with a view to advantage), and to those who are attached to one another by the motive of pleasure (as children are), we may perhaps also be allowed to call such persons friends, and say there are several species of Friendship; primarily and specially that of the good, in that they are good, and the rest only in the way of resemblance: I mean, people connected otherwise are friends in that way in which there arises to them somewhat good and some mutual resemblance (because, we must remember the pleasurable is good to those who are fond of it).

These secondary Friendships, however, do not combine very well; that is to say, the same persons do not become friends by reason of advantage and by reason of the pleasurable, for these matters of result are not often combined. And Friendship having been divided into these kinds, bad men will be friends by reason of pleasure or profit, this being their point of resemblance; while the good are friends for one another's sake, that is, in so far as they are good.

These last may be termed abstractedly and simply friends, the former as a matter of result and termed friends from their resemblance to these last.

V

Further; just as in respect of the different virtues some men are termed good in respect of a certain inward state, others in respect of acts of working, so is it in respect of Friendship: I mean, they who live together take pleasure in, and impart good to, one another: but they who are asleep or are locally separated do not perform acts, but only are in such a state as to act in a friendly way if they acted at all: distance has in itself no direct effect upon Friendship, but only prevents the acting it out: yet, if the absence be protracted, it is thought to cause a forgetfulness even of the Friendship: and hence it has been said, "many and many a Friendship doth want of intercourse destroy."

Accordingly, neither the old nor the morose appear to be calculated for Friendship, because the pleasurableness in them is small, and no one can spend his days in company with that which is positively painful or even not pleasurable; since to avoid the painful and aim at the pleasurable is one of the most obvious tendencies of human nature. They who get on with one another very fairly, but are not in habits of intimacy, are rather like people having kindly feelings towards one another than friends; nothing being so characteristic of friends as the living with one another, because the necessitous desire assistance, and the happy companionship, they being the last persons in the world for solitary existence: but people cannot spend their time together unless they are mutually pleasurable and take pleasure in the same objects, a quality which is thought to appertain to the Friendship of companionship.

The connection then subsisting between the good is Friendship par excellence, as has already been frequently said: since that which is abstractedly good or pleasant is thought to be an object of Friendship and choiceworthy, and to each individual whatever is such to him; and the good man to the good man for both these reasons. (Now the entertaining the sentiment is like a feeling, but Friendship itself like a state: because the former may have for its object even things inanimate, but requital of Friendship is attended with moral choice which proceeds from a moral state: and again, men wish good to the objects of their Friendship for their sakes, not in the way of a mere feeling but of moral state.).

And the good, in loving their friend, love their own good (inasmuch as the good man, when brought into that relation, becomes a good to him with whom he is so connected), so that either party loves his own good, and repays his friend equally both in wishing well and in the pleasurable: for equality is said to be a tie of Friendship. Well, these points belong most to the Friendship between good men.

But between morose or elderly men Friendship is less apt to arise, because they are somewhat awkward-tempered, and take less pleasure in intercourse and society; these being thought to be specially friendly and productive of Friendship: and so young men become friends quickly, old men not so (because people do not become friends with any, unless they take pleasure in them); and in like manner neither do the morose. Yet men of these classes entertain kindly feelings towards one another: they wish good to one another and render mutual assistance in respect of their needs, but they are not quite friends, because they neither spend their time together nor take pleasure in one another, which circumstances are thought specially to belong to Friendship.

To be a friend to many people, in the way of the perfect Friendship, is not possible; just as you cannot be in love with many at once: it is, so to speak, a state of excess which naturally has but one object; and besides, it is not an easy thing for one man to be very much pleased with many people at the same time, nor perhaps to find many really good. Again, a man needs experience, and to be in habits of close intimacy, which is very difficult.

But it is possible to please many on the score of advantage and pleasure: because there are many men of the kind, and the services may be rendered in a very short time.

Of the two imperfect kinds that which most resembles the perfect is the Friendship based upon pleasure, in which the same results accrue from both and they take pleasure in one another or in the same objects; such as are the Friendships of the young, because a generous spirit is most found in these. The Friendship because of advantage is the connecting link of shopkeepers.

Then again, the very happy have no need of persons who are profitable, but of pleasant ones they have because they wish to have people to live intimately with; and what is painful they bear for a short time indeed, but continuously no one could support it, nay, not even the Chief Good itself, if it were painful to him individually: and so they look out for pleasant friends: perhaps they ought to require such to be good also; and good moreover to themselves individually, because then they will have all the proper requisites of Friendship.

Men in power are often seen to make use of several distinct friends: for some are useful to them and others pleasurable, but the two are not often united: because they do not, in fact, seek such as shall combine pleasantness and goodness, nor such as shall be useful for honourable purposes: but with a view to attain what is pleasant they look out for men of easy-pleasantry; and again, for men who are clever at executing any business put into their hands: and these qualifications are not commonly found united in the same man.

It has been already stated that the good man unites the qualities of pleasantness and usefulness: but then such a one will not be a friend to a superior unless he be also his superior in goodness: for if this be not the case, he cannot, being surpassed in one point, make things equal by a proportionate degree of Friendship. And characters who unite superiority of station and goodness are not common. Now all the kinds of Friendship which have been already mentioned exist in a state of equality, inasmuch as either the same results accrue to both and they wish the same things to one another, or else they barter one thing against another; pleasure, for instance, against profit: it has been said already that Friendships of this latter kind are less intense in degree and less permanent.

And it is their resemblance or dissimilarity to the same thing which makes them to be thought to be and not to be Friendships: they show like Friendships in right of their likeness to that which is based on virtue (the one kind having the pleasurable, the other the profitable, both of which belong also to the other); and again, they do not show like Friendships by reason of their unlikeness to that true kind; which unlikeness consists herein, that while that is above calumny and so permanent these quickly change and differ in many other points.

VI

But there is another form of Friendship, that, namely, in which the one party is superior to the other; as between father and son, elder and younger, husband and wife, ruler and ruled. These also differ one from another: I mean, the Friendship between parents and children is not the same as between ruler and the ruled, nor has the father the same towards the son as the son towards the father, nor the husband towards the wife as she towards him; because the work, and therefore the excellence, of each of these is different, and different therefore are the causes of their feeling Friendship; distinct and different therefore are their feelings and states of Friendship.

And the same results do not accrue to each from the other, nor in fact ought they to be looked for: but, when children render to their parents what they ought to the authors of their being, and parents to their sons what they ought to their offspring, the Friendship between such parties will be permanent and equitable.

Further; the feeling of Friendship should be in a due proportion in all Friendships which are between superior and inferior; I mean, the better man, or the more profitable, and so forth, should be the object of a stronger feeling than he himself entertains, because when the feeling of Friendship comes to be after a certain rate then equality in a certain sense is produced, which is thought to be a requisite in Friendship.

(It must be remembered, however, that the equal is not in the same case as regards Justice and Friendship: for in strict Justice the exactly proportioned equal ranks first, and the actual numerically equal ranks second, while in Friendship this is exactly reversed.)

And that equality is thus requisite is plainly shown by the occurrence of a great difference of goodness or badness, or prosperity, or something else: for in this case, people are not any longer friends, nay they do not even feel that they ought to be. The clearest illustration is perhaps the case of the gods, because they are most superior in all good things. It is obvious too, in the case of kings, for they who are greatly their inferiors do not feel entitled to be friends to them; nor do people very insignificant to be friends to those of very high excellence or wisdom. Of course, in such cases it is out of the question to attempt to define up to what point they may continue friends: for you may remove many points of agreement and the Friendship last nevertheless; but when one of the parties is very far separated (as a god from men), it cannot continue any longer.

This has given room for a doubt, whether friends do really wish to their friends the very highest goods, as that they may be gods: because, in case the wish were accomplished, they would no longer have them for friends, nor in fact would they have the good things they had, because friends are good things. If then it has been rightly said that a friend wishes to his friend good things for that friend's sake, it must be understood that he is to remain such as he now is: that is to say, he will wish the greatest good to him of which as man he is capable: yet perhaps not all, because each man desires good for himself most of all.

VII

It is thought that desire for honour makes the mass of men wish rather to be the objects of the feeling of Friendship than to entertain it themselves (and for this reason they are fond of flatterers, a flatterer being a friend inferior or at least pretending to be such and rather to entertain towards another the feeling of Friendship than to be himself the object of it), since the former is thought to be nearly the same as being honoured, which the mass of men desire. And yet men seem to choose honour, not for its own sake, but incidentally: I mean, the common run of men delight to be honoured by those in power because of the hope it raises; that is they think they shall get from them anything they may happen to be in want of, so they delight in honour as an earnest of future benefit. They again who grasp at honour at the hands of the good and those who are really acquainted with their merits desire to confirm their own opinion about themselves: so they take pleasure in the conviction that they are good, which is based on the sentence of those who assert it. But in being the objects of Friendship men delight for its own sake, and so this may be judged to be higher than being honoured and Friendship to be in itself choiceworthy. Friendship, moreover, is thought to consist in feeling, rather than being the object of, the sentiment of Friendship, which is proved by the delight mothers have in the feeling: some there are who give their children to be adopted and brought up by others, and knowing them bear this feeling towards them never seeking to have it returned, if both are not possible; but seeming to be content with seeing them well off and bearing this feeling themselves towards them, even though they, by reason of ignorance, never render to them any filial regard or love.

Since then Friendship stands rather in the entertaining, than in being the object of, the sentiment, and they are praised who are fond of their friends, it seems that entertaining--the sentiment is the Excellence of friends; and so, in whomsoever this exists in due proportion these are stable friends and their Friendship is permanent. And in this way may they who are unequal best be friends, because they may thus be made equal.

Equality, then, and similarity are a tie to Friendship, and specially the similarity of goodness, because good men, being stable in themselves, are also stable as regards others, and neither ask degrading services nor render them, but, so to say, rather prevent them: for it is the part of the good neither to do wrong themselves nor to allow their friends in so doing.

The bad, on the contrary, have no principle of stability: in fact, they do not even continue like themselves: only they come to be friends for a short time from taking delight in one another's wickedness. Those connected by motives of profit, or pleasure, hold together somewhat longer: so long, that is to say, as they can give pleasure or profit mutually.

The Friendship based on motives of profit is thought to be most of all formed out of contrary elements: the poor man, for instance, is thus a friend of the rich, and the ignorant of the man of information; that is to say, a man desiring that of which he is, as it happens, in want, gives something else in exchange for it. To this same class we may refer the lover and beloved, the beautiful and the ill-favoured. For this reason lovers sometimes show in a ridiculous light by claiming to be the objects of as intense a feeling as they themselves entertain: of course if they are equally fit objects of Friendship they are perhaps entitled to claim this, but if they have nothing of the kind it is ridiculous.

Perhaps, moreover, the contrary does not aim at its contrary for its own sake but incidentally: the mean is really what is grasped at; it being good for the dry, for instance, not to become wet but to attain the mean, and so of the hot, etc. However, let us drop these questions, because they are in fact somewhat foreign to our purpose.

VIII

It seems too, as was stated at the commencement, that Friendship and Justice have the same object-matter, and subsist between the same persons: I mean that in every Communion there is thought to be some principle of Justice and also some Friendship: men address as friends, for instance, those who are their comrades by sea, or in war, and in like manner also those who are brought into Communion with them in other ways: and the Friendship, because also the Justice, is co-extensive with the Communion, This justifies the common proverb, "the goods of friends are common," since Friendship rests upon Communion.

Now brothers and intimate companions have all in common, but other people have their property separate, and some have more in common and others less, because the Friendships likewise differ in degree. So too do the various principles of Justice involved, not being the same between parents and children as between brothers, nor between companions as between fellow-citizens merely, and so on of all the other conceivable Friendships. Different also are the principles of Injustice as regards these different grades, and the acts become intensified by being done to friends; for instance, it is worse to rob your companion than one who is merely a fellow-citizen; to refuse help to a brother than to a stranger; and to strike your father than any one else. So then the Justice naturally increases with the degree of Friendship, as being between the same parties and of equal extent.

All cases of Communion are parts, so to say, of the great Social one, since in them men associate with a view to some advantage and to procure some of those things which are needful for life; and the great Social Communion is thought originally to have been associated and to continue for the sake of some advantage: this being the point at which legislators aim, affirming that to be just which is generally expedient. All the other cases of Communion aim at advantage in particular points; the crew of a vessel at that which is to result from the voyage which is undertaken with a view to making money, or some such object; comrades in war at that which is to result from the war, grasping either at wealth or victory, or it may be a political position; and those of the same tribe, or Demus, in like manner.

Some of them are thought to be formed for pleasure's sake, those, for instance, of bacchanals or club-fellows, which are with a view to Sacrifice or merely company. But all these seem to be ranged under the great Social one, inasmuch as the aim of this is, not merely the expediency of the moment but, for life and at all times; with a view to which the members of it institute sacrifices and their attendant assemblies, to render honour to the gods and procure for themselves respite from toil combined with pleasure. For it appears that sacrifices and religious assemblies in old times were made as a kind of first-fruits after the ingathering of the crops, because at such seasons they had most leisure.

So then it appears that all the instances of Communion are parts of the great Social one: and corresponding Friendships will follow upon such Communions.

IX

Of Political Constitutions there are three kinds; and equal in number are the deflections from them, being, so to say, corruptions of them.

The former are Kingship, Aristocracy, and that which recognises the principle of wealth, which it seems appropriate to call Timocracy (I give to it the name of a political constitution because people commonly do so). Of these the best is Monarchy, and Timocracy the worst.

From Monarchy the deflection is Despotism; both being Monarchies but widely differing from each other; for the Despot looks to his own advantage, but the King to that of his subjects: for he is in fact no King who is not thoroughly independent and superior to the rest in all good things, and he that is this has no further wants: he will not then have to look to his own advantage but to that of his subjects, for he that is not in such a position is a mere King elected by lot for the nonce.

But Despotism is on a contrary footing to this Kingship, because the Despot pursues his own good: and in the case of this its inferiority is most evident, and what is worse is contrary to what is best. The Transition to Despotism is made from Kingship, Despotism being a corrupt form of Monarchy, that is to say, the bad King comes to be a Despot.

From Aristocracy to Oligarchy the transition is made by the fault of the Rulers in distributing the public property contrary to right proportion; and giving either all that is good, or the greatest share, to themselves; and the offices to the same persons always, making wealth their idol; thus a few bear rule and they bad men in the place of the best.

From Timocracy the transition is to Democracy, they being contiguous: for it is the nature of Timocracy to be in the hands of a multitude, and all in the same grade of property are equal. Democracy is the least vicious of all, since herein the form of the constitution undergoes least change.

Well, these are generally the changes to which the various Constitutions are liable, being the least in degree and the easiest to make.

Likenesses, and, as it were, models of them, one may find even in Domestic life: for instance, the Communion between a Father and his Sons presents the figure of Kingship, because the children are the Father's care: and hence Homer names Jupiter Father because Kingship is intended to be a paternal rule. Among the Persians, however, the Father's rule is Despotic, for they treat their Sons as slaves. (The relation of Master to Slaves is of the nature of Despotism because the point regarded herein is the Master's interest): this now strikes me to be as it ought, but the Persian custom to be mistaken; because for different persons there should be different rules. Between Husband and Wife the relation takes the form of Aristocracy, because he rules by right and in such points only as the Husband should, and gives to the Wife all that befits her to have. Where the Husband lords it in everything he changes the relation into an Oligarchy; because he does it contrary to right and not as being the better of the two. In some instances the Wives take the reins of government, being heiresses: here the rule is carried on not in right of goodness but by reason of wealth and power, as it is in Oligarchies.

Timocracy finds its type in the relation of Brothers: they being equal except as to such differences as age introduces: for which reason, if they are very different in age, the Friendship comes to be no longer a fraternal one: while Democracy is represented specially by families which have no head (all being there equal), or in which the proper head is weak and so every member does that which is right in his own eyes.

X

Attendant then on each form of Political Constitution there plainly is Friendship exactly co-extensive with the principle of Justice; that between a King and his Subjects being in the relation of a superiority of benefit, inasmuch as he benefits his subjects; it being assumed that he is a good king and takes care of their welfare as a shepherd tends his flock; whence Homer (to quote him again) calls Agamemnon, "shepherd of the people." And of this same kind is the Paternal Friendship, only that it exceeds the former in the greatness of the benefits done; because the father is the author of being (which is esteemed the greatest benefit) and of maintenance and education (these things are also, by the way, ascribed to ancestors generally): and by the law of nature the father has the right of rule over his sons, ancestors over their descendants, and the king over his subjects.

These friendships are also between superiors and inferiors, for which reason parents are not merely loved but also honoured. The principle of Justice also between these parties is not exactly the same but according to proportiton, because so also is the Friendship.

Now between Husband and Wife there is the same Friendship as in Aristocracy: for the relation is determined by relative excellence, and the better person has the greater good and each has what befits: so too also is the principle of Justice between them.

The Fraternal Friendship is like that of Companions, because brothers are equal and much of an age, and such persons have generally like feelings and like dispositions. Like to this also is the Friendship of a Timocracy, because the citizens are intended to be equal and equitable: rule, therefore, passes from hand to hand, and is distributed on equal terms: so too is the Friendship accordingly.

In the deflections from the constitutional forms, just as the principle of Justice is but small so is the Friendship also: and least of all in the most perverted form: in Despotism there is little or no Friendship. For generally wherever the ruler and the ruled have nothing in common there is no Friendship because there is no Justice; but the case is as between an artisan and his tool, or between soul and body, and master and slave; all these are benefited by those who use them, but towards things inanimate there is neither Friendship nor Justice: nor even towards a horse or an ox, or a slave quâ slave, because there is nothing in common: a slave as such is an animate tool, a tool an inanimate slave. Quâ slave, then, there is no Friendship towards him, only quâ man: for it is thought that there is some principle of Justice between every man, and every other who can share in law and be a party to an agreement; and so somewhat of Friendship, in so far as he is man. So in Despotisms the Friendships and the principle of Justice are inconsiderable in extent, but in Democracies they are most considerable because they who are equal have much in common.

XI

Now of course all Friendship is based upon Communion, as has been already stated: but one would be inclined to separate off from the rest the Friendship of Kindred, and that of Companions: whereas those of men of the same city, or tribe, or crew, and all such, are more peculiarly, it would seem, based upon Communion, inasmuch as they plainly exist in right of some agreement expressed or implied: among these one may rank also the Friendship of Hospitality,

The Friendship of Kindred is likewise of many kinds, and appears in all its varieties to depend on the Parental: parents, I mean, love their children as being a part of themselves, children love their parents as being themselves somewhat derived from them. But parents know their offspring more than these know that they are from the parents, and the source is more closely bound to that which is produced than that which is produced is to that which formed it: of course, whatever is derived from one's self is proper to that from which it is so derived (as, for instance, a tooth or a hair, or any other thing whatever to him that has it): but the source to it is in no degree proper, or in an inferior degree at least.

Then again the greater length of time comes in: the parents love their offspring from the first moment of their being, but their offspring them only after a lapse of time when they have attained intelligence or instinct. These considerations serve also to show why mothers have greater strength of affection than fathers.

Now parents love their children as themselves (since what is derived from themselves becomes a kind of other Self by the fact of separation), but children their parents as being sprung from them. And brothers love one another from being sprung from the same; that is, their sameness with the common stock creates a sameness with one another; whence come the phrases, "same blood," "root," and so on. In fact they are the same, in a sense, even in the separate distinct individuals.

Then again the being brought up together, and the nearness of age, are a great help towards Friendship, for a man likes one of his own age and persons who are used to one another are companions, which accounts for the resemblance between the Friendship of Brothers and that of Companions.

And cousins and all other relatives derive their bond of union from these, that is to say, from their community of origin: and the strength of this bond varies according to their respective distances from the common ancestor.

Further: the Friendship felt by children towards parents, and by men towards the gods, is as towards something good and above them; because these have conferred the greatest possible benefits, in that they are the causes of their being and being nourished, and of their having been educated after they were brought into being.

And Friendship of this kind has also the pleasurable and the profitable more than that between persons unconnected by blood, in proportion as their life is also more shared in common. Then again in the Fraternal Friendship there is all that there is in that of Companions, and more in the good, and generally in those who are alike; in proportion as they are more closely tied and from their very birth have a feeling of affection for one another to begin with, and as they are more like in disposition who spring from the same stock and have grown up together and been educated alike: and besides this they have the greatest opportunities in respect of time for proving one another, and can therefore depend most securely upon the trial. The elements of Friendship between other consanguinities will be of course proportionably similar.

Between Husband and Wife there is thought to be Friendship by a law of nature: man being by nature disposed to pair, more than to associate in Communities: in proportion as the family is prior in order of time and more absolutely necessary than the Community. And procreation is more common to him with other animals; all the other animals have Communion thus far, but human creatures cohabit not merely for the sake of procreation but also with a view to life in general: because in this connection the works are immediately divided, and some belong to the man, others to the woman: thus they help one the other, putting what is peculiar to each into the common stock.

And for these reasons this Friendship is thought to combine the profitable and the pleasurable: it will be also based upon virtue if they are good people; because each has goodness and they may take delight in this quality in each other. Children too are thought to be a tie: accordingly the childless sooner separate, for the children are a good common to both and anything in common is a bond of union.

The question how a man is to live with his wife, or (more generally) one friend with another, appears to be no other than this, how it is just that they should: because plainly there is not the same principle of Justice between a friend and friend, as between strangers, or companions, or mere chance fellow-travellers.

XII

There are then, as was stated at the commencement of this book, three kinds of Friendship, and in each there may be friends on a footing of equality and friends in the relation of superior and inferior; we find, I mean, that people who are alike in goodness, become friends, and better with worse, and so also pleasant people; again, because of advantage people are friends, either balancing exactly their mutual profitableness or differing from one another herein. Well then, those who are equal should in right of this equality be equalised also by the degree of their Friendship and the other points, and those who are on a footing of inequality by rendering Friendship in proportion to the superiority of the other party.

Fault-finding and blame arises, either solely or most naturally, in Friendship of which utility is the motive: for they who are friends by reason of goodness, are eager to do kindnesses to one another because this is a natural result of goodness and Friendship; and when men are vying with each other for this End there can be no fault-finding nor contention: since no one is annoyed at one who entertains for him the sentiment of Friendship and does kindnesses to him, but if of a refined mind he requites him with kind actions. And suppose that one of the two exceeds the other, yet as he is attaining his object he will not find fault with his friend, for good is the object of each party.

Neither can there well be quarrels between men who are friends for pleasure's sake: because supposing them to delight in living together then both attain their desire; or if not a man would be put in a ridiculous light who should find fault with another for not pleasing him, since it is in his power to forbear intercourse with him. But the Friendship because of advantage is very liable to fault-finding;

because, as the parties use one another with a view to advantage, the requirements are continually enlarging, and they think they have less than of right belongs to them, and find fault because though justly entitled they do not get as much as they want: while they who do the kindnesses, can never come up to the requirements of those to whom they are being done.

It seems also, that as the Just is of two kinds, the unwritten and the legal, so Friendship because of advantage is of two kinds, what may be called the Moral, and the Legal: and the most fruitful source of complaints is that parties contract obligations and discharge them not in the same line of Friendship. The Legal is upon specified conditions, either purely tradesmanlike from hand to hand or somewhat more gentlemanly as regards time but still by agreement a quid pro quo.

In this Legal kind the obligation is clear and admits of no dispute, the friendly element is the delay in requiring its discharge: and for this reason in some countries no actions can be maintained at Law for the recovery of such debts, it being held that they who have dealt on the footing of credit must be content to abide the issue.

That which may be termed the Moral kind is not upon specified conditions, but a man gives as to his friend and so on: but still he expects to receive an equivalent, or even more, as though he had not given but lent: he also will find fault, because he does not get the obligation discharged in the same way as it was contracted.

Now this results from the fact, that all men, or the generality at least, wish what is honourable, but, when tested, choose what is profitable; and the doing kindnesses disinterestedly is honourable while receiving benefits is profitable. In such cases one should, if able, make a return proportionate to the good received, and do so willingly, because one ought not to make a disinterested friend of a man against his inclination: one should act, I say, as having made a mistake originally in receiving kindness from one from whom one ought not to have received it, he being not a friend nor doing the act disinterestedly; one should therefore discharge one's self of the obligation as having received a kindness on specified terms: and if able a man would engage to repay the kindness, while if he were unable even the doer of it would not expect it of him: so that if he is able he ought to repay it. But one ought at the first to ascertain from whom one is receiving kindness, and on what understanding, that on that same understanding one may accept it or not.

A question admitting of dispute is whether one is to measure a kindness by the good done to the receiver of it, and make this the standard by which to requite, or by the kind intention of the doer?

For they who have received kindnesses frequently plead in depreciation that they have received from their benefactors such things as were small for them to give, or such as they themselves could have got from others: while the doers of the kindnesses affirm that they gave the best they had, and what could not have been got from others, and under danger, or in such-like straits.

May we not say, that as utility is the motive of the Friendship the advantage conferred on the receiver must be the standard? because he it is who requests the kindness and the other serves him in his need on the understanding that he is to get an equivalent: the assistance rendered is then exactly proportionate to the advantage which the receiver has obtained, and he should therefore repay as much as he gained by it, or even more, this being more creditable.

In Friendships based on goodness, the question, of course, is never raised, but herein the motive of the doer seems to be the proper standard, since virtue and moral character depend principally on motive.

XIII

Quarrels arise also in those Friendships in which the parties are unequal because each party thinks himself entitled to the greater share, and of course, when this happens, the Friendship is broken up.

The man who is better than the other thinks that having the greater share pertains to him of right, for that more is always awarded to the good man: and similarly the man who is more profitable to another than that other to him: "one who is useless," they say, "ought not to share equally, for it comes to a tax, and not a Friendship, unless the fruits of the Friendship are reaped in proportion to the works done:" their notion being, that as in a money partnership they who contribute more receive more so should it be in Friendship likewise.

On the other hand, the needy man and the less virtuous advance the opposite claim: they urge that "it is the very business of a good friend to help those who are in need, else what is the use of having a good or powerful friend if one is not to reap the advantage at all?"

Now each seems to advance a right claim and to be entitled to get more out of the connection than the other, only not more of the same thing: but the superior man should receive more respect, the needy man more profit: respect being the reward of goodness and beneficence, profit being the aid of need.

This is plainly the principle acted upon in Political Communities: he receives no honour who gives no good to the common stock: for the property of the Public is given to him who does good to the Public, and honour is the property of the Public; it is not possible both to make money out of the Public and receive honour likewise; because no one will put up with the less in every respect: so to him who suffers loss as regards money they award honour, but money to him who can be paid by gifts: since, as has been stated before, the observing due proportion equalises and preserves Friendship.

Like rules then should be observed in the intercourse of friends who are unequal; and to him who advantages another in respect of money, or goodness, that other should repay honour, making requital according to his power; because Friendship requires what is possible, not what is strictly due, this being not possible in all cases, as in the honours paid to the gods and to parents: no man could ever make the due return in these cases, and so he is thought to be a good man who pays respect according to his ability.

For this reason it may be judged never to be allowable for a son to disown his father, whereas a father may his son: because he that owes is bound to pay; now a son can never, by anything he has done, fully requite the benefits first conferred on him by his father, and so is always a debtor. But they to whom anything is owed may cast off their debtors: therefore the father may his son. But at the same time it must perhaps be admitted, that it seems no father ever would sever himself utterly from a son, except in a case of exceeding depravity: because, independently of the natural Friendship, it is like human nature not to put away from one's self the assistance which a son might render. But to the son, if depraved, assisting his father is a thing to be avoided, or at least one which he will not be very anxious to do; most men being willing enough to receive kindness, but averse to doing it as unprofitable.

Let thus much suffice on these points.

BOOK IX

I

Well, in all the Friendships the parties to which are dissimilar it is the proportionate which equalises and preserves the Friendship, as has been already stated: I mean, in the Social Friendship the cobbler, for instance, gets an equivalent for his shoes after a certain rate; and the weaver, and all others in like manner. Now in this case a common measure has been provided in money, and to this accordingly all things are referred and by this are measured: but in the Friendship of Love the complaint is sometimes from the lover that, though he loves exceedingly, his love is not requited; he having perhaps all the time nothing that can be the object of Friendship: again, oftentimes from the object of love that he who as a suitor promised any and every thing now performs nothing. These cases occur because the Friendship of the lover for the beloved object is based upon pleasure, that of the other for him upon utility, and in one of the parties the requisite quality is not found: for, as these are respectively the grounds of the Friendship, the Friendship comes to be broken up because the motives to it cease to exist: the parties loved not one another but qualities in one another which are not permanent, and so neither are the Friendships: whereas the Friendship based upon the moral character of the parties, being independent and disinterested, is permanent, as we have already stated.

Quarrels arise also when the parties realise different results and not those which they desire; for the not attaining one's special object is all one, in this case, with getting nothing at all: as in the well-known case where a man made promises to a musician, rising in proportion to the excellence of his music; but when, the next morning, the musician claimed the performance of his promises, he said that he had given him pleasure for pleasure: of course, if each party had intended this, it would have been all right: but if the one desires amusement and the other gain, and the one gets his object but the other not, the dealing cannot be fair: because a man fixes his mind upon what he happens to want, and will give so and so for that specific thing.

The question then arises, who is to fix the rate? the man who first gives, or the man who first takes? because, prima facie, the man who first gives seems to leave the rate to be fixed by the other party. This, they say, was in fact the practice of Protagoras: when he taught a man anything he would bid the learner estimate the worth of the knowledge gained by his own private opinion; and then he used to take so much from him. In such cases some people adopt the rule,

"With specified reward a friend should be content."

They are certainly fairly found fault with who take the money in advance and then do nothing of what they said they would do, their promises having been so far beyond their ability; for such men do not perform what they agreed, The Sophists, however, are perhaps obliged to take this course, because no one would give a sixpence for their knowledge. These then, I say, are fairly found fault with, because they do not what they have already taken money for doing.

In cases where no stipulation as to the respective services is made they who disinterestedly do the first service will not raise the question (as we have said before), because it is the nature of Friendship, based on mutual goodness to be reference to the intention of the other, the intention being characteristic of the true friend and of goodness.

And it would seem the same rule should be laid down for those who are connected with one another as teachers and learners of philosophy; for here the value of the commodity cannot be measured by money, and, in fact, an exactly equivalent price cannot be set upon it, but perhaps it is sufficient to do what one can, as in the case of the gods or one's parents.

But where the original giving is not upon these terms but avowedly for some return, the most proper course is perhaps for the requital to be such as both shall allow to be proportionate, and, where this cannot be, then for the receiver to fix the value would seem to be not only necessary but also fair: because when the first giver gets that which is equivalent to the advantage received by the other, or to what he would have given to secure the pleasure he has had, then he has the value from him: for not only is this seen to be the course adopted in matters of buying and selling but also in some places the law does not allow of actions upon voluntary dealings; on the principle that when one man has trusted another he must be content to have the obligation discharged in the same spirit as he originally contracted it: that is to say, it is thought fairer for the trusted, than for the trusting, party, to fix the value. For, in general, those who have and those who wish to get things do not set the same value on them: what is their own, and what they give in each case, appears to them worth a great deal: but yet the return is made according to the estimate of those who have received first, it should perhaps be added that the receiver should estimate what he has received, not by the value he sets upon it now that he has it, but by that which he set upon it before he obtained it.

II

Questions also arise upon such points as the following: Whether one's father has an unlimited claim on one's services and obedience, or whether the sick man is to obey his physician? or, in an election of a general, the warlike qualities of the candidates should be alone regarded?

In like manner whether one should do a service rather to one's friend or to a good man? whether one should rather requite a benefactor or give to one's companion, supposing that both are not within one's power?

Is not the true answer that it is no easy task to determine all such questions accurately, inasmuch as they involve numerous differences of all kinds, in respect of amount and what is honourable and what is necessary? It is obvious, of course, that no one person can unite in himself all claims. Again, the requital of benefits is, in general, a higher duty than doing unsolicited kindnesses to one's companion; in other words, the discharging of a debt is more obligatory upon one than the duty of giving to a companion. And yet this rule may admit of exceptions; for instance, which is the higher duty? for one who has been ransomed out of the hands of robbers to ransom in return his ransomer, be he who he may, or to repay him on his demand though he has not been taken by robbers, or to ransom his own father? for it would seem that a man ought to ransom his father even in preference to himself.

Well then, as has been said already, as a general rule the debt should be discharged, but if in a particular case the giving greatly preponderates as being either honourable or necessary, we must be swayed by these considerations: I mean, in some cases the requital of the obligation previously existing may not be equal; suppose, for instance, that the original benefactor has conferred a kindness on a good man, knowing him to be such, whereas this said good man has to repay it believing him to be a scoundrel.

And again, in certain cases no obligation lies on a man to lend to one who has lent to him; suppose, for instance, that a bad man lent to him, as being a good man, under the notion that he should get repaid, whereas the said good man has no hope of repayment from him being a bad man. Either then the case is really as we have supposed it and then the claim is not equal, or it is not so but supposed to be; and still in so acting people are not to be thought to act wrongly. In short, as has been oftentimes stated before, all statements regarding feelings and actions can be definite only in proportion as their object-matter is so; it is of course quite obvious that all people have not the same claim upon one, nor are the claims of one's father unlimited; just as Jupiter does not claim all kinds of sacrifice without distinction: and since the claims of parents, brothers, companions, and benefactors, are all different, we must give to each what belongs to and befits each.

And this is seen to be the course commonly pursued: to marriages men commonly invite their relatives, because these are from a common stock and therefore all the actions in any way pertaining thereto are common also: and to funerals men think that relatives ought to assemble in preference to other people, for the same reason.

And it would seem that in respect of maintenance it is our duty to assist our parents in preference to all others, as being their debtors, and because it is more honourable to succour in these respects the authors of our existence than ourselves. Honour likewise we ought to pay to our parents just as to the gods, but then, not all kinds of honour: not the same, for instance, to a father as to a mother: nor again to a father the honour due to a scientific man or to a general but that which is a father's due, and in like manner to a mother that which is a mother's.

To all our elders also the honour befitting their age, by rising up in their presence, turning out of the way for them, and all similar marks of respect: to our companions again, or brothers, frankness and free participation in all we have. And to those of the same family, or tribe, or city, with ourselves, and all similarly connected with us, we should constantly try to render their due, and to discriminate what belongs to each in respect of nearness of connection, or goodness, or intimacy: of course in the case of those of the same class the discrimination is easier; in that of those who are in different classes it is a matter of more trouble. This, however, should not be a reason for giving up the attempt, but we must observe the distinctions so far as it is practicable to do so.

III

A question is also raised as to the propriety of dissolving or not dissolving those Friendships the parties to which do not remain what they were when the connection was formed.

Now surely in respect of those whose motive to Friendship is utility or pleasure there can be nothing wrong in breaking up the connection when they no longer have those qualities; because they were friends [not of one another, but] of those qualities: and, these having failed, it is only reasonable to expect that they should cease to entertain the sentiment.

But a man has reason to find fault if the other party, being really attached to him because of advantage or pleasure, pretended to be so because of his moral character: in fact, as we said at the commencement, the most common source of quarrels between friends is their not being friends on the same grounds as they suppose themselves to be.

Now when a man has been deceived in having supposed himself to excite the sentiment of Friendship by reason of his moral character, the other party doing nothing to indicate he has but himself to blame: but when he has been deceived by the pretence of the other he has a right to find fault with the man who has so deceived him, aye even more than with utterers of false coin, in proportion to the greater preciousness of that which is the object-matter of the villany.

But suppose a man takes up another as being a good man, who turns out, and is found by him, to be a scoundrel, is he bound still to entertain Friendship for him? or may we not say at once it is impossible? since it is not everything which is the object-matter of Friendship, but only that which is good; and so there is no obligation to be a bad man's friend, nor, in fact, ought one to be such: for one ought not to be a lover of evil, nor to be assimilated to what is base; which would be implied, because we have said before, like is friendly to like.

Are we then to break with him instantly? not in all cases; only where our friends are incurably depraved; when there is a chance of amendment we are bound to aid in repairing the moral character of our friends even more than their substance, in proportion as it is better and more closely related to Friendship. Still he who should break off the connection is not to be judged to act wrongly, for he never was a friend to such a character as the other now is, and therefore, since the man is changed and he cannot reduce him to his original state, he backs out of the connection.

To put another case: suppose that one party remains what he was when the Friendship was formed, while the other becomes morally improved and widely different from his friend in goodness; is the improved character to treat the other as a friend?

May we not say it is impossible? The case of course is clearest where there is a great difference, as in the Friendships of boys: for suppose that of two boyish friends the one still continues a boy in mind and the other becomes a man of the highest character, how can they be friends? since they neither are pleased with the same objects nor like and dislike the same things: for these points will not belong to them as regards one another, and without them it was assumed they cannot be friends because they cannot live in intimacy: and of the case of those who cannot do so we have spoken before.

Well then, is the improved party to bear himself towards his former friend in no way differently to what he would have done had the connection never existed?

Surely he ought to bear in mind the intimacy of past times, and just as we think ourselves bound to do favours for our friends in preference to strangers, so to those who have been friends and are so no longer we should allow somewhat on the score of previous Friendship, whenever the cause of severance is not excessive depravity on their part.

IV

Now the friendly feelings which are exhibited towards our friends, and by which Friendships are characterised, seem to have sprung out of those which we entertain toward ourselves. I mean, people define a friend to be "one who intends and does what is good (or what he believes to be good) to another for that other's sake," or "one who wishes his friend to be and to live for that friend's own sake" (which is the feeling of mothers towards their children, and of friends who have come into collision). Others again, "one who lives with another and chooses the same objects," or "one who sympathises with his friend in his sorrows and in his joys" (this too is especially the case with mothers).

Well, by some one of these marks people generally characterise Friendship: and each of these the good man has towards himself, and all others have them in so far as they suppose themselves to be good. (For, as has been said before, goodness, that is the good man, seems to be a measure to every one else.)

For he is at unity in himself, and with every part of his soul he desires the same objects; and he wishes for himself both what is, and what he believes to be, good; and he does it (it being characteristic of the good man to work at what is good), and for the sake of himself, inasmuch as he does it for the sake of his Intellectual Principle which is generally thought to be a man's Self. Again, he wishes himself And specially this Principle whereby he is an intelligent being, to live and be preserved in life, because existence is a good to him that is a good man.

But it is to himself that each individual wishes what is good, and no man, conceiving the possibility of his becoming other than he now is, chooses that that New Self should have all things indiscriminately: a god, for instance, has at the present moment the Chief Good, but he has it in right of being whatever he actually now is: and the Intelligent Principle must be judged to be each man's Self, or at least eminently so [though other Principles help, of course, to constitute him the man he is]. Furthermore, the good man wishes to continue to live with himself; for he can do it with pleasure, in that his memories of past actions are full of delight and his anticipations of the future are good and such are pleasurable. Then, again, he has good store of matter for his Intellect to contemplate, and he most especially sympathises with his Self in its griefs and joys, because the objects which give him pain and pleasure are at all times the same, not one thing to-day and a different one to-morrow: because he is not given to repentance, if one may so speak. It is then because each of these feelings are entertained by the good man towards his own Self and a friend feels towards a friend as towards himself (a friend being in fact another Self), that Friendship is thought to be some one of these things and they are accounted friends in whom they are found. Whether or no there can really be Friendship between a man and his Self is a question we will not at present entertain: there may be thought to be Friendship, in so far as there are two or more of the aforesaid requisites, and because the highest degree of Friendship, in the usual acceptation of that term, resembles the feeling entertained by a man towards himself.

But it may be urged that the aforesaid requisites are to all appearance found in the common run of men, though they are men of a low stamp.

May it not be answered, that they share in them only in so far as they please themselves, and conceive themselves to be good? for certainly, they are not either really, or even apparently, found in any one of those who are very depraved and villainous; we may almost say not even in those who are bad men at all: for they are at variance with themselves and lust after different things from those which in cool reason they wish for, just as men who fail of Self-Control: I mean, they choose things which, though hurtful, are pleasurable, in preference to those which in their own minds they believe to be good: others again, from cowardice and indolence, decline to do what still they are convinced is best for them: while they who from their depravity have actually done many dreadful actions hate and avoid life, and accordingly kill themselves: and the wicked seek others in whose company to spend their time, but fly from themselves because they have many unpleasant subjects of memory, and can only look forward to others like them when in solitude but drown their remorse in the company of others: and as they have nothing to raise the sentiment of Friendship so they never feel it towards themselves.

Neither, in fact, can they who are of this character sympathise with their Selves in their joys and sorrows, because their soul is, as it were, rent by faction, and the one principle, by reason of the depravity in them, is grieved at abstaining from certain things, while the other and better principle is pleased thereat; and the one drags them this way and the other that way, as though actually tearing them asunder. And though it is impossible actually to have at the same time the sensations of pain and pleasure; yet after a little time the man is sorry for having been pleased, and he could wish that those objects had not given him pleasure; for the wicked are full of remorse.

It is plain then that the wicked man cannot be in the position of a friend even towards himself, because he has in himself nothing which can excite the sentiment of Friendship. If then to be thus is exceedingly wretched it is a man's duty to flee from wickedness with all his might and to strive to be good, because thus may he be friends with himself and may come to be a friend to another.

V

Kindly Feeling, though resembling Friendship, is not identical with it, because it may exist in reference to those whom we do not know and without the object of it being aware of its existence, which Friendship cannot. (This, by the way, has also been said before.) And further, it is not even Affection because it does not imply intensity nor yearning, which are both consequences of Affection. Again Affection requires intimacy but Kindly Feeling may arise quite suddenly, as happens sometimes in respect of men against whom people are matched in any way, I mean they come to be kindly disposed to them and sympathise in their wishes, but still they would not join them in any action, because, as we said, they conceive this feeling of kindness suddenly and so have but a superficial liking.

What it does seem to be is the starting point of a Friendship; just as pleasure, received through the sight, is the commencement of Love: for no one falls in love without being first pleased with the personal appearance of the beloved object, and yet he who takes pleasure in it does not therefore necessarily love, but when he wearies for the object in its absence and desires its presence. Exactly in the same way men cannot be friends without having passed through the stage of Kindly Feeling, and yet they who are in that stage do not necessarily advance to Friendship: they merely have an inert wish for the good of those toward whom they entertain the feeling, but would not join them in any action, nor put themselves out of the way for them. So that, in a metaphorical way of speaking, one might say that it is dormant Friendship, and when it has endured for a space and ripened into intimacy comes to be real Friendship; but not that whose object is advantage or pleasure, because such motives cannot produce even Kindly Feeling.

I mean, he who has received a kindness requites it by Kindly Feeling towards his benefactor, and is right in so doing: but he who wishes another to be prosperous, because he has hope of advantage through his instrumentality, does not seem to be kindly disposed to that person but rather to himself; just as neither is he his friend if he pays court to him for any interested purpose.

Kindly Feeling always arises by reason of goodness and a certain amiability, when one man gives another the notion of being a fine fellow, or brave man, etc., as we said was the case sometimes with those matched against one another.

VI

Unity of Sentiment is also plainly connected with Friendship, and therefore is not the same as Unity of Opinion, because this might exist even between people unacquainted with one another.

Nor do men usually say people are united in sentiment merely because they agree in opinion on any point, as, for instance, on points of astronomical science (Unity of Sentiment herein not having any connection with Friendship), but they say that Communities have Unity of Sentiment when they agree respecting points of expediency and take the same line and carry out what has been determined in common consultation.

Thus we see that Unity of Sentiment has for its object matters of action, and such of these as are of importance, and of mutual, or, in the case of single States, common, interest: when, for instance, all agree in the choice of magistrates, or forming alliance with the Lacedæmonians, or appointing Pittacus ruler (that is to say, supposing he himself was willing). But when each wishes himself to be in power (as the brothers in the Phoenissæ), they quarrel and form parties: for, plainly, Unity of Sentiment does not merely imply that each entertains the same idea be it what it may, but that they do so in respect of the same object, as when both the populace and the sensible men of a State desire that the best men should be in office, because then all attain their object.

Thus Unity of Sentiment is plainly a social Friendship, as it is also said to be: since it has for its object-matter things expedient and relating to life.

And this Unity exists among the good: for they have it towards themselves and towards one another, being, if I may be allowed the expression, in the same position: I mean, the wishes of such men are steady and do not ebb and flow like the Euripus, and they wish what is just and expedient and aim at these things in common.

The bad, on the contrary, can as little have Unity of Sentiment as they can be real friends, except to a very slight extent, desiring as they do unfair advantage in things profitable while they shirk labour and service for the common good: and while each man wishes for these things for himself he is jealous of and hinders his neighbour: and as they do not watch over the common good it is lost. The result is that they quarrel while they are for keeping one another to work but are not willing to perform their just share.

VII

Benefactors are commonly held to have more Friendship for the objects of their kindness than these for them: and the fact is made a subject of discussion and inquiry, as being contrary to reasonable expectation.

The account of the matter which satisfies most persons is that the one are debtors and the others creditors: and therefore that, as in the case of actual loans the debtors wish their creditors out of the way while the creditors are anxious for the preservation of their debtors, so those who have done kindnesses desire the continued existence of the people they have done them to, under the notion of getting a return of their good offices, while these are not particularly anxious about requital.

Epicharmus, I suspect, would very probably say that they who give this solution judge from their own baseness; yet it certainly is like human nature, for the generality of men have short memories on these points, and aim rather at receiving than conferring benefits.

But the real cause, it would seem, rests upon nature, and the case is not parallel to that of creditors; because in this there is no affection to the persons, but merely a wish for their preservation with a view to the return: whereas, in point of fact, they who have done kindnesses feel friendship and love for those to whom they have done them, even though they neither are, nor can by possibility hereafter be, in a position to serve their benefactors.

And this is the case also with artisans; every one, I mean, feels more affection for his own work than that work possibly could for him if it were animate. It is perhaps specially the case with poets: for these entertain very great affection for their poems, loving them as their own children. It is to this kind of thing I should be inclined to compare the case of benefactors: for the object of their kindness is their own work, and so they love this more than this loves its creator.

And the account of this is that existence is to all a thing choiceworthy and an object of affection; now we exist by acts of working, that is, by living and acting; he then that has created a given work exists, it may be said, by his act of working: therefore he loves his work because he loves existence. And this is natural, for the work produced displays in act what existed before potentially.

Then again, the benefactor has a sense of honour in right of his action, so that he may well take pleasure in him in whom this resides; but to him who has received the benefit there is nothing honourable in respect of his benefactor, only something advantageous which is both less pleasant and less the object of Friendship.

Again, pleasure is derived from the actual working out of a present action, from the anticipation of a future one, and from the recollection of a past one: but the highest pleasure and special object of affection is that which attends on the actual working. Now the benefactor's work abides (for the honourable is enduring), but the advantage of him who has received the kindness passes away.

Again, there is pleasure in recollecting honourable actions, but in recollecting advantageous ones there is none at all or much less (by the way though, the contrary is true of the expectation of advantage).

Further, the entertaining the feeling of Friendship is like acting on another; but being the object of the feeling is like being acted upon.

So then, entertaining the sentiment of Friendship, and all feelings connected with it, attend on those who, in the given case of a benefaction, are the superior party.

Once more: all people value most what has cost them much labour in the production; for instance, people who have themselves made their money are fonder of it than those who have inherited it: and receiving kindness is, it seems, unlaborious, but doing it is laborious. And this is the reason why the female parents are most fond of their offspring; for their part in producing them is attended with most labour, and they know more certainly that they are theirs. This feeling would seem also to belong to benefactors.

VIII

A question is also raised as to whether it is right to love one's Self best, or some one else: because men find fault with those who love themselves best, and call them in a disparaging way lovers of Self; and the bad man is thought to do everything he does for his own sake merely, and the more so the more depraved he is; accordingly men reproach him with never doing anything unselfish: whereas the good man acts from a sense of honour (and the more so the better man he is), and for his friend's sake, and is careless of his own interest.

But with these theories facts are at variance, and not unnaturally: for it is commonly said also that a man is to love most him who is most his friend, and he is most a friend who wishes good to him to whom he wishes it for that man's sake even though no one knows. Now these conditions, and in fact all the rest by which a friend is characterised, belong specially to each individual in respect of his Self: for we have said before that all the friendly feelings are derived to others from those which have Self primarily for their object. And all the current proverbs support this view; for instance, "one soul," "the goods of friends are common," "equality is a tie of Friendship," "the knee is nearer than the shin." For all these things exist specially with reference to a man's own Self: he is specially a friend to himself and so he is bound to love himself the most.

It is with good reason questioned which of the two parties one should follow, both having plausibility on their side. Perhaps then, in respect of theories of this kind, the proper course is to distinguish and define how far each is true, and in what way. If we could ascertain the sense in which each uses the term "Self-loving," this point might be cleared up.

Well now, they who use it disparagingly give the name to those who, in respect of wealth, and honours, and pleasures of the body, give to themselves the larger share: because the mass of mankind grasp after these and are earnest about them as being the best things; which is the reason why they are matters of contention. They who are covetous in regard to these gratify their lusts and passions in general, that is to say the irrational part of their soul: now the mass of mankind are so disposed, for which reason the appellation has taken its rise from that mass which is low and bad. Of course they are justly reproached who are Self-loving in this sense.

And that the generality of men are accustomed to apply the term to denominate those who do give such things to themselves is quite plain: suppose, for instance, that a man were anxious to do, more than other men, acts of justice, or self-mastery, or any other virtuous acts, and, in general, were to secure to himself that which is abstractedly noble and honourable, no one would call him Self-loving, nor blame him.

Yet might such an one be judged to be more truly Self-loving: certainly he gives to himself the things which are most noble and most good, and gratifies that Principle of his nature which is most rightfully authoritative, and obeys it in everything: and just as that which possesses the highest authority is thought to constitute a Community or any other system, so also in the case of Man: and so he is most truly Self-loving who loves and gratifies this Principle.

Again, men are said to have, or to fail of having, self-control, according as the Intellect controls or not, it being plainly implied thereby that this Principle constitutes each individual; and people are thought to have done of themselves, and voluntarily, those things specially which are done with Reason.

It is plain, therefore, that this Principle does, either entirely or specially constitute the individual man, and that the good man specially loves this. For this reason then he must be specially Self-loving, in a kind other than that which is reproached, and as far superior to it as living in accordance with Reason is to living at the beck and call of passion, and aiming at the truly noble to aiming at apparent advantage.

Now all approve and commend those who are eminently earnest about honourable actions, and if all would vie with one another in respect of the [Greek: kalhon], and be intent upon doing what is most truly noble and honourable, society at large would have all that is proper while each individual in particular would have the greatest of goods, Virtue being assumed to be such.

And so the good man ought to be Self-loving: because by doing what is noble he will have advantage himself and will do good to others: but the bad man ought not to be, because he will harm himself and his neighbours by following low and evil passions. In the case of the bad man, what he ought to do and what he does are at variance, but the good man does what he ought to do, because all Intellect chooses what is best for itself and the good man puts himself under the direction of Intellect.

Of the good man it is true likewise that he does many things for the sake of his friends and his country, even to the extent of dying for them, if need be: for money and honours, and, in short, all the good things which others fight for, he will throw away while eager to secure to himself the [Greek: kalhon]: he will prefer a brief and great joy to a tame and enduring one, and to live nobly for one year rather than ordinarily for many, and one great and noble action to many trifling ones. And this is perhaps that which befals men who die for their country and friends; they choose great glory for themselves: and they will lavish their own money that their friends may receive more, for hereby the friend gets the money but the man himself the [Greek: kalhon]; so, in fact he gives to himself the greater good. It is the same with honours and offices; all these things he will give up to his friend, because this reflects honour and praise on himself: and so with good reason is he esteemed a fine character since he chooses the honourable before all things else. It is possible also to give up the opportunities of action to a friend; and to have caused a friend's doing a thing may be more noble than having done it one's self.

In short, in all praiseworthy things the good man does plainly give to himself a larger share of the honourable. In this sense it is right to be Self-loving, in the vulgar acceptation of the term it is not.

IX

A question is raised also respecting the Happy man, whether he will want Friends, or no?

Some say that they who are blessed and independent have no need of Friends, for they already have all that is good, and so, as being independent, want nothing further: whereas the notion of a friend's office is to be as it were a second Self and procure for a man what he cannot get by himself: hence the saying,

"When Fortune gives us good, what need we Friends?"

On the other hand, it looks absurd, while we are assigning to the Happy man all other good things, not to give him Friends, which are, after all, thought to be the greatest of external goods.

Again, if it is more characteristic of a friend to confer than to receive kindnesses, and if to be beneficent belongs to the good man and to the character of virtue, and if it is more noble to confer kindnesses on friends than strangers, the good man will need objects for his benefactions. And out of this last consideration springs a question whether the need of Friends be greater in prosperity or adversity, since the unfortunate man wants people to do him kindnesses and they who are fortunate want objects for their kind acts.

Again, it is perhaps absurd to make our Happy man a solitary, because no man would choose the possession of all goods in the world on the condition of solitariness, man being a social animal and formed by nature for living with others: of course the Happy man has this qualification since he has all those things which are good by nature: and it is obvious that the society of friends and good men must be preferable to that of strangers and ordinary people, and we conclude, therefore, that the Happy man does need Friends.

But then, what do they mean whom we quoted first, and how are they right? Is it not that the mass of mankind mean by Friends those who are useful? and of course the Happy man will not need such because he has all good things already; neither will he need such as are Friends with a view to the pleasurable, or at least only to a slight extent; because his life, being already pleasurable, does not want pleasure imported from without; and so, since the Happy man does not need Friends of these kinds, he is thought not to need any at all.

But it may be, this is not true: for it was stated originally, that Happiness is a kind of Working; now Working plainly is something that must come into being, not be already there like a mere piece of property.

If then the being happy consists in living and working, and the good man's working is in itself excellent and pleasurable (as we said at the commencement of the treatise), and if what is our own reckons among things pleasurable, and if we can view our neighbours better than ourselves and their actions better than we can our own, then the actions of their Friends who are good men are pleasurable to the good; inasmuch as they have both the requisites which are naturally pleasant. So the man in the highest state of happiness will need Friends of this kind, since he desires to contemplate good actions, and actions of his own, which those of his friend, being a good man, are. Again, common opinion requires that the Happy man live with pleasure to himself: now life is burthensome to a man in solitude, for it is not easy to work continuously by one's self, but in company with, and in regard to others, it is easier, and therefore the working, being pleasurable in itself will be more continuous (a thing which should be in respect of the Happy man); for the good man, in that he is good takes pleasure in the actions which accord with Virtue and is annoyed at those which spring from Vice, just as a musical man is pleased with beautiful music and annoyed by bad. And besides, as Theognis says, Virtue itself may be improved by practice, from living with the good.

And, upon the following considerations more purely metaphysical, it will probably appear that the good friend is naturally choiceworthy to the good man. We have said before, that whatever is naturally good is also in itself good and pleasant to the good man; now the fact of living, so far as animals are concerned, is characterised generally by the power of sentience, in man it is characterised by that of sentience, or of rationality (the faculty of course being referred to the actual operation of the faculty, certainly the main point is the actual operation of it); so that living seems mainly to consist in the act of sentience or exerting rationality: now the fact of living is in itself one of the things that are good and pleasant (for it is a definite totality, and whatever is such belongs to the nature of good), but what is naturally good is good to the good man: for which reason it seems to be pleasant to all. (Of course one must not suppose a life which is depraved and corrupted, nor one spent in pain, for that which is such is indefinite as are its inherent qualities: however, what is to be said of pain will be clearer in what is to follow.)

If then the fact of living is in itself good and pleasant (and this appears from the fact that all desire it, and specially those who are good and in high happiness; their course of life being most choiceworthy and their existence most choiceworthy likewise), then also he that sees perceives that he sees; and he that hears perceives that he hears; and he that walks perceives that he walks; and in all the other instances in like manner there is a faculty which reflects upon and perceives the fact that we are working, so that we can perceive that we perceive and intellectually know that we intellectually know: but to perceive that we perceive or that we intellectually know is to perceive that we exist, since existence was defined to be perceiving or intellectually knowing. Now to perceive that one lives is a thing pleasant in itself, life being a thing naturally good, and the perceiving of the presence in ourselves of things naturally good being pleasant.

Therefore the fact of living is choiceworthy, and to the good specially so since existence is good and pleasant to them: for they receive pleasure from the internal consciousness of that which in itself is good.

But the good man is to his friend as to himself, friend being but a name for a second Self; therefore as his own existence is choiceworthy to each so too, or similarly at least, is his friend's existence. But the ground of one's own existence being choiceworthy is the perceiving of one's self being good, any such perception being in itself pleasant. Therefore one ought to be thoroughly conscious of one's friend's existence, which will result from living with him, that is sharing in his words and thoughts: for this is the meaning of the term as applied to the human species, not mere feeding together as in the case of brutes.

If then to the man in a high state of happiness existence is in itself choiceworthy, being naturally good and pleasant, and so too a friend's existence, then the friend also must be among things choiceworthy. But whatever is choiceworthy to a man he should have or else he will be in this point deficient. The man therefore who is to come up to our notion "Happy" will need good Friends. Are we then to make our friends as numerous as possible? or, as in respect of acquaintance it is thought to have been well said "have not thou many acquaintances yet be not without;" so too in respect of Friendship may we adopt the precept, and say that a man should not be without friends, nor again have exceeding many friends?

Now as for friends who are intended for use, the maxim I have quoted will, it seems, fit in exceedingly well, because to requite the services of many is a matter of labour, and a whole life would not be long enough to do this for them. So that, if more numerous than what will suffice for one's own life, they become officious, and are hindrances in respect of living well: and so we do not want them. And again of those who are to be for pleasure a few are quite enough, just like sweetening in our food.

X

But of the good are we to make as many as ever we can, or is there any measure of the number of friends, as there is of the number to constitute a Political Community? I mean, you cannot make one out of ten men, and if you increase the number to one hundred thousand it is not any longer a Community. However, the number is not perhaps some one definite number but any between certain extreme limits.

Well, of friends likewise there is a limited number, which perhaps may be laid down to be the greatest number with whom it would be possible to keep up intimacy; this being thought to be one of the greatest marks of Friendship, and it being quite obvious that it is not possible to be intimate with many, in other words, to part one's self among many. And besides it must be remembered that they also are to be friends to one another if they are all to live together: but it is a matter of difficulty to find this in many men at once.

It comes likewise to be difficult to bring home to one's self the joys and sorrows of many: because in all probability one would have to sympathise at the same time with the joys of this one and the sorrows of that other.

Perhaps then it is well not to endeavour to have very many friends but so many as are enough for intimacy: because, in fact, it would seem not to be possible to be very much a friend to many at the same time: and, for the same reason, not to be in love with many objects at the same time: love being a kind of excessive Friendship which implies but one object: and all strong emotions must be limited in the number towards whom they are felt.

And if we look to facts this seems to be so: for not many at a time become friends in the way of companionship, all the famous Friendships of the kind are between two persons: whereas they who have many friends, and meet everybody on the footing of intimacy, seem to be friends really to no one except in the way of general society; I mean the characters denominated as over-complaisant.

To be sure, in the way merely of society, a man may be a friend to many without being necessarily over-complaisant, but being truly good: but one cannot be a friend to many because of their virtue, and for the persons' own sake; in fact, it is a matter for contentment to find even a few such.

XI

Again: are friends most needed in prosperity or in adversity? they are required, we know, in both states, because the unfortunate need help and the prosperous want people to live with and to do kindnesses to: for they have a desire to act kindly to some one.

To have friends is more necessary in adversity, and therefore in this case useful ones are wanted; and to have them in prosperity is more honourable, and this is why the prosperous want good men for friends, it being preferable to confer benefits on, and to live with, these. For the very presence of friends is pleasant even in adversity: since men when grieved are comforted by the sympathy of their friends.

And from this, by the way, the question might be raised, whether it is that they do in a manner take part of the weight of calamities, or only that their presence, being pleasurable, and the consciousness of their sympathy, make the pain of the sufferer less. However, we will not further discuss whether these which have been suggested or some other causes produce the relief, at least the effect we speak of is a matter of plain fact.

But their presence has probably a mixed effect: I mean, not only is the very seeing friends pleasant, especially to one in misfortune, and actual help towards lessening the grief is afforded (the natural tendency of a friend, if he is gifted with tact, being to comfort by look and word, because he is well acquainted with the sufferer's temper and disposition and therefore knows what things give him pleasure and pain), but also the perceiving a friend to be grieved at his misfortunes causes the sufferer pain, because every one avoids being cause of pain to his friends. And for this reason they who are of a manly nature are cautious not to implicate their friends in their pain; and unless a man is exceedingly callous to the pain of others he cannot bear the pain which is thus caused to his friends: in short, he does not admit men to wail with him, not being given to wail at all: women, it is true, and men who resemble women, like to have others to groan with them, and love such as friends and sympathisers. But it is plain that it is our duty in all things to imitate the highest character.

On the other hand, the advantages of friends in our prosperity are the pleasurable intercourse and the consciousness that they are pleased at our good fortune.

It would seem, therefore, that we ought to call in friends readily on occasion of good fortune, because it is noble to be ready to do good to others: but on occasion of bad fortune, we should do so with reluctance; for we should as little as possible make others share in our ills; on which principle goes the saying, "I am unfortunate, let that suffice." The most proper occasion for calling them in is when with small trouble or annoyance to themselves they can be of very great use to the person who needs them.

But, on the contrary, it is fitting perhaps to go to one's friends in their misfortunes unasked and with alacrity (because kindness is the friend's office and specially towards those who are in need and who do not demand it as a right, this being more creditable and more pleasant to both); and on occasion of their good fortune to go readily, if we can forward it in any way (because men need their friends for this likewise), but to be backward in sharing it, any great eagerness to receive advantage not being creditable.

One should perhaps be cautious not to present the appearance of sullenness in declining the sympathy or help of friends, for this happens occasionally.

It appears then that the presence of friends is, under all circumstances, choiceworthy.

May we not say then that, as seeing the beloved object is most prized by lovers and they choose this sense rather than any of the others because Love

"Is engendered in the eyes,
With gazing fed,"

in like manner intimacy is to friends most choiceworthy, Friendship being communion? Again, as a man is to himself so is he to his friend; now with respect to himself the perception of his own existence is choiceworthy, therefore is it also in respect of his friend.

And besides, their Friendship is acted out in intimacy, and so with good reason they desire this. And whatever in each man's opinion constitutes existence, or whatsoever it is for the sake of which they choose life, herein they wish their friends to join with them; and so some men drink together, others gamble, others join in gymnastic exercises or hunting, others study philosophy together: in each case spending their days together in that which they like best of all things in life, for since they wish to be intimate with their friends they do and partake in those things whereby they think to attain this object.

Therefore the Friendship of the wicked comes to be depraved; for, being unstable, they share in what is bad and become depraved in being made like to one another: but the Friendship of the good is good, growing with their intercourse; they improve also, as it seems, by repeated acts, and by mutual correction, for they receive impress from one another in the points which give them pleasure; whence says the poet,

"Thou from the good, good things shalt surely learn."

Here then we will terminate our discourse of Friendship. The next thing is to go into the subject of Pleasure.

BOOK X

I

Next, it would seem, follows a discussion respecting Pleasure, for it is thought to be most closely bound up with our kind: and so men train the young, guiding them on their course by the rudders of Pleasure and Pain. And to like and dislike what one ought is judged to be most important for the formation of good moral character: because these feelings extend all one's life through, giving a bias towards and exerting an influence on the side of Virtue and Happiness, since men choose what is pleasant and avoid what is painful.

Subjects such as these then, it would seem, we ought by no means to pass by, and specially since they involve much difference of opinion. There are those who call Pleasure the Chief Good; there are others who on the contrary maintain that it is exceedingly bad; some perhaps from a real conviction that such is the case, others from a notion that it is better, in reference to our life and conduct, to show up Pleasure as bad, even if it is not so really; arguing that, as the mass of men have a bias towards it and are the slaves of their pleasures, it is right to draw them to the contrary, for that so they may possibly arrive at the mean.

I confess I suspect the soundness of this policy; in matters respecting men's feelings and actions theories are less convincing than facts: whenever, therefore, they are found conflicting with actual experience, they not only are despised but involve the truth in their fall: he, for instance, who deprecates Pleasure, if once seen to aim at it, gets the credit of backsliding to it as being universally such as he said it was, the mass of men being incapable of nice distinctions.

Real accounts, therefore, of such matters seem to be most expedient, not with a view to knowledge merely but to life and conduct: for they are believed as being in harm with facts, and so they prevail with the wise to live in accordance with them.

But of such considerations enough: let us now proceed to the current maxims respecting Pleasure.

II

Now Eudoxus thought Pleasure to be the Chief Good because he saw all, rational and irrational alike, aiming at it: and he argued that, since in all what was the object of choice must be good and what most so the best, the fact of all being drawn to the same thing proved this thing to be the best for all: "For each," he said, "finds what is good for itself just as it does its proper nourishment, and so that which is good for all, and the object of the aim of all, is their Chief Good."

(And his theories were received, not so much for their own sake, as because of his excellent moral character; for he was thought to be eminently possessed of perfect self-mastery, and therefore it was not thought that he said these things because he was a lover of Pleasure but that he really was so convinced.)

And he thought his position was not less proved by the argument from the contrary: that is, since Pain was in itself an object of avoidance to all the contrary must be in like manner an object of choice.

Again he urged that that is most choiceworthy which we choose, not by reason of, or with a view to, anything further; and that Pleasure is confessedly of this kind because no one ever goes on to ask to what purpose he is pleased, feeling that Pleasure is in itself choiceworthy.

Again, that when added to any other good it makes it more choiceworthy; as, for instance, to actions of justice, or perfected self-mastery; and good can only be increased by itself.

However, this argument at least seems to prove only that it belongs to the class of goods, and not that it does so more than anything else: for every good is more choiceworthy in combination with some other than when taken quite alone. In fact, it is by just such an argument that Plato proves that Pleasure is not the Chief Good: "For," says he, "the life of Pleasure is more choiceworthy in combination with Practical Wisdom than apart from it; but, if the compound better then simple Pleasure cannot be the Chief Good; because the very Chief Good cannot by any addition become choiceworthy than it is already:" and it is obvious that nothing else can be the Chief Good, which by combination with any of the things in themselves good comes to be more choiceworthy.

What is there then of such a nature? (meaning, of course, whereof we can partake; because that which we are in search of must be such).

As for those who object that "what all aim at is not necessarily good," I confess I cannot see much in what they say, because what all think we say is. And he who would cut away this ground from under us will not bring forward things more dependable: because if the argument had rested on the desires of irrational creatures there might have been something in what he says, but, since the rational also desire Pleasure, how can his objection be allowed any weight? and it may be that, even in the lower animals, there is some natural good principle above themselves which aims at the good peculiar to them.

Nor does that seem to be sound which is urged respecting the argument from the contrary: I mean, some people say "it does not follow that Pleasure must be good because Pain is evil, since evil may be opposed to evil, and both evil and good to what is indifferent:" now what they say is right enough in itself but does not hold in the present instance. If both Pleasure and Pain were bad both would have been objects of avoidance; or if neither then neither would have been, at all events they must have fared alike: but now men do plainly avoid the one as bad and choose the other as good, and so there is a complete opposition.

III

Nor again is Pleasure therefore excluded from being good because it does not belong to the class of qualities: the acts of virtue are not qualities, neither is Happiness [yet surely both are goods].

Again, they say the Chief Good is limited but Pleasure unlimited, in that it admits of degrees.

Now if they judge this from the act of feeling Pleasure then the same thing will apply to justice and all the other virtues, in respect of which clearly it is said that men are more or less of such and such characters (according to the different virtues), they are more just or more brave, or one may practise justice and self-mastery more or less.

If, on the other hand, they judge in respect of the Pleasures themselves then it may be they miss the true cause, namely that some are unmixed and others mixed: for just as health being in itself limited, admits of degrees, why should not Pleasure do so and yet be limited? in the former case we account for it by the fact that there is not the same adjustment of parts in all men, nor one and the same always in the same individual: but health, though relaxed, remains up to a certain point, and differs in degrees; and of course the same may be the case with Pleasure.

Again, assuming the Chief Good to be perfect and all Movements and Generations imperfect, they try to shew that Pleasure is a Movement and a Generation.

Yet they do not seem warranted in saying even that it is a Movement: for to every Movement are thought to belong swiftness and slowness, and if not in itself, as to that of the universe, yet relatively: but to Pleasure neither of these belongs: for though one may have got quickly into the state Pleasure, as into that of anger, one cannot be in the state quickly, nor relatively to the state of any other person; but we can walk or grow, and so on, quickly or slowly.

Of course it is possible to change into the state of Pleasure quickly or slowly, but to act in the state (by which, I mean, have the perception of Pleasure) quickly, is not possible. And how can it be a Generation? because, according to notions generally held, not anything is generated from anything, but a thing resolves itself into that out of which it was generated: whereas of that of which Pleasure is a Generation Pain is a Destruction.

Again, they say that Pain is a lack of something suitable to nature and Pleasure a supply of it.

But these are affections of the body: now if Pleasure really is a supplying of somewhat suitable to nature, that must feel the Pleasure in which the supply takes place, therefore the body of course: yet this is not thought to be so: neither then is Pleasure a supplying, only a person of course will be pleased when a supply takes place just as he will be pained when he is cut.

This notion would seem to have arisen out of the Pains and Pleasures connected with natural nourishment; because, when people have felt a lack and so have had Pain first, they, of course, are pleased with the supply of their lack.

But this is not the case with all Pleasures: those attendant on mathematical studies, for instance, are unconnected with any Pain; and of such as attend on the senses those which arise through the sense of Smell; and again, many sounds, and sights, and memories, and hopes: now of what can these be Generations? because there has been here no lack of anything to be afterwards supplied.

And to those who bring forward disgraceful Pleasures we may reply that these are not really pleasant things; for it does not follow because they are pleasant to the ill-disposed that we are to admit that they are pleasant except to them; just as we should not say that those things are really wholesome, or sweet, or bitter, which are so to the sick, or those objects really white which give that impression to people labouring under ophthalmia.

Or we might say thus, that the Pleasures are choiceworthy but not as derived from these sources: just as wealth is, but not as the price of treason; or health, but not on the terms of eating anything however loathsome. Or again, may we not say that Pleasures differ in kind? those derived from honourable objects, for instance are different from those arising from disgraceful ones; and it is not possible to experience the Pleasure of the just man without being just, or of the musical man without being musical; and so on of others.

The distinction commonly drawn between the friend and the flatterer would seem to show clearly either that Pleasure is not a good, or that there are different kinds of Pleasure: for the former is thought to have good as the object of his intercourse, the latter Pleasure only; and this last is reproached, but the former men praise as having different objects in his intercourse.

Again, no one would choose to live with a child's intellect all his life through, though receiving the highest possible Pleasure from such objects as children receive it from; or to take Pleasure in doing any of the most disgraceful things, though sure never to be pained.

There are many things also about which we should be diligent even though they brought no Pleasure; as seeing, remembering, knowing, possessing the various Excellences; and the fact that Pleasures do follow on these naturally makes no difference, because we should certainly choose them even though no Pleasure resulted from them.

It seems then to be plain that Pleasure is not the Chief Good, nor is every kind of it choiceworthy: and that there are some choiceworthy in themselves, differing in kind, i.e. in the sources from which they are derived. Let this then suffice by way of an account of the current maxims respecting Pleasure and Pain.

IV

Now what it is, and how characterised, will be more plain if we take up the subject afresh.

An act of Sight is thought to be complete at any moment; that is to say, it lacks nothing the accession of which subsequently will complete its whole nature.

Well, Pleasure resembles this: because it is a whole, as one may say; and one could not at any moment of time take a Pleasure whose whole nature would be completed by its lasting for a longer time. And for this reason it is not a Movement: for all Movement takes place in time of certain duration and has a certain End to accomplish; for instance, the Movement of house-building is then only complete when the builder has produced what he intended, that is, either in the whole time [necessary to complete the whole design], or in a given portion. But all the subordinate Movements are incomplete in the parts of the time, and are different in kind from the whole movement and from one another (I mean, for instance, that the fitting the stones together is a Movement different from that of fluting the column, and both again from the construction of the Temple as a whole: but this last is complete as lacking nothing to the result proposed; whereas that of the basement, or of the triglyph, is incomplete, because each is a Movement of a part merely).

As I said then, they differ in kind, and you cannot at any time you choose find a Movement complete in its whole nature, but, if at all, in the whole time requisite.

And so it is with the Movement of walking and all others: for, if motion be a Movement from one place to another place, then of it too there are different kinds, flying, walking, leaping, and such-like. And not only so, but there are different kinds even in walking: the where-from and where-to are not the same in the whole Course as in a portion of it; nor in one portion as in another; nor is crossing this line the same as crossing that: because a man is not merely crossing a line but a line in a given place, and this is in a different place from that.

Of Movement I have discoursed exactly in another treatise. I will now therefore only say that it seems not to be complete at any given moment; and that most movements are incomplete and specifically different, since the whence and whither constitute different species.

But of Pleasure the whole nature is complete at any given moment: it is plain then that Pleasure and Movement must be different from one another, and that Pleasure belongs to the class of things whole and complete. And this might appear also from the impossibility of moving except in a definite time, whereas there is none with respect to the sensation of Pleasure, for what exists at the very present moment is a kind of "whole."

From these considerations then it is plain that people are not warranted in saying that Pleasure is a Movement or a Generation: because these terms are not applicable to all things, only to such as are divisible and not "wholes:" I mean that of an act of Sight there is no Generation, nor is there of a point, nor of a monad, nor is any one of these a Movement or a Generation: neither then of Pleasure is there Movement or Generation, because it is, as one may say, "a whole."

Now since every Percipient Faculty works upon the Object answering to it, and perfectly the

Faculty in a good state upon the most excellent of the Objects within its range (for Perfect Working is thought to be much what I have described; and we will not raise any question about saying "the Faculty" works, instead of, "that subject wherein the Faculty resides"), in each case the best Working is that of the Faculty in its best state upon the best of the Objects answering to it. And this will be, further, most perfect and most pleasant: for Pleasure is attendant upon every Percipient Faculty, and in like manner on every intellectual operation and speculation; and that is most pleasant which is most perfect, and that most perfect which is the Working of the best Faculty upon the most excellent of the Objects within its range.

And Pleasure perfects the Working. But Pleasure does not perfect it in the same way as the Faculty and Object of Perception do, being good; just as health and the physician are not in similar senses causes of a healthy state.

And that Pleasure does arise upon the exercise of every Percipient Faculty is evident, for we commonly say that sights and sounds are pleasant; it is plain also that this is especially the case when the Faculty is most excellent and works upon a similar Object: and when both the Object and Faculty of Perception are such, Pleasure will always exist, supposing of course an agent and a patient.

Furthermore, Pleasure perfects the act of Working not in the way of an inherent state but as a supervening finish, such as is bloom in people at their prime. Therefore so long as the Object of intellectual or sensitive Perception is such as it should be and also the Faculty which discerns or realises the Object, there will be Pleasure in the Working: because when that which has the capacity of being acted on and that which is apt to act are alike and similarly related, the same result follows naturally.

How is it then that no one feels Pleasure continuously? is it not that he wearies, because all human faculties are incapable of unintermitting exertion; and so, of course, Pleasure does not arise either, because that follows upon the act of Working. But there are some things which please when new, but afterwards not in the like way, for exactly the same reason: that at first the mind is roused and works on these Objects with its powers at full tension; just as they who are gazing stedfastly at anything; but afterwards the act of Working is not of the kind it was at first, but careless, and so the Pleasure too is dulled.

Again, a person may conclude that all men grasp at Pleasure, because all aim likewise at Life and Life is an act of Working, and every man works at and with those things which also he best likes; the musical man, for instance, works with his hearing at music; the studious man with his intellect at speculative questions, and so forth. And Pleasure perfects the acts of Working, and so Life after which men grasp. No wonder then that they aim also at Pleasure, because to each it perfects Life, which is itself choiceworthy. (We will take leave to omit the question whether we choose Life for Pleasure's sake of Pleasure for Life's sake; because these two plainly are closely connected and admit not of separation; since Pleasure comes not into being without Working, and again, every Working Pleasure perfects.)

And this is one reason why Pleasures are thought to differ in kind, because we suppose that things which differ in kind must be perfected by things so differing: it plainly being the case with the productions of Nature and Art; as animals, and trees, and pictures, and statues, and houses, and furniture; and so we suppose that in like manner acts of Working which are different in kind are perfected by things differing in kind. Now Intellectual Workings differ specifically from those of the Senses, and these last from one another; therefore so do the Pleasures which perfect them.

This may be shown also from the intimate connection subsisting between each Pleasure and the Working which it perfects: I mean, that the Pleasure proper to any Working increases that Working; for they who work with Pleasure sift all things more closely and carry them out to a greater degree of nicety; for instance, those men become geometricians who take Pleasure in geometry, and they apprehend particular points more completely: in like manner men who are fond of music, or architecture, or anything else, improve each on his own pursuit, because they feel Pleasure in them. Thus the Pleasures aid in increasing the Workings, and things which do so aid are proper and peculiar: but the things which are proper and peculiar to others specifically different are themselves also specifically different.

Yet even more clearly may this be shown from the fact that the Pleasures arising from one kind of Workings hinder other Workings; for instance, people who are fond of flute-music cannot keep their attention to conversation or discourse when they catch the sound of a flute; because they take more Pleasure in flute-playing than in the Working they are at the time engaged on; in other words, the Pleasure attendant on flute-playing destroys the Working of conversation or discourse. Much the same kind of thing takes place in other cases, when a person is engaged in two different Workings at the same time: that is, the pleasanter of the two keeps pushing out the other, and, if the disparity in pleasantness be great, then more and more till a man even ceases altogether to work at the other.

This is the reason why, when we are very much pleased with anything whatever, we do nothing else, and it is only when we are but moderately pleased with one occupation that we vary it with another: people, for instance, who eat sweetmeats in the theatre do so most when the performance is indifferent.

Since then the proper and peculiar Pleasure gives accuracy to the Workings and makes them more enduring and better of their kind, while those Pleasures which are foreign to them mar them, it is plain there is a wide difference between them: in fact, Pleasures foreign to any Working have pretty much the same effect as the Pains proper to it, which, in fact, destroy the Workings; I mean, if one man dislikes writing, or another calculation, the one does not write, the other does not calculate; because, in each case, the Working is attended with some Pain: so then contrary effects are produced upon the Workings by the Pleasures and Pains proper to them, by which I mean those which arise upon the Working, in itself, independently of any other circumstances. As for the Pleasures foreign to a Working, we have said already that they produce a similar effect to the Pain proper to it; that is they destroy the Working, only not in like way.

Well then, as Workings differ from one another in goodness and badness, some being fit objects of choice, others of avoidance, and others in their nature indifferent, Pleasures are similarly related; since its own proper Pleasure attends or each Working: of course that proper to a good Working is good, that proper to a bad, bad: for even the desires for what is noble are praiseworthy, and for what is base blameworthy.

Furthermore, the Pleasures attendant on Workings are more closely connected with them even than the desires after them: for these last are separate both in time and nature, but the former are close to the Workings, and so indivisible from them as to raise a question whether the Working and the Pleasure are identical; but Pleasure does not seem to be an Intellectual Operation nor a Faculty of Perception, because that is absurd; but yet it gives some the impression of being the same from not being separated from these.

As then the Workings are different so are their Pleasures; now Sight differs from Touch in purity, and Hearing and Smelling from Taste; therefore, in like manner, do their Pleasures; and again, Intellectual Pleasures from these Sensual, and the different kinds both of Intellectual and Sensual from one another.

It is thought, moreover, that each animal has a Pleasure proper to itself, as it has a proper Work; that Pleasure of course which is attendant on the Working. And the soundness of this will appear upon particular inspection: for horse, dog, and man have different Pleasures; as Heraclitus says, an ass would sooner have hay than gold; in other words, provender is pleasanter to asses than gold. So then the Pleasures of animals specifically different are also specifically different, but those of the same, we may reasonably suppose, are without difference.

Yet in the case of human creatures they differ not a little: for the very same things please some and pain others: and what are painful and hateful to some are pleasant to and liked by others. The same is the case with sweet things: the same will not seem so to the man in a fever as to him who is in health: nor will the invalid and the person in robust health have the same notion of warmth. The same is the case with other things also.

Now in all such cases that is held to be which impresses the good man with the notion of being such and such; and if this is a second maxim (as it is usually held to be), and Virtue, that is, the Good man, in that he is such, is the measure of everything, then those must be real Pleasures which gave him the impression of being so and those things pleasant in which he takes Pleasure. Nor is it at all astonishing that what are to him unpleasant should give another person the impression of being pleasant, for men are liable to many corruptions and marrings; and the things in question are not pleasant really, only to these particular persons, and to them only as being thus disposed.

Well of course, you may say, it is obvious that we must assert those which are confessedly disgraceful to be real Pleasures, except to depraved tastes: but of those which are thought to be good what kind, or which, must we say is The Pleasure of Man? is not the answer plain from considering the Workings, because the Pleasures follow upon these?

Whether then there be one or several Workings which belong to the perfect and blessed man, the Pleasures which perfect these Workings must be said to be specially and properly The Pleasures of Man; and all the rest in a secondary sense, and in various degrees according as the Workings are related to those highest and best ones.

V

Now that we have spoken about the Excellences of both kinds, and Friendship in its varieties, and Pleasures, it remains to sketch out Happiness, since we assume that to be the one End of all human things: and we shall save time and trouble by recapitulating what was stated before.

Well then, we said that it is not a State merely; because, if it were, it might belong to one who slept all his life through and merely vegetated, or to one who fell into very great calamities: and so, if these possibilities displease us and we would rather put it into the rank of some kind of Working (as was also said before), and Workings are of different kinds (some being necessary and choiceworthy with a view to other things, while others are so in themselves), it is plain we must rank Happiness among those choiceworthy for their own sakes and not among those which are so with a view to something further: because Happiness has no lack of anything but is self-sufficient.

By choiceworthy in themselves are meant those from which nothing is sought beyond the act of Working: and of this kind are thought to be the actions according to Virtue, because doing what is noble and excellent is one of those things which are choiceworthy for their own sake alone.

And again, such amusements as are pleasant; because people do not choose them with any further purpose: in fact they receive more harm than profit from them, neglecting their persons and their property. Still the common run of those who are judged happy take refuge in such pastimes, which is the reason why they who have varied talent in such are highly esteemed among despots; because they make themselves pleasant in those things which these aim at, and these accordingly want such men.

Now these things are thought to be appurtenances of Happiness because men in power spend their leisure herein: yet, it may be, we cannot argue from the example of such men: because there is neither Virtue nor Intellect necessarily involved in having power, and yet these are the only sources of good Workings: nor does it follow that because these men, never having tasted pure and generous Pleasure, take refuge in bodily ones, we are therefore to believe them to be more choiceworthy: for children too believe that those things are most excellent which are precious in their eyes.

We may well believe that as children and men have different ideas as to what is precious so too have the bad and the good: therefore, as we have many times said, those things are really precious and pleasant which seem so to the good man: and as to each individual that Working is most choiceworthy which is in accordance with his own state to the good man that is so which is in accordance with Virtue.

Happiness then stands not in amusement; in fact the very notion is absurd of the End being amusement, and of one's toiling and enduring hardness all one's life long with a view to amusement: for everything in the world, so to speak, we choose with some further End in view, except Happiness, for that is the End comprehending all others. Now to take pains and to labour with a view to amusement is plainly foolish and very childish: but to amuse one's self with a view to steady employment afterwards, as Anacharsis says, is thought to be right: for amusement is like rest, and men want rest because unable to labour continuously.

Rest, therefore, is not an End, because it is adopted with a view to Working afterwards.

Again, it is held that the Happy Life must be one in the way of Excellence, and this is accompanied by earnestness and stands not in amusement. Moreover those things which are done in earnest, we say, are better than things merely ludicrous and joined with amusement: and we say that the Working of the better part, or the better man, is more earnest; and the Working of the better is at once better and more capable of Happiness.

Then, again, as for bodily Pleasures, any ordinary person, or even a slave, might enjoy them, just as well as the best man living but Happiness no one supposes a slave to share except so far as it is implied in life: because Happiness stands not in such pastimes but in the Workings in the way of Excellence, as has also been stated before.

VI

Now if Happiness is a Working in the way of Excellence of course that Excellence must be the highest, that is to say, the Excellence of the best Principle. Whether then this best Principle is Intellect or some other which is thought naturally to rule and to lead and to conceive of noble and divine things, whether being in its own nature divine or the most divine of all our internal Principles, the Working of this in accordance with its own proper Excellence must be the perfect Happiness.

That it is Contemplative has been already stated: and this would seem to be consistent with what we said before and with truth: for, in the first place, this Working is of the highest kind, since the Intellect is the highest of our internal Principles and the subjects with which it is conversant the highest of all which fall within the range of our knowledge.

Next, it is also most Continuous: for we are better able to contemplate than to do anything else whatever, continuously.

Again, we think Pleasure must be in some way an ingredient in Happiness, and of all Workings in accordance with Excellence that in the way of Science is confessedly most pleasant: at least the pursuit of Science is thought to contain Pleasures admirable for purity and permanence; and it is reasonable to suppose that the employment is more pleasant to those who have mastered, than to those who are yet seeking for, it.

And the Self-Sufficiency which people speak of will attach chiefly to the Contemplative Working: of course the actual necessaries of life are needed alike by the man of science, and the just man, and all the other characters; but, supposing all sufficiently supplied with these, the just man needs people towards whom, and in concert with whom, to practise his justice; and in like manner the man of perfected self-mastery, and the brave man, and so on of the rest; whereas the man of science can contemplate and speculate even when quite alone, and the more entirely he deserves the appellation the more able is he to do so: it may be he can do better for having fellow-workers but still he is certainly most Self-Sufficient.

Again, this alone would seem to be rested in for its own sake, since nothing results from it beyond the fact of having contemplated; whereas from all things which are objects of moral action we do mean to get something beside the doing them, be the same more or less.

Also, Happiness is thought to stand in perfect rest; for we toil that we may rest, and war that we may be at peace. Now all the Practical Virtues require either society or war for their Working, and the actions regarding these are thought to exclude rest; those of war entirely, because no one chooses war, nor prepares for war, for war's sake: he would indeed be thought a bloodthirsty villain who should make enemies of his friends to secure the existence of fighting and bloodshed. The Working also of the statesman excludes the idea of rest, and, beside the actual work of government, seeks for power and dignities or at least Happiness for the man himself and his fellow-citizens: a Happiness distinct the national Happiness which we evidently seek as being different and distinct.

If then of all the actions in accordance with the various virtues those of policy and war are pre-eminent in honour and greatness, and these are restless, and aim at some further End and are not choiceworthy for their own sakes, but the Working of the Intellect, being apt for contemplation, is thought to excel in earnestness, and to aim at no End beyond itself and to have Pleasure of its own which helps to increase the Working, and if the attributes of Self-Sufficiency, and capacity of rest, and unweariedness (as far as is compatible with the infirmity of human nature), and all other attributes of the highest Happiness, plainly belong to this Working, this must be perfect Happiness, if attaining a complete duration of life, which condition is added because none of the points of Happiness is incomplete.

But such a life will be higher than mere human nature, because a man will live thus, not in so far as he is man but in so far as there is in him a divine Principle: and in proportion as this Principle excels his composite nature so far does the Working thereof excel that in accordance with any other kind of Excellence: and therefore, if pure Intellect, as compared with human nature, is divine, so too will the life in accordance with it be divine compared with man's ordinary life. Yet must we not give ear to those who bid one as man to mind only man's affairs, or as mortal only mortal things; but, so far as we can, make ourselves like immortals and do all with a view to living in accordance with the highest Principle in us, for small as it may be in bulk yet in power and preciousness it far more excels all the others.

In fact this Principle would seem to constitute each man's "Self," since it is supreme and above all others in goodness it would be absurd then for a man not to choose his own life but that of some other.

And here will apply an observation made before, that whatever is proper to each is naturally best and pleasantest to him: such then is to Man the life in accordance with pure Intellect (since this Principle is most truly Man), and if so, then it is also the happiest.

VII

And second in degree of Happiness will be that Life which is in accordance with the other kind of Excellence, for the Workings in accordance with this are proper to Man: I mean, we do actions of justice, courage, and the other virtues, towards one another, in contracts, services of different kinds, and in all kinds of actions and feelings too, by observing what is befitting for each: and all these plainly are proper to man. Further, the Excellence of the Moral character is thought to result in some points from physical circumstances, and to be, in many, very closely connected with the passions.

Again, Practical Wisdom and Excellence of the Moral character are very closely united; since the Principles of Practical Wisdom are in accordance with the Moral Virtues and these are right when they accord with Practical Wisdom.

These moreover, as bound up with the passions, must belong to the composite nature, and the Excellences or Virtues of the composite nature are proper to man: therefore so too will be the life and Happiness which is in accordance with them. But that of the Pure Intellect is separate and distinct: and let this suffice upon the subject, since great exactness is beyond our purpose,

It would seem, moreover, to require supply of external goods to a small degree, or certainly less than the Moral Happiness: for, as far as necessaries of life are concerned, we will suppose both characters to need them equally (though, in point of fact, the man who lives in society does take more pains about his person and all that kind of thing; there will really be some little difference), but when we come to consider their Workings there will be found a great difference.

I mean, the liberal man must have money to do his liberal actions with, and the just man to meet his engagements (for mere intentions are uncertain, and even those who are unjust make a pretence of wishing to do justly), and the brave man must have power, if he is to perform any of the actions which appertain to his particular Virtue, and the man of perfected self-mastery must have opportunity of temptation, else how shall he or any of the others display his real character?

(By the way, a question is sometimes raised, whether the moral choice or the actions have most to do with Virtue, since it consists in both: it is plain that the perfection of virtuous action requires both: but for the actions many things are required, and the greater and more numerous they are the more.) But as for the man engaged in Contemplative Speculation, not only are such things unnecessary for his Working, but, so to speak, they are even hindrances: as regards the Contemplation at least; because of course in so far as he is Man and lives in society he chooses to do what Virtue requires, and so he will need such things for maintaining his character as Man though not as a speculative philosopher.

And that the perfect Happiness must be a kind of Contemplative Working may appear also from the following consideration: our conception of the gods is that they are above all blessed and happy: now what kind of Moral actions are we to attribute to them? those of justice? nay, will they not be set in a ridiculous light if represented as forming contracts, and restoring deposits, and so on? well then, shall we picture them performing brave actions, withstanding objects of fear and meeting dangers, because it is noble to do so? or liberal ones? but to whom shall they be giving? and further, it is absurd to think they have money or anything of the kind. And as for actions of perfected self-mastery, what can theirs be? would it not be a degrading praise that they have no bad desires? In short, if one followed the subject into all details all the circumstances connected with Moral actions would appear trivial and unworthy of gods.

Still, every one believes that they live, and therefore that they Work because it is not supposed that they sleep their time away like Endymion: now if from a living being you take away Action, still more if Creation, what remains but Contemplation? So then the Working of the Gods, eminent in blessedness, will be one apt for Contemplative Speculation; and of all human Workings that will have the greatest capacity for Happiness which is nearest akin to this.

A corroboration of which position is the fact that the other animals do not partake of Happiness, being completely shut out from any such Working.

To the gods then all their life is blessed; and to men in so far as there is in it some copy of such Working, but of the other animals none is happy because it in no way shares in Contemplative Speculation.

Happiness then is co-extensive with this Contemplative Speculation, and in proportion as people have the act of Contemplation so far have they also the being happy, not incidentally, but in the way of Contemplative Speculation because it is in itself precious.

So Happiness must be a kind of Contemplative Speculation; but since it is Man we are speaking of he will need likewise External Prosperity, because his Nature is not by itself sufficient for Speculation, but there must be health of body, and nourishment, and tendance of all kinds.

However, it must not be thought, because without external goods a man cannot enjoy high Happiness, that therefore he will require many and great goods in order to be happy: for neither Self-sufficiency, nor Action, stand in Excess, and it is quite possible to act nobly without being ruler of sea and land, since even with moderate means a man may act in accordance with Virtue.

And this may be clearly seen in that men in private stations are thought to act justly, not merely no less than men in power but even more: it will be quite enough that just so much should belong to a man as is necessary, for his life will be happy who works in accordance with Virtue.

Solon perhaps drew a fair picture of the Happy, when he said that they are men moderately supplied with external goods, and who have achieved the most noble deeds, as he thought, and who have lived with perfect self-mastery: for it is quite possible for men of moderate means to act as they ought.

Anaxagoras also seems to have conceived of the Happy man not as either rich or powerful, saying that he should not wonder if he were accounted a strange man in the judgment of the multitude: for they judge by outward circumstances of which alone they have any perception.

And thus the opinions of the Wise seem to be accordant with our account of the matter: of course such things carry some weight, but truth, in matters of moral action, is judged from facts and from actual life, for herein rests the decision. So what we should do is to examine the preceding statements by referring them to facts and to actual life, and when they harmonise with facts we may accept them, when they are at variance with them conceive of them as mere theories.

Now he that works in accordance with, and pays observance to, Pure Intellect, and tends this, seems likely to be both in the best frame of mind and dearest to the Gods: because if, as is thought, any care is bestowed on human things by the Gods then it must be reasonable to think that they take pleasure in what is best and most akin to themselves (and this must be the Pure Intellect); and that they requite with kindness those who love and honour this most, as paying observance to what is dear to them, and as acting rightly and nobly. And it is quite obvious that the man of Science chiefly combines all these: he is therefore dearest to the Gods, and it is probable that he is at the same time most Happy.

Thus then on this view also the man of Science will be most Happy.

VIII

Now then that we have said enough in our sketchy kind of way on these subjects; I mean, on the Virtues, and also on Friendship and Pleasure; are we to suppose that our original purpose is completed? Must we not rather acknowledge, what is commonly said, that in matters of moral action mere Speculation and Knowledge is not the real End but rather Practice: and if so, then neither in respect of Virtue is Knowledge enough; we must further strive to have and exert it, and take whatever other means there are of becoming good.

Now if talking and writing were of themselves sufficient to make men good, they would justly, as Theognis observes have reaped numerous and great rewards, and the thing to do would be to provide them: but in point of fact, while they plainly have the power to guide and stimulate the generous among the young and to base upon true virtuous principle any noble and truly high-minded disposition, they as plainly are powerless to guide the mass of men to Virtue and goodness; because it is not their nature to be amenable to a sense of shame but only to fear; nor to abstain from what is low and mean because it is disgraceful to do it but because of the punishment attached to it: in fact, as they live at the beck and call of passion, they pursue their own proper pleasures and the means of securing them, and they avoid the contrary pains; but as for what is noble and truly pleasurable they have not an idea of it, inasmuch as they have never tasted of it.

Men such as these then what mere words can transform? No, indeed! it is either actually impossible, or a task of no mean difficulty, to alter by words what has been of old taken into men's very dispositions: and, it may be, it is a ground for contentment if with all the means and appliances for goodness in our hands we can attain to Virtue.

The formation of a virtuous character some ascribe to Nature, some to Custom, and some to Teaching. Now Nature's part, be it what it may, obviously does not rest with us, but belongs to those who in the truest sense are fortunate, by reason of certain divine agency,

Then, as for Words and Precept, they, it is to be feared, will not avail with all; but it may be necessary for the mind of the disciple to have been previously prepared for liking and disliking as he ought; just as the soil must, to nourish the seed sown. For he that lives in obedience to passion cannot hear any advice that would dissuade him, nor, if he heard, understand: now him that is thus how can one reform? in fact, generally, passion is not thought to yield to Reason but to brute force. So then there must be, to begin with, a kind of affinity to Virtue in the disposition; which must cleave to what is honourable and loath what is disgraceful. But to get right guidance towards Virtue from the earliest youth is not easy unless one is brought up under laws of such kind; because living with self-mastery and endurance is not pleasant to the mass of men, and specially not to the young. For this reason the food, and manner of living generally, ought to be the subject of legal regulation, because things when become habitual will not be disagreeable.

Yet perhaps it is not sufficient that men while young should get right food and tendance, but, inasmuch as they will have to practise and become accustomed to certain things even after they have attained to man's estate, we shall want laws on these points as well, and, in fine, respecting one's whole life, since the mass of men are amenable to compulsion rather than Reason, and to punishment rather than to a sense of honour.

And therefore some men hold that while lawgivers should employ the sense of honour to exhort and guide men to Virtue, under the notion that they will then obey who have been well trained in habits; they should impose chastisement and penalties on those who disobey and are of less promising nature; and the incurable expel entirely: because the good man and he who lives under a sense of honour will be obedient to reason; and the baser sort, who grasp at pleasure, will be kept in check, like beasts of burthen by pain. Therefore also they say that the pains should be such as are most contrary to the pleasures which are liked.

As has been said already, he who is to be good must have been brought up and habituated well, and then live accordingly under good institutions, and never do what is low and mean, either against or with his will. Now these objects can be attained only by men living in accordance with some guiding Intellect and right order, with power to back them.

As for the Paternal Rule, it possesses neither strength nor compulsory power, nor in fact does the Rule of any one man, unless he is a king or some one in like case: but the Law has power to compel, since it is a declaration emanating from Practical Wisdom and Intellect. And people feel enmity towards their fellow-men who oppose their impulses, however rightly they may do so: the Law, on the contrary, is not the object of hatred, though enforcing right rules.

The Lacedæmonian is nearly the only State in which the framer of the Constitution has made any provision, it would seem, respecting the food and manner of living of the people: in most States these points are entirely neglected, and each man lives just as he likes, ruling his wife and children Cyclops-Fashion.

Of course, the best thing would be that there should be a right Public System and that we should be able to carry it out: but, since as a public matter those points are neglected, the duty would seem to devolve upon each individual to contribute to the cause of Virtue with his own children and friends, or at least to make this his aim and purpose: and this, it would seem, from what has been said, he will be best able to do by making a Legislator of himself: since all public systems, it is plain, are formed by the instrumentality of laws and those are good which are formed by that of good laws: whether they are written or unwritten, whether they are applied to the training of one or many, will not, it seems, make any difference, just as it does not in music, gymnastics, or any other such accomplishments, which are gained by practice.

For just as in Communities laws and customs prevail, so too in families the express commands of the Head, and customs also: and even more in the latter, because of blood-relationship and the benefits conferred: for there you have, to begin with, people who have affection and are naturally obedient to the authority which controls them.

Then, furthermore, Private training has advantages over Public, as in the case of the healing art: for instance, as a general rule, a man who is in a fever should keep quiet, and starve; but in a particular case, perhaps, this may not hold good; or, to take a different illustration, the boxer will not use the same way of fighting with all antagonists.

It would seem then that the individual will be most exactly attended to under Private care, because so each will be more likely to obtain what is expedient for him. Of course, whether in the art of healing, or gymnastics, or any other, a man will treat individual cases the better for being acquainted with general rules; as, "that so and so is good for all, or for men in such and such cases:" because general maxims are not only said to be but are the object-matter of sciences: still this is no reason against the possibility of a man's taking excellent care of some one case, though he possesses no scientific knowledge but from experience is exactly acquainted with what happens in each point; just as some people are thought to doctor themselves best though they would be wholly unable to administer relief to others. Yet it may seem to be necessary nevertheless, for one who wishes to become a real artist and well acquainted with the theory of his profession, to have recourse to general principles and ascertain all their capacities: for we have already stated that these are the object-matter of sciences.

If then it appears that we may become good through the instrumentality of laws, of course whoso wishes to make men better by a system of care and training must try to make a Legislator of himself; for to treat skilfully just any one who may be put before you is not what any ordinary person can do, but, if any one, he who has knowledge; as in the healing art, and all others which involve careful practice and skill.

Will not then our next business be to inquire from what sources, or how one may acquire this faculty of Legislation; or shall we say, that, as in similar cases, Statesmen are the people to learn from, since this faculty was thought to be a part of the Social Science? Must we not admit that the Political Science plainly does not stand on a similar footing to that of other sciences and faculties? I mean, that while in all other cases those who impart the faculties and themselves exert them are identical (physicians and painters for instance) matters of Statesmanship the Sophists profess to teach, but not one of them practises it, that being left to those actually engaged in it: and these might really very well be thought to do it by some singular knack and by mere practice rather than by any intellectual process: for they neither write nor speak on these matters (though it might be more to their credit than composing speeches for the courts or the assembly), nor again have they made Statesmen of their own sons or their friends.

One can hardly suppose but that they would have done so if they could, seeing that they could have bequeathed no more precious legacy to their communities, nor would they have preferred, for themselves or their dearest friends, the possession of any faculty rather than this.

Practice, however, seems to contribute no little to its acquisition; merely breathing the atmosphere of politics would never have made Statesmen of them, and therefore we may conclude that they who would acquire a knowledge of Statesmanship must have in addition practice.

But of the Sophists they who profess to teach it are plainly a long way off from doing so: in fact, they have no knowledge at all of its nature and objects; if they had, they would never have put it on the same footing with Rhetoric or even on a lower: neither would they have conceived it to be "an easy matter to legislate by simply collecting such laws as are famous because of course one could select the best," as though the selection were not a matter of skill, and the judging aright a very great matter, as in Music: for they alone, who have practical knowledge of a thing, can judge the performances rightly or understand with what means and in what way they are accomplished, and what harmonises with what: the unlearned must be content with being able to discover whether the result is good or bad, as in painting.

Now laws may be called the performances or tangible results of Political Science; how then can a man acquire from these the faculty of Legislation, or choose the best? we do not see men made physicians by compilations: and yet in these treatises men endeavour to give not only the cases but also how they may be cured, and the proper treatment in each case, dividing the various bodily habits. Well, these are thought to be useful to professional men, but to the unprofessional useless. In like manner it may be that collections of laws and Constitutions would be exceedingly useful to such as are able to speculate on them, and judge what is well, and what ill, and what kind of things fit in with what others: but they who without this qualification should go through such matters cannot have right judgment, unless they have it by instinct, though they may become more intelligent in such matters.

Since then those who have preceded us have left uninvestigated the subject of Legislation, it will be better perhaps for us to investigate it ourselves, and, in fact, the whole subject of Polity, that thus what we may call Human Philosophy may be completed as far as in us lies.

First then, let us endeavour to get whatever fragments of good there may be in the statements of our predecessors, next, from the Polities we have collected, ascertain what kind of things preserve or destroy Communities, and what, particular Constitutions; and the cause why some are well and others ill managed, for after such inquiry, we shall be the better able to take a concentrated view as to what kind of Constitution is best, what kind of regulations are best for each, and what laws and customs.

To this let us now proceed.

Politics

INTRODUCTION

The Politics of Aristotle is the second part of a treatise of which the Ethics is the first part. It looks back to the Ethics as the Ethics looks forward to the Politics. For Aristotle did not separate, as we are inclined to do, the spheres of the statesman and the moralist. In the Ethics he has described the character necessary for the good life, but that life is for him essentially to be lived in society, and when in the last chapters of the Ethics he comes to the practical application of his inquiries, that finds expression not in moral exhortations addressed to the individual but in a description of the legislative opportunities of the statesman. It is the legislator's task to frame a society which shall make the good life possible. Politics for Aristotle is not a struggle between individuals or classes for power, nor a device for getting done such elementary tasks as the maintenance of order and security without too great encroachments on individual liberty. The state is "a community of well-being in families and aggregations of families for the sake of a perfect and self-sufficing life." The legislator is a craftsman whose material is society and whose aim is the good life.

In an early dialogue of Plato's, the Protagoras, Socrates asks Protagoras why it is not as easy to find teachers of virtue as it is to find teachers of swordsmanship, riding, or any other art. Protagoras' answer is that there are no special teachers of virtue, because virtue is taught by the whole community. Plato and Aristotle both accept the view of moral education implied in this answer. In a passage of the Republic (492 b) Plato repudiates the notion that the sophists have a corrupting moral influence upon young men. The public themselves, he says, are the real sophists and the most complete and thorough educators. No private education can hold out against the irresistible force of public opinion and the ordinary moral standards of society. But that makes it all the more essential that public opinion and social environment should not be left to grow up at haphazard as they ordinarily do, but should be made by the wise legislator the expression of the good and be informed in all their details by his knowledge. The legislator is the only possible teacher of virtue.

Such a programme for a treatise on government might lead us to expect in the Politics mainly a description of a Utopia or ideal state which might inspire poets or philosophers but have little direct effect upon political institutions. Plato's Republic is obviously impracticable, for its author had turned away in despair from existing politics. He has no proposals, in that dialogue at least, for making the best of things as they are. The first lesson his philosopher has to learn is to turn away from this world of becoming and decay, and to look upon the unchanging eternal world of ideas. Thus his ideal city is, as he says, a pattern laid up in heaven by which the just man may rule his life, a pattern therefore in the meantime for the individual and not for the statesman. It is a city, he admits in the Laws, for gods or the children of gods, not for men as they are.

Aristotle has none of the high enthusiasm or poetic imagination of Plato. He is even unduly impatient of Plato's idealism, as is shown by the criticisms in the second book. But he has a power to see the possibilities of good in things that are imperfect, and the patience of the true politician who has learned that if he would make men what they ought to be, he must take them as he finds them. His ideal is constructed not of pure reason or poetry, but from careful and sympathetic study of a wide range of facts. His criticism of Plato in the light of history, in Book II. chap, v., though as a criticism it is curiously inept, reveals his own attitude admirably: "Let us remember that we should not disregard the experience of ages; in the multitude of years, these things, if they were good, would certainly not have been unknown; for almost everything has been found out, although sometimes they are not put together; in other cases men do not use the knowledge which they have." Aristotle in his Constitutions had made a study of one hundred and fifty-eight constitutions of the states of his day, and the fruits of that study are seen in the continual reference to concrete political experience, which makes the Politics in some respects a critical history of the workings of the institutions of the Greek city state. In Books IV., V., and VI. the ideal state seems far away, and we find a dispassionate survey of imperfect states, the best ways of preserving them, and an analysis of the causes of their instability. It is as though Aristotle were saying: "I have shown you the proper and normal type of constitution, but if you will not have it and insist on living under a perverted form, you may as well know how to make the best of it." In this way the Politics, though it defines the state in the light of its ideal, discusses states and institutions as they are. Ostensibly it is merely a continuation of the Ethics, but it comes to treat political questions from a purely political standpoint.

This combination of idealism and respect for the teachings of experience constitutes in some ways the strength and value of the Politics, but it also makes it harder to follow. The large nation states to which we are accustomed make it difficult for us to think that the state could be constructed and modelled to express the good life. We can appreciate Aristotle's critical analysis of constitutions, but find it hard to take seriously his advice to the legislator. Moreover, the idealism and the empiricism of the Politics are never really reconciled by Aristotle himself.

It may help to an understanding of the Politics if something is said on those two points.

We are accustomed since the growth of the historical method to the belief that states are "not made but grow," and are apt to be impatient with the belief which Aristotle and Plato show in the powers of the lawgiver. But however true the maxim may be of the modern nation state, it was not true of the much smaller and more self-conscious Greek city. When Aristotle talks of the legislator, he is not talking in the air. Students of the Academy had been actually called on to give new constitutions to Greek states. For the Greeks the constitution was not merely as it is so often with us, a matter of political machinery. It was regarded as a way of life. Further, the constitution within the framework of which the ordinary process of administration and passing of decrees went on, was always regarded as the work of a special man or body of men, the lawgivers. If we study Greek history, we find that the position of the legislator corresponds to that assigned to him by Plato and Aristotle. All Greek states, except those perversions which Aristotle criticises as being "above law," worked under rigid constitutions, and the constitution was only changed when the whole people gave a commission to a lawgiver to draw up a new one. Such was the position of the AEsumnetes, whom Aristotle describes in Book III. chap. xiv., in earlier times, and of the pupils of the Academy in the fourth century. The lawgiver was not an ordinary politician. He was a state doctor, called in to prescribe for an ailing constitution. So Herodotus recounts that when the people of Cyrene asked the oracle of Delphi to help them in their dissensions, the oracle told them to go to Mantinea, and the Mantineans lent them Demonax, who acted as a "setter straight" and drew up a new constitution for Cyrene. So again the Milesians, Herodotus tells us, were long troubled by civil discord, till they asked help from Paros, and the Parians sent ten commissioners who gave Miletus a new constitution. So the Athenians, when they were founding their model new colony at Thurii, employed Hippodamus of Miletus, whom Aristotle mentions in Book II, as the best expert in town-planning, to plan the streets of the city, and Protagoras as the best expert in law-making, to give the city its laws. In the Laws Plato represents one of the persons of the dialogue as having been asked by the people of Gortyna to draw up laws for a colony which they were founding. The situation described must have occurred frequently in actual life. The Greeks thought administration should be democratic and law-making the work of experts. We think more naturally of law-making as the special right of the people and administration as necessarily confined to experts.

Aristotle's Politics, then, is a handbook for the legislator, the expert who is to be called in when a state wants help. We have called him a state doctor. It is one of the most marked characteristics of Greek political theory that Plato and Aristotle think of the statesman as one who has knowledge of what ought to be done, and can help those who call him in to prescribe for them, rather than one who has power to control the forces of society. The desire of society for the statesman's advice is taken for granted, Plato in the Republic says that a good constitution is only possible when the ruler does not want to rule; where men contend for power, where they have not learnt to distinguish between the art of getting hold of the helm of state and the art of steering, which alone is statesmanship, true politics is impossible.

With this position much that Aristotle has to say about government is in agreement. He assumes the characteristic Platonic view that all men seek the good, and go wrong through ignorance, not through evil will, and so he naturally regards the state as a community which exists for the sake of the good life. It is in the state that that common seeking after the good which is the profoundest truth about men and nature becomes explicit and knows itself. The state is for Aristotle prior to the family and the village, although it succeeds them in time, for only when the state with its conscious organisation is reached can man understand the secret of his past struggles after something he knew not what. If primitive society is understood in the light of the state, the state is understood in the light of its most perfect form, when the good after which all societies are seeking is realised in its perfection. Hence for Aristotle as for Plato, the natural state or the state as such is the ideal state, and the ideal state is the starting-point of political inquiry.

In accordance with the same line of thought, imperfect states, although called perversions, are regarded by Aristotle as the result rather of misconception and ignorance than of perverse will. They all represent, he says, some kind of justice. Oligarchs and democrats go wrong in their conception of the good. They have come short of the perfect state through misunderstanding of the end or through ignorance of the proper means to the end. But if they are states at all, they embody some common conception of the good, some common aspirations of all their members.

The Greek doctrine that the essence of the state consists in community of purpose is the counterpart of the notion often held in modern times that the essence of the state is force. The existence of force is for Plato and Aristotle a sign not of the state but of the state's failure. It comes from the struggle between conflicting misconceptions of the good. In so far as men conceive the good rightly they are united. The state represents their common agreement, force their failure to make that agreement complete. The cure, therefore, of political ills is knowledge of the good life, and the statesman is he who has such knowledge, for that alone can give men what they are always seeking.

If the state is the organisation of men seeking a common good, power and political position must be given to those who can forward this end. This is the principle expressed in Aristotle's account of political justice, the principle of "tools to those who can use them." As the aim of the state is differently conceived, the qualifications for government will vary. In the ideal state power will be given to the man with most knowledge of the good; in other states to the men who are most truly capable of achieving that end which the citizens have set themselves to pursue. The justest distribution of political power is that in which there is least waste of political ability.

Further, the belief that the constitution of a state is only the outward expression of the common aspirations and beliefs of its members, explains the paramount political importance which Aristotle assigns to education. It is the great instrument by which the legislator can ensure that the future citizens of his state will share those common beliefs which make the state possible. The Greeks with their small states had a far clearer apprehension than we can have of the dependence of a constitution upon the people who have to work it.

Such is in brief the attitude in which Aristotle approaches political problems, but in working out its application to men and institutions as they are, Aristotle admits certain compromises which are not really consistent with it.

1. Aristotle thinks of membership of a state as community in pursuit of the good. He wishes to confine membership in it to those who are capable of that pursuit in the highest and most explicit manner. His citizens, therefore, must be men of leisure, capable of rational thought upon the end of life. He does not recognise the significance of that less conscious but deep-seated membership of the state which finds its expression in loyalty and patriotism. His definition of citizen includes only a small part of the population of any Greek city. He is forced to admit that the state is not possible without the co-operation of men whom he will not admit to membership in it, either because they are not capable of sufficient rational appreciation of political ends, like the barbarians whom he thought were natural slaves, or because the leisure necessary for citizenship can only be gained by the work of the artisans who by that very work make themselves incapable of the life which they make possible for others. "The artisan only attains excellence in proportion as he becomes a slave," and the slave is only a living instrument of the good life. He exists for the state, but the state does not exist for him.

2. Aristotle in his account of the ideal state seems to waver between two ideals. There is the ideal of an aristocracy and the ideal of what he calls constitutional government, a mixed constitution. The principle of "tools to those who can use them" ought to lead him, as it does Plato, to an aristocracy. Those who have complete knowledge of the good must be few, and therefore Plato gave entire power in his state into the hands of the small minority of philosopher guardians. It is in accordance with this principle that Aristotle holds that kingship is the proper form of government when there is in the state one man of transcendent virtue. At the same time, Aristotle always holds that absolute government is not properly political, that government is not like the rule of a shepherd over his sheep, but the rule of equals over equals. He admits that the democrats are right in insisting that equality is a necessary element in the state, though he thinks they do not admit the importance of other equally necessary elements. Hence he comes to say that ruling and being ruled over by turns is an essential feature of constitutional government, which he admits as an alternative to aristocracy. The end of the state, which is to be the standard of the distribution of political power, is conceived sometimes as a good for the apprehension and attainment of which "virtue" is necessary and sufficient (this is the principle of aristocracy), and sometimes as a more complex good, which needs for its attainment not only "virtue" but wealth and equality. This latter conception is the principle on which the mixed constitution is based. This in its distribution of political power gives some weight to "virtue," some to wealth, and some to mere number. But the principle of "ruling and being ruled by turns" is not really compatible with an unmodified principle of "tools to those who can use them." Aristotle is right in seeing that political government demands equality, not in the sense that all members of the state should be equal in ability or should have equal power, but in the sense that none of them can properly be regarded simply as tools with which the legislator works, that each has a right to say what will be made of his own life. The

analogy between the legislator and the craftsman on which Plato insists, breaks down because the legislator is dealing with men like himself, men who can to some extent conceive their own end in life and cannot be treated merely as means to the end of the legislator. The sense of the value of "ruling and being ruled in turn" is derived from the experience that the ruler may use his power to subordinate the lives of the citizens of the state not to the common good but to his own private purposes. In modern terms, it is a simple, rough-and-ready attempt to solve that constant problem of politics, how efficient government is to be combined with popular control. This problem arises from the imperfection of human nature, apparent in rulers as well as in ruled, and if the principle which attempts to solve it be admitted as a principle of importance in the formation of the best constitution, then the starting-point of politics will be man's actual imperfection, not his ideal nature. Instead, then, of beginning with a state which would express man's ideal nature, and adapting it as well as may be to man's actual shortcomings from that ideal, we must recognise that the state and all political machinery are as much the expression of man's weakness as of his ideal possibilities. The state is possible only because men have common aspirations, but government, and political power, the existence of officials who are given authority to act in the name of the whole state, are necessary because men's community is imperfect, because man's social nature expresses itself in conflicting ways, in the clash of interests, the rivalry of parties, and the struggle of classes, instead of in the united seeking after a common good. Plato and Aristotle were familiar with the legislator who was called in by the whole people, and they tended therefore to take the general will or common consent of the people for granted. Most political questions are concerned with the construction and expression of the general will, and with attempts to ensure that the political machinery made to express the general will shall not be exploited for private or sectional ends.

Aristotle's mixed constitution springs from a recognition of sectional interests in the state. For the proper relation between the claims of "virtue," wealth, and numbers is to be based not upon their relative importance in the good life, but upon the strength of the parties which they represent. The mixed constitution is practicable in a state where the middle class is strong, as only the middle class can mediate between the rich and the poor. The mixed constitution will be stable if it represents the actual balance of power between different classes in the state. When we come to Aristotle's analysis of existing constitutions, we find that while he regards them as imperfect approximations to the ideal, he also thinks of them as the result of the struggle between classes. Democracy, he explains, is the government not of the many but of the poor; oligarchy a government not of the few but of the rich. And each class is thought of, not as trying to express an ideal, but as struggling to acquire power or maintain its position. If ever the class existed in unredeemed nakedness, it was in the Greek cities of the fourth century, and its existence is abundantly recognised by Aristotle. His account of the causes of revolutions in Book V. shows how far were the existing states of Greece from the ideal with which he starts. His analysis of the facts forces him to look upon them as the scene of struggling factions. The causes of revolutions are not described as primarily changes in the conception of the common good, but changes in the military or economic power of the several classes in the state. The aim which he sets before oligarchs or democracies is not the good life, but simple stability or permanence of the existing constitution.

With this spirit of realism which pervades Books IV., V., and VI. the idealism of Books I., II., VII., and VIII. is never reconciled. Aristotle is content to call existing constitutions perversions of the true form. But we cannot read the Politics without recognising and profiting from the insight into the nature of the state which is revealed throughout. Aristotle's failure does not lie in this, that he is both idealist and realist, but that he keeps these two tendencies too far apart. He thinks too much of his ideal state, as something to be reached once for all by knowledge, as a fixed type to which actual states approximate or from which they are perversions. But if we are to think of actual politics as intelligible in the light of the ideal, we must think of that ideal as progressively revealed in history, not as something to be discovered by turning our back on experience and having recourse to abstract reasoning. If we stretch forward from what exists to an ideal, it is to a better which may be in its turn transcended, not to a single immutable best. Aristotle found in the society of his time men who were not capable of political reflection, and who, as he thought, did their best work under superintendence. He therefore called them natural slaves. For, according to Aristotle, that is a man's natural condition in which he does his best work. But Aristotle also thinks of nature as something fixed and immutable; and therefore sanctions the institution of slavery, which assumes that what men are that they will always be, and sets up an artificial barrier to their ever becoming anything else. We see in Aristotle's defence of slavery how the conception of nature as the ideal can have a debasing influence upon views of practical politics. His high ideal of citizenship offers to those who can satisfy its claims the prospect of a fair life; those who fall short are deemed to be different in nature and shut out entirely from approach to the ideal.

A. D. LINDSAY.

BOOK I

CHAPTER I

As we see that every city is a society, and every society Ed. is established for some good purpose; for an apparent good is the spring of all human actions; it is evident that this is the principle upon which they are every one founded, and this is more especially true of that which has for its object the best possible, and is itself the most excellent, and comprehends all the rest. Now this is called a city, and the society thereof a political society; for those who think that the principles of a political, a regal, a family, and a herile government are the same are mistaken, while they suppose that each of these differ in the numbers to whom their power extends, but not in their constitution: so that with them a herile government is one composed of a very few, a domestic of more, a civil and a regal of still more, as if there was no difference between a large family and a small city, or that a regal government and a political one are the same, only that in the one a single person is continually at the head of public affairs; in the other, that each member of the state has in his turn a share in the government, and is at one time a magistrate, at another a private person, according to the rules of political science. But now this is not true, as will be evident to any one who will consider this question in the most approved method. As, in an inquiry into every other subject, it is necessary to separate the different parts of which it is compounded, till we arrive at their first elements, which are the most minute parts thereof; so by the same proceeding we shall acquire a knowledge of the primary parts of a city and see wherein they differ from each other, and whether the rules of art will give us any assistance in examining into each of these things which are mentioned.

CHAPTER II

Now if in this particular science any one would attend to its original seeds, and their first shoot, he would then as in others have the subject perfectly before him; and perceive, in the first place, that it is requisite that those should be joined together whose species cannot exist without each other, as the male and the female, for the business of propagation; and this not through choice, but by that natural impulse which acts both upon plants and animals also, for the purpose of their leaving behind them others like themselves. It is also from natural causes that some beings command and others obey, that each may obtain their mutual safety; for a being who is endowed with a mind capable of reflection and forethought is by nature the superior and governor, whereas he whose excellence is merely corporeal is formect to be a slave; whence it follows that the different state of master and slave is equally advantageous to both. But there is a natural difference between a female and a slave: for nature is not like the artists who make the Delphic swords for the use of the poor, but for every particular purpose she has her separate instruments, and thus her ends are most complete, for whatsoever is employed on one subject only, brings that one to much greater perfection than when employed on many; and yet among the barbarians, a female and a slave are upon a level in the community, the reason for which is, that amongst them there are none qualified by nature to govern, therefore their society can be nothing but between slaves of different sexes. For which reason the poets say, it is proper for the Greeks to govern the barbarians, as if a barbarian and a slave were by nature one. Now of these two societies the domestic is the first, and Hesiod is right when he says, "First a house, then a wife, then an ox for the plough," for the poor man has always an ox before a household slave. That society then which nature has established for daily support is the domestic, and those who compose it are called by Charondas homosipuoi, and by Epimenides the Cretan homokapnoi; but the society of many families, which was first instituted for their lasting, mutual advantage, is called a village, and a village is most naturally composed of the descendants of one family, whom some persons call homogalaktes, the children and the children's children thereof: for which reason cities were originally governed by kings, as the barbarian states now are, which are composed of those who had before submitted to kingly government; for every family is governed by the elder, as are the branches thereof, on account of their relationship thereunto, which is what Homer says, "Each one ruled his wife and child;" and in this scattered manner they formerly lived. And the opinion which universally prevails, that the gods themselves are subject to kingly government, arises from hence, that all men formerly were, and many are so now; and as they imagined themselves to be made in the likeness of the gods, so they supposed their manner of life must needs be the same. And when many villages so entirely join themselves together as in every respect to form but one society, that society is a city, and contains in itself, if I may so speak, the end and perfection of government: first founded that we might live, but continued that we may live happily. For which reason every city must be allowed to be the work of nature, if we admit that the original society between male and female is; for to this as their end all subordinate societies tend, and the end of everything is the nature of it. For what every being is in its most perfect state, that certainly is the nature of that being, whether it be a man, a horse, or a house: besides, whatsoever produces the final cause and the end which we desire, must be best; but a government complete in itself is that final cause and what is best. Hence it is evident that a city is a natural production, and that man is naturally a political animal, and that whosoever is naturally and not accidentally unfit for society, must be either inferior or superior to man: thus the man in Homer, who is reviled for being "without society, without law, without family." Such a one must naturally be of a quarrelsome disposition, and as solitary as the birds. The gift of speech also evidently proves that man is a more social animal than the bees, or any of the herding cattle: for nature, as we say, does nothing in vain, and man is the only animal who enjoys it. Voice indeed, as being the token of pleasure and pain, is imparted to others also, and thus much their nature is capable of, to perceive pleasure and pain, and to impart these sensations to others; but it is by speech that we are enabled to express what is useful for us, and what is hurtful, and of course what is just and what is unjust: for in this particular man differs from other animals, that he alone has a perception of good and evil, of just and unjust, and it is a participation of these common sentiments which forms a family and a city. Besides, the notion of a city naturally precedes that of a family or an individual, for the whole must necessarily be prior to the parts, for if you take away the whole man, you cannot say a foot or a hand remains, unless by equivocation, as supposing a hand of stone to be made, but that would only be a dead one; but everything is understood to be this or that by its energic qualities and powers, so that when these no longer remain, neither can that be said to be the same, but something of the same name. That a city then precedes an individual is plain, for if an individual is not in himself sufficient to compose a perfect government, he is to a city as other parts are to a whole; but he that is incapable of society, or so complete in himself as not to want it, makes no part of a city, as a beast or a god. There is then in all persons a natural impetus to associate with each other in this manner, and he who first founded civil society was the cause of the greatest good; for as by the completion of it man is the most excellent of all living beings, so without law and justice he would be the worst of all, for nothing is so difficult to subdue as injustice in arms: but these arms man is born with, namely, prudence and valour, which he may apply to the most opposite purposes, for he who abuses them will be the most wicked, the most cruel, the most lustful, and most gluttonous being imaginable; for justice is a political virtue, by the rules of it the state is regulated, and these rules are the criterion of what is right.

CHAPTER III

SINCE it is now evident of what parts a city is composed, it will be necessary to treat first of family government, for every city is made up of families, and every family has again its separate parts of which it is composed. When a family is complete, it consists of freemen and slaves; but as in every subject we should begin with examining into the smallest parts of which it consists, and as the first and smallest parts of a family are the master and slave, the husband and wife, the father and child, let us first inquire into these three, what each of them may be, and what they ought to be; that is to say, the herile, the nuptial, and the paternal. Let these then be considered as the three distinct parts of a family: some think that the providing what is necessary for the family is something different from the government of it, others that this is the greatest part of it; it shall be considered separately; but we will first speak of a master and a slave, that we may both understand the nature of those things which are absolutely necessary, and also try if we can learn anything better on this subject than what is already known. Some persons have thought that the power of the master over his slave originates from his superior knowledge, and that this knowledge is the same in the master, the magistrate, and the king, as we have already said; but others think that herile government is contrary to nature, and that it is the law which makes one man a slave and another free, but that in nature there is no difference; for which reason that power cannot be founded in justice, but in force.

CHAPTER IV

Since then a subsistence is necessary in every family, the means of procuring it certainly makes up part of the management of a family, for without necessaries it is impossible to live, and to live well. As in all arts which are brought to perfection it is necessary that they should have their proper instruments if they would complete their works, so is it in the art of managing a family: now of instruments some of them are alive, others inanimate; thus with respect to the pilot of the ship, the tiller is without life, the sailor is alive; for a servant is as an instrument in many arts. Thus property is as an instrument to living; an estate is a multitude of instruments; so a slave is an animated instrument, but every one that can minister of himself is more valuable than any other instrument; for if every instrument, at command, or from a preconception of its master's will, could accomplish its work (as the story goes of the statues of Daedalus; or what the poet tells us of the tripods of Vulcan, "that they moved of their own accord into the assembly of the gods "), the shuttle would then weave, and the lyre play of itself; nor would the architect want servants, or the master slaves. Now what are generally called instruments are the efficients of something else, but possessions are what we simply use: thus with a shuttle we make something else for our use; but we only use a coat, or a bed: since then making and using differ from each other in species, and they both require their instruments, it is necessary that these should be different from each other. Now life is itself what we use, and not what we employ as the efficient of something else; for which reason the services of a slave are for use. A possession may be considered in the same nature as a part of anything; now a part is not only a part of something, but also is nothing else; so is a possession; therefore a master is only the master of the slave, but no part of him; but the slave is not only the slave of the master, but nothing else but that. This fully explains what is the nature of a slave, and what are his capacities; for that being who by nature is nothing of himself, but totally another's, and is a man, is a slave by nature; and that man who is the property of another, is his mere chattel, though he continues a man; but a chattel is an instrument for use, separate from the body.

CHAPTER V

But whether any person is such by nature, and whether it is advantageous and just for any one to be a slave or no, or whether all slavery is contrary to nature, shall be considered hereafter; not that it is difficult to determine it upon general principles, or to understand it from matters of fact; for that some should govern, and others be governed, is not only necessary but useful, and from the hour of their birth some are marked out for those purposes, and others for the other, and there are many species of both sorts. And the better those are who are governed the better also is the government, as for instance of man, rather than the brute creation: for the more excellent the materials are with which the work is finished, the more excellent certainly is the work; and wherever there is a governor and a governed, there certainly is some work produced; for whatsoever is composed of many parts, which jointly become one, whether conjunct or separate, evidently show the marks of governing and governed; and this is true of every living thing in all nature; nay, even in some things which partake not of life, as in music; but this probably would be a disquisition too foreign to our present purpose. Every living thing in the first place is composed of soul and body, of these the one is by nature the governor, the other the governed; now if we would know what is natural, we ought to search for it in those subjects in which nature appears most perfect, and not in those which are corrupted; we should therefore examine into a man who is most perfectly formed both in soul and body, in whom this is evident, for in the depraved and vicious the body seems to rule rather than the soul, on account of their being corrupt and contrary to nature. We may then, as we affirm, perceive in an animal the first principles of herile and political government; for the soul governs the body as the master governs his slave; the mind governs the appetite with a political or a kingly power, which shows that it is both natural and advantageous that the body should be governed by the soul, and the pathetic part by the mind, and that part which is possessed of reason; but to have no ruling power, or an improper one, is hurtful to all; and this holds true not only of man, but of other animals also, for tame animals are naturally better than wild ones, and it is advantageous that both should be under subjection to man; for this is productive of their common safety: so is it naturally with the male and the female; the one is superior, the other inferior; the one governs, the other is governed; and the same rule must necessarily hold good with respect to all mankind. Those men therefore who are as much inferior to others as the body is to the soul, are to be thus disposed of, as the proper use of them is their bodies, in which their excellence consists; and if what I have said be true, they are slaves by nature, and it is advantageous to them to be always under government. He then is by nature formed a slave who is qualified to become the chattel of another person, and on that account is so, and who has just reason enough to know that there is such a faculty, without being indued with the use of it; for other animals have no perception of reason, but are entirely guided by appetite, and indeed they vary very little in their use from each other; for the advantage which we receive, both from slaves and tame animals, arises from their bodily strength administering to our necessities; for it is the intention of nature to make the bodies of slaves and freemen different from each other, that the one should be robust for their necessary purposes, the others erect, useless indeed for what slaves are employed in, but fit for civil life, which is divided into the duties of war and peace; though these rules do not always take place, for slaves have sometimes the bodies of freemen, sometimes the souls; if then it is evident that if some bodies are as much more excellent than others as the statues of the gods excel the human form, every one will allow that the inferior ought to be slaves to the superior; and if this is true with respect to the body, it is still juster to determine in the same manner, when we consider the soul; though it is not so easy to perceive the beauty of the soul as it is of the body. Since then some men are slaves by nature, and others are freemen, it is clear that where slavery is advantageous to any one, then it is just to make him a slave.

CHAPTER VI

But it is not difficult to perceive that those who maintain the contrary opinion have some reason on their side; for a man may become a slave two different ways; for he may be so by law also, and this law is a certain compact, by which whatsoever is taken in battle is adjudged to be the property of the conquerors: but many persons who are conversant in law call in question this pretended right, and say that it would be hard that a man should be compelled by violence to be the slave and subject of another who had the power to compel him, and was his superior in strength; and upon this subject, even of those who are wise, some think one way and some another; but the cause of this doubt and variety of opinions arises from hence, that great abilities, when accompanied with proper means, are generally able to succeed by force: for victory is always owing to a superiority in some advantageous circumstances; so that it seems that force never prevails but in consequence of great abilities. But still the dispute concerning the justice of it remains; for some persons think, that justice consists in benevolence, others think it just that the powerful should govern: in the midst of these contrary opinions, there are no reasons sufficient to convince us, that the right of being master and governor ought not to be placed with those who have the greatest abilities. Some persons, entirely resting upon the right which the law gives (for that which is legal is in some respects just), insist upon it that slavery occasioned by war is just, not that they say it is wholly so, for it may happen that the principle upon which the wars were commenced is unjust; moreover no one will say that a man who is unworthily in slavery is therefore a slave; for if so, men of the noblest families might happen to be slaves, and the descendants of slaves, if they should chance to be taken prisoners in war and sold: to avoid this difficulty they say that such persons should not be called slaves, but barbarians only should; but when they say this, they do nothing more than inquire who is a slave by nature, which was what we at first said; for we must acknowledge that there are some persons who, wherever they are, must necessarily be slaves, but others in no situation; thus also it is with those of noble descent: it is not only in their own country that they are Esteemed as such, but everywhere, but the barbarians are respected on this account at home only; as if nobility and freedom were of two sorts, the one universal, the other not so. Thus says the Helen of Theodectes:

"Who dares reproach me with the name of slave? When from the immortal gods, on either side, I draw my lineage."

Those who express sentiments like these, shew only that they distinguish the slave and the freeman, the noble and the ignoble from each other by their virtues and their vices; for they think it reasonable, that as a man begets a man, and a beast a beast, so from a good man, a good man should be descended; and this is what nature desires to do, but frequently cannot accomplish it. It is evident then that this doubt has some reason in it, and that these persons are not slaves, and those freemen, by the appointment of nature; and also that in some instances it is sufficiently clear, that it is advantageous to both parties for this man to be a slave, and that to be a master, and that it is right and just, that some should be governed, and others govern, in the manner that nature intended; of which sort of government is that which a master exercises over a slave. But to govern ill is disadvantageous to both; for the same thing is useful to the part and to the whole, to the body and to the soul; but the slave is as it were a part of the master, as if he were an animated part of his body, though separate. For which reason a mutual utility and friendship may subsist between the master and the slave, I mean when they are placed by nature in that relation to each other, for the contrary takes place amongst those who are reduced to slavery by the law, or by conquest.

CHAPTER VII

It is evident from what has been said, that a herile and a political government are not the same, or that all governments are alike to each other, as some affirm; for one is adapted to the nature of freemen, the other to that of slaves. Domestic government is a monarchy, for that is what prevails in every house; but a political state is the government of free men and equals. The master is not so called from his knowing how to manage his slave, but because he is so; for the same reason a slave and a freeman have their respective appellations. There is also one sort of knowledge proper for a master, another for a slave; the slave's is of the nature of that which was taught by a slave at Syracuse; for he for a stipulated sum instructed the boys in all the business of a household slave, of which there are various sorts to be learnt, as the art of cookery, and other such-like services, of which some are allotted to some, and others to others; some employments being more honourable, others more necessary; according to the proverb, "One slave excels another, one master excels another:" in such-like things the knowledge of a slave consists. The knowledge of the master is to be able properly to employ his slaves, for the mastership of slaves is the employment, not the mere possession of them; not that this knowledge contains anything great or respectable; for what a slave ought to know how to do, that a master ought to know how to order; for which reason, those who have it in their power to be free from these low attentions, employ a steward for this business, and apply themselves either to public affairs or philosophy: the knowledge of procuring what is necessary for a family is different from that which belongs either to the master or the slave: and to do this justly must be either by war or hunting. And thus much of the difference between a master and a slave.

CHAPTER VIII

As a slave is a particular species of property, let us by all means inquire into the nature of property in general, and the acquisition of money, according to the manner we have proposed. In the first place then, some one may doubt whether the getting of money is the same thing as economy, or whether it is a part of it, or something subservient to it; and if so, whether it is as the art of making shuttles is to the art of weaving, or the art of making brass to that of statue founding, for they are not of the same service; for the one supplies the tools, the other the matter: by the matter I mean the subject out of which the work is finished, as wool for the cloth and brass for the statue. It is evident then that the getting of money is not the same thing as economy, for the business of the one is to furnish the means of the other to use them; and what art is there employed in the management of a family but economy, but whether this is a part of it, or something of a different species, is a doubt; for if it is the business of him who is to get money to find out how riches and possessions may be procured, and both these arise from various causes, we must first inquire whether the art of husbandry is part of money-getting or something different, and in general, whether the same is not true of every acquisition and every attention which relates to provision. But as there are many sorts of provision, so are the methods of living both of man and the brute creation very various; and as it is impossible to live without food, the difference in that particular makes the lives of animals so different from each other. Of beasts, some live in herds, others separate, as is most convenient for procuring themselves food; as some of them live upon flesh, others on fruit, and others on whatsoever they light on, nature having so distinguished their course of life, that they can very easily procure themselves subsistence; and as the same things are not agreeable to all, but one animal likes one thing and another another, it follows that the lives of those beasts who live upon flesh must be different from the lives of those who live on fruits; so is it with men, their lives differ greatly from each other; and of all these the shepherd's is the idlest, for they live upon the flesh of tame animals, without any trouble, while they are obliged to change their habitations on account of their flocks, which they are compelled to follow, cultivating, as it were, a living farm. Others live exercising violence over living creatures, one pursuing this thing, another that, these preying upon men; those who live near lakes and marshes and rivers, or the sea itself, on fishing, while others are fowlers, or hunters of wild beasts; but the greater part of mankind live upon the produce of the earth and its cultivated fruits; and the manner in which all those live who follow the direction of nature, and labour for their own subsistence, is nearly the same, without ever thinking to procure any provision by way of exchange or merchandise, such are shepherds, husband-men, robbers, fishermen, and hunters: some join different employments together, and thus live very agreeably; supplying those deficiencies which were wanting to make their subsistence depend upon themselves only: thus, for instance, the same person shall be a shepherd and a robber, or a husbandman and a hunter; and so with respect to the rest, they pursue that mode of life which necessity points out. This provision then nature herself seems to have furnished all animals with, as well immediately upon their first origin as also when they are arrived at a state of maturity; for at the first of these periods some of them are provided in the womb with proper nourishment, which continues till that which is born can get food for itself, as is the case with worms and birds; and as to those which bring forth their young alive, they have the means for their subsistence for a certain time within themselves, namely milk. It is evident then that we may conclude of those things that are, that plants are created for the sake of animals, and animals for the sake of men; the tame for our use and provision; the wild, at least the greater part, for our provision also, or for some other advantageous purpose, as furnishing us with clothes, and the like. As nature therefore makes nothing either imperfect or in vain, it necessarily follows that she has made all these things for men: for which reason what we gain in war is in a certain degree a natural acquisition; for hunting is a part of it, which it is necessary for us to employ against wild beasts; and those men who being intended by nature for slavery are unwilling to submit to it, on which occasion such a. war is by nature just: that species of acquisition then only which is according to nature is part of economy; and this ought to be at hand, or if not, immediately procured, namely, what is necessary to be kept in store to live upon, and which are useful as well for the state as the family. And true riches seem to consist in these; and the acquisition of those possessions which are necessary for a happy life is not infinite; though Solon says otherwise in this verse:

"No bounds to riches can be fixed for man;"

for they may be fixed as in other arts; for the instruments of no art whatsoever are infinite, either in their number or their magnitude; but riches are a number of instruments in domestic and civil economy; it is therefore evident that the acquisition of certain things according to nature is a part both of domestic and civil economy, and for what reason.

CHAPTER IX

There is also another species of acquisition which they particularly call pecuniary, and with great propriety; and by this indeed it seems that there are no bounds to riches and wealth. Now many persons suppose, from their near relation to each other, that this is one and the same with that we have just mentioned, but it is not the same as that, though not very different; one of these is natural, the other is not, but rather owing to some art and skill; we will enter into a particular examination of this subject. The uses of every possession are two, both dependent upon the thing itself, but not in the same manner, the one supposing an inseparable connection with it, the other not; as a shoe, for instance, which may be either worn, or exchanged for something else, both these are the uses of the shoe; for he who exchanges a shoe with some man who wants one, for money or provisions, uses the shoe as a shoe, but not according to the original intention, for shoes were not at first made to be exchanged. The same thing holds true of all other possessions; for barter, in general, had its original beginning in nature, some men having a surplus, others too little of what was necessary for them: hence it is evident, that the selling provisions for money is not according to the natural use of things; for they were obliged to use barter for those things which they wanted; but it is plain that barter could have no place in the first, that is to say, in family society; but must have begun when the number of those who composed the community was enlarged: for the first of these had all things in common; but when they came to be separated they were obliged to exchange with each other many different things which both parties wanted. Which custom of barter is still preserved amongst many barbarous nations, who procure one necessary with another, but never sell anything; as giving and receiving wine for corn and the like. This sort of barter is not contradictory to nature, nor is it any species of money-getting; but is necessary in procuring that subsistence which is so consonant thereunto. But this barter introduced the use of money, as might be expected; for a convenient place from whence to import what you wanted, or to export what you had a surplus of, being often at a great distance, money necessarily made its way into commerce; for it is not everything which is naturally most useful that is easiest of carriage; for which reason they invented something to exchange with each other which they should mutually give and take, that being really valuable itself, should have the additional advantage of being of easy conveyance, for the purposes of life, as iron and silver, or anything else of the same nature: and this at first passed in value simply according to its weight or size; but in process of time it had a certain stamp, to save the trouble of weighing, which stamp expressed its value.

Money then being established as the necessary medium of exchange, another species of money-getting soon took place, namely, by buying and selling, at probably first in a simple manner, afterwards with more skill and experience, where and how the greatest profits might be made. For which reason the art of money-getting seems to be chiefly conversant about trade, and the business of it to be able to tell where the greatest profits can be made, being the means of procuring abundance of wealth and possessions: and thus wealth is very often supposed to consist in the quantity of money which any one possesses, as this is the medium by which all trade is conducted and a fortune made, others again regard it as of no value, as being of none by nature, but arbitrarily made so by compact; so that if those who use it should alter their sentiments, it would be worth nothing, as being of no service for any necessary purpose. Besides, he who abounds in money often wants necessary food; and it is impossible to say that any person is in good circumstances when with all his possessions he may perish with hunger.

Like Midas in the fable, who from his insatiable wish had everything he touched turned into gold. For which reason others endeavour to procure other riches and other property, and rightly, for there are other riches and property in nature; and these are the proper objects of economy: while trade only procures money, not by all means, but by the exchange of it, and for that purpose it is this which it is chiefly employed about, for money is the first principle and the end of trade; nor are there any bounds to be set to what is thereby acquired. Thus also there are no limits to the art of medicine, with respect to the health which it attempts to procure; the same also is true of all other arts; no line can be drawn to terminate their bounds, the several professors of them being desirous to extend them as far as possible. (But still the means to be employed for that purpose are limited; and these are the limits beyond which the art cannot proceed.) Thus in the art of acquiring riches there are no limits, for the object of that is money and possessions; but economy has a boundary, though this has not: for acquiring riches is not the business of that, for which reason it should seem that some boundary should be set to riches, though we see the contrary to this is what is practised; for all those who get riches add to their money without end; the cause of which is the near connection of these two arts with each other, which sometimes occasions the one to change employments with the other, as getting of money is their common object: for economy requires the possession of wealth, but not on its own account but with another view, to purchase things necessary therewith; but the other procures it merely to increase it: so that some persons are confirmed in their belief, that this is the proper object of economy, and think that for this purpose money should be saved and hoarded up without end; the reason for which disposition is, that they are intent upon living, but not upon living well; and this desire being boundless in its extent, the means which they aim at for that purpose are boundless also; and those who propose to live well, often confine that to the enjoyment of the pleasures of sense; so that as this also seems to depend upon what a man has, all their care is to get money, and hence arises the other cause for this art; for as this enjoyment is excessive in its degree, they endeavour to procure means proportionate to supply it; and if they cannot do this merely by the art of dealing in money, they will endeavour to do it by other ways, and apply all their powers to a purpose they were not by nature intended for. Thus, for instance, courage was intended to inspire fortitude, not to get money by; neither is this the end of the soldier's or the physician's art, but victory and health. But such persons make everything subservient to money-getting, as if this was the only end; and to the end everything ought to refer.

We have now considered that art of money-getting which is not necessary, and have seen in what manner we became in want of it; and also that which is necessary, which is different from it; for that economy which is natural, and whose object is to provide food, is not like this unlimited in its extent, but has its bounds.

CHAPTER X

We have now determined what was before doubtful, whether or no the art of getting money is his business who is at the head of a family or a state, and though not strictly so, it is however very necessary; for as a politician does not make men, but receiving them from the hand of nature employs them to proper purposes; thus the earth, or the sea, or something else ought to supply them with provisions, and this it is the business of the master of the family to manage properly; for it is not the weaver's business to make yarn, but to use it, and to distinguish what is good and useful from what is bad and of no service; and indeed some one may inquire why getting money should be a part of economy when the art of healing is not, as it is as requisite that the family should be in health as that they should eat, or have anything else which is necessary; and as it is indeed in some particulars the business both of the master of the family, and he to whom the government of the state is entrusted, to see after the health of those under their care, but in others not, but the physician's; so also as to money; in some respects it is the business of the master of the family, in others not, but of the servant; but as we have already said, it is chiefly nature's, for it is her part to supply her offspring with food; for everything finds nourishment left for it in what produced it; for which reason the natural riches of all men arise from fruits and animals. Now money-making, as we say, being twofold, it may be applied to two purposes, the service of the house or retail trade; of which the first is necessary and commendable, the other justly censurable; for it has not its origin in nature, but by it men gain from each other; for usury is most reasonably detested, as it is increasing our fortune by money itself, and not employing it for the purpose it was originally intended, namely exchange.

And this is the explanation of the name (TOKOS), which means the breeding of money. For as offspring resemble their parents, so usury is money bred of money. Whence of all forms of money-making it is most against nature.

CHAPTER XI

Having already sufficiently considered the general principles of this subject, let us now go into the practical part thereof; the one is a liberal employment for the mind, the other necessary. These things are useful in the management of one's affairs; to be skilful in the nature of cattle, which are most profitable, and where, and how; as for instance, what advantage will arise from keeping horses, or oxen, or sheep, or any other live stock; it is also necessary to be acquainted with the comparative value of these things, and which of them in particular places are worth most; for some do better in one place, some in another. Agriculture also should be understood, and the management of arable grounds and orchards; and also the care of bees, and fish, and birds, from whence any profit may arise; these are the first and most proper parts of domestic management.

With respect to gaining money by exchange, the principal method of doing this is by merchandise, which is carried on in three different ways, either by sending the commodity for sale by sea or by land, or else selling it on the place where it grows; and these differ from each other in this, that the one is more profitable, the other safer. The second method is by usury. The third by receiving wages for work done, and this either by being employed in some mean art, or else in mere bodily labour. There is also a third species of improving a fortune, that is something between this and the first; for it partly depends upon nature, partly upon exchange; the subject of which is, things that are immediately from the earth, or their produce, which, though they bear no fruit, are yet useful, such as selling of timber and the whole art of metallurgy, which includes many different species, for there are various sorts of things dug out of the earth.

These we have now mentioned in general, but to enter into particulars concerning each of them, though it might be useful to the artist, would be tiresome to dwell on. Now of all the works of art, those are the most excellent wherein chance has the least to do, and those are the meanest which deprave the body, those the most servile in which bodily strength alone is chiefly wanted, those most illiberal which require least skill; but as there are books written on these subjects by some persons, as by Chares the Panian, and Apollodorus the Lemnian, upon husbandry and planting; and by others on other matters, let those who have occasion consult them thereon; besides, every person should collect together whatsoever he hears occasionally mentioned, by means of which many of those who aimed at making a fortune have succeeded in their intentions; for all these are useful to those who make a point of getting money, as in the contrivance of Thales the Milesian (which was certainly a gainful one, but as it was his it was attributed to his wisdom, though the method he used was a general one, and would universally succeed), when they reviled him for his poverty, as if the study of philosophy was useless: for they say that he, perceiving by his skill in astrology that there would be great plenty of olives that year, while it was yet winter, having got a little money, he gave earnest for all the oil works that were in Miletus and Chios, which he hired at a low price, there being no one to bid against him; but when the season came for making oil, many persons wanting them, he all at once let them upon what terms he pleased; and raising a large sum of money by that means, convinced them that it was easy for philosophers to be rich if they chose it, but that that was not what they aimed at; in this manner is Thales said to have shown his wisdom. It indeed is, as we have said, generally gainful for a person to contrive to make a monopoly of anything; for which reason some cities also take this method when they want money, and monopolise their commodities. There was a certain person in Sicily who laid out a sum of money which was deposited in his hand in buying up all the iron from the iron merchants; so that when the dealers came from the markets to purchase, there was no one had any to sell but himself; and though he put no great advance upon it, yet by laying out fifty talents he made an hundred. When Dionysius heard this he permitted him to take his money with him, but forbid him to continue any longer in Sicily, as being one who contrived means for getting money inconsistent with his affairs. This man's view and Thales's was exactly the same; both of them contrived to procure a monopoly for themselves: it is useful also for politicians to understand these things, for many states want to raise money and by such means, as well as private families, nay more so; for which reason some persons who are employed in the management of public affairs confine themselves to this province only.

CHAPTER XII

There are then three parts of domestic government, the masters, of which we have already treated, the fathers, and the husbands; now the government of the wife and children should both be that of free persons, but not the same; for the wife should be treated as a citizen of a free state, the children should be under kingly power; for the male is by nature superior to the female, except when something happens contrary to the usual course of nature, as is the elder and perfect to the younger and imperfect. Now in the generality of free states, the governors and the governed alternately change place; for an equality without any preference is what nature chooses; however, when one governs and another is governed, she endeavours that there should be a distinction between them in forms, expressions, and honours; according to what Amasis said of his laver. This then should be the established rule between the man and the woman. The government of children should be kingly; for the power of the father over the child is founded in affection and seniority, which is a species of kingly government; for which reason Homer very properly calls Jupiter "the father of gods and men," who was king of both these; for nature requires that a king should be of the same species with those whom he governs, though superior in some particulars, as is the case between the elder and the younger, the father and the son.

CHAPTER XIII

It is evident then that in the due government of a family, greater attention should be paid to the several members of it and their virtues than to the possessions or riches of it; and greater to the freemen than the slaves: but here some one may doubt whether there is any other virtue in a slave than his organic services, and of higher estimation than these, as temperance, fortitude, justice, and such-like habits, or whether they possess only bodily qualities: each side of the question has its difficulties; for if they possess these virtues, wherein do they differ from freemen? and that they do not, since they are men, and partakers of reason, is absurd. Nearly the same inquiry may be made concerning a woman and a child, whether these also have their proper virtues; whether a woman ought to be temperate, brave, and just, and whether a child is temperate or no; and indeed this inquiry ought to be general, whether the virtues of those who, by nature, either govern or are governed, are the same or different; for if it is necessary that both of them should partake of the fair and good, why is it also necessary that, without exception, the one should govern, the other always be governed? for this cannot arise from their possessing these qualities in different degrees; for to govern, and to be governed, are things different in species, but more or less are not. And yet it is wonderful that one party ought to have them, and the other not; for if he who is to govern should not be temperate and just, how can he govern well? or if he is to be governed, how can he be governed well? for he who is intemperate and a coward will never do what he ought: it is evident then that both parties ought to be virtuous; but there is a difference between them, as there is between those who by nature command and who by nature obey, and this originates in the soul; for in this nature has planted the governing and submitting principle, the virtues of which we say are different, as are those of a rational and an irrational being. It is plain then that the same principle may be extended farther, and that there are in nature a variety of things which govern and are governed; for a freeman is governed in a different manner from a slave, a male from a female, and a man from a child: and all these have parts of mind within them, but in a different manner. Thus a slave can have no power of determination, a woman but a weak one, a child an imperfect one. Thus also must it necessarily be with respect to moral virtues; all must be supposed to possess them, but not in the same manner, but as is best suited to every one's employment; on which account he who is to govern ought to be perfect in moral virtue, for his business is entirely that of an architect, and reason is the architect; while others want only that portion of it which may be sufficient for their station; from whence it is evident, that although moral virtue is common to all those we have spoken of, yet the temperance of a man and a woman are not the same, nor their courage, nor their justice, though Socrates thought otherwise; for the courage of the man consists in commanding, the woman's in obeying; and the same is true in other particulars: and this will be evident to those who will examine different virtues separately; for those who use general terms deceive themselves when they say, that virtue consists in a good disposition of mind, or doing what is right, or something of this sort. They do much better who enumerate the different virtues as Georgias did, than those who thus define them; and as Sophocles speaks of a woman, we think of all persons, that their 'virtues should be applicable to their characters, for says he,

"Silence is a woman's ornament,"

but it is not a man's; and as a child is incomplete, it is evident that his virtue is not to be referred to himself in his present situation, but to that in which he will be complete, and his preceptor. In like manner the virtue of a slave is to be referred to his master; for we laid it down as a maxim, that the use of a slave was to employ him in what you wanted; so that it is clear enough that few virtues are wanted in his station, only that he may not neglect his work through idleness or fear: some person may question if what I have said is true, whether virtue is not necessary for artificers in their calling, for they often through idleness neglect their work, but the difference between them is very great; for a slave is connected with you for life, but the artificer not so nearly: as near therefore as the artificer approaches to the situation of a slave, just so much ought he to have of the virtues of one; for a mean artificer is to a certain point a slave; but then a slave is one of those things which are by nature what they are, but this is not true of a shoemaker, or any other artist. It is evident then that a slave ought to be trained to those virtues which are proper for his situation by his master; and not by him who has the power of a master, to teach him any particular art. Those therefore are in the wrong who would deprive slaves of reason, and say that they have only to follow their orders; for slaves want more instruction than children, and thus we determine this matter. It is necessary, I am sensible, for every one who treats upon government, to enter particularly into the relations of husband and wife, and of parent and child, and to show what are the virtues of each and their respective connections with each other; what is right and what is wrong; and how the one ought to be followed, and the other avoided. Since then every family is part of a city, and each of those individuals is part of a family, and the virtue of the parts ought to correspond to the virtue of the whole; it is necessary, that both the wives and children of the community should be instructed correspondent to the nature thereof, if it is of consequence to the virtue of the state, that the wives and children therein should be virtuous, and of consequence it certainly is, for the wives are one half of the free persons; and of the children the succeeding citizens are to be formed. As then we have determined these points, we will leave the rest to be spoken to in another place, as if the subject was now finished; and beginning again anew, first consider the sentiments of those who have treated of the most perfect forms of government.

BOOK II

CHAPTER I

Since then we propose to inquire what civil society is of all others best for those who have it in their power to live entirely as they wish, it is necessary to examine into the polity of those states which are allowed to be well governed; and if there should be any others which some persons have described, and which appear properly regulated, to note what is right and useful in them; and when we point out wherein they have failed, let not this be imputed to an affectation of wisdom, for it is because there are great defects in all those which are already established, that I have been induced to undertake this work. We will begin with that part of the subject which naturally presents itself first to our consideration. The members of every state must of necessity have all things in common, or some things common, and not others, or nothing at all common. To have nothing in common is evidently impossible, for society itself is one species of community; and the first thing necessary thereunto is a common place of habitation, namely the city, which must be one, and this every citizen must have a share in. But in a government which is to be well founded, will it be best to admit of a community in everything which is capable thereof, or only in some particulars, but in others not? for it is possible that the citizens may have their wives, and children, and goods in common, as in Plato's Commonwealth; for in that Socrates affirms that all these particulars ought to be so. Which then shall we prefer? the custom which is already established, or the laws which are proposed in that treatise?

CHAPTER II

Now as a community of wives is attended with many other difficulties, so neither does the cause for which he would frame his government in this manner seem agreeable to reason, nor is it capable of producing that end which he has proposed, and for which he says it ought to take place; nor has he given any particular directions for putting it in practice. Now I also am willing to agree with Socrates in the principle which he proceeds upon, and admit that the city ought to be one as much as possible; and yet it is evident that if it is contracted too much, it will be no longer a city, for that necessarily supposes a multitude; so that if we proceed in this manner, we shall reduce a city to a family, and a family to a single person: for we admit that a family is one in a greater degree than a city, and a single person than a family; so that if this end could be obtained, it should never be put in practice, as it would annihilate the city; for a city does not only consist of a large number of inhabitants, but there must also be different sorts; for were they all alike, there could be no city; for a confederacy and a city are two different things; for a confederacy is valuable from its numbers, although all those who compose it are men of the same calling; for this is entered into for the sake of mutual defence, as we add an additional weight to make the scale go down. The same distinction prevails between a city and a nation when the people are not collected into separate villages, but live as the Arcadians. Now those things in which a city should be one are of different sorts, and in preserving an alternate reciprocation of power between these, the safety thereof consists (as I have already mentioned in my treatise on Morals), for amongst freemen and equals this is absolutely necessary; for all cannot govern at the same time, but either by the year, or according to some other regulation or time, by which means every one in his turn will be in office; as if the shoemakers and carpenters should exchange occupations, and not always be employed in the same calling. But as it is evidently better, that these should continue to exercise their respective trades; so also in civil society, where it is possible, it would be better that the government should continue in the same hands; but where it is not (as nature has made all men equal, and therefore it is just, be the administration good or bad, that all should partake of it), there it is best to observe a rotation, and let those who are their equals by turns submit to those who are at that time magistrates, as they will, in their turns, alternately be governors and governed, as if they were different men: by the same method different persons will execute different offices. From hence it is evident, that a city cannot be one in the manner that some persons propose; and that what has been said to be the greatest good which it could enjoy, is absolutely its destruction, which cannot be: for the good of anything is that which preserves it. For another reason also it is clear, that it is not for the best to endeavour to make a city too much one, because a family is more sufficient in itself than a single person, a city than a family; and indeed Plato supposes that a city owes its existence to that sufficiency in themselves which the members of it enjoy. If then this sufficiency is so desirable, the less the city is one the better.

CHAPTER III

But admitting that it is most advantageous for a city to be one as much as possible, it does not seem to follow that this will take place by permitting all at once to say this is mine, and this is not mine (though this is what Socrates regards as a proof that a city is entirely one), for the word All is used in two senses; if it means each individual, what Socrates proposes will nearly take place; for each person will say, this is his own son, and his own wife, and his own property, and of everything else that may happen to belong to him, that it is his own. But those who have their wives and children in common will not say so, but all will say so, though not as individuals; therefore, to use the word all is evidently a fallacious mode of speech; for this word is sometimes used distributively, and sometimes collectively, on account of its double meaning, and is the cause of inconclusive syllogisms in reasoning. Therefore for all persons to say the same thing was their own, using the word all in its distributive sense, would be well, but is impossible: in its collective sense it would by no means contribute to the concord of the state. Besides, there would be another inconvenience attending this proposal, for what is common to many is taken least care of; for all men regard more what is their own than what others share with them in, to which they pay less attention than is incumbent on every one: let me add also, that every one is more negligent of what another is to see to, as well as himself, than of his own private business; as in a family one is often worse served by many servants than by a few. Let each citizen then in the state have a thousand children, but let none of them be considered as the children of that individual, but let the relation of father and child be common to them all, and they will all be neglected. Besides, in consequence of this, whenever any citizen behaved well or ill, every person, be the number what it would, might say, this is my son, or this man's or that; and in this manner would they speak, and thus would they doubt of the whole thousand, or of whatever number the city consisted; and it would be uncertain to whom each child belonged, and when it was born, who was to take care of it: and which do you think is better, for every one to say this is mine, while they may apply it equally to two thousand or ten thousand; or as we say, this is mine in our present forms of government, where one man calls another his son, another calls that same person his brother, another nephew, or some other relation, either by blood or marriage, and first extends his care to him and his, while another regards him as one of the same parish and the same tribe; and it is better for any one to be a nephew in his private capacity than a son after that manner. Besides, it will be impossible to prevent some persons from suspecting that they are brothers and sisters, fathers and mothers to each other; for, from the mutual likeness there is between the sire and the offspring, they will necessarily conclude in what relation they stand to each other, which circumstance, we are informed by those writers who describe different parts of the world, does sometimes happen; for in Upper Africa there are wives in common who yet deliver their children to their respective fathers, being guided by their likeness to them. There are also some mares and cows which naturally bring forth their young so like the male, that we can easily distinguish by which of them they were impregnated: such was the mare called Just, in Pharsalia.

CHAPTER IV

Besides, those who contrive this plan of community cannot easily avoid the following evils; namely, blows, murders involuntary or voluntary, quarrels, and reproaches, all which it would be impious indeed to be guilty of towards our fathers and mothers, or those who are nearly related to us; though not to those who are not connected to us by any tie of affinity: and certainly these mischiefs must necessarily happen oftener amongst those who do not know how they are connected to each other than those who do; and when they do happen, if it is among the first of these, they admit of a legal expiation, but amongst the latter that cannot be done. It is also absurd for those who promote a community of children to forbid those who love each other from indulging themselves in the last excesses of that passion, while they do not restrain them from the passion itself, or those intercourses which are of all things most improper, between a Father and a son, a brother and a brother, and indeed the thing itself is most absurd. It is also ridiculous to prevent this intercourse between the nearest relations, for no other reason than the violence of the pleasure, while they think that the relation of father and daughter, the brother and sister, is of no consequence at all. It seems also more advantageous for the state, that the husbandmen should have their wives and children in common than the military, for there will be less affection among them in that case than when otherwise; for such persons ought to be under subjection, that they may obey the laws, and not seek after innovations. Upon the whole, the consequences of such a law as this would be directly contrary to those things which good laws ought to establish, and which Socrates endeavoured to establish by his regulations concerning women and children: for we think that friendship is the greatest good which can happen to any city, as nothing so much prevents seditions: and amity in a city is what Socrates commends above all things, which appears to be, as indeed he says, the effect of friendship; as we learn from Aristophanes in the Erotics, who says, that those who love one another from the excess of that passion, desire to breathe the same soul, and from being two to be blended into one: from whence it would necessarily follow, that both or one of them must be destroyed. But now in a city which admits of this community, the tie of friendship must, from that very cause, be extremely weak, when no father can say, this is my son; or son, this is my father; for as a very little of what is sweet, being mixed with a great deal of water is imperceptible after the mixture, so must all family connections, and the names they go by, be necessarily disregarded in such a community, it being then by no means necessary that the father should have any regard for him he called a son, or the brothers for those they call brothers. There are two things which principally inspire mankind with care and love of their offspring, knowing it is their own, and what ought to be the object of their affection, neither of which can take place in this sort of community. As for exchanging the children of the artificers and husbandmen with those of the military, and theirs reciprocally with these, it will occasion great confusion in whatever manner it shall be done; for of necessity, those who carry the children must know from whom they took and to whom they gave them; and by this means those evils which I have already mentioned will necessarily be the more likely to happen, as blows, incestuous love, murders, and the like; for those who are given from their own parents to other citizens, the military, for instance, will not call them brothers, sons, fathers, or mothers. The same thing would happen to those of the military who were placed among the other citizens; so that by this means every one would be in fear how to act in consequence of consanguinity. And thus let us determine concerning a community of wives and children.

CHAPTER V

We proceed next to consider in what manner property should be regulated in a state which is formed after the most perfect mode of government, whether it should be common or not; for this may be considered as a separate question from what had been determined concerning wives and children; I mean, whether it is better that these should be held separate, as they now everywhere are, or that not only possessions but also the usufruct of them should be in common; or that the soil should have a particular owner, but that the produce should be brought together and used as one common stock, as some nations at present do; or on the contrary, should the soil be common, and should it also be cultivated in common, while the produce is divided amongst the individuals for their particular use, which is said to be practised by some barbarians; or shall both the soil and the fruit be common? When the business of the husbandman devolves not on the citizen, the matter is much easier settled; but when those labour together who have a common right of possession, this may occasion several difficulties; for there may not be an equal proportion between their labour and what they consume; and those who labour hard and have but a small proportion of the produce, will certainly complain of those who take a large share of it and do but little for that. Upon the whole, as a community between man and man so entire as to include everything possible, and thus to have all things that man can possess in common, is very difficult, so is it particularly so with respect to property; and this is evident from that community which takes place between those who go out to settle a colony; for they frequently have disputes with each other upon the most common occasions, and come to blows upon trifles: we find, too, that we oftenest correct those slaves who are generally employed in the common offices of the family: a community of property then has these and other inconveniences attending it.

But the manner of life which is now established, more particularly when embellished with good morals and a system of equal laws, is far superior to it, for it will have the advantage of both; by both I mean properties being common, and divided also; for in some respects it ought to be in a manner common, but upon the whole private: for every man's attention being employed on his own particular concerns, will prevent mutual complaints against each other; nay, by this means industry will be increased, as each person will labour to improve his own private property; and it will then be, that from a principle of virtue they will mutually perform good offices to each other, according to the proverb, "All things are common amongst friends;" and in some cities there are traces of this custom to be seen, so that it is not impracticable, and particularly in those which are best governed; some things are by this means in a manner common, and others might be so; for there, every person enjoying his own private property, some things he assists his friend with, others are considered as in common; as in Lacedaemon, where they use each other's slaves, as if they were, so to speak, their own, as they do their horses and dogs, or even any provision they may want in a journey.

It is evident then that it is best to have property private, but to make the use of it common; but how the citizens are to be brought to it is the particular business of the legislator. And also with respect to pleasure, it is unspeakable how advantageous it is, that a man should think he has something which he may call his own; for it is by no means to no purpose, that each person should have an affection for himself, for that is natural, and yet to be a self-lover is justly censured; for we mean by that, not one that simply loves himself, but one that loves himself more than he ought; in like manner we blame a money-lover, and yet both money and self is what all men love. Besides, it is very pleasing to us to oblige and assist our friends and companions, as well as those whom we are connected with by the rights of hospitality; and this cannot be done without the establishment of private property, which cannot take place with those who make a city too much one; besides, they prevent every opportunity of exercising two principal virtues, modesty and liberality. Modesty with respect to the female sex, for this virtue requires you to abstain from her who is another's; liberality, which depends upon private property, for without that no one can appear liberal, or do any generous action; for liberality consists in imparting to others what is our own.

This system of polity does indeed recommend itself by its good appearance and specious pretences to humanity; and when first proposed to any one, must give him great pleasure, as he will conclude it to be a wonderful bond of friendship, connecting all to all; particularly when any one censures the evils which are now to be found in society, as arising from properties not being common, I mean the disputes which happen between man and man, upon their different contracts with each other; those judgments which are passed in court in consequence of fraud, and perjury, and flattering the rich, none of which arise from properties being private, but from the vices of mankind. Besides, those who live in one general community, and have all things in common, oftener dispute with each other than those who have their property separate; from the very small number indeed of those who have their property in common, compared with those where it is appropriated, the instances of their quarrels are but few. It is also but right to mention, not only the inconveniences they are preserved from who live in a communion of goods, but also the advantages they are deprived of; for when the whole comes to be considered, this manner of life will be found impracticable.

We must suppose, then, that Socrates's mistake arose from the principle he set out with being false; we admit, indeed, that both a family and a city ought to be one in some particulars, but not entirely; for there is a point beyond which if a city proceeds in reducing itself to one, it will be no longer a city.

There is also another point at which it will still continue to be a city, but it will approach so near to not being one, that it will be worse than none; as if any one should reduce the voices of those who sing in concert to one, or a verse to a foot. But the people ought to be made one, and a community, as I have already said, by education; as property at Lacedaemon, and their public tables at Crete, were made common by their legislators. But yet, whosoever shall introduce any education, and think thereby to make his city excellent and respectable, will be absurd, while he expects to form it by such regulations, and not by manners, philosophy, and laws. And whoever would establish a government upon a community of goods, ought to know that he should consult the experience of many years, which would plainly enough inform him whether such a scheme is useful; for almost all things have already been found out, but some have been neglected, and others which have been known have not been put in practice. But this would be most evident, if any one could see such a government really established: for it would be impossible to frame such a city without dividing and separating it into its distinct parts, as public tables, wards, and tribes; so that here the laws will do nothing more than forbid the military to engage in agriculture, which is what the Lacedaemonians are at present endeavouring to do.

Nor has Socrates told us (nor is it easy to say) what plan of government should be pursued with respect to the individuals in the state where there is a community of goods established; for though the majority of his citizens will in general consist of a multitude of persons of different occupations, of those he has determined nothing; whether the property of the husbandman ought to be in common, or whether each person should have his share to himself; and also, whether their wives and children ought to be in common: for if all things are to be alike common to all, where will be the difference between them and the military, or what would they get by submitting to their government? and upon what principles would they do it, unless they should establish the wise practice of the Cretans? for they, allowing everything else to their slaves, forbid them only gymnastic exercises and the use of arms. And if they are not, but these should be in the same situation with respect to their property which they are in other cities, what sort of a community will there be? in one city there must of necessity be two, and those contrary to each other; for he makes the military the guardians of the state, and the husbandman, artisans, and others, citizens; and all those quarrels, accusations, and things of the like sort, which he says are the bane of other cities, will be found in his also: notwithstanding Socrates says they will not want many laws in consequence of their education, but such only as may be necessary for regulating the streets, the markets, and the like, while at the same time it is the education of the military only that he has taken any care of. Besides, he makes the husbandmen masters of property upon paying a tribute; but this would be likely to make them far more troublesome and high-spirited than the Helots, the Penestise, or the slaves which others employ; nor has he ever determined whether it is necessary to give any attention to them in these particulars, nor thought of what is connected therewith, their polity, their education, their laws; besides, it is of no little consequence, nor is it easy to determine, how these should be framed so as to preserve the community of the military.

Besides, if he makes the wives common, while the property continues separate, who shall manage the domestic concerns with the same care which the man bestows upon his fields? nor will the inconvenience be remedied by making property as well as wives common; and it is absurd to draw a comparison from the brute creation, and say, that the same principle should regulate the connection of a man and a woman which regulates theirs amongst whom there is no family association.

It is also very hazardous to settle the magistracy as Socrates has done; for he would have persons of the same rank always in office, which becomes the cause of sedition even amongst those who are of no account, but more particularly amongst those who are of a courageous and warlike disposition; it is indeed evidently necessary that he should frame his community in this manner; for that golden particle which God has mixed up in the soul of man flies not from one to the other, but always continues with the same; for he says, that some of our species have gold, and others silver, blended in their composition from the moment of their birth: but those who are to be husbandmen and artists, brass and iron; besides, though he deprives the military of happiness, he says, that the legislator ought to make all the citizens happy; but it is impossible that the whole city can be happy, without all, or the greater, or some part of it be happy. For happiness is not like that numerical equality which arises from certain numbers when added together, although neither of them may separately contain it; for happiness cannot be thus added together, but must exist in every individual, as some properties belong to every integral; and if the military are not happy, who else are so? for the artisans are not, nor the multitude of those who are employed in inferior offices. The state which Socrates has described has all these defects, and others which are not of less consequence.

CHAPTER VI

It is also nearly the same in the treatise upon Laws which was writ afterwards, for which reason it will be proper in this place to consider briefly what he has there said upon government, for Socrates has thoroughly settled but very few parts of it; as for instance, in what manner the community of wives and children ought to be regulated, how property should be established, and government conducted.

Now he divides the inhabitants into two parts, husbandmen and soldiers, and from these he select a third part who are to be senators and govern the city; but he has not said whether or no the husbandman and artificer shall have any or what share in the government, or whether they shall have arms, and join with the others in war, or not. He thinks also that the women ought to go to war, and have the same education as the soldiers; as to other particulars, he has filled his treatise with matter foreign to the purpose; and with respect to education, he has only said what that of the guards ought to be.

As to his book of Laws, laws are the principal thing which that contains, for he has there said but little concerning government; and this government, which he was so desirous of framing in such a manner as to impart to its members a more entire community of goods than is to be found in other cities, he almost brings round again to be the same as that other government which he had first proposed; for except the community of wives and goods, he has framed both his governments alike, for the education of the citizens is to be the same in both; they are in both to live without any servile employ, and their common tables are to be the same, excepting that in that he says the women should have common tables, and that there should be a thousand men-at-arms, in this, that there should be five thousand.

All the discourses of Socrates are masterly, noble, new, and inquisitive; but that they are all true it may probably be too much to say. For now with respect to the number just spoken of, it must be acknowledged that he would want the country of Babylonia for them, or some one like it, of an immeasurable extent, to support five thousand idle persons, besides a much greater number of women and servants. Every one, it is true, may frame an hypothesis as he pleases, but yet it ought to be possible. It has been said, that a legislator should have two things in view when he frames his laws, the country and the people. He will also do well, if he has some regard to the neighbouring states, if he intends that his community should maintain any political intercourse with them, for it is not only necessary that they should understand that practice of war which is adapted to their own country, but to others also; for admitting that any one chooses not this life either in public or private, yet there is not the less occasion for their being formidable to their enemies, not only when they invade their country, but also when they retire out of it.

It may also be considered whether the quantity of each person's property may not be settled in a different manner from what he has done it in, by making it more determinate; for he says, that every one ought to have enough whereon to live moderately, as if any one had said to live well, which is the most comprehensive expression. Besides, a man may live moderately and miserably at the same time; he had therefore better have proposed, that they should live both moderately and liberally; for unless these two conspire, luxury will come in on the one hand, or wretchedness on the other, since these two modes of living are the only ones applicable to the employment of our substance; for we cannot say with respect to a man's fortune, that he is mild or courageous, but we may say that he is prudent and liberal, which are the only qualities connected therewith.

It is also absurd to render property equal, and not to provide for the increasing number of the citizens; but to leave that circumstance uncertain, as if it would regulate itself according to the number of women who should happen to be childless, let that be what it would because this seems to take place in other cities; but the case would not be the same in such a state which he proposes and those which now actually unite; for in these no one actually wants, as the property is divided amongst the whole community, be their numbers what they will; but as it could not then be divided, the supernumeraries, whether they were many or few, would have nothing at all. But it is more necessary than even to regulate property, to take care that the increase of the people should not exceed a certain number; and in determining that, to take into consideration those children who will die, and also those women who will be barren; and to neglect this, as is done in several cities, is to bring certain poverty on the citizens; and poverty is the cause of sedition and evil. Now Phidon the Corinthian, one of the oldest legislators, thought the families and the number of the citizens should continue the same; although it should happen that all should have allotments at the first, disproportionate to their numbers.

In Plato's Laws it is however different; we shall mention hereafter what we think would be best in these particulars. He has also neglected in that treatise to point out how the governors are to be distinguished from the governed; for he says, that as of one sort of wool the warp ought to be made, and of another the woof, so ought some to govern, and others to be governed. But since he admits, that all their property may be increased fivefold, why should he not allow the same increase to the country? he ought also to consider whether his allotment of the houses will be useful to the community, for he appoints two houses to each person, separate from each other; but it is inconvenient for a person to inhabit two houses. Now he is desirous to have his whole plan of government neither a democracy nor an oligarchy, but something between both, which he calls a polity, for it is to be composed of men-at-arms. If Plato intended to frame a state in which more than in any other everything should be common, he has certainly given it a right name; but if he intended it to be the next in perfection to that which he had already framed, it is not so; for perhaps some persons will give the preference to the Lacedaemonian form of government, or some other which may more completely have attained to the aristocratic form.

Some persons say, that the most perfect government should be composed of all others blended together, for which reason they commend that of Lacedaemon; for they say, that this is composed of an oligarchy, a monarchy, and a democracy, their kings representing the monarchical part, the senate the oligarchical; and, that in the ephori may be found the democratical, as these are taken from the people. But some say, that in the ephori is absolute power, and that it is their common meal and daily course of life, in which the democratical form is represented. It is also said in this treatise of Laws, that the best form of government must, be one composed of a democracy and a tyranny; though such a mixture no one else would ever allow to be any government at all, or if it is, the worst possible; those propose what is much better who blend many governments together; for the most perfect is that which is formed of many parts. But now in this government of Plato's there are no traces of a monarchy, only of an oligarchy and democracy, though he seems to choose that it should rather incline to an oligarchy, as is evident from the appointment of the magistrates; for to choose them by lot is common to both; but that a man of fortune must necessarily be a member of the assembly, or to elect the magistrates, or take part in the management of public affairs, while others are passed over, makes the state incline to an oligarchy; as does the endeavouring that the greater part of the rich may be in office, and that the rank of their appointments may correspond with their fortunes.

The same principle prevails also in the choice of their senate; the manner of electing which is favourable also to an oligarchy; for all are obliged to vote for those who are senators of the first class, afterwards they vote for the same number out of the second, and then out of the third; but this compulsion to vote at the election of senators does not extend to the third and fourth classes and the first and second class only are obliged to vote for the fourth. By this means he says he shall necessarily have an equal number of each rank, but he is mistaken--for the majority will always consist of those of the first rank, and the most considerable people; and for this reason, that many of the commonalty not being obliged to it, will not attend the elections. From hence it is evident, that such a state will not consist of a democracy and a monarchy, and this will be further proved by what we shall say when we come particularly to consider this form of government.

There will also great danger arise from the manner of electing the senate, when those who are elected themselves are afterwards to elect others; for by this means, if a certain number choose to combine together, though not very considerable, the election will always fall according to their pleasure. Such are the things which Plato proposes concerning government in his book of Laws.

CHAPTER VII

There are also some other forms of government, which have been proposed either by private persons, or philosophers, or politicians, all of which come much nearer to those which have been really established, or now exist, than these two of Plato's; for neither have they introduced the innovation of a community of wives and children, and public tables for the women, but have been contented to set out with establishing such rules as are absolutely necessary.

There are some persons who think, that the first object of government should be to regulate well everything relating to private property; for they say, that a neglect herein is the source of all seditions whatsoever. For this reason, Phaleas the Chalcedonian first proposed, that the fortunes of the citizens should be equal, which he thought was not difficult to accomplish when a community was first settled, but that it was a work of greater difficulty in one that had been long established; but yet that it might be effected, and an equality of circumstances introduced by these means, that the rich should give marriage portions, but never receive any, while the poor should always receive, but never give.

But Plato, in his treatise of Laws, thinks that a difference in circumstances should be permitted to a certain degree; but that no citizen should be allowed to possess more than five times as much as the lowest census, as we have already mentioned. But legislators who would establish this principle are apt to overlook what they ought to consider; that while they regulate the quantity of provisions which each individual shall possess, they ought also to regulate the number of his children; for if these exceed the allotted quantity of provision, the law must necessarily be repealed; and yet, in spite of the repeal, it will have the bad effect of reducing many from wealth to poverty, so difficult is it for innovators not to fall into such mistakes. That an equality of goods was in some degree serviceable to strengthen the bands of society, seems to have been known to some of the ancients; for Solon made a law, as did some others also, to restrain persons from possessing as much land as they pleased. And upon the same principle there are laws which forbid men to sell their property, as among the Locrians, unless they can prove that some notorious misfortune has befallen them. They were also to preserve their ancient patrimony, which custom being broken through by the Leucadians, made their government too democratic; for by that means it was no longer necessary to be possessed of a certain fortune to be qualified to be a magistrate. But if an equality of goods is established, this may be either too much, when it enables the people to live luxuriously, or too little, when it obliges them to live hard. Hence it is evident, that it is not proper for the legislator to establish an equality of circumstances, but to fix a proper medium. Besides, if any one should regulate the division of property in such a manner that there should be a moderate sufficiency for all, it would be of no use; for it is of more consequence that the citizen should entertain a similarity of sentiments than an equality of circumstances; but this can never be attained unless they are properly educated under the direction of the law. But probably Phaleas may say, that this in what he himself mentions; for he both proposes a equality of property and one plan of education in his city. But he should have said particularly what education he intended, nor is it of any service to have this to much one; for this education may be one, and yet such as will make the citizens over-greedy, to grasp after honours, or riches, or both. Besides, not only an inequality of possessions, but also of honours, will occasion seditions, but this upon contrary grounds; for the vulgar will be seditious if there be an inequality of goods, by those of more elevated sentiments, if there is an equality of honours.

"When good and bad do equal honours share."

For men are not guilty of crimes for necessaries only (for which he thinks an equality of goods would be a sufficient remedy, as they would then have no occasion to steal cold or hunger), but that they may enjoy what they desire, and not wish for it in vain; for if their desire extend beyond the common necessaries of life, they were be wicked to gratify them; and not only so, but if their wishes point that way, they will do the same to enjoy those pleasures which are free from the alloy of pain. What remedy then shall we find for these three disorders? And first, to prevent stealing from necessity, let every one be supplied with a moderate subsistence, which may make the addition of his own industry necessary; second to prevent stealing to procure the luxuries of life, temperance be enjoined; and thirdly, let those who wish for pleasure in itself seek for it only in philosophy, all others want the assistance of men.

Since then men are guilty of the greatest crimes from ambition, and not from necessity, no one, for instance aims at being a tyrant to keep him from the cold, hence great honour is due to him who kills not a thief, but tyrant; so that polity which Phaleas establishes would only be salutary to prevent little crimes. He has also been very desirous to establish such rules as will conduce to perfect the internal policy of his state, and he ought also to have done the same with respect to its neighbours and all foreign nations; for the considerations of the military establishment should take place in planning every government, that it may not be unprovided in case of a war, of which he has said nothing; so also with respect to property, it ought not only to be adapted to the exigencies of the state, but also to such dangers as may arise from without.

Thus it should not be so much as to tempt those who are near, and more powerful to invade it, while those who possess it are not able to drive out the invaders, nor so little as that the state should not be able to go to war with those who are quite equal to itself, and of this he has determined nothing; it must indeed be allowed that it is advantageous to a community to be rather rich than poor; probably the proper boundary is this, not to possess enough to make it worth while for a more powerful neighbour to attack you, any more than he would those who had not so much as yourself; thus when Autophradatus proposed to besiege Atarneus, Eubulus advised him to consider what time it would require to take the city, and then would have him determine whether it would answer, for that he should choose, if it would even take less than he proposed, to quit the place; his saying this made Autophradatus reflect upon the business and give over the siege. There is, indeed, some advantage in an equality of goods amongst the citizens to prevent seditions; and yet, to say truth, no very great one; for men of great abilities will stomach their being put upon a level with the rest of the community. For which reason they will very often appear ready for every commotion and sedition; for the wickedness of mankind is insatiable. For though at first two oboli might be sufficient, yet when once it is become customary, they continually want something more, until they set no limits to their expectations; for it is the nature of our desires to be boundless, and many live only to gratify them. But for this purpose the first object is, not so much to establish an equality of fortune, as to prevent those who are of a good disposition from desiring more than their own, and those who are of a bad one from being able to acquire it; and this may be done if they are kept in an inferior station, and not exposed to injustice. Nor has he treated well the equality of goods, for he has extended his regulation only to land; whereas a man's substance consists not only in this, but also in slaves, cattle, money, and all that variety of things which fall under the name of chattels; now there must be either an equality established in all these, or some certain rule, or they must be left entirely at large. It appears too by his laws, that he intends to establish only a small state, as all the artificers are to belong to the public, and add nothing to the complement of citizens; but if all those who are to be employed in public works are to be the slaves of the public, it should be done in the same manner as it is at Epidamnum, and as Diophantus formerly regulated it at Athens. From these particulars any one may nearly judge whether Phaleas's community is well or ill established.

CHAPTER VIII

Hippodamus, the son of Euruphon a Milesian, contrived the art of laying out towns, and separated the Pireus. This man was in other respects too eager after notice, and seemed to many to live in a very affected manner, with his flowing locks and his expensive ornaments, and a coarse warm vest which he wore, not only in the winter, but also in the hot weather. As he was very desirous of the character of a universal scholar, he was the first who, not being actually engaged in the management of public affairs, sat himself to inquire what sort of government was best; and he planned a state, consisting of ten thousand persons, divided into three parts, one consisting of artisans, another of husbandmen, and the third of soldiers; he also divided the lands into three parts, and allotted one to sacred purposes, another to the public, and the third to individuals. The first of these was to supply what was necessary for the established worship of the gods; the second was to be allotted to the support of the soldiery; and the third was to be the property of the husbandman. He thought also that there need only be three sorts of laws, corresponding to the three sorts of actions which can be brought, namely, for assault, trespasses, or death. He ordered also that there should be a particular court of appeal, into which all causes might be removed which were supposed to have been unjustly determined elsewhere; which court should be composed of old men chosen for that purpose. He thought also that they should not pass sentence by votes; but that every one should bring with him a tablet, on which he should write, that he found the party guilty, if it was so, but if not, he should bring a plain tablet; but if he acquitted him of one part of the indictment but not of the other, he should express that also on the tablet; for he disapproved of that general custom already established, as it obliges the judges to be guilty of perjury if they determined positively either on the one side or the other. He also made a law, that those should be rewarded who found out anything for the good of the city, and that the children of those who fell in battle should be educated at the public expense; which law had never been proposed by any other legislator, though it is at present in use at Athens as well as in other cities, he would have the magistrates chosen out of the people in general, by whom he meant the three parts before spoken of; and that those who were so elected should be the particular guardians of what belonged to the public, to strangers, and to orphans.

These are the principal parts and most worthy of notice in Hippodamus's plan. But some persons might doubt the propriety of his division of the citizens into three parts; for the artisans, the husbandmen, and the soldiers are to compose one community, where the husbandmen are to have no arms, and the artisans neither arms nor land, which would in a manner render them slaves to the soldiery. It is also impossible that the whole community should partake of all the honourable employments in it--for the generals and the guardians of the state must necessarily be appointed out of the soldiery, and indeed the most honourable magistrates; but as the two other parts will not have their share in the government, how can they be expected to have any affection for it? But it is necessary that the soldiery should be superior to the other two parts, and this superiority will not be easily gained without they are very numerous; and if they are so, why should the community consist of any other members? why should any others have a right to elect the magistrates? Besides, of what use are the husbandmen to this community? Artisans, 'tis true, are necessary, for these every city wants, and they can live upon their business. If the husbandmen indeed furnished the soldiers with provisions, they would be properly part of the community; but these are supposed to have their private property, and to cultivate it for their own use. Moreover, if the soldiers themselves are to cultivate that common land which is appropriated for their support, there will be no distinction between the soldier and the husbandman, which the legislator intended there should be; and if there should be any others who are to cultivate the private property of the husbandman and the common lands of the military, there will be a fourth order in the state which will have no share in it, and always entertain hostile sentiments towards it. If any one should propose that the same persons should cultivate their own lands and the public ones also, then there would be a deficiency of provisions to supply two families, as the lands would not immediately yield enough for themselves and the soldiers also; and all these things would occasion great confusion.

Nor do I approve of his method of determining causes, when he would have the judge split the case which comes simply before him; and thus, instead of being a judge, become an arbitrator. Now when any matter is brought to arbitration, it is customary for many persons to confer together upon the business that is before them; but when a cause is brought before judges it is not so; and many legislators take care that the judges shall not have it in their power to communicate their sentiments to each other. Besides, what can prevent confusion on the bench when one judge thinks a fine should be different from what another has set it at; one proposing twenty minae, another ten, or be it more or less, another four, and another five; and it is evident, that in this manner they will differ from each other, while some will give the whole damages sued for, and others nothing; in this situation, how shall their determinations be settled? Besides, a judge cannot be obliged to perjure himself who simply acquits or condemns, if the action is fairly and justly brought; for he who acquits the party does not say that he ought not to pay any fine at all, but that he ought not to pay a fine of twenty minae. But he that condemns him is guilty of perjury if he sentences him to pay twenty minae while he believes the damages ought not to be so much.

Now with respect to these honours which he proposes to bestow on those who can give any information useful to the community, this, though very pleasing in speculation, is what the legislator should not settle, for it would encourage informers, and probably occasion commotions in the state. And this proposal of his gives rise also to further conjectures and inquiries; for some persons have doubted whether it is useful or hurtful to alter the established law of any country, if even for the better; for which reason one cannot immediately determine upon what he here says, whether it is advantageous to alter the law or not. We know, indeed, that it is possible to propose to new model both the laws and government as a common good; and since we have mentioned this subject, it may be very proper to enter into a few particulars concerning it, for it contains some difficulties, as I have already said, and it may appear better to alter them, since it has been found useful in other sciences.

Thus the science of physic is extended beyond its ancient bounds; so is the gymnastic, and indeed all other arts and powers; so that one may lay it down for certain that the same thing will necessarily hold good in the art of government. And it may also be affirmed, that experience itself gives a proof of this; for the ancient laws are too simple and barbarous; which allowed the Greeks to wear swords in the city, and to buy their wives of each other. And indeed all the remains of old laws which we have are very simple; for instance, a law in Cuma relative to murder. If any person who prosecutes another for murder can produce a certain number of witnesses to it of his own relations, the accused person shall be held guilty. Upon the whole, all persons ought to endeavour to follow what is right, and not what is established; and it is probable that the first men, whether they sprung out of the earth, or were saved from some general calamity, had very little understanding or knowledge, as is affirmed of these aborigines; so that it would be absurd to continue in the practice of their rules. Nor is it, moreover, right to permit written laws always to remain without alteration; for as in all other sciences, so in politics, it is impossible to express everything in writing with perfect exactness; for when we commit anything to writing we must use general terms, but in every action there is something particular to itself, which these may not comprehend; from whence it is evident, that certain laws will at certain times admit of alterations. But if we consider this matter in another point of view, it will appear to require great caution; for when the advantage proposed is trifling, as the accustoming the people easily to abolish their laws is of bad consequence, it is evidently better to pass over some faults which either the legislator or the magistrates may have committed; for the alterations will not be of so much service as a habit of disobeying the magistrates will be of disservice. Besides, the instance brought from the arts is fallacious; for it is not the same thing to alter the one as the other. For a law derives all its strength from custom, and this requires long time to establish; so that, to make it an easy matter to pass from the established laws to other new ones, is to weaken the power of laws. Besides, here is another question; if the laws are to be altered, are they all to be altered, and in every government or not, and whether at the pleasure of one person or many? all which particulars will make a great difference; for which reason we will at present drop the inquiry, to pursue it at some other time.

CHAPTER IX

There are two considerations which offer themselves with respect to the government established at Lacedaemon and Crete, and indeed in almost all other states whatsoever; one is whether their laws do or do not promote the best establishment possible? the other is whether there is anything, if we consider either the principles upon which it is founded or the executive part of it, which prevents the form of government that they had proposed to follow from being observed; now it is allowed that in every well-regulated state the members of it should be free from servile labour; but in what manner this shall be effected is not so easy to determine; for the Penestse have very often attacked the Thessalians, and the Helots the Lacedaemonians, for they in a manner continually watch an opportunity for some misfortune befalling them. But no such thing has ever happened to the Cretans; the reason for which probably is, that although they are engaged in frequent wars with the neighbouring cities, yet none of these would enter into an alliance with the revolters, as it would be disadvantageous for them, who themselves also have their villains. But now there is perpetual enmity between the Lacedaemonians and all their neighbours, the Argives, the Messenians, and the Arcadians. Their slaves also first revolted from the Thessalians while they were engaged in wars with their neighbours the Acheans, the Perrabeans, and the Magnesians. It seems to me indeed, if nothing else, yet something very troublesome to keep upon proper terms with them; for if you are remiss in your discipline they grow insolent, and think themselves upon an equality with their masters; and if they are hardly used they are continually plotting against you and hate you. It is evident, then, that those who employ slaves have not as yet hit upon the right way of managing them.

As to the indulging of women in any particular liberties, it is hurtful to the end of government and the prosperity of the city; for as a man and his wife are the two parts of a family, if we suppose a city to be divided into two parts, we must allow that the number of men and women will be equal.

In whatever city then the women are not under good regulations, we must look upon one half of it as not under the restraint of law, as it there happened; for the legislator, desiring to make his whole city a collection of warriors with respect to the men, he most evidently accomplished his design; but in the meantime the women were quite neglected, for they live without restraint in every improper indulgence and luxury. So that in such a state riches will necessarily be in general esteem, particularly if the men are governed by their wives, which has been the case with many a brave and warlike people except the Celts, and those other nations, if there are any such, who openly practise pederasty. And the first mythologists seem not improperly to have joined Mars and Venus together; for all nations of this character are greatly addicted either to the love of women or of boys, for which reason it was thus at Lacedaemon; and many things in their state were done by the authority of the women. For what is the difference, if the power is in the hands of the women, or in the hands of those whom they themselves govern? it must turn to the same account. As this boldness of the women can be of no use in any common occurrences, if it was ever so, it must be in war; but even here we find that the Lacedaemonian women were of the greatest disservice, as was proved at the time of the Theban invasion, when they were of no use at all, as they are in other cities, but made more disturbance than even the enemy.

The origin of this indulgence which the Lacedaemonian women enjoy is easily accounted for, from the long time the men were absent from home upon foreign expeditions against the Argives, and afterwards the Arcadians and Messenians, so that, when these wars were at an end, their military life, in which there is no little virtue, prepared them to obey the precepts of their law-giver; but we are told, that when Lycurgus endeavoured also to reduce the women to an obedience to his laws, upon their refusal he declined it. It may indeed be said that the women were the causes of these things, and of course all the fault was theirs. But we are not now considering where the fault lies, or where it does not lie, but what is right and what is wrong; and when the manners of the women are not well regulated, as I have already said, it must not only occasion faults which are disgraceful to the state, but also increase the love of money. In the next place, fault may be found with his unequal division of property, for some will have far too much, others too little; by which means the land will come into few hands, which business is badly regulated by his laws. For he made it infamous for any one either to buy or sell their possessions, in which he did right; but he permitted any one that chose it to give them away, or bequeath them, although nearly the same consequences will arise from one practice as from the other. It is supposed that near two parts in five of the whole country is the property of women, owing to their being so often sole heirs, and having such large fortunes in marriage; though it would be better to allow them none, or a little, or a certain regulated proportion. Now every one is permitted to make a woman his heir if he pleases; and if he dies intestate, he who succeeds as heir at law gives it to whom he pleases. From whence it happens that although the country is able to support fifteen hundred horse and thirty thousand foot, the number does not amount to one thousand.

And from these facts it is evident, that this particular is badly regulated; for the city could not support one shock, but was ruined for want of men. They say, that during the reigns of their ancient kings they used to present foreigners with the freedom of their city, to prevent there being a want of men while they carried on long wars; it is also affirmed that the number of Spartans was formerly ten thousand; but be that as it will, an equality of property conduces much to increase the number of the people. The law, too, which he made to encourage population was by no means calculated to correct this inequality; for being willing that the Spartans should be as numerous as possible, to make them desirous of having large families he ordered that he who had three children should be excused the night-watch, and that he who had four should pay no taxes: though it is very evident, that while the land was divided in this manner, that if the people increased there must many of them be very poor.

Nor was he less blamable for the manner in which he constituted the ephori; for these magistrates take cognisance of things of the last importance, and yet they are chosen out of the people in general; so that it often happens that a very poor person is elected to that office, who, from that circumstance, is easily bought. There have been many instances of this formerly, as well as in the late affair at Andros. And these men, being corrupted with money, went as far as they could to ruin the city: and, because their power was too great and nearly tyrannical, their kings were obliged to natter them, which contributed greatly to hurt the state; so that it altered from an aristocracy to a democracy. This magistracy is indeed the great support of the state; for the people are easy, knowing that they are eligible to the first office in it; so that, whether it took place by the intention of the legislator, or whether it happened by chance, this is of great service to their affairs; for it is necessary that every member of the state should endeavour that each part of the government should be preserved, and continue the same. And upon this principle their kings have always acted, out of regard to their honour; the wise and good from their attachment to the senate, a seat wherein they consider as the reward of virtue; and the common people, that they may support the ephori, of whom they consist. And it is proper that these magistrates should be chosen out of the whole community, not as the custom is at present, which is very ridiculous. The ephori are the supreme judges in causes of the last consequence; but as it is quite accidental what sort of persons they may be, it is not right that they should determine according to their own opinion, but by a written law or established custom. Their way of life also is not consistent with the manners of the city, for it is too indulgent; whereas that of others is too severe; so that they cannot support it, but are obliged privately to act contrary to law, that they may enjoy some of the pleasures of sense. There are also great defects in the institution of their senators. If indeed they were fitly trained to the practice of every human virtue, every one would readily admit that they would be useful to the government; but still it might be debated whether they should be continued judges for life, to determine points of the greatest moment, since the mind has its old age as well as the body; but as they are so brought up, that even the legislator could not depend upon them as good men, their power must be inconsistent with the safety of the state: for it is known that the members of that body have been guilty both of bribery and partiality in many public affairs; for which reason it had been much better if they had been made answerable for their conduct, which they are not. But it may be said the ephori seem to have a check upon all the magistrates. They have indeed in this particular very great power; but I affirm that they should not be entrusted with this control in the manner they are. Moreover, the mode of choice which they make use of at the election of their senators is very childish. Nor is it right for any one to solicit for a place he is desirous of; for every person, whether he chooses it or not, ought to execute any office he is fit for. But his intention was evidently the same in this as in the other parts of his government. For making his citizens ambitious after honours, with men of that disposition he has filled his senate, since no others will solicit for that office; and yet the principal part of those crimes which men are deliberately guilty of arise from ambition and avarice.

We will inquire at another time whether the office of a king is useful to the state: thus much is certain, that they should be chosen from a consideration of their conduct and not as they are now. But that the legislator himself did not expect to make all his citizens honourable and completely virtuous is evident from this, that he distrusts them as not being good men; for he sent those upon the same embassy that were at variance with each other; and thought, that in the dispute of the kings the safety of the state consisted. Neither were their common meals at first well established: for these should rather have been provided at the public expense, as at Crete, where, as at Lacedaemon, every one was obliged to buy his portion, although he might be very poor, and could by no means bear the expense, by which means the contrary happened to what the legislator desired: for he intended that those public meals should strengthen the democratic part of his government: but this regulation had quite the contrary effect, for those who were very poor could not take part in them; and it was an observation of their forefathers, that the not allowing those who could not contribute their proportion to the common tables to partake of them, would be the ruin of the state. Other persons have censured his laws concerning naval affairs, and not without reason, as it gave rise to disputes. For the commander of the fleet is in a manner set up in opposition to the kings, who are generals of the army for life.

There is also another defect in his laws worthy of censure, which Plato has given in his book of Laws; that the whole constitution was calculated only for the business of war: it is indeed excellent to make them conquerors; for which reason the preservation of the state depended thereon. The destruction of it commenced with their victories: for they knew not how to be idle, or engage in any other employment than war. In this particular also they were mistaken, that though they rightly thought, that those things which are the objects of contention amongst mankind are better procured by virtue than vice, yet they wrongfully preferred the things themselves to virtue. Nor was the public revenue well managed at Sparta, for the state was worth nothing while they were obliged to carry on the most extensive wars, and the subsidies were very badly raised; for as the Spartans possessed a large extent of country, they were not exact upon each other as to what they paid in. And thus an event contrary to the legislator's intention took place; for the state was poor, the individuals avaricious. Enough of the Lacedaemonian government; for these seem the chief defects in it.

CHAPTER X

The government of Crete bears a near resemblance to this, in some few particulars it is not worse, but in general it is far inferior in its contrivance. For it appears and is allowed in many particulars the constitution of Lacedaemon was formed in imitation of that of Crete; and in general most new things are an improvement upon the old. For they say, that when Lycurgus ceased to be guardian to King Charilles he went abroad and spent a long time with his relations in Crete, for the Lycians are a colony of the Lacedaemonians; and those who first settled there adopted that body of laws which they found already established by the inhabitants; in like manner also those who now live near them have the very laws which Minos first drew up.

This island seems formed by nature to be the mistress of Greece, for it is entirely surrounded by a navigable ocean which washes almost all the maritime parts of that country, and is not far distant on the one side from Peloponnesus, on the other, which looks towards Asia, from Triopium and Rhodes. By means of this situation Minos acquired the empire of the sea and the islands; some of which he subdued, in others planted colonies: at last he died at Camicus while he was attacking Sicily. There is this analogy between the customs of the Lacedaemonians and the Cretans, the Helots cultivate the grounds for the one, the domestic slaves for the other. Both states have their common meals, and the Lacedaemonians called these formerly not psiditia but andpia, as the Cretans do; which proves from whence the custom arose. In this particular their governments are also alike: the ephori have the same power with those of Crete, who are called kosmoi; with this difference only, that the number of the one is five, of the other ten. The senators are the same as those whom the Cretans call the council. There was formerly also a kingly power in Crete; but it was afterwards dissolved, and the command of their armies was given to the kosmoi. Every one also has a vote in their public assembly; but this has only the power of confirming what has already passed the council and the kosmoi.

The Cretans conducted their public meals better than the Lacedaemonians, for at Lacedaemon each individual was obliged to furnish what was assessed upon him; which if he could not do, there was a law which deprived him of the rights of a citizen, as has been already mentioned: but in Crete they were furnished by the community; for all the corn and cattle, taxes and contributions, which the domestic slaves were obliged to furnish, were divided into parts and allotted to the gods, the exigencies of the state, and these public meals; so that all the men, women, and children were maintained from a common stock. The legislator gave great attention to encourage a habit of eating sparingly, as very useful to the citizens. He also endeavoured, that his community might not be too populous, to lessen the connection with women, by introducing the love of boys: whether in this he did well or ill we shall have some other opportunity of considering. But that the public meals were better ordered at Crete than at Lacedaemon is very evident.

The institution of the kosmoi, was still worse than that of the ephori: for it contained all the faults incident to that magistracy and some peculiar to itself; for in both cases it is uncertain who will be elected: but the Lacedaemonians have this advantage which the others have not, that as all are eligible, the whole community have a share in the highest honours, and therefore all desire to preserve the state:

whereas among the Cretans the kosmoi are not chosen out of the people in general, but out of some certain families, and the senate out of the kosmoi. And the same observations which may be made on the senate at Lacedaemon may be applied to these; for their being under no control, and their continuing for life, is an honour greater than they merit; and to have their proceedings not regulated by a written law, but left to their own discretion, is dangerous. (As to there being no insurrections, although the people share not in the management of public affairs, this is no proof of a well-constituted government, as the kosmoi have no opportunity of being bribed like the ephori, as they live in an island far from those who would corrupt them.) But the method they take to correct that fault is absurd, impolitic, and tyrannical: for very often either their fellow-magistrates or some private persons conspire together and turn out the kosmoi. They are also permitted to resign their office before their time is elapsed, and if all this was done by law it would be well, and not at the pleasure of the individuals, which is a bad rule to follow. But what is worst of all is, that general confusion which those who are in power introduce to impede the ordinary course of justice; which sufficiently shows what is the nature of the government, or rather lawless force: for it is usual with the principal persons amongst them to collect together some of the common people and their friends, and then revolt and set up for themselves, and come to blows with each other. And what is the difference, if a state is dissolved at once by such violent means, or if it gradually so alters in process of time as to be no longer the same constitution? A state like this would ever be exposed to the invasions of those who were powerful and inclined to attack it; but, as has been already mentioned, its situation preserves it, as it is free from the inroads of foreigners; and for this reason the family slaves still remain quiet at Crete, while the Helots are perpetually revolting: for the Cretans take no part in foreign affairs, and it is but lately that any foreign troops have made an attack upon the island; and their ravages soon proved the ineffectualness of their laws. And thus much for the government of Crete.

CHAPTER XI

The government of Carthage seems well established, and in many respects superior to others; in some particulars it bears a near resemblance to the Lacedaemonians; and indeed these three states, the Cretans, the Lacedaemonians and the Carthaginians are in some things very like each other, in others they differ greatly. Amongst many excellent constitutions this may show how well their government is framed, that although the people are admitted to a share in the administration, the form of it remains unaltered, without any popular insurrections, worth notice, on the one hand, or degenerating into a tyranny on the other. Now the Carthaginians have these things in common with the Lacedaemonians: public tables for those who are connected together by the tie of mutual friendship, after the manner of their Phiditia; they have also a magistracy, consisting of an hundred and four persons, similar to the ephori, or rather selected with more judgment; for amongst the Lacedaemonians, all the citizens are eligible, but amongst the Carthaginians, they are chosen out of those of the better sort: there is also some analogy between the king and the senate in both these governments, though the Carthaginian method of appointing their kings is best, for they do not confine themselves to one family; nor do they permit the election to be at large, nor have they any regard to seniority; for if amongst the candidates there are any of greater merit than the rest, these they prefer to those who may be older; for as their power is very extensive, if they are persons of no account, they may be very hurtful to the state, as they have always been to the Lacedaemonians; also the greater part of those things which become reprehensible by their excess are common to all those governments which we have described.

Now of those principles on which the Carthaginians have established their mixed form of government, composed of an aristocracy and democracy, some incline to produce a democracy, others an oligarchy: for instance, if the kings and the senate are unanimous upon any point in debate, they can choose whether they will bring it before the people or no; but if they disagree, it is to these they must appeal, who are not only to hear what has been approved of by the senate, but are finally to determine upon it; and whosoever chooses it, has a right to speak against any matter whatsoever that may be proposed, which is not permitted in other cases. The five, who elect each other, have very great and extensive powers; and these choose the hundred, who are magistrates of the highest rank: their power also continues longer than any other magistrates, for it commences before they come into office, and is prolonged after they are out of it; and in this particular the state inclines to an oligarchy: but as they are not elected by lot, but by suffrage, and are not permitted to take money, they are the greatest supporters imaginable of an aristocracy.

The determining all causes by the same magistrates, and not orae in one court and another in another, as at Lacedaemon, has the same influence. The constitution of Carthage is now shifting from an aristocracy to an oligarchy, in consequence of an opinion which is favourably entertained by many, who think that the magistrates in the community ought not to be persons of family only, but of fortune also; as it is impossible for those who are in bad circumstances to support the dignity of their office, or to be at leisure to apply to public business. As choosing men of fortune to be magistrates make a state incline to an oligarchy, and men of abilities to an aristocracy, so is there a third method of proceeding which took place in the polity of Carthage; for they have an eye to these two particulars when they elect their officers, particularly those of the highest rank, their kings and their generals. It must be admitted, that it was a great fault in their legislator not to guard against the constitution's degenerating from an aristocracy; for this is a most necessary thing to provide for at first, that those citizens who have the best abilities should never be obliged to do anything unworthy their character, but be always at leisure to serve the public, not only when in office, but also when private persons; for if once you are obliged to look among the wealthy, that you may have men at leisure to serve you, your greatest offices, of king and general, will soon become venal; in consequence of which, riches will be more honourable than virtue and a love of money be the ruling principle in the city-for what those who have the chief power regard as honourable will necessarily be the object which the citizens in general will aim at; and where the first honours are not paid to virtue, there the aristocratic form of government cannot flourish: for it is reasonable to conclude, that those who bought their places should generally make an advantage of what they laid out their money for; as it is absurd to suppose, that if a man of probity who is poor should be desirous of gaining something, a bad man should not endeavour to do the same, especially to reimburse himself; for which reason the magistracy should be formed of those who are most able to support an aristocracy. It would have been better for the legislature to have passed over the poverty of men of merit, and only to have taken care to have ensured them sufficient leisure, when in office, to attend to public affairs.

It seems also improper, that one person should execute several offices, which was approved of at Carthage; for one business is best done by one person; and it is the duty of the legislator to look to this, and not make the same person a musician and a shoemaker: so that where the state is not small it is more politic and more popular to admit many persons to have a share in the government; for, as I just now said, it is not only more usual, but everything is better and sooner done, when one thing only is allotted to one person: and this is evident both in the army and navy, where almost every one, in his turn, both commands and is under command. But as their government inclines to an oligarchy, they avoid the ill effects of it by always appointing some of the popular party to the government of cities to make their fortunes. Thus they consult this fault in their constitution and render it stable; but this is depending on chance; whereas the legislator ought to frame his government, that there the no room for insurrections. But now, if there should be any general calamity, and the people should revolt from their rulers, there is no remedy for reducing them to obedience by the laws. And these are the particulars of the Lacedaemonian, the Cretan, and the Carthaginian governments which seem worthy of commendation.

CHAPTER XII

Some of those persons who have written upon government had never any share in public affairs, but always led a private life. Everything worthy of notice in their works we have already spoke to. Others were legislators, some in their own cities, others were employed in regulating the governments of foreign states. Some of them only composed a body of laws; others formed the constitution also, as Lycurgus; and Solon, who did both. The Lacedaemonians have been already mentioned. Some persons think that Solon was an excellent legislator, who could dissolve a pure oligarchy, and save the people from that slavery which hung over them, and establish the ancient democratic form of government in his country; wherein every part of it was so framed as to be well adapted to the whole. In the senate of Areopagus an oligarchy was preserved; by the manner of electing their magistrates, an aristocracy; and in their courts of justice, a democracy.

Solon seems not to have altered the established form of government, either with respect to the senate or the mode of electing their magistrates; but to have raised the people to great consideration in the state by allotting the supreme judicial department to them; and for this some persons blame him, as having done what would soon overturn that balance of power he intended to establish; for by trying all causes whatsoever before the people, who were chosen by lot to determine them, it was necessary to flatter a tyrannical populace who had got this power; which contributed to bring the government to that pure democracy it now is.

Both Ephialtes and Pericles abridged the power of the Areopagites, the latter of whom introduced the method of paying those who attended the courts of justice: and thus every one who aimed at being popular proceeded increasing the power of the people to what we now see it. But it is evident that this was not Solon's intention, but that it arose from accident; for the people being the cause of the naval victory over the Medes, assumed greatly upon it, and enlisted themselves under factious demagogues, although opposed by the better part of the citizens. He thought it indeed most necessary to entrust the people with the choice of their magistrates and the power of calling them to account; for without that they must have been slaves and enemies to the other citizens: but he ordered them to elect those only who were persons of good account and property, either out of those who were worth five hundred medimns, or those who were called xeugitai, or those of the third census, who were called horsemen.

As for those of the fourth, which consisted of mechanics, they were incapable of any office. Zaleucus was the legislator of the Western Locrians, as was Charondas, the Catanean, of his own cities, and those also in Italy and Sicily which belonged to the Calcidians. Some persons endeavour to prove that Onomacritus, the Locrian, was the first person of note who drew up laws; and that he employed himself in that business while he was at Crete, where he continued some time to learn the prophetic art: and they say, that Thales was his companion; and that Lycurgus and Zaleucus were the scholars of Thales, and Charondas of Zaleucus; but those who advance this, advance what is repugnant to chronology. Philolaus also, of the family of the Bacchiades, was a Theban legislator. This man was very fond of Diocles, a victor in the Olympic games, and when he left his country from a disgust at an improper passion which his mother Alithoe had entertained for him, and settled at Thebes, Philolaus followed him, where they both died, and where they still show their tombs placed in view of each other, but so disposed, that one of them looks towards Corinth, the other does not; the reason they give for this is, that Diodes, from his detestation of his mother's passion, would have his tomb so placed that no one could see Corinth from it; but Philolaus chose that it might be seen from his: and this was the cause of their living at Thebes.

As Philolaus gave them laws concerning many other things, so did he upon adoption, which they call adoptive laws; and this he in particular did to preserve the number of families. Charondas did nothing new, except in actions for perjury, which he was the first person who took into particular consideration. He also drew up his laws with greater elegance and accuracy than even any of our present legislators. Philolaus introduced the law for the equal distribution of goods; Plato that for the community of women, children, and goods, and also for public tables for the women; and one concerning drunkenness, that they might observe sobriety in their symposiums. He also made a law concerning their warlike exercises; that they should acquire a habit of using both hands alike, as it was necessary that one hand should be as useful as the other.

As for Draco's laws, they were published when the government was already established, and they have nothing particular in them worth mentioning, except their severity on account of the enormity of their punishments. Pittacus was the author of some laws, but never drew up any form of government; one of which was this, that if a drunken man beat any person he should be punished more than if he did it when sober; for as people are more apt to be abusive when drunk than sober, he paid no consideration to the excuse which drunkenness might claim, but regarded only the common benefit. Andromadas Regmus was also a lawgiver to the Thracian talcidians. There are some laws of his concerning murders and heiresses extant, but these contain nothing that any one can say is new and his own. And thus much for different sorts of governments, as well those which really exist as those which different persons have proposed.

BOOK III

CHAPTER I

Every one who inquires into the nature of government, and what are its different forms, should make this almost his first question, What is a city? For upon this there is a dispute: for some persons say the city did this or that, while others say, not the city, but the oligarchy, or the tyranny. We see that the city is the only object which both the politician and legislator have in view in all they do: but government is a certain ordering of those who inhabit a city. As a city is a collective body, and, like other wholes, composed of many parts, it is evident our first inquiry must be, what a citizen is: for a city is a certain number of citizens. So that we must consider whom we ought to call citizen, and who is one; for this is often doubtful: for every one will not allow that this character is applicable to the same person; for that man who would be a citizen in a republic would very often not be one in an oligarchy. We do not include in this inquiry many of those who acquire this appellation out of the ordinary way, as honorary persons, for instance, but those only who have a natural right to it.

Now it is not residence which constitutes a man a citizen; for in this sojourners and slaves are upon an equality with him; nor will it be sufficient for this purpose, that you have the privilege of the laws, and may plead or be impleaded, for this all those of different nations, between whom there is a mutual agreement for that purpose, are allowed; although it very often happens, that sojourners have not a perfect right therein without the protection of a patron, to whom they are obliged to apply, which shows that their share in the community is incomplete. In like manner, with respect to boys who are not yet enrolled, or old men who are past war, we admit that they are in some respects citizens, but not completely so, but with some exceptions, for these are not yet arrived to years of maturity, and those are past service; nor is there any difference between them. But what we mean is sufficiently intelligible and clear, we want a complete citizen, one in whom there is no deficiency to be corrected to make him so. As to those who are banished, or infamous, there may be the same objections made and the same answer given. There is nothing that more characterises a complete citizen than having a share in the judicial and executive part of the government.

With respect to offices, some are fixed to a particular time, so that no person is, on any account, permitted to fill them twice; or else not till some certain period has intervened; others are not fixed, as a juryman's, and a member of the general assembly: but probably some one may say these are not offices, nor have the citizens in these capacities any share in the government; though surely it is ridiculous to say that those who have the principal power in the state bear no office in it. But this objection is of no weight, for it is only a dispute about words; as there is no general term which can be applied both to the office of a juryman and a member of the assembly. For the sake of distinction, suppose we call it an indeterminate office: but I lay it down as a maxim, that those are citizens who could exercise it. Such then is the description of a citizen who comes nearest to what all those who are called citizens are. Every one also should know, that of the component parts of those things which differ from each other in species, after the first or second remove, those which follow have either nothing at all or very little common to each.

Now we see that governments differ from each other in their form, and that some of them are defective, others as excellent as possible: for it is evident, that those which have many deficiencies and degeneracies in them must be far inferior to those which are without such faults. What I mean by degeneracies will be hereafter explained. Hence it is clear that the office of a citizen must differ as governments do from each other: for which reason he who is called a citizen has, in a democracy, every privilege which that station supposes. In other forms of government he may enjoy them; but not necessarily: for in some states the people have no power; nor have they any general assembly, but a few select men.

The trial also of different causes is allotted to different persons; as at Lacedaemon all disputes concerning contracts are brought before some of the ephori: the senate are the judges in cases of murder, and so on; some being to be heard by one magistrate, others by another: and thus at Carthage certain magistrates determine all causes. But our former description of a citizen will admit of correction; for in some governments the office of a juryman and a member of the general assembly is not an indeterminate one; but there are particular persons appointed for these purposes, some or all of the citizens being appointed jurymen or members of the general assembly, and this either for all causes and all public business whatsoever, or else for some particular one: and this may be sufficient to show what a citizen is; for he who has a right to a share in the judicial and executive part of government in any city, him we call a citizen of that place; and a city, in one word, is a collective body of such persons sufficient in themselves to all the purposes of life.

CHAPTER II

In common use they define a citizen to be one who is sprung from citizens on both sides, not on the father's or the mother's only. Others carry the matter still further, and inquire how many of his ancestors have been citizens, as his grandfather, great-grandfather, etc., but some persons have questioned how the first of the family could prove themselves citizens, according to this popular and careless definition. Gorgias of Leontium, partly entertaining the same doubt, and partly in jest, says, that as a mortar is made by a mortar-maker, so a citizen is made by a citizen-maker, and a Larisssean by a Larisssean-maker. This is indeed a very simple account of the matter; for if citizens are so, according to this definition, it will be impossible to apply it to the first founders or first inhabitants of states, who cannot possibly claim in right either of their father or mother. It is probably a matter of still more difficulty to determine their rights as citizens who are admitted to their freedom after any revolution in the state. As, for instance, at Athens, after the expulsion of the tyrants, when Clisthenes enrolled many foreigners and city-slaves amongst the tribes; and the doubt with respect to them was, not whether they were citizens or no, but whether they were legally so or not. Though indeed some persons may have this further doubt, whether a citizen can be a citizen when he is illegally made; as if an illegal citizen, and one who is no citizen at all, were in the same predicament: but since we see some persons govern unjustly, whom yet we admit to govern, though not justly, and the definition of a citizen is one who exercises certain offices, for such a one we have defined a citizen to be, it is evident, that a citizen illegally created yet continues to be a citizen, but whether justly or unjustly so belongs to the former inquiry.

CHAPTER III

It has also been doubted what was and what was not the act of the city; as, for instance, when a democracy arises out of an aristocracy or a tyranny; for some persons then refuse to fulfil their contracts; as if the right to receive the money was in the tyrant and not in the state, and many other things of the same nature; as if any covenant was founded for violence and not for the common good. So in like manner, if anything is done by those who have the management of public affairs where a democracy is established, their actions are to be considered as the actions of the state, as well as in the oligarchy or tyranny.

And here it seems very proper to consider this question, When shall we say that a city is the same, and when shall we say that it is different?

It is but a superficial mode of examining into this question to begin with the place and the people; for it may happen that these may be divided from that, or that some one of them may live in one place, and some in another (but this question may be regarded as no very knotty one; for, as a city may acquire that appellation on many accounts, it may be solved many ways); and in like manner, when men inhabit one common place, when shall we say that they inhabit the same city, or that the city is the same? for it does not depend upon the walls; for I can suppose Peloponnesus itself surrounded with a wall, as Babylon was, and every other place, which rather encircles many nations than one city, and that they say was taken three days when some of the inhabitants knew nothing of it: but we shall find a proper time to determine this question; for the extent of a city, how large it should be, and whether it should consist of more than one people, these are particulars that the politician should by no means be unacquainted with. This, too, is a matter of inquiry, whether we shall say that a city is the same while it is inhabited by the same race of men, though some of them are perpetually dying, others coming into the world, as we say that a river or a fountain is the same, though the waters are continually changing; or when a revolution takes place shall we say the men are the same, but the city is different: for if a city is a community, it is a community of citizens; but if the mode of government should alter, and become of another sort, it would seem a necessary consequence that the city is not the same; as we regard the tragic chorus as different from the comic, though it may probably consist of the same performers: thus every other community or composition is said to be different if the species of composition is different; as in music the same hands produce different harmony, as the Doric and Phrygian. If this is true, it is evident, that when we speak of a city as being the same we refer to the government there established; and this, whether it is called by the same name or any other, or inhabited by the same men or different. But whether or no it is right to dissolve the community when the constitution is altered is another question.

CHAPTER IV

What has been said, it follows that we should consider whether the same virtues which constitute a good man make a valuable citizen, or different; and if a particular inquiry is necessary for this matter we must first give a general description of the virtues of a good citizen; for as a sailor is one of those who make up a community, so is a citizen, although the province of one sailor may be different from another's (for one is a rower, another a steersman, a third a boatswain, and so on, each having their several appointments), it is evident that the most accurate description of any one good sailor must refer to his peculiar abilities, yet there are some things in which the same description may be applied to the whole crew, as the safety of the ship is the common business of all of them, for this is the general centre of all their cares: so also with respect to citizens, although they may in a few particulars be very different, yet there is one care common to them all, the safety of the community, for the community of the citizens composes the state; for which reason the virtue of a citizen has necessarily a reference to the state. But if there are different sorts of governments, it is evident that those actions which constitute the virtue of an excellent citizen in one community will not constitute it in another; wherefore the virtue of such a one cannot be perfect: but we say, a man is good when his virtues are perfect; from whence it follows, that an excellent citizen does not possess that virtue which constitutes a good man. Those who are any ways doubtful concerning this question may be convinced of the truth of it by examining into the best formed states: for, if it is impossible that a city should consist entirely of excellent citizens (while it is necessary that every one should do well in his calling, in which consists his excellence, as it is impossible that all the citizens should have the same qualifications) it is impossible that the virtue of a citizen and a good man should be the same; for all should possess the virtue of an excellent citizen: for from hence necessarily arise the perfection of the city: but that every one should possess the virtue of a good man is impossible without all the citizens in a well-regulated state were necessarily virtuous. Besides, as a city is composed of dissimilar parts, as an animal is of life and body; the soul of reason and appetite; a family of a man and his wife--property of a master and a slave; in the same manner, as a city is composed of all these and many other very different parts, it necessarily follows that the virtue of all the citizens cannot be the same; as the business of him who leads the band is different from the other dancers. From all which proofs it is evident that the virtues of a citizen cannot be one and the same. But do we never find those virtues united which constitute a good man and excellent citizen? for we say, such a one is an excellent magistrate and a prudent and good man; but prudence is a necessary qualification for all those who engage in public affairs. Nay, some persons affirm that the education of those who are intended to command should, from the beginning, be different from other citizens, as the children of kings are generally instructed in riding and warlike exercises; and thus Euripides says:

"... No showy arts Be mine, but teach me what the state requires."

As if those who are to rule were to have an education peculiar to themselves. But if we allow, that the virtues of a good man and a good magistrate may be the same, and a citizen is one who obeys the magistrate, it follows that the virtue of the one cannot in general be the same as the virtue of the other, although it may be true of some particular citizen; for the virtue of the magistrate must be different from the virtue of the citizen. For which reason Jason declared that was he deprived of his kingdom he should pine away with regret, as not knowing how to live a private man. But it is a great recommendation to know how to command as well as to obey; and to do both these things well is the virtue of an accomplished citizen. If then the virtue of a good man consists only in being able to command, but the virtue of a good citizen renders him equally fit for the one as well as the other, the commendation of both of them is not the same. It appears, then, that both he who commands and he who obeys should each of them learn their separate business: but that the citizen should be master of and take part in both these, as any one may easily perceive; in a family government there is no occasion for the master to know how to perform the necessary offices, but rather to enjoy the labour of others; for to do the other is a servile part. I mean by the other, the common family business of the slave.

There are many sorts of slaves; for their employments are various: of these the handicraftsmen are one, who, as their name imports, get their living by the labour of their hands, and amongst these all mechanics are included; for which reasons such workmen, in some states, were not formerly admitted into any share in the government; till at length democracies were established: it is not therefore proper for any man of honour, or any citizen, or any one who engages in public affairs, to learn these servile employments without they have occasion for them for their own use; for without this was observed the distinction between a master and a slave would be lost. But there is a government of another sort, in which men govern those who are their equals in rank, and freemen, which we call a political government, in which men learn to command by first submitting to obey, as a good general of horse, or a commander-in-chief, must acquire a knowledge of their duty by having been long under the command of another, and the like in every appointment in the army: for well is it said, no one knows how to command who has not himself been under command of another. The virtues of those are indeed different, but a good citizen must necessarily be endowed with them; he ought also to know in what manner freemen ought to govern, as well as be governed: and this, too, is the duty of a good man. And if the temperance and justice of him who commands is different from his who, though a freeman, is under command, it is evident that the virtues of a good citizen cannot be the same as justice, for instance but must be of a different species in these two different situations, as the temperance and courage of a man and a woman are different from each other; for a man would appear a coward who had only that courage which would be graceful in a woman, and a woman would be thought a talker who should take as large a part in the conversation as would become a man of consequence.

The domestic employments of each of them are also different; it is the man's business to acquire subsistence, the woman's to take care of it. But direction and knowledge of public affairs is a virtue peculiar to those who govern, while all others seem to be equally requisite for both parties; but with this the governed have no concern, it is theirs to entertain just notions: they indeed are like flute-makers, while those who govern are the musicians who play on them. And thus much to show whether the virtue of a good man and an excellent citizen is the same, or if it is different, and also how far it is the same, and how far different.

CHAPTER V

But with respect to citizens there is a doubt remaining, whether those only are truly so who are allowed to share in the government, or whether the mechanics also are to be considered as such? for if those who are not permitted to rule are to be reckoned among them, it is impossible that the virtue of all the citizens should be the same, for these also are citizens; and if none of them are admitted to be citizens, where shall they be ranked? for they are neither sojourners nor foreigners? or shall we say that there will no inconvenience arise from their not being citizens, as they are neither slaves nor freedmen: for this is certainly true, that all those are not citizens who are necessary to the existence of a city, as boys are not citizens in the same manner that men are, for those are perfectly so, the others under some conditions; for they are citizens, though imperfect ones: for in former times among some people the mechanics were either slaves or foreigners, for which reason many of them are so now: and indeed the best regulated states will not permit a mechanic to be a citizen; but if it be allowed them, we cannot then attribute the virtue we have described to every citizen or freeman, but to those only who are disengaged from servile offices. Now those who are employed by one person in them are slaves; those who do them for money are mechanics and hired servants: hence it is evident on the least reflection what is their situation, for what I have said is fully explained by appearances. Since the number of communities is very great, it follows necessarily that there will be many different sorts of citizens, particularly of those who are governed by others, so that in one state it may be necessary to admit mechanics and hired servants to be citizens, but in others it may be impossible; as particularly in an aristocracy, where honours are bestowed on virtue and dignity: for it is impossible for one who lives the life of a mechanic or hired servant to acquire the practice of virtue. In an oligarchy also hired servants are not admitted to be citizens; because there a man's right to bear any office is regulated by his fortune; but mechanics are, for many citizens are very rich.

There was a law at Thebes that no one could have a share in the government till he had been ten years out of trade. In many states the law invites strangers to accept the freedom of the city; and in some democracies the son of a free-woman is himself free. The same is also observed in many others with respect to natural children; but it is through want of citizens regularly born that they admit such: for these laws are always made in consequence of a scarcity of inhabitants; so, as their numbers increase, they first deprive the children of a male or female slave of this privilege, next the child of a free-woman, and last of all they will admit none but those whose fathers and mothers were both free.

That there are many sorts of citizens, and that he may be said to be as completely who shares the honours of the state, is evident from what has been already said. Thus Achilles, in Homer, complains of Agamemnon's treating him like an unhonoured stranger; for a stranger or sojourner is one who does not partake of the honours of the state: and whenever the right to the freedom of the city is kept obscure, it is for the sake of the inhabitants. From what has been said it is plain whether the virtue of a good man and an excellent citizen is the same or different: and we find that in some states it is the same, in others not; and also that this is not true of each citizen, but of those only who take the lead, or are capable of taking the lead, in public affairs, either alone or in conjunction with others.

CHAPTER VI

Having established these points, we proceed next to consider whether one form of government only should be established, or more than one; and if more, how many, and of what sort, and what are the differences between them. The form of government is the ordering and regulating of the city, and all the offices in it, particularly those wherein the supreme power is lodged; and this power is always possessed by the administration; but the administration itself is that particular form of government which is established in any state: thus in a democracy the supreme power is lodged in the whole people; on the contrary, in an oligarchy it is in the hands of a few. We say then, that the form of government in these states is different, and we shall find the same thing hold good in others. Let us first determine for whose sake a city is established; and point out the different species of rule which man may submit to in social life.

I have already mentioned in my treatise on the management of a family, and the power of the master, that man is an animal naturally formed for society, and that therefore, when he does not want any foreign assistance, he will of his own accord desire to live with others; not but that mutual advantage induces them to it, as far as it enables each person to live more agreeably; and this is indeed the great object not only to all in general, but also to each individual: but it is not merely matter of choice, but they join in society also, even that they may be able to live, which probably is not without some share of merit, and they also support civil society, even for the sake of preserving life, without they are grievously overwhelmed with the miseries of it: for it is very evident that men will endure many calamities for the sake of living, as being something naturally sweet and desirable. It is easy to point out the different modes of government, and we have already settled them in our exoteric discourses. The power of the master, though by nature equally serviceable, both to the master and to the slave, yet nevertheless has for its object the benefit of the master, while the benefit of the slave arises accidentally; for if the slave is destroyed, the power of the master is at an end: but the authority which a man has over his wife, and children, and his family, which we call domestic government, is either for the benefit of those who are under subjection, or else for the common benefit of the whole: but its particular object is the benefit of the governed, as we see in other arts; in physic, for instance, and the gymnastic exercises, wherein, if any benefit arise to the master, it is accidental; for nothing forbids the master of the exercises from sometimes being himself one of those who exercises, as the steersman is always one of the sailors; but both the master of the exercises and the steersman consider the good of those who are under their government. Whatever good may happen to the steersman when he is a sailor, or to the master of the exercises when he himself makes one at the games, is not intentional, or the object of their power; thus in all political governments which are established to preserve and defend the equality of the citizens it is held right to rule by turns. Formerly, as was natural, every one expected that each of his fellow-citizens should in his turn serve the public, and thus administer to his private good, as he himself when in office had done for others; but now every one is desirous of being continually in power, that he may enjoy the advantage which he makes of public business and being in office; as if places were a never-failing remedy for every complaint, and were on that account so eagerly sought after.

It is evident, then, that all those governments which have a common good in view are rightly established and strictly just, but those who have in view only the good of the rulers are all founded on wrong principles, and are widely different from what a government ought to be, for they are tyranny over slaves, whereas a city is a community of freemen.

CHAPTER VII

Having established these particulars, we come to consider next the different number of governments which there are, and what they are; and first, what are their excellencies: for when we have determined this, their defects will be evident enough.

It is evident that every form of government or administration, for the words are of the same import, must contain a supreme power over the whole state, and this supreme power must necessarily be in the hands of one person, or a few, or many; and when either of these apply their power for the common good, such states are well governed; but when the interest of the one, the few, or the many who enjoy this power is alone consulted, then ill; for you must either affirm that those who make up the community are not citizens, or else let these share in the advantages of government. We usually call a state which is governed by one person for the common good, a kingdom; one that is governed by more than one, but by a few only, an aristocracy; either because the government is in the hands of the most worthy citizens, or because it is the best form for the city and its inhabitants. When the citizens at large govern for the public good, it is called a state; which is also a common name for all other governments, and these distinctions are consonant to reason; for it will not be difficult to find one person, or a very few, of very distinguished abilities, but almost impossible to meet with the majority of a people eminent for every virtue; but if there is one common to a whole nation it is valour; for this is created and supported by numbers: for which reason in such a state the profession of arms will always have the greatest share in the government.

Now the corruptions attending each of these governments are these; a kingdom may degenerate into a tyranny, an aristocracy into an oligarchy, and a state into a democracy. Now a tyranny is a monarchy where the good of one man only is the object of government, an oligarchy considers only the rich, and a democracy only the poor; but neither of them have a common good in view.

CHAPTER VIII

It will be necessary to enlarge a little more upon the nature of each of these states, which is not without some difficulty, for he who would enter into a philosophical inquiry into the principles of them, and not content himself with a superficial view of their outward conduct, must pass over and omit nothing, but explain the true spirit of each of them. A tyranny then is, as has been said, a monarchy, where one person has an absolute and despotic power over the whole community and every member therein: an oligarchy, where the supreme power of the state is lodged with the rich: a democracy, on the contrary, is where those have it who are worth little or nothing. But the first difficulty that arises from the distinctions which we have laid down is this, should it happen that the majority of the inhabitants who possess the power of the state (for this is a democracy) should be rich, the question is, how does this agree with what we have said? The same difficulty occurs, should it ever happen that the poor compose a smaller part of the people than the rich, but from their superior abilities acquire the supreme power; for this is what they call an oligarchy; it should seem then that our definition of the different states was not correct: nay, moreover, could any one suppose that the majority of the people were poor, and the minority rich, and then describe the state in this manner, that an oligarchy was a government in which the rich, being few in number, possessed the supreme power, and that a democracy was a state in which the poor, being many in number, possessed it, still there will be another difficulty; for what name shall we give to those states we have been describing? I mean, that in which the greater number are rich, and that in which the lesser number are poor (where each of these possess the supreme power), if there are no other states than those we have described. It seems therefore evident to reason, that whether the supreme power is vested in the hands of many or few may be a matter of accident; but that it is clear enough, that when it is in the hands of the few, it will be a government of the rich; when in the hands of the many, it will be a government of the poor; since in all countries there are many poor and few rich: it is not therefore the cause that has been already assigned (namely, the number of people in power) that makes the difference between the two governments; but an oligarchy and democracy differ in this from each other, in the poverty of those who govern in the one, and the riches of those who govern in the other; for when the government is in the hands of the rich, be they few or be they more, it is an oligarchy; when it is in the hands of the poor, it is a democracy: but, as we have already said, the one will be always few, the other numerous, but both will enjoy liberty; and from the claims of wealth and liberty will arise continual disputes with each other for the lead in public affairs.

CHAPTER IX

Let us first determine what are the proper limits of an oligarchy and a democracy, and what is just in each of these states; for all men have some natural inclination to justice; but they proceed therein only to a certain degree; nor can they universally point out what is absolutely just; as, for instance, what is equal appears just, and is so; but not to all; only among those who are equals: and what is unequal appears just, and is so; but not to all, only amongst those who are unequals; which circumstance some people neglect, and therefore judge ill; the reason for which is, they judge for themselves, and every one almost is the worst judge in his own cause. Since then justice has reference to persons, the same distinctions must be made with respect to persons which are made with respect to things, in the manner that I have already described in my Ethics.

As to the equality of the things, these they agree in; but their dispute is concerning the equality of the persons, and chiefly for the reason above assigned; because they judge ill in their own cause; and also because each party thinks, that if they admit what is right in some particulars, they have done justice on the whole: thus, for instance, if some persons are unequal in riches, they suppose them unequal in the whole; or, on the contrary, if they are equal in liberty, they suppose them equal in the whole: but what is absolutely just they omit; for if civil society was founded for the sake of preserving and increasing property, every one's right in the city would be equal to his fortune; and then the reasoning of those who insist upon an oligarchy would be valid; for it would not be right that he who contributed one mina should have an equal share in the hundred along with him who brought in all the rest, either of the original money or what was afterwards acquired.

Nor was civil society founded merely to preserve the lives of its members; but that they might live well: for otherwise a state might be composed of slaves, or the animal creation: but this is not so; for these have no share in the happiness of it; nor do they live after their own choice; nor is it an alliance mutually to defend each other from injuries, or for a commercial intercourse: for then the Tyrrhenians and Carthaginians, and all other nations between whom treaties of commerce subsist, would be citizens of one city; for they have articles to regulate their exports and imports, and engagements for mutual protection, and alliances for mutual defence; but yet they have not all the same magistrates established among them, but they are different among the different people; nor does the one take any care, that the morals of the other should be as they ought, or that none of those who have entered into the common agreements should be unjust, or in any degree vicious, only that they do not injure any member of the confederacy. But whosoever endeavours to establish wholesome laws in a state, attends to the virtues and the vices of each individual who composes it; from whence it is evident, that the first care of him who would found a city, truly deserving that name, and not nominally so, must be to have his citizens virtuous; for otherwise it is merely an alliance for self-defence; differing from those of the same cast which are made between different people only in place: for law is an agreement and a pledge, as the sophist Lycophron says, between the citizens of their intending to do justice to each other, though not sufficient to make all the citizens just and good: and that this is fact is evident, for could any one bring different places together, as, for instance, enclose Megara and Corinth in a wall, yet they would not be one city, not even if the inhabitants intermarried with each other, though this inter-community contributes much to make a place one city. Besides, could we suppose a set of people to live separate from each other, but within such a distance as would admit of an intercourse, and that there were laws subsisting between each party, to prevent their injuring one another in their mutual dealings, supposing one a carpenter, another a husbandman, shoemaker, and the like, and that their numbers were ten thousand, still all that they would have together in common would be a tariff for trade, or an alliance for mutual defence, but not the same city. And why? not because their mutual intercourse is not near enough, for even if persons so situated should come to one place, and every one should live in his own house as in his native city, and there should be alliances subsisting between each party to mutually assist and prevent any injury being done to the other, still they would not be admitted to be a city by those who think correctly, if they preserved the same customs when they were together as when they were separate.

It is evident, then, that a city is not a community of place; nor established for the sake of mutual safety or traffic with each other; but that these things are the necessary consequences of a city, although they may all exist where there is no city: but a city is a society of people joining together with their families and their children to live agreeably for the sake of having their lives as happy and as independent as possible: and for this purpose it is necessary that they should live in one place and intermarry with each other: hence in all cities there are family-meetings, clubs, sacrifices, and public entertainments to promote friendship; for a love of sociability is friendship itself; so that the end then for which a city is established is, that the inhabitants of it may live happy, and these things are conducive to that end: for it is a community of families and villages for the sake of a perfect independent life; that is, as we have already said, for the sake of living well and happily. It is not therefore founded for the purpose of men's merely living together, but for their living as men ought; for which reason those who contribute most to this end deserve to have greater power in the city than those who are their equals in family and freedom, but their inferiors in civil virtue, or those who excel them in wealth but are below them in worth. It is evident from what has been said, that in all disputes upon government each party says something that is just.

CHAPTER X

It may also be a doubt where the supreme power ought to be lodged. Shall it be with the majority, or the wealthy, with a number of proper persons, or one better than the rest, or with a tyrant? But whichever of these we prefer some difficulty will arise. For what? shall the poor have it because they are the majority? they may then divide among themselves, what belongs to the rich: nor is this unjust; because truly it has been so judged by the supreme power. But what avails it to point out what is the height of injustice if this is not? Again, if the many seize into their own hands everything which belongs to the few, it is evident that the city will be at an end. But virtue will never destroy what is virtuous; nor can what is right be the ruin of the state: therefore such a law can never be right, nor can the acts of a tyrant ever be wrong, for of necessity they must all be just; for he, from his unlimited power, compels every one to obey his command, as the multitude oppress the rich. Is it right then that the rich, the few, should have the supreme power? and what if they be guilty of the same rapine and plunder the possessions of the majority, that will be as right as the other: but that all things of this sort are wrong and unjust is evident. Well then, these of the better sort shall have it: but must not then all the other citizens live unhonoured, without sharing the offices of the city; for the offices of a city are its honours, and if one set of men are always in power, it is evident that the rest must be without honour. Well then, let it be with one person of all others the fittest for it: but by this means the power will be still more contracted, and a greater number than before continue unhonoured. But some one may say, that it is wrong to let man have the supreme power and not the law, as his soul is subject to so many passions. But if this law appoints an aristocracy, or a democracy, how will it help us in our present doubts? for those things will happen which we have already mentioned.

CHAPTER XI

Other particulars we will consider separately; but it seems proper to prove, that the supreme power ought to be lodged with the many, rather than with those of the better sort, who are few; and also to explain what doubts (and probably just ones) may arise: now, though not one individual of the many may himself be fit for the supreme power, yet when these many are joined together, it does not follow but they may be better qualified for it than those; and this not separately, but as a collective body; as the public suppers exceed those which are given at one person's private expense: for, as they are many, each person brings in his share of virtue and wisdom; and thus, coming together, they are like one man made up of a multitude, with many feet, many hands, and many intelligences: thus is it with respect to the manners and understandings of the multitude taken together; for which reason the public are the best judges of music and poetry; for some understand one part, some another, and all collectively the whole; and in this particular men of consequence differ from each of the many; as they say those who are beautiful do from those who are not so, and as fine pictures excel any natural objects, by collecting the several beautiful parts which were dispersed among different originals into one, although the separate parts, as the eye or any other, might be handsomer than in the picture.

But if this distinction is to be made between every people and every general assembly, and some few men of consequence, it may be doubtful whether it is true; nay, it is clear enough that, with respect to a few, it is not; since the same conclusion might be applied even to brutes: and indeed wherein do some men differ from brutes? Not but that nothing prevents what I have said being true of the people in some states. The doubt then which we have lately proposed, with all its consequences, may be settled in this manner; it is necessary that the freemen who compose the bulk of the people should have absolute power in some things; but as they are neither men of property, nor act uniformly upon principles of virtue, it is not safe to trust them with the first offices in the state, both on account of their iniquity and their ignorance; from the one of which they will do what is wrong, from the other they will mistake: and yet it is dangerous to allow them no power or share in the government; for when there are many poor people who are incapable of acquiring the honours of their country, the state must necessarily have many enemies in it; let them then be permitted to vote in the public assemblies and to determine causes; for which reason Socrates, and some other legislators, gave them the power of electing the officers of the state, and also of inquiring into their conduct when they came out of office, and only prevented their being magistrates by themselves; for the multitude when they are collected together have all of them sufficient understanding for these purposes, and, mixing among those of higher rank, are serviceable to the city, as some things, which alone are improper for food, when mixed with others make the whole more wholesome than a few of them would be.

But there is a difficulty attending this form of government, for it seems, that the person who himself was capable of curing any one who was then sick, must be the best judge whom to employ as a physician; but such a one must be himself a physician; and the same holds true in every other practice and art: and as a physician ought to give an account of his practice to a physician, so ought it to be in other arts: those whose business is physic may be divided into three sorts, the first of these is he who makes up the medicines; the second prescribes, and is to the other as the architect is to the mason; the third is he who understands the science, but never practises it: now these three distinctions may be found in those who understand all other arts; nor have we less opinion of their judgment who are only instructed in the principles of the art than of those who practise it: and with respect to elections the same method of proceeding seems right; for to elect a proper person in any science is the business of those who are skilful therein; as in geometry, of geometricians; in steering, of steersmen: but if some individuals should know something of particular arts and works, they do not know more than the professors of them: so that even upon this principle neither the election of magistrates, nor the censure of their conduct, should be entrusted to the many.

But probably all that has been here said may not be right; for, to resume the argument I lately used, if the people are not very brutal indeed, although we allow that each individual knows less of these affairs than those who have given particular attention to them, yet when they come together they will know them better, or at least not worse; besides, in some particular arts it is not the workman only who is the best judge; namely, in those the works of which are understood by those who do not profess them: thus he who builds a house is not the only judge of it, for the master of the family who inhabits it is a better; thus also a steersman is a better judge of a tiller than he who made it; and he who gives an entertainment than the cook. What has been said seems a sufficient solution of this difficulty; but there is another that follows: for it seems absurd that the power of the state should be lodged with those who are but of indifferent morals, instead of those who are of excellent characters. Now the power of election and censure are of the utmost consequence, and this, as has been said, in some states they entrust to the people; for the general assembly is the supreme court of all, and they have a voice in this, and deliberate in all public affairs, and try all causes, without any objection to the meanness of their circumstances, and at any age: but their treasurers, generals, and other great officers of state are taken from men of great fortune and worth. This difficulty also may be solved upon the same principle; and here too they may be right, for the power is not in the man who is member of the assembly, or council, but the assembly itself, and the council, and the people, of which each individual of the whole community are the parts, I mean as senator, adviser, or judge; for which reason it is very right, that the many should have the greatest powers in their own hands; for the people, the council, and the judges are composed of them, and the property of all these collectively is more than the property of any person or a few who fill the great offices of the state: and thus I determine these points.

The first question that we stated shows plainly, that the supreme power should be lodged in laws duly made and that the magistrate or magistrates, either one or more, should be authorised to determine those cases which the laws cannot particularly speak to, as it is impossible for them, in general language, to explain themselves upon everything that may arise: but what these laws are which are established upon the best foundations has not been yet explained, but still remains a matter of some question: but the laws of every state will necessarily be like every state, either trifling or excellent, just or unjust; for it is evident, that the laws must be framed correspondent to the constitution of the government; and, if so, it is plain, that a well-formed government will have good laws, a bad one, bad ones.

CHAPTER XII

Since in every art and science the end aimed at is always good, so particularly in this, which is the most excellent of all, the founding of civil society, the good wherein aimed at is justice; for it is this which is for the benefit of all. Now, it is the common opinion, that justice is a certain equality; and in this point all the philosophers are agreed when they treat of morals: for they say what is just, and to whom; and that equals ought to receive equal: but we should know how we are to determine what things are equal and what unequal; and in this there is some difficulty, which calls for the philosophy of the politician. Some persons will probably say, that the employments of the state ought to be given according to every particular excellence of each citizen, if there is no other difference between them and the rest of the community, but they are in every respect else alike: for justice attributes different things to persons differing from each other in their character, according to their respective merits. But if this is admitted to be true, complexion, or height, or any such advantage will be a claim for a greater share of the public rights. But that this is evidently absurd is clear from other arts and sciences; for with respect to musicians who play on the flute together, the best flute is not given to him who is of the best family, for he will play never the better for that, but the best instrument ought to be given to him who is the best artist.

If what is now said does not make this clear, we will explain it still further: if there should be any one, a very excellent player on the flute, but very deficient in family and beauty, though each of them are more valuable endowments than a skill in music, and excel this art in a higher degree than that player excels others, yet the best flutes ought to be given to him; for the superiority in beauty and fortune should have a reference to the business in hand; but these have none. Moreover, according to this reasoning, every possible excellence might come in comparison with every other; for if bodily strength might dispute the point with riches or liberty, even any bodily strength might do it; so that if one person excelled in size more than another did in virtue, and his size was to qualify him to take place of the other's virtue, everything must then admit of a comparison with each other; for if such a size is greater than virtue by so much, it is evident another must be equal to it: but, since this is impossible, it is plain that it would be contrary to common sense to dispute a right to any office in the state from every superiority whatsoever: for if one person is slow and the other swift, neither is the one better qualified nor the other worse on that account, though in the gymnastic races a difference in these particulars would gain the prize; but a pretension to the offices of the state should be founded on a superiority in those qualifications which are useful to it: for which reason those of family, independency, and fortune, with great propriety, contend with each other for them; for these are the fit persons to fill them: for a city can no more consist of all poor men than it can of all slaves But if such persons are requisite, it is evident that those also who are just and valiant are equally so; for without justice and valour no state can be supported, the former being necessary for its existence, the latter for its happiness.

CHAPTER XIII

It seems, then, requisite for the establishment of a state, that all, or at least many of these particulars should be well canvassed and inquired into; and that virtue and education may most justly claim the right of being considered as the necessary means of making the citizens happy, as we have already said. As those who are equal in one particular are not therefore equal in all, and those who are unequal in one particular are not therefore unequal in all, it follows that all those governments which are established upon a principle which supposes they are, are erroneous.

We have already said, that all the members of the community will dispute with each other for the offices of the state; and in some particulars justly, but not so in general; the rich, for instance, because they have the greatest landed property, and the ultimate right to the soil is vested in the community; and also because their fidelity is in general most to be depended on. The freemen and men of family will dispute the point with each other, as nearly on an equality; for these latter have a right to a higher regard as citizens than obscure persons, for honourable descent is everywhere of great esteem: nor is it an improper conclusion, that the descendants of men of worth will be men of worth themselves; for noble birth is the fountain of virtue to men of family: for the same reason also we justly say, that virtue has a right to put in her pretensions. Justice, for instance, is a virtue, and so necessary to society, that all others must yield her the precedence.

Let us now see what the many have to urge on their side against the few; and they may say, that if, when collectively taken, they are compared with them, they are stronger, richer, and better than they are. But should it ever happen that all these should inhabit the same city, I mean the good, the rich, the noble, as well as the many, such as usually make up the community, I ask, will there then be any reason to dispute concerning who shall govern, or will there not? for in every community which we have mentioned there is no dispute where the supreme power should be placed; for as these differ from each other, so do those in whom that is placed; for in one state the rich enjoy it, in others the meritorious, and thus each according to their separate manners. Let us however consider what is to be done when all these happen at the same time to inhabit the same city. If the virtuous should be very few in number, how then shall we act? shall we prefer the virtuous on account of their abilities, if they are capable of governing the city? or should they be so many as almost entirely to compose the state?

There is also a doubt concerning the pretensions of all those who claim the honours of government: for those who found them either on fortune or family have nothing which they can justly say in their defence; since it is evident upon their principle, that if any one person can be found richer than all the rest, the right of governing all these will be justly vested in this one person. In the same manner, one man who is of the best family will claim it from those who dispute the point upon family merit: and probably in an aristocracy the same dispute might arise on the score of virtue, if there is one man better than all the other men of worth who are in the same community; it seems just, by the same reasoning, that he should enjoy the supreme power. And upon this principle also, while the many suppose they ought to have the supreme command, as being more powerful than the few, if one or more than one, though a small number should be found stronger than themselves, these ought rather to have it than they.

All these things seem to make it plain, that none of these principles are justly founded on which these persons would establish their right to the supreme power; and that all men whatsoever ought to obey them: for with respect to those who claim it as due to their virtue or their fortune, they might have justly some objection to make; for nothing hinders but that it may sometimes happen, that the many may be better or richer than the few, not as individuals, but in their collective capacity.

As to the doubt which some persons have proposed and objected, we may answer it in this manner; it is this, whether a legislator, who would establish the most perfect system of laws, should calculate them for the use of the better part of the citizens, or the many, in the circumstances we have already mentioned? The rectitude of anything consists in its equality; that therefore which is equally right will be advantageous to the whole state, and to every member of it in common.

Now, in general, a citizen is one who both shares in the government and also in his turn submits to be governed; their condition, it is true, is different in different states: the best is that in which a man is enabled to choose and to persevere in a course of virtue during his whole life, both in his public and private state. But should there be one person, or a very few, eminent for an uncommon degree of virtue, though not enough to make up a civil state, so that the virtue of the many, or their political abilities, should be too inferior to come in comparison with theirs, if more than one; or if but one, with his only; such are not to be considered as part of the city; for it would be doing them injustice to rate them on a level with those who are so far their inferiors in virtue and political abilities, that they appear to them like a god amongst men. From whence it is evident, that a system of laws must be calculated for those who are equal to each other in nature and power. Such men, therefore, are not the object of law; for they are themselves a law: and it would be ridiculous in any one to endeavour to include them in the penalties of a law: for probably they might say what Antisthenes tells us the lions did to the hares when they demanded to be admitted to an equal share with them in the government. And it is on this account that democratic states have established the ostracism; for an equality seems the principal object of their government. For which reason they compel all those who are very eminent for their power, their fortune, their friendships, or any other cause which may give them too great weight in the government, to submit to the ostracism, and leave the city for a stated time; as the fabulous histories relate the Argonauts served Hercules, for they refused to take him with them in the ship Argo on account of his superior valour. For which reason those who hate a tyranny and find fault with the advice which Periander gave to Thrasybulus, must not think there was nothing to be said in its defence; for the story goes, that Periander said nothing to the messenger in answer to the business he was consulted about, but striking off those ears of corn which were higher than the rest, reduced the whole crop to a level; so that the messenger, without knowing the cause of what was done, related the fact to Thrasybulus, who understood by it that he must take off all the principal men in the city. Nor is this serviceable to tyrants only; nor is it tyrants only who do it; for the same thing is practised both in oligarchies and democracies: for the ostracism has in a manner nearly the same power, by restraining and banishing those who are too great; and what is done in one city is done also by those who have the supreme power in separate states; as the Athenians with respect to the Samians, the Chians, and the Lesbians; for when they suddenly acquired the superiority over all Greece, they brought the other states into subjection, contrary to the treaties which subsisted between them. The King of Persia also very often reduces the Medes and Babylonians when they assume upon their former power: and this is a principle which all governments whatsoever keep in their eye; even those which are best administered, as well as those which are not, do it; these for the sake of private utility, the others for the public good.

The same thing is to be perceived in the other arts and sciences; for a painter would not represent an animal with a foot disproportionally large, though he had drawn it remarkably beautiful; nor would the shipwright make the prow or any other part of the vessel larger than it ought to be; nor will the master of the band permit any who sings louder and better than the rest to sing in concert with them. There is therefore no reason that a monarch should not act in agreement with free states, to support his own power, if they do the same thing for the benefit of their respective communities; upon which account when there is any acknowledged difference in the power of the citizens, the reason upon which the ostracism is founded will be politically just; but it is better for the legislator so to establish his state at the beginning as not to want this remedy: but if in course of time such an inconvenience should arise, to endeavour to amend it by some such correction. Not that this was the use it was put to: for many did not regard the benefit of their respective communities, but made the ostracism a weapon in the hand of sedition.

It is evident, then, that in corrupt governments it is partly just and useful to the individual, though probably it is as clear that it is not entirely just: for in a well-governed state there may be great doubts about the use of it, not on account of the pre-eminence which one may have in strength, riches, or connection: but when the pre-eminence is virtue, what then is to be done? for it seems not right to turn out and banish such a one; neither does it seem right to govern him, for that would be like desiring to share the power with Jupiter and to govern him: nothing then remains but what indeed seems natural, and that is for all persons quietly to submit to the government of those who are thus eminently virtuous, and let them be perpetually kings in the separate states.

CHAPTER XIV

What has been now said, it seems proper to change our subject and to inquire into the nature of monarchies; for we have already admitted them to be one of those species of government which are properly founded. And here let us consider whether a kingly government is proper for a city or a country whose principal object is the happiness of the inhabitants, or rather some other. But let us first determine whether this is of one kind only, or more; and it is easy to know that it consists of many different species, and that the forms of government are not the same in all: for at Sparta the kingly power seems chiefly regulated by the laws; for it is not supreme in all circumstances; but when the king quits the territories of the state he is their general in war; and all religious affairs are entrusted to him: indeed the kingly power with them is chiefly that of a general who cannot be called to an account for his conduct, and whose command is for life: for he has not the power of life and death, except as a general; as they frequently had in their expeditions by martial law, which we learn from Homer; for when Agamemnon is affronted in council, he restrains his resentment, but when he is in the field and armed with this power, he tells the Greeks:

"Whoe'er I know shall shun th' impending fight,
To dogs and vultures soon shall be a prey; For death is mine...."

This, then, is one species of monarchical government in which the kingly power is in a general for life; and is sometimes hereditary, sometimes elective: besides, there is also another, which is to be met with among some of the barbarians, in which the kings are invested with powers nearly equal to a tyranny, yet are, in some respects, bound by the laws and the customs of their country; for as the barbarians are by nature more prone to slavery than the Greeks, and those in Asia more than those in Europe, they endure without murmuring a despotic government; for this reason their governments are tyrannies; but yet not liable to be overthrown, as being customary and according to law. Their guards also are such as are used in a kingly government, not a despotic one; for the guards of their kings are his citizens, but a tyrant's are foreigners. The one commands, in the manner the law directs, those who willingly obey; the other, arbitrarily, those who consent not. The one, therefore, is guarded by the citizens, the other against them.

These, then, are the two different sorts of these monarchies, and another is that which in ancient Greece they called aesumnetes; which is nothing more than an elective tyranny; and its difference from that which is to be found amongst the barbarians consists not in its not being according to law, but only in its not being according to the ancient customs of the country. Some persons possessed this power for life, others only for a particular time or particular purpose, as the people of Mitylene elected Pittacus to oppose the exiles, who were headed by Antimenides and Alcaeus the poet, as we learn from a poem of his; for he upbraids the Mitylenians for having chosen Pittacus for their tyrant, and with one voice extolling him to the skies who was the ruin of a rash and devoted people. These sorts of government then are, and ever were, despotic, on account of their being tyrannies; but inasmuch as they are elective, and over a free people, they are also kingly.

A fourth species of kingly government is that which was in use in the heroic times, when a free people submitted to a kingly government, according to the laws and customs of their country. For those who were at first of benefit to mankind, either in arts or arms, or by collecting them into civil society, or procuring them an establishment, became the kings of a willing people, and established an hereditary monarchy. They were particularly their generals in war, and presided over their sacrifices, excepting such only as belonged to the priests: they were also the supreme judges over the people; and in this case some of them took an oath, others did not; they did, the form of swearing was by their sceptre held out.

In ancient times the power of the kings extended to everything whatsoever, both civil, domestic, and foreign; but in after-times they relinquished some of their privileges, and others the people assumed, so that, in some states, they left their kings only the right of presiding over the sacrifices; and even those whom it were worth while to call by that name had only the right of being commander-in-chief in their foreign wars.

These, then, are the four sorts of kingdoms: the first is that of the heroic times; which was a government over a free people, with its rights in some particulars marked out; for the king was their general, their judge, and their high priest. The second, that of the barbarians; which is an hereditary despotic government regulated by laws: the third is that which they call aesumnetic, which is an elective tyranny. The fourth is the Lacedaemonian; and this, in few words, is nothing more than an hereditary generalship: and in these particulars they differ from each other. There is a fifth species of kingly government, which is when one person has a supreme power over all things whatsoever, in the manner that every state and every city has over those things which belong to the public: for as the master of a family is king in his own house, so such a king is master of a family in his own city or state.

CHAPTER XV

But the different sorts of kingly governments may, if I may so say, be reduced to two; which we will consider more particularly. The last spoken of, and the Lacedaemonian, for the chief of the others are placed between these, which are as it were at the extremities, they having less power than an absolute government, and yet more than the Lacedaemonians; so that the whole matter in question may be reduced to these two points; the one is, whether it is advantageous to the citizens to have the office of general continue in one person for life, and whether it should be confined to any particular families or whether every one should be eligible: the other, whether it is advantageous for one person to have the supreme power over everything or not. But to enter into the particulars concerning the office of a Lacedaemonian general would be rather to frame laws for a state than to consider the nature and utility of its constitution, since we know that the appointing of a general is what is done in every state. Passing over this question then, we will proceed to consider the other part of their government, which is the polity of the state; and this it will be necessary to examine particularly into, and to go through such questions as may arise.

Now the first thing which presents itself to our consideration is this, whether it is best to be governed by a good man, or by good laws? Those who prefer a kingly government think that laws can only speak a general language, but cannot adapt themselves to particular circumstances; for which reason it is absurd in any science to follow written rule; and even in Egypt the physician was allowed to alter the mode of cure which the law prescribed to him, after the fourth day; but if he did it sooner it was at his own peril: from whence it is evident, on the very same account, that a government of written laws is not the best; and yet general reasoning is necessary to all those who are to govern, and it will be much more perfect in those who are entirely free from passions than in those to whom they are natural. But now this is a quality which laws possess; while the other is natural to the human soul. But some one will say in answer to this, that man will be a better judge of particulars. It will be necessary, then, for a king to be a lawgiver, and that his laws should be published, but that those should have no authority which are absurd, as those which are not, should. But whether is it better for the community that those things which cannot possibly come under the cognisance of the law either at all or properly should be under the government of every worthy citizen, as the present method is, when the public community, in their general assemblies, act as judges and counsellors, where all their determinations are upon particular cases, for one individual, be he who he will, will be found, upon comparison, inferior to a whole people taken collectively: but this is what a city is, as a public entertainment is better than one man's portion: for this reason the multitude judge of many things better than any one single person. They are also less liable to corruption from their numbers, as water is from its quantity: besides, the judgment of an individual must necessarily be perverted if he is overcome by anger or any other passion; but it would be hard indeed if the whole community should be misled by anger. Moreover, let the people be free, and they will do nothing but in conformity to the law, except only in those cases which the law cannot speak to. But though what I am going to propose may not easily be met with, yet if the majority of the state should happen to be good men, should they prefer one uncorrupt governor or many equally good, is it not evident that they should choose the many? But there may be divisions among these which cannot happen when there is but one. In answer to this it may be replied that all their souls will be as much animated with virtue as this one man's.

If then a government of many, and all of them good men, compose an aristocracy, and the government of one a kingly power, it is evident that the people should rather choose the first than the last; and this whether the state is powerful or not, if many such persons so alike can be met with: and for this reason probable it was, that the first governments were generally monarchies; because it was difficult to find a number of persons eminently virtuous, more particularly as the world was then divided into small communities; besides, kings were appointed in return for the benefits they had conferred on mankind; but such actions are peculiar to good men: but when many persons equal in virtue appeared at the time, they brooked not a superiority, but sought after an equality and established a free state; but after this, when they degenerated, they made a property of the public; which probably gave rise to oligarchies; for they made wealth meritorious, and the honours of government were reserved for the rich: and these afterwards turned to tyrannies and these in their turn gave rise to democracies; for the power of the tyrants continually decreasing, on account of their rapacious avarice, the people grew powerful enough to frame and establish democracies: and as cities after that happened to increase, probably it was not easy for them to be under any other government than a democracy. But if any person prefers a kingly government in a state, what is to be done with the king's children? Is the family also to reign? But should they have such children as some persons usually have, it will be very detrimental. It may be said, that then the king who has it in his power will never permit such children to succeed to his kingdom. But it is not easy to trust to that; for it is very hard and requires greater virtue than is to be met with in human nature. There is also a doubt concerning the power with which a king should be entrusted: whether he should be allowed force sufficient to compel those who do not choose to be obedient to the laws, and how he is to support his government? for if he is to govern according to law and do nothing of his own will which is contrary thereunto, at the same time it will be necessary to protect that power with which he guards the law, This matter however may not be very difficult to determine; for he ought to have a proper power, and such a one is that which will be sufficient to make the king superior to any one person or even a large part of the community, but inferior to the whole, as the ancients always appointed guards for that person whom they created aesumnetes or tyrant; and some one advised the Syracusians, when Dionysius asked for guards, to allow him such.

CHAPTER XVI

We will next consider the absolute monarch that we have just mentioned, who does everything according to his own will: for a king governing under the direction of laws which he is obliged to follow does not of himself create any particular species of government, as we have already said: for in every state whatsoever, either aristocracy or democracy, it is easy to appoint a general for life; and there are many who entrust the administration of affairs to one person only; such is the government at Dyrrachium, and nearly the same at Opus. As for an absolute monarchy as it is called, that is to say, when the whole state is wholly subject to the will of one person, namely the king, it seems to many that it is unnatural that one man should have the entire rule over his fellow-citizens when the state consists of equals: for nature requires that the same right and the same rank should necessarily take place amongst all those who are equal by nature: for as it would be hurtful to the body for those who are of different constitutions to observe the same regimen, either of diet or clothing, so is it with respect to the honours of the state as hurtful, that those who are equal in merit should be unequal in rank; for which reason it is as much a man's duty to submit to command as to assume it, and this also by rotation; for this is law, for order is law; and it is more proper that law should govern than any one of the citizens: upon the same principle, if it is advantageous to place the supreme power in some particular persons, they should be appointed to be only guardians, and the servants of the laws, for the supreme power must be placed somewhere; but they say, that it is unjust that where all are equal one person should continually enjoy it. But it seems unlikely that man should be able to adjust that which the law cannot determine; it may be replied, that the law having laid down the best rules possible, leaves the adjustment and application of particulars to the discretion of the magistrate; besides, it allows anything to be altered which experience proves may be better established. Moreover, he who would place the supreme power in mind, would place it in God and the laws; but he who entrusts man with it, gives it to a wild beast, for such his appetites sometimes make him; for passion influences those who are in power, even the very best of men: for which reason law is reason without desire.

The instance taken from the arts seems fallacious: wherein it is said to be wrong for a sick person to apply for a remedy to books, but that it would be far more eligible to employ those who are skilful in physic; for these do nothing contrary to reason from motives of friendship but earn their money by curing the sick, whereas those who have the management of public affairs do many things through hatred or favour. And, as a proof of what we have advanced, it may be observed, that whenever a sick person suspects that his physician has been persuaded by his enemies to be guilty of any foul practice to him in his profession, he then rather chooses to apply to books for his cure: and not only this but even physicians themselves when they are ill call in other physicians: and those who teach others the gymnastic exercises, exercise with those of the same profession, as being incapable from self-partiality to form a proper judgment of what concerns themselves. From whence it is evident, that those who seek for what is just, seek for a mean; now law is a mean. Moreover; the moral law is far superior and conversant with far superior objects than the written law; for the supreme magistrate is safer to be trusted to than the one, though he is inferior to the other. But as it is impossible that one person should have an eye to everything himself, it will be necessary that the supreme magistrate should employ several subordinate ones under him; why then should not this be done at first, instead of appointing one person in this manner? Besides, if, according to what has been already said, the man of worth is on that account fit to govern, two men of worth are certainly better than one: as, for instance, in Homer, "Let two together go:" and also Agamemnon's wish; "Were ten such faithful counsel mine!" Not but that there are even now some particular magistrates invested with supreme power to decide, as judges, those things which the law cannot, as being one of those cases which comes not properly under its jurisdiction; for of those which can there is no doubt: since then laws comprehend some things, but not all, it is necessary to enquire and consider which of the two is preferable, that the best man or the best law should govern; for to reduce every subject which can come under the deliberation of man into a law is impossible.

No one then denies, that it is necessary that there should be some person to decide those cases which cannot come under the cognisance of a written law: but we say, that it is better to have many than one; for though every one who decides according to the principles of the law decides justly; yet surely it seems absurd to suppose, that one person can see better with two eyes, and hear better with two ears, or do better with two hands and two feet, than many can do with many: for we see that absolute monarchs now furnish themselves with many eyes and ears and hands and feet; for they entrust those who are friends to them and their government with part of their power; for if they are not friends to the monarch, they will not do what he chooses; but if they are friends to him, they are friends also to his government: but a friend is an equal and like his friend: if then he thinks that such should govern, he thinks that his equal also should govern. These are nearly the objections which are usually made to a kingly power.

CHAPTER XVII

Probably what we have said may be true of some persons, but not of others; for some men are by nature formed to be under the government of a master; others, of a king; others, to be the citizens of a free state, just and useful; but a tyranny is not according to nature, nor the other perverted forms of government; for they are contrary to it. But it is evident from what has been said, that among equals it is neither advantageous nor right that one person should be lord over all where there are no established laws, but his will is the law; or where there are; nor is it right that one who is good should have it over those who are good; or one who is not good over those who are not good; nor one who is superior to the rest in worth, except in a particular manner, which shall be described, though indeed it has been already mentioned. But let us next determine what people are best qualified for a kingly government, what for an aristocratic, and what for a democratic. And, first, for a kingly; and it should be those who are accustomed by nature to submit the civil government of themselves to a family eminent for virtue: for an aristocracy, those who are naturally framed to bear the rule of free men, whose superior virtue makes them worthy of the management of others: for a free state, a war-like people, formed by nature both to govern and be governed by laws which admit the poorest citizen to share the honours of the commonwealth according to his worth. But whenever a whole family or any one of another shall happen so far to excel in virtue as to exceed all other persons in the community, then it is right that the kingly power should be in them, or if it is an individual who does so, that he should be king and lord of all; for this, as we have just mentioned, is not only correspondent to that principle of right which all founders of all states, whether aristocracies, oligarchies, or democracies, have a regard to (for in placing the supreme power they all think it right to fix it to excellence, though not the same); but it is also agreeable to what has been already said; as it would not be right to kill, or banish, or ostracise such a one for his superior merit. Nor would it be proper to let him have the supreme power only in turn; for it is contrary to nature that what is highest should ever be lowest: but this would be the case should such a one ever be governed by others. So that there can nothing else be done but to submit, and permit him continually to enjoy the supreme power. And thus much with respect to kingly power in different states, and whether it is or is not advantageous to them, and to what, and in what manner.

CHAPTER XVIII

Since then we have said that there are three sorts of regular governments, and of these the best must necessarily be that which is administered by the best men (and this must be that which happens to have one man, or one family, or a number of persons excelling all the rest in virtue, who are able to govern and be governed in such a manner as will make life most agreeable, and we have already shown that the virtue of a good man and of a citizen in the most perfect government will be the same), it is evident, that in the same manner, and for those very qualities which would procure a man the character of good, any one would say, that the government of a state was a well-established aristocracy or kingdom; so that it will be found to be education and morals that are almost the whole which go to make a good man, and the same qualities will make a good citizen or good king.

These particulars being treated of, we will now proceed to consider what sort of government is best, how it naturally arises, and how it is established; for it is necessary to make a proper inquiry concerning this.

BOOK IV

CHAPTER I

In every art and science which is not conversant in parts but in some one genus in which it is complete, it is the business of that art alone to determine what is fitted to its particular genus; as what particular exercise is fitted to a certain particular body, and suits it best: for that body which is formed by nature the most perfect and superior to others necessarily requires the best exercise-and also of what one kind that must be which will suit the generality; and this is the business of the gymnastic arts: and although any one should not desire to acquire an exact knowledge and skill in these exercises, yet it is not, on that account, the less necessary that he who professes to be a master and instruct the youth in them should be perfect therein: and we see that this is what equally befalls the healing, shipbuilding, cloth-making, and indeed all other arts; so that it evidently belongs to the same art to find out what kind of government is best, and would of all others be most correspondent to our wish, while it received no molestation from without: and what particular species of it is adapted to particular persons; for there are many who probably are incapable of enjoying the best form: so that the legislator, and he who is truly a politician, ought to be acquainted not only with that which is most perfect imaginable, but also that which is the best suited to any given circumstances. There is, moreover, a third sort, an imaginary one, and he ought, if such a one should be presented to his consideration, to be able to discern what sort of one it would be at the beginning; and, when once established, what would be the proper means to preserve it a long time. I mean, for instance, if a state should happen not to have the best form of government, or be deficient in what was necessary, or not receive every advantage possible, but something less. And, besides all this, it is necessary to know what sort of government is best fitting for all cities: for most of those writers who have treated this subject, however speciously they may handle other parts of it, have failed in describing the practical parts: for it is not enough to be able to perceive what is best without it is what can be put in practice. It should also be simple, and easy for all to attain to. But some seek only the most subtile forms of government. Others again, choosing rather to treat of what is common, censure those under which they live, and extol the excellence of a particular state, as the Lacedaemonian, or some other: but every legislator ought to establish such a form of government as from the present state and disposition of the people who are to receive it they will most readily submit to and persuade the community to partake of: for it is not a business of less trouble to correct the mistakes of an established government than to form a new one; as it is as difficult to recover what we have forgot as to learn anything afresh. He, therefore, who aspires to the character of a legislator, ought, besides all we have already said, to be able to correct the mistakes of a government already established, as we have before mentioned. But this is impossible to be done by him who does not know how many different forms of government there are: some persons think that there is only one species both of democracy and oligarchy; but this is not true: so that every one should be acquainted with the difference of these governments, how great they are, and whence they arise; and should have equal knowledge to perceive what laws are best, and what are most suitable to each particular government: for all laws are, and ought to be, framed agreeable to the state that is to be governed by them, and not the state to the laws: for government is a certain ordering in a state which particularly respects the magistrates in what manner they shall be regulated, and where the supreme power shall be placed; and what shall be the final object which each community shall have in view; but the laws are something different from what regulates and expresses the form of the constitution-it is their office to direct the conduct of the magistrate in the execution of his office and the punishment of offenders. From whence it is evident, that the founders of laws should attend both to the number and the different sorts of government; for it is impossible that the same laws should be calculated for all sorts of oligarchies and all sorts of democracies, for of both these governments there are many species, not one only.

CHAPTER II

Since, then, according to our first method in treating of the different forms of government, we have divided those which are regular into three sorts, the kingly, the aristocratical, the free states, and shown the three excesses which these are liable to: the kingly, of becoming tyrannical; the aristocratical, oligarchical; and the free state, democratical: and as we have already treated of the aristocratical and kingly; for to enter into an inquiry what sort of government is best is the same thing as to treat of these two expressly; for each of them desires to be established upon the principles of virtue: and as, moreover, we have already determined wherein a kingly power and an aristocracy differ from each other, and when a state may be said to be governed by a king, it now remains that we examine into a free state, and also these other governments, an oligarchy, a democracy, and a tyranny; and it is evident of these three excesses which must be the worst of all, and which next to it; for, of course, the excesses of the best and most holy must be the worst; for it must necessarily happen either that the name of king only will remain, or else that the king will assume more power than belongs to him, from whence tyranny will arise, the worst excess imaginable, a government the most contrary possible to a free state. The excess next hurtful is an oligarchy; for an aristocracy differs much from this sort of government: that which is least so is a democracy. This subject has been already treated of by one of those writers who have gone before me, though his sentiments are not the same as mine: for he thought, that of all excellent constitutions, as a good oligarchy or the like, a democracy was the worst, but of all bad ones, the best.

Now I affirm, that all these states have, without exception, fallen into excess; and also that he should not have said that one oligarchy was better than another, but that it was not quite so bad. But this question we shall not enter into at present. We shall first inquire how many different sorts of free states there are; since there are many species of democracies and oligarchies; and which of them is the most comprehensive, and most desirable after the best form of government; or if there is any other like an aristocracy, well established; and also which of these is best adapted to most cities, and which of them is preferable for particular persons: for, probably, some may suit better with an oligarchy than a democracy, and others better with a democracy than an oligarchy; and afterwards in what manner any one ought to proceed who desires to establish either of these states, I mean every species of democracy, and also of oligarchy. And to conclude, when we shall have briefly gone through everything that is necessary, we will endeavour to point out the sources of corruption, and stability, in government, as well those which are common to all as those which are peculiar to each state, and from what causes they chiefly arise.

CHAPTER III

The reason for there being many different sorts of governments is this, that each state consists of a great number of parts; for, in the first place, we see that all cities are made up of families: and again, of the multitude of these some must be rich, some poor, and others in the middle station; and that, both of the rich and poor, some will be used to arms, others not. We see also, that some of the common people are husbandmen, others attend the market, and others are artificers. There is also a difference between the nobles in their wealth, and the dignity in which they live: for instance, in the number of horses they breed; for this cannot be supported without a large fortune: for which reason, in former times, those cities whose strength consisted in horse became by that means oligarchies; and they used horse in their expeditions against the neighbouring cities; as the Eretrians the Chalcidians, the Magnetians, who lived near the river Meander, and many others in Asia. Moreover, besides the difference of fortune, there is that which arises from family and merit; or, if there are any other distinctions which make part of the city, they have been already mentioned in treating of an aristocracy, for there we considered how many parts each city must necessarily be composed of; and sometimes each of these have a share in the government, sometimes a few, sometimes more.

It is evident then, that there must be many forms of government, differing from each other in their particular constitution: for the parts of which they are composed each differ from the other. For government is the ordering of the magistracies of the state; and these the community share between themselves, either as they can attain them by force, or according to some common equality which there is amongst them, as poverty, wealth, or something which they both partake of. There must therefore necessarily be as many different forms of governments as there are different ranks in the society, arising from the superiority of some over others, and their different situations. And these seem chiefly to be two, as they say, of the winds: namely, the north and the south; and all the others are declinations from these. And thus in politics, there is the government of the many and the government of the few; or a democracy and an oligarchy: for an aristocracy may be considered as a species of oligarchy, as being also a government of the few; and what we call a free state may be considered as a democracy: as in the winds they consider the west as part of the north, and the east as part of the south: and thus it is in music, according to some, who say there are only two species of it, the Doric and the Phrygian, and all other species of composition they call after one of these names; and many people are accustomed to consider the nature of government in the same light; but it is both more convenient and more correspondent to truth to distinguish governments as I have done, into two species: one, of those which are established upon proper principles; of which there may be one or two sorts: the other, which includes all the different excesses of these; so that we may compare the best form of government to the most harmonious piece of music; the oligarchic and despotic to the more violent tunes; and the democratic to the soft and gentle airs.

CHAPTER IV

We ought not to define a democracy as some do, who say simply, that it is a government where the supreme power is lodged in the people; for even in oligarchies the supreme power is in the majority. Nor should they define an oligarchy a government where the supreme power is in the hands of a few: for let us suppose the number of a people to be thirteen hundred, and that of these one thousand were rich, who would not permit the three hundred poor to have any share in the government, although they were free, and their equal in everything else; no one would say, that this government was a democracy. In like manner, if the poor, when few in number, should acquire the power over the rich, though more than themselves, no one would say, that this was an oligarchy; nor this, when the rest who are rich have no share in the administration. We should rather say, that a democracy is when the supreme power is in the hands of the freemen; an oligarchy, when it is in the hands of the rich: it happens indeed that in the one case the many will possess it, in the other the few; because there are many poor and few rich. And if the power of the state was to be distributed according to the size of the citizens, as they say it is in Ethiopia, or according to their beauty, it would be an oligarchy: for the number of those who are large and beautiful is small.

Nor are those things which we have already mentioned alone sufficient to describe these states; for since there are many species both of a democracy and an oligarchy, the matter requires further consideration; as we cannot admit, that if a few persons who are free possess the supreme power over the many who are not free, that this government is a democracy: as in Apollonia, in Ionia, and in Thera: for in each of these cities the honours of the state belong to some few particular families, who first founded the colonies. Nor would the rich, because they are superior in numbers, form a democracy, as formerly at Colophon; for there the majority had large possessions before the Lydian war: but a democracy is a state where the freemen and the poor, being the majority, are invested with the power of the state. An oligarchy is a state where the rich and those of noble families, being few, possess it.

We have now proved that there are various forms of government and have assigned a reason for it; and shall proceed to show that there are even more than these, and what they are, and why; setting out with the principle we have already laid down. We admit that every city consists not of one, but many parts: thus, if we should endeavour to comprehend the different species of animals we should first of all note those parts which every animal must have, as a certain sensorium, and also what is necessary to acquire and retain food, as a mouth and a belly; besides certain parts to enable it to move from place to place. If, then, these are the only parts of an animal and there are differences between them; namely, in their various sorts of stomachs, bellies, and sensoriums: to which we must add their motive powers; the number of the combinations of all these must necessarily make up the different species of animals. For it is not possible that the same kind of animal should have any very great difference in its mouth or ears; so that when all these are collected, who happen to have these things similar in all, they make up a species of animals of which there are as many as there are of these general combinations of necessary parts.

The same thing is true of what are called states; for a city is not made of one but many parts, as has already been often said; one of which is those who supply it with provisions, called husbandmen, another called mechanics, whose employment is in the manual arts, without which the city could not be inhabited; of these some are busied about what is absolutely necessary, others in what contribute to the elegancies and pleasures of life; the third sort are your exchange-men, I mean by these your buyers, sellers, merchants, and victuallers; the fourth are your hired labourers or workmen; the fifth are the men-at-arms, a rank not less useful than the other, without you would have the community slaves to every invader; but what cannot defend itself is unworthy of the name of a city; for a city is self-sufficient, a slave not. So that when Socrates, in Plato's Republic, says that a city is necessarily composed of four sorts of people, he speaks elegantly but not correctly, and these are, according to him, weavers, husbandmen, shoe-makers, and builders; he then adds, as if these were not sufficient, smiths, herdsmen for what cattle are necessary, and also merchants and victuallers, and these are by way of appendix to his first list; as if a city was established for necessity, and not happiness, or as if a shoe-maker and a husbandman were equally useful. He reckons not the military a part before the increase of territory and joining to the borders of the neighbouring powers will make war necessary: and even amongst them who compose his four divisions, or whoever have any connection with each other, it will be necessary to have some one to distribute justice, and determine between man and man. If, then, the mind is a more valuable part of man than the body, every one would wish to have those things more regarded in his city which tend to the advantage of these than common matters, such are war and justice; to which may be added council, which is the business of civil wisdom (nor is it of any consequence whether these different employments are filled by different persons or one, as the same man is oftentimes both a soldier and a husbandman): so that if both the judge and the senator are parts of the city, it necessarily follows that the soldier must be so also. The seventh sort are those who serve the public in expensive employments at their own charge: these are called the rich. The eighth are those who execute the different offices of the state, and without these it could not possibly subsist: it is therefore necessary that there should be some persons capable of governing and filling the places in the city; and this either for life or in rotation: the office of senator, and judge, of which we have already sufficiently treated, are the only ones remaining. If, then, these things are necessary for a state, that it may be happy and just, it follows that the citizens who engage in public affairs should be men of abilities therein. Several persons think, that different employments may be allotted to the same person; as a soldier's, a husbandman's, and an artificer's; as also that others may be both senators and judges.

Besides, every one supposes himself a man of political abilities, and that he is qualified for almost every department in the state. But the same person cannot at once be poor and rich: for which reason the most obvious division of the city is into two parts, the poor and rich; moreover, since for the generality the one are few, the other many, they seem of all the parts of a city most contrary to each other; so that as the one or the other prevail they form different states; and these are the democracy and the oligarchy.

But that there are many different states, and from what causes they arise, has been already mentioned: and that there are also different species both of democracies and oligarchies we will now show. Though this indeed is evident from what we have already said: there are also many different sorts of common people, and also of those who are called gentlemen. Of the different sorts of the first are husbandmen, artificers, exchange-men, who are employed in buying and selling, seamen, of which some are engaged in war, some in traffic, some in carrying goods and passengers from place to place, others in fishing, and of each of these there are often many, as fishermen at Tarentum and Byzantium, masters of galleys at Athens, merchants at AEgina and Chios, those who let ships on freight at Tenedos; we may add to these those who live by their manual labour and have but little property; so that they cannot live without some employ: and also those who are not free-born on both sides, and whatever other sort of common people there may be. As for gentlemen, they are such as are distinguished either by their fortune, their birth, their abilities, or their education, or any such-like excellence which is attributed to them.

The most pure democracy is that which is so called principally from that equality which prevails in it: for this is what the law in that state directs; that the poor shall be in no greater subjection than the rich; nor that the supreme power shall be lodged with either of these, but that both shall share it. For if liberty and equality, as some persons suppose, are chiefly to be found in a democracy, it must be most so by every department of government being alike open to all; but as the people are the majority, and what they vote is law, it follows that such a state must be a democracy. This, then, is one species thereof. Another is, when the magistrates are elected by a certain census; but this should be but small, and every one who was included in it should be eligible, but as soon as he was below it should lose that right. Another sort is, in which every citizen who is not infamous has a share in the government, but where the government is in the laws. Another, where every citizen without exception has this right. Another is like these in other particulars, but there the people govern, and not the law: and this takes place when everything is determined by a majority of votes, and not by a law; which happens when the people are influenced by the demagogues: for where a democracy is governed by stated laws there is no room for them, but men of worth fill the first offices in the state: but where the power is not vested in the laws, there demagogues abound: for there the people rule with kingly power: the whole composing one body; for they are supreme, not as individuals but in their collective capacity.

Homer also discommends the government of many; but whether he means this we are speaking of, or where each person exercises his power separately, is uncertain. When the people possess this power they desire to be altogether absolute, that they may not be under the control of the law, and this is the time when flatterers are held in repute. Nor is there any difference between such a people and monarchs in a tyranny: for their manners are the same, and they both hold a despotic power over better persons than themselves. For their decrees are like the others' edicts; their demagogues like the others' flatterers: but their greatest resemblance consists in the mutual support they give to each other, the flatterer to the tyrant, the demagogue to the people: and to them it is owing that the supreme power is lodged in the votes of the people, and not in the laws; for they bring everything before them, as their influence is owing to their being supreme whose opinions they entirely direct; for these are they whom the multitude obey. Besides, those who accuse the magistrates insist upon it, that the right of determining on their conduct lies in the people, who gladly receive their complaints as the means of destroying all their offices.

Any one, therefore, may with great justice blame such a government as being a democracy, and not a free state; for where the government is not in the laws, then there is no free state, for the law ought to be supreme over all things; and particular incidents which arise should be determined by the magistrates or the state. If, therefore, a democracy is to be reckoned a free state, it is evident that any such establishment which centres all power in the votes of the people cannot, properly speaking, be a democracy: for their decrees cannot be general in their extent. Thus, then, we may describe the several species of democracies.

CHAPTER V

Of the different species of oligarchies one is, when the right to the offices is regulated by a certain census; so that the poor, although the majority, have no share in it; while all those who are included therein take part in the management of public affairs. Another sort is, when the magistrates are men of very small fortune, who upon any vacancy do themselves fill it up: and if they do this out of the community at large, the state approaches to an aristocracy; if out of any particular class of people, it will be an oligarchy. Another sort of oligarchy is, when the power is an hereditary nobility. The fourth is, when the power is in the same hands as the other, but not under the control of law; and this sort of oligarchy exactly corresponds to a tyranny in monarchies, and to that particular species of democracies which I last mentioned in treating of that state: this has the particular name of a dynasty. These are the different sorts of oligarchies and democracies.

It should also be known, that it often happens that a free state, where the supreme power is in the laws, may not be democratic, and yet in consequence of the established manners and customs of the people, may be governed as if it was; so, on the other hand, where the laws may countenance a more democratic form of government, these may make the state inclining to an oligarchy; and this chiefly happens when there has been any alteration in the government; for the people do not easily change, but love their own ancient customs; and it is by small degrees only that one thing takes place of another; so that the ancient laws will remain, while the power will be in the hands of those who have brought about a revolution in the state.

CHAPTER VI

It is evident from what has been said, that there are as many different sorts of democracies and oligarchies as I have reckoned up: for, of necessity, either all ranks of the people which I have enumerated must have a share in the government, or some only, and others not; for when the husbandmen, and those only who possess moderate fortunes, have the supreme power, they will govern according to law; for as they must get their livings by their employs, they have but little leisure for public business: they will therefore establish proper laws, and never call public assemblies but when there is a necessity for them; and they will readily let every one partake with them in the administration of public affairs as soon as they possess that fortune which the law requires for their qualification: every one, therefore, who is qualified will have his share in the government: for to exclude any would be to make the government an oligarchy, and for all to have leisure to attend without they had a subsistence would be impossible: for these reasons, therefore, this government is a species of democracy. Another species is distinguished by the mode of electing their magistrates, in which every one is eligible, to whose birth there are no objections, provided he is supposed to have leisure to attend: for which reason in such a democracy the supreme power will be vested in the laws, as there will be nothing paid to those who go to the public assemblies. A third species is where every freeman has a right to a share in the government, which he will not accept for the cause already assigned; for which reason here also the supreme power will be in the law. The fourth species of democracy, the last which was established in order of time, arose when cities were greatly enlarged to what they were at first, and when the public revenue became something considerable; for then the populace, on account of their numbers, were admitted to share in the management of public affairs, for then even the poorest people were at leisure to attend to them, as they received wages for so doing; nay, they were more so than others, as they were not hindered by having anything of their own to mind, as the rich had; for which reason these last very often did not frequent the public assemblies and the courts of justice: thus the supreme power was lodged in the poor, and not in the laws. These are the different sorts of democracies, and such are the causes which necessarily gave birth to them.

The first species of oligarchy is, when the generality of the state are men of moderate and not too large property; for this gives them leisure for the management of public affairs: and, as they are a numerous body, it necessarily follows that the supreme power must be in the laws, and not in men; for as they are far removed from a monarchical government, and have not sufficient fortune to neglect their private affairs, while they are too many to be supported by the public, they will of course determine to be governed by the laws, and not by each other. But if the men of property in the state are but few, and their property is large, then an oligarchy of the second sort will take place; for those who have most power will think that they have a right to lord it over the others; and, to accomplish this, they will associate to themselves some who have an inclination for public affairs, and as they are not powerful enough to govern without law, they will make a law for that purpose. And if those few who have large fortunes should acquire still greater power, the oligarchy will then alter into one of the third sort; for they will get all the offices of the state into their own hands by a law which directs the son to succeed upon the death of his father; and, after that, when, by means of their increasing wealth and powerful connections, they extend still further their oppression, a monarchical dynasty will directly succeed wherein men will be supreme, and not the law; and this is the fourth species of an oligarchy correspondent to the last-mentioned class of democracies.

CHAPTER VII

There are besides two other states, a democracy and an oligarchy, one of which all speak of, and it is always esteemed a species of the four sorts; and thus they reckon them up; a monarchy, an oligarchy, a democracy, and this fourth which they call an aristocracy. There is also a fifth, which bears a name that is also common to the other four, namely, a state: but as this is seldom to be met with, it has escaped those who have endeavoured to enumerate the different sorts of governments, which they fix at four only, as does Plato in his Republic.

An aristocracy, of which I have already treated in the first book, is rightly called so; for a state governed by the best men, upon the most virtuous principles, and not upon any hypothesis, which even good men may propose, has alone a right to be called an aristocracy, for it is there only that a man is at once a good man and a good citizen; while in other states men are good only relative to those states. Moreover, there are some other states which are called by the same name, that differ both from oligarchies and free states, wherein not only the rich but also the virtuous have a share in the administration; and have therefore acquired the name of aristocracies; for in those governments wherein virtue is not their common care, there are still men of worth and approved goodness. Whatever state, then, like the Carthaginians, favours the rich, the virtuous, and the citizens at large, is a sort of aristocracy: when only the two latter are held in esteem, as at Lacedaemon, and the state is jointly composed of these, it is a virtuous democracy. These are the two species of aristocracies after the first, which is the best of all governments. There is also a third, which is, whenever a free state inclines to the dominion of a few.

CHAPTER VIII

It now remains for us to treat of that government which is particularly called a free state, and also of a tyranny; and the reason for my choosing to place that free state here is, because this, as well as those aristocracies already mentioned, although they do not seem excesses, yet, to speak true, they have all departed from what a perfect government is. Nay, they are deviations both of them equally from other forms, as I said at the beginning. It is proper to mention a tyranny the last of all governments, for it is of all others the least like one: but as my intention is to treat of all governments in general, for this reason that also, as I have said, will be taken into consideration in its proper place.

I shall now inquire into a free state and show what it is; and we shall the better understand its positive nature as we have already described an oligarchy and a democracy; for a free state is indeed nothing more than a mixture of them, and it has been usual to call those which incline most to a democracy, a free state; those which incline most to an oligarchy, an aristocracy, because those who are rich are generally men of family and education; besides, they enjoy those things which others are often guilty of crimes to procure: for which reason they are regarded as men of worth and honour and note.

Since, then, it is the genius of an aristocracy to allot the larger part of the government to the best citizens, they therefore say, that an oligarchy is chiefly composed of those men who are worthy and honourable: now it seems impossible that where the government is in the hands of the good, there the laws should not be good, but bad; or, on the contrary, that where the government is in the hands of the bad, there the laws should be good; nor is a government well constituted because the laws are, without at the same time care is taken that they are observed; for to enforce obedience to the laws which it makes is one proof of a good constitution in the state-another is, to have laws well calculated for those who are to abide by them; for if they are improper they must be obeyed: and this may be done two ways, either by their being the best relative to the particular state, or the best absolutely. An aristocracy seems most likely to confer the honours of the state on the virtuous; for virtue is the object of an aristocracy, riches of an oligarchy, and liberty of a democracy; for what is approved of by the majority will prevail in all or in each of these three different states; and that which seems good to most of those who compose the community will prevail: for what is called a state prevails in many communities, which aim at a mixture of rich and poor, riches and liberty: as for the rich, they are usually supposed to take the place of the worthy and honourable. As there are three things which claim an equal rank in the state, freedom, riches, and virtue (for as for the fourth, rank, it is an attendant on two of the others, for virtue and riches are the origin of family), it is evident, that the conjuncture of the rich and the poor make up a free state; but that all three tend to an aristocracy more than any other, except that which is truly so, which holds the first rank.

We have already seen that there are governments different from a monarchy, a democracy, and an oligarchy; and what they are, and wherein they differ from each other; and also aristocracies and states properly so called, which are derived from them; and it is evident that these are not much unlike each other.

CHAPTER IX

We shall next proceed to show how that government which is peculiarly called a state arises alongside of democracy and oligarchy, and how it ought to be established; and this will at the same time show what are the proper boundaries of both these governments, for we must mark out wherein they differ from one another, and then from both these compose a state of such parts of each of them as will show from whence they were taken.

There are three different ways in which two states may be blended and joined together; for, in the first place, all those rules may be adopted which the laws of each of them have ordered; as for instance in the judicial department, for in an oligarchy the rich are fined if they do not come to the court as jurymen, but the poor are not paid for their attendance; but in democracies they are, while the rich are not fined for their neglect. Now these things, as being common to both, are fit to be observed in a free state which is composed of both. This, then, is one way in which they may be joined together. In the second place, a medium may be taken between the different methods which each state observes; for instance, in a democracy the right to vote in the public assembly is either confined by no census at all, or limited by a very small one; in an oligarchy none enjoy it but those whose census is high: therefore, as these two practices are contrary to each other, a census between each may be established in such a state. In the third place, different laws of each community may be adopted; as, for instance, as it seems correspondent to the nature of a democracy, that the magistrates should be chosen by lot, but an aristocracy by vote, and in the one state according to a census, but not in the other: let, then, an aristocracy and a free state copy something from each of them; let them follow an oligarchy in choosing their magistrates by vote, but a democracy in not admitting of any census, and thus blend together the different customs of the two governments. But the best proof of a happy mixture of a democracy and an oligarchy is this, when a person may properly call the same state a democracy and an oligarchy. It is evident that those who speak of it in this manner are induced to it because both these governments are there well blended together: and indeed this is common to all mediums, that the extremes of each side should be discerned therein, as at Lacedaemon; for many affirm that it is a democracy from the many particulars in which it follows that form of government; as for instance, in the first place, in the bringing up of their children, for the rich and poor are brought up in the same manner; and their education is such that the children of the poor may partake of it; and the same rules are observed when they are youths and men, there is no distinction between a rich person and a poor one; and in their public tables the same provision is served to all. The rich also wear only such clothes as the poorest man is able to purchase. Moreover, with respect to two magistracies of the highest rank, one they have a right to elect to, the other to fill; namely, the senate and the ephori. Others consider it as an oligarchy, the principles of which it follows in many things, as in choosing all their officers by vote, and not by lot; in there being but a few who have a right to sit in judgment on capital causes and the like. Indeed, a state which is well composed of two others ought to resemble them both, and neither, Such a state ought to have its means of preservation in itself, and not without; and when I say in itself, I do not mean that it should owe this to the forbearance of their neighbours, for this may happen to a bad government, but to every member of the community's not being willing that there should be the least alteration in their constitution. Such is the method in which a free state or aristocracy ought to be established.

CHAPTER X

It now remains to treat of a tyranny; not that there is much to be said on that subject, but as it makes part of our plan, since we enumerated it amongst our different sorts of governments. In the beginning of this work we inquired into the nature of kingly government, and entered into a particular examination of what was most properly called so, and whether it was advantageous to a state or not, and what it should be, and how established; and we divided a tyranny into two pieces when we were upon this subject, because there is something analogous between this and a kingly government, for they are both of them established by law; for among some of the barbarians they elect a monarch with absolute power, and formerly among the Greeks there were some such, whom they called sesumnetes. Now these differ from each other; for some possess only kingly power regulated by law, and rule those who voluntarily submit to their government; others rule despotically according to their own will. There is a third species of tyranny, most properly so called, which is the very opposite to kingly power; for this is the government of one who rules over his equals and superiors without being accountable for his conduct, and whose object is his own advantage, and not the advantage of those he governs; for which reason he rules by compulsion, for no freemen will ever willingly submit to such a government. These are the different species of tyrannies, their principles, and their causes.

CHAPTER XI

We proceed now to inquire what form of government and what manner of life is best for communities in general, not adapting it to that superior virtue which is above the reach of the vulgar, or that education which every advantage of nature and fortune only can furnish, nor to those imaginary plans which may be formed at pleasure; but to that mode of life which the greater part of mankind can attain to, and that government which most cities may establish: for as to those aristocracies which we have now mentioned, they are either too perfect for a state to support, or one so nearly alike to that state we now going to inquire into, that we shall treat of them both as one.

The opinions which we form upon these subjects must depend upon one common principle: for if what I have said in my treatise on Morals is true, a happy life must arise from an uninterrupted course of virtue; and if virtue consists in a certain medium, the middle life must certainly be the happiest; which medium is attainable by every one. The boundaries of virtue and vice in the state must also necessarily be the same as in a private person; for the form of government is the life of the city. In every city the people are divided into three sorts; the very rich, the very poor, and those who are between them. If this is universally admitted, that the mean is best, it is evident that even in point of fortune mediocrity is to be preferred; for that state is most submissive to reason; for those who are very handsome, or very strong, or very noble, or very rich; or, on the contrary; those who are very poor, or very weak, or very mean, with difficulty obey it; for the one are capricious and greatly flagitious, the other rascally and mean, the crimes of each arising from their different excesses: nor will they go through the different offices of the state; which is detrimental to it: besides, those who excel in strength, in riches, or friends, or the like, neither know how nor are willing to submit to command: and this begins at home when they are boys; for there they are brought up too delicately to be accustomed to obey their preceptors: as for the very poor, their general and excessive want of what the rich enjoy reduces them to a state too mean: so that the one know not how to command, but to be commanded as slaves, the others know not how to submit to any command, nor to command themselves but with despotic power.

A city composed of such men must therefore consist of slaves and masters, not freemen; where one party must hate, and the other despise, where there could be no possibility of friendship or political community: for community supposes affection; for we do not even on the road associate with our enemies. It is also the genius of a city to be composed as much as possible of equals; which will be most so when the inhabitants are in the middle state: from whence it follows, that that city must be best framed which is composed of those whom we say are naturally its proper members. It is men of this station also who will be best assured of safety and protection; for they will neither covet what belongs to others, as the poor do; nor will others covet what is theirs, as the poor do what belongs to the rich; and thus, without plotting against any one, or having any one plot against them, they will live free from danger: for which reason Phocylides wisely wishes for the middle state, as being most productive of happiness. It is plain, then, that the most perfect political community must be amongst those who are in the middle rank, and those states are best instituted wherein these are a larger and more respectable part, if possible, than both the other; or, if that cannot be, at least than either of them separate; so that being thrown into the balance it may prevent either scale from preponderating.

It is therefore the greatest happiness which the citizens can enjoy to possess a moderate and convenient fortune; for when some possess too much, and others nothing at all, the government must either be in the hands of the meanest rabble or else a pure oligarchy; or, from the excesses of both, a tyranny; for this arises from a headstrong democracy or an oligarchy, but very seldom when the members of the community are nearly on an equality with each other. We will assign a reason for this when we come to treat of the alterations which different states are likely to undergo. The middle state is therefore best, as being least liable to those seditions and insurrections which disturb the community; and for the same reason extensive governments are least liable to these inconveniences; for there those in a middle state are very numerous, whereas in small ones it is easy to pass to the two extremes, so as hardly to have any in a medium remaining, but the one half rich, the other poor: and from the same principle it is that democracies are more firmly established and of longer continuance than oligarchies; but even in those when there is a want of a proper number of men of middling fortune, the poor extend their power too far, abuses arise, and the government is soon at an end.

We ought to consider as a proof of what I now advance, that the best lawgivers themselves were those in the middle rank of life, amongst whom was Solon, as is evident from his poems, and Lycurgus, for he was not a king, and Charondas, and indeed most others. What has been said will show us why of so many free states some have changed to democracies, others to oligarchies: for whenever the number of those in the middle state has been too small, those who were the more numerous, whether the rich or the poor, always overpowered them and assumed to themselves the administration of public affairs; from hence arose either a democracy or an oligarchy. Moreover, when in consequence of their disputes and quarrels with each other, either the rich get the better of the poor, or the poor of the rich, neither of them will establish a free state; but, as the record of their victory, one which inclines to their own principles, and form either a democracy or an oligarchy.

Those who made conquests in Greece, having all of them an eye to the respective forms of government in their own cities, established either democracies or oligarchies, not considering what was serviceable to the state, but what was similar to their own; for which reason a government has never been established where the supreme power has been placed amongst those of the middling rank, or very seldom; and, amongst a few, one man only of those who have yet been conquerors has been persuaded to give the preference to this order of men: it is indeed an established custom with the inhabitants of most cities not to desire an equality, but either to aspire to govern, or when they are conquered, to submit.

Thus we have shown what the best state is, and why. It will not be difficult to perceive of the many states which there are, for we have seen that there are various forms both of democracies and oligarchies, to which we should give the first place, to which the second, and in the same manner the next also; and to observe what are the particular excellences and defects of each, after we have first described the best possible; for that must be the best which is nearest to this, that worst which is most distant from the medium, without any one has a particular plan of his own which he judges by. I mean by this, that it may happen, that although one form of government may be better than another, yet there is no reason to prevent another from being preferable thereunto in particular circumstances and for particular purposes.

CHAPTER XII

After what has been said, it follows that we should now show what particular form of government is most suitable for particular persons; first laying this down as a general maxim, that that party which desires to support the actual administration of the state ought always to be superior to that which would alter it. Every city is made up of quality and quantity: by quality I mean liberty, riches, education, and family, and by quantity its relative populousness: now it may happen that quality may exist in one of those parts of which the city is composed, and quantity in another; thus the number of the ignoble may be greater than the number of those of family, the number of the poor than that of the rich; but not so that the quantity of the one shall overbalance the quality of the other; those must be properly adjusted to each other; for where the number of the poor exceeds the proportion we have mentioned, there a democracy will rise up, and if the husbandry should have more power than others, it will be a democracy of husbandmen; and the democracy will be a particular species according to that class of men which may happen to be most numerous: thus, should these be the husbandmen, it will be of these, and the best; if of mechanics and those who hire themselves out, the worst possible: in the same manner it may be of any other set between these two. But when the rich and the noble prevail more by their quality than they are deficient in quantity, there an oligarchy ensues; and this oligarchy may be of different species, according to the nature of the prevailing party. Every legislator in framing his constitution ought to have a particular regard to those in the middle rank of life; and if he intends an oligarchy, these should be the object of his laws; if a democracy, to these they should be entrusted; and whenever their number exceeds that of the two others, or at least one of them, they give stability to the constitution; for there is no fear that the rich and the poor should agree to conspire together against them, for neither of these will choose to serve the other. If any one would choose to fix the administration on the widest basis, he will find none preferable to this; for to rule by turns is what the rich and the poor will not submit to, on account of their hatred to each other. It is, moreover, allowed that an arbitrator is the most proper person for both parties to trust to; now this arbitrator is the middle rank.

Those who would establish aristocratical governments are mistaken not only in giving too much power to the rich, but also in deceiving the common people; for at last, instead of an imaginary good, they must feel a real evil, for the encroachments of the rich are more destructive to the state than those of the poor.

CHAPTER XIII

There are five particulars in which, under fair pretences, the rich craftily endeavour to undermine the rights of the people, these are their public assemblies, their offices of state, their courts of justice, their military power, and their gymnastic exercises. With respect to their public assemblies, in having them open to all, but in fining the rich only, or others very little, for not attending; with respect to offices, in permitting the poor to swear off, but not granting this indulgence to those who are within the census; with respect to their courts of justice, in fining the rich for non-attendance, but the poor not at all, or those a great deal, and these very little, as was done by the laws of Charondas. In some places every citizen who was enrolled had a right to attend the public assemblies and to try causes; which if they did not do, a very heavy fine was laid upon them; that through fear of the fine they might avoid being enrolled, as they were then obliged to do neither the one nor the other. The same spirit of legislation prevailed with respect to their bearing arms and their gymnastic exercises; for the poor are excused if they have no arms, but the rich are fined; the same method takes place if they do not attend their gymnastic exercises, there is no penalty on one, but there is on the other: the consequence of which is, that the fear of this penalty induces the rich to keep the one and attend the other, while the poor do neither. These are the deceitful contrivances of oligarchical legislators.

The contrary prevails in a democracy; for there they make the poor a proper allowance for attending the assemblies and the courts, but give the rich nothing for doing it: whence it is evident, that if any one would properly blend these customs together, they must extend both the pay and the fine to every member of the community, and then every one would share in it, whereas part only now do. The citizens of a free state ought to consist of those only who bear arms: with respect to their census it is not easy to determine exactly what it ought to be, but the rule that should direct upon this subject should be to make it as extensive as possible, so that those who are enrolled in it make up a greater part of the people than those who are not; for those who are poor, although they partake not of the offices of the state, are willing to live quiet, provided that no one disturbs them in their property: but this is not an easy matter; for it may not always happen, that those who are at the head of public affairs are of a humane behaviour. In time of war the poor are accustomed to show no alacrity without they have provisions found them; when they have, then indeed they are willing to fight.

In some governments the power is vested not only in those who bear arms, but also in those who have borne them. Among the Malienses the state was composed of these latter only, for all the officers were soldiers who had served their time. And the first states in Greece which succeeded those where kingly power was established, were governed by the military. First of all the horse, for at that time the strength and excellence of the army depended on the horse, for as to the heavy-armed foot they were useless without proper discipline; but the art of tactics was not known to the ancients, for which reason their strength lay in their horse: but when cities grew larger, and they depended more on their foot, greater numbers partook of the freedom of the city; for which reason what we call republics were formerly called democracies. The ancient governments were properly oligarchies or kingdoms; for on account of the few persons in each state, it would have been impossible to have found a sufficient number of the middle rank; so these being but few, and those used to subordination, they more easily submitted to be governed.

We have now shown why there are many sorts of governments, and others different from those we have treated of: for there are more species of democracies than one, and the like is true of other forms, and what are their differences, and whence they arise; and also of all others which is the best, at least in general; and which is best suited for particular people.

CHAPTER XIV

We will now proceed to make some general reflections upon the governments next in order, and also to consider each of them in particular; beginning with those principles which appertain to each: now there are three things in all states which a careful legislator ought well to consider, which are of great consequence to all, and which properly attended to the state must necessarily be happy; and according to the variation of which the one will differ from the other. The first of these is the public assembly; the second the officers of the state, that is, who they ought to be, and with what power they should be entrusted, and in what manner they should be appointed; the third, the judicial department.

Now it is the proper business of the public assembly to determine concerning war and peace, making or breaking off alliances, to enact laws, to sentence to death, banishment, or confiscation of goods, and to call the magistrates to account for their behaviour when in office. Now these powers must necessarily be entrusted to the citizens in general, or all of them to some; either to one magistrate or more; or some to one, and some to another, or some to all, but others to some: to entrust all to all is in the spirit of a democracy, for the people aim at equality. There are many methods of delegating these powers to the citizens at large, one of which is to let them execute them by turn, and not altogether, as was done by Tellecles, the Milesian, in his state. In others the supreme council is composed of the different magistrates, and they succeed to the offices of the community by proper divisions of tribes, wards, and other very small proportions, till every one in his turn goes through them: nor does the whole community ever meet together, without it is when new laws are enacted, or some national affair is debated, or to hear what the magistrates have to propose to them. Another method is for the people to meet in a collective body, but only for the purpose of holding the comitia, making laws, determining concerning war or peace, and inquiring into the conduct of their magistrates, while the remaining part of the public business is conducted by the magistrates, who have their separate departments, and are chosen out of the whole community either by vote or ballot. Another method is for the people in general to meet for the choice of the magistrates, and to examine into their conduct; and also to deliberate concerning war and alliances, and to leave other things to the magistrates, whoever happen to be chosen, whose particular employments are such as necessarily require persons well skilled therein. A fourth method is for every person to deliberate upon every subject in public assembly, where the magistrates can determine nothing of themselves, and have only the privilege of giving their opinions first; and this is the method of the most pure democracy, which is analogous to the proceedings in a dynastic oligarchy and a tyrannic monarchy.

These, then, are the methods in which public business is conducted in a democracy. When the power is in the hands of part of the community only, it is an oligarchy and this also admits of different customs; for whenever the officers of the state are chosen out of those who have a moderate fortune, and these from that circumstance are many, and when they depart not from that line which the law has laid down, but carefully follow it, and when all within the census are eligible, certainly it is then an oligarchy, but founded on true principles of government from its moderation. When the people in general do not partake of the deliberative power, but certain persons chosen for that purpose, who govern according to law; this also, like the first, is an oligarchy. When those who have the deliberative power elect each other, and the son succeeds to the father, and when they can supersede the laws, such a government is of necessity a strict oligarchy. When some persons determine on one thing, and others on another, as war and peace, and when all inquire into the conduct of their magistrates, and other things are left to different officers, elected either by vote or lot, then the government is an aristocracy or a free state. When some are chosen by vote and others by lot, and these either from the people in general, or from a certain number elected for that purpose, or if both the votes and the lots are open to all, such a state is partly an aristocracy, partly a free government itself. These are the different methods in which the deliberative power is vested in different states, all of whom follow some regulation here laid down. It is advantageous to a democracy, in the present sense of the word, by which I mean a state wherein the people at large have a supreme power, even over the laws, to hold frequent public assemblies; and it will be best in this particular to imitate the example of oligarchies in their courts of justice; for they fine those who are appointed to try causes if they do not attend, so should they reward the poor for coming to the public assemblies: and their counsels will be best when all advise with each other, the citizens with the nobles, the nobles with the citizens. It is also advisable when the council is to be composed of part of the citizens, to elect, either by vote or lot, an equal number of both ranks. It is also proper, if the common people in the state are very numerous, either not to pay every one for his attendance, but such a number only as will make them equal to the nobles, or to reject many of them by lot.

In an oligarchy they should either call up some of the common people to the council, or else establish a court, as is done in some other states, whom they call pre-advisers or guardians of the laws, whose business should be to propose first what they should afterwards enact. By this means the people would have a place in the administration of public affairs, without having it in their power to occasion any disorder in the government. Moreover, the people may be allowed to have a vote in whatever bill is proposed, but may not themselves propose anything contrary thereto; or they may give their advice, while the power of determining may be with the magistrates only. It is also necessary to follow a contrary practice to what is established in democracies, for the people should be allowed the power of pardoning, but not of condemning, for the cause should be referred back again to the magistrates: whereas the contrary takes place in republics; for the power of pardoning is with the few, but not of condemning, which is always referred to the people at large. And thus we determine concerning the deliberative power in any state, and in whose hands it shall be.

CHAPTER XV

We now proceed to consider the choice of magistrates; for this branch of public business contains many different Parts, as how many there shall be, what shall be their particular office, and with respect to time how long each of them shall continue in place; for some make it six months, others shorter, others for a year, others for a much longer time; or whether they should be perpetual or for a long time, or neither; for the same person may fill the same office several times, or he may not be allowed to enjoy it even twice, but only once: and also with respect to the appointment of magistrates, who are to be eligible, who is to choose them, and in what manner; for in all these particulars we ought properly to distinguish the different ways which may be followed; and then to show which of these is best suited to such and such governments.

Now it is not easy to determine to whom we ought properly to give the name of magistrate, for a government requires many persons in office; but every one of those who is either chosen by vote or lot is not to be reckoned a magistrate. The priests, for instance, in the first place; for these are to be considered as very different from civil magistrates: to these we may add the choregi and heralds; nay, even ambassadors are elected: there are some civil employments which belong to the citizens; and these are either when they are all engaged in one thing, as when as soldiers they obey their general, or when part of them only are, as in governing the women or educating the youth; and also some economic, for they often elect corn-meters: others are servile, and in which, if they are rich, they employ slaves. But indeed they are most properly called magistrates, who are members of the deliberative council, or decide causes, or are in some command, the last more especially, for to command is peculiar to magistrates. But to speak truth, this question is of no great consequence, nor is it the province of the judges to decide between those who dispute about words; it may indeed be an object of speculative inquiry; but to inquire what officers are necessary in a state, and how many, and what, though not most necessary, may yet be advantageous in a well-established government, is a much more useful employment, and this with respect to all states in general, as well as to small cities.

In extensive governments it is proper to allot one employment to one person, as there are many to serve the public in so numerous a society, where some may be passed over for a long time, and others never be in office but once; and indeed everything is better done which has the whole attention of one person, than when that attention is divided amongst many; but in small states it is necessary that a few of the citizens should execute many employments; for their numbers are so small it will not be convenient to have many of them in office at the same time; for where shall we find others to succeed them in turn? Small states will sometimes want the same magistrates and the same laws as large ones; but the one will not want to employ them so often as the other; so that different charges may be intrusted to the same person without any inconvenience, for they will not interfere with each other, and for want of sufficient members in the community it will be necessary. If we could tell how many magistrates are necessary in every city, and how many, though not necessary, it is yet proper to have, we could then the better know how many different offices one might assign to one magistrate. It is also necessary to know what tribunals in different places should have different things under their jurisdiction, and also what things should always come under the cognisance of the same magistrate; as, for instance, decency of manners, shall the clerk of the market take cognisance of that if the cause arises in the market, and another magistrate in another place, or the same magistrate everywhere: or shall there be a distinction made of the fact, or the parties? as, for instance, in decency of manners, shall it be one cause when it relates to a man, another when it relates to a woman?

In different states shall the magistrates be different or the same? I mean, whether in a democracy, an oligarchy, an aristocracy, and a monarchy, the same persons shall have the same power? or shall it vary according to the different formation of the government? as in an aristocracy the offices of the state are allotted to those who are well educated; in an oligarchy to those who are rich; in a democracy to the freemen? Or shall the magistrates differ as the communities differ? For it may happen that the very same may be sometimes proper, sometimes otherwise: in this state it may be necessary that the magistrate have great powers, in that but small. There are also certain magistrates peculiar to certain states--as the pre-advisers are not proper in a democracy, but a senate is; for one such order is necessary, whose business shall be to consider beforehand and prepare those bills which shall be brought before the people that they may have leisure to attend to their own affairs; and when these are few in number the state inclines to an oligarchy. The pre-advisers indeed must always be few for they are peculiar to an oligarchy: and where there are both these offices in the same state, the pre-adviser's is superior to the senator's, the one having only a democratical power, the other an oligarchical: and indeed the power of the senate is lost in those democracies, in which the people, meeting in one public assembly, take all the business into their own hands; and this is likely to happen either when the community in general are in easy circumstances, or when they are paid for their attendance; for they are then at leisure often to meet together and determine everything for themselves. A magistrate whose business is to control the manners of the boys, or women, or who takes any department similar to this, is to be found in an aristocracy, not in a democracy; for who can forbid the wives of the poor from appearing in public? neither is such a one to be met with in an oligarchy; for the women there are too delicate to bear control. And thus much for this subject. Let us endeavour to treat at large of the establishment of magistrates, beginning from first principles. Now, they differ from each other in three ways, from which, blended together, all the varieties which can be imagined arise. The first of these differences is in those who appoint the magistrates, the second consists in those who are appointed, the third in the mode of appointment; and each of these three differ in three manners; for either all the citizens may appoint collectively, or some out of their whole body, or some out of a particular order in it, according to fortune, family, or virtue, or some other rule (as at Megara, where the right of election was amongst those who had returned together to their country, and had reinstated themselves by force of arms) and this either by vote or lot. Again, these several modes may be differently formed together, as some magistrates may be chosen by part of the community, others by the whole; some out of part, others out of the whole; some by vote, others by lot: and each of these different modes admit of a four-fold subdivision; for either all may elect all by vote or by lot; and when all elect, they may either proceed without any distinction, or they may elect by a certain division of tribes, wards, or companies, till they have gone through the whole community: and some magistrates may be elected one way, and others another. Again, if some magistrates are elected either by vote or lot of all the citizens, or by the vote of some and the lot of some, or some one way and some another; that is to say, some by the vote of all, others by the lot of all, there will then be twelve different methods of electing the magistrates, without blending the two together. Of these there are two adapted to a democracy; namely, to have all the magistrates chosen out of all the people, either by vote or lot, or both; that is to say, some of them by lot, some by vote. In a free state the whole community should not elect at the same time, but some out of the whole, or out of some particular rank; and this either by lot, or vote, or both: and they should elect either out of the whole community, or out of some particular persons in it, and this both by lot and vote. In an oligarchy it is proper to choose some magistrates out of the whole body of the citizens, some by vote, some by lot, others by both: by lot is most correspondent to that form of government. In a free aristocracy, some magistrates should be chosen out of the community in general, others out of a particular rank, or these by choice, those by lot. In a pure oligarchy, the magistrates should be chosen out of certain ranks, and by certain persons, and some of those by lot, others by both methods; but to choose them out of the whole community is not correspondent to the nature of this government. It is proper in an aristocracy for the whole community to elect their magistrates out of particular persons, and this by vote. These then are all the different ways of electing of magistrates; and they have been allotted according to the nature of the different communities; but what mode of proceeding is proper for different communities, or how the offices ought to be established, or with what powers shall be particularly explained. I mean by the powers of a magistrate, what should be his particular province, as the management of the finances or the laws of the state; for different magistrates have different powers, as that of the general of the army differs from the clerk of the market.

CHAPTER XVI

Of the three parts of which a government is formed, we now come to consider the judicial; and this also we shall divide in the same manner as we did the magisterial, into three parts. Of whom the judges shall consist, and for what causes, and how. When I say of whom, I mean whether they shall be the whole people, or some particulars; by for what causes I mean, how many different courts shall be appointed; by how, whether they shall be elected by vote or lot. Let us first determine how many different courts there ought to be. Now these are eight. The first of these is the court of inspection over the behaviour of the magistrates when they have quitted their office; the second is to punish those who have injured the public; the third is to take cognisance of those causes in which the state is a party; the fourth is to decide between magistrates and private persons, who appeal from a fine laid upon them; the fifth is to determine disputes which may arise concerning contracts of great value; the sixth is to judge between foreigners, and of murders, of which there are different species; and these may all be tried by the same judges or by different ones; for there are murders of malice prepense and of chance-medley; there is also justifiable homicide, where the fact is admitted, and the legality of it disputed.

There is also another court called at Athens the Court of Phreattae, which determines points relating to a murder committed by one who has run away, to decide whether he shall return; though such an affair happens but seldom, and in very large cities; the seventh, to determine causes wherein strangers are concerned, and this whether they are between stranger and stranger or between a stranger and a citizen. The eighth and last is for small actions, from one to five drachma's, or a little more; for these ought also to be legally determined, but not to be brought before the whole body of the judges. But without entering into any particulars concerning actions for murder, and those wherein strangers are the parties, let us particularly treat of those courts which have the jurisdiction of those matters which more particularly relate to the affairs of the community and which if not well conducted occasion seditions and commotions in the state. Now, of necessity, either all persons must have a right to judge of all these different causes, appointed for that purpose, either by vote or lot, or all of all, some of them by vote, and others by lot, or in some causes by vote, in others by lot. Thus there will be four sorts of judges. There will be just the same number also if they are chosen out of part of the people only; for either all the judges must be chosen out of that part either by vote or lot, or some by lot and some by vote, or the judges in particular causes must be chosen some by vote, others by lot; by which means there will be the same number of them also as was mentioned. Besides, different judges may be joined together; I mean those who are chosen out of the whole people or part of them or both; so that all three may sit together in the same court, and this either by vote, lot, or both. And thus much for the different sorts of judges. Of these appointments that which admits all the community to be judges in all causes is most suitable to a democracy; the second, which appoints that certain persons shall judge all causes, to an oligarchy; the third, which appoints the whole community to be judges in some causes, but particular persons in others, to an aristocracy or free state.

BOOK V

CHAPTER I

We have now gone through those particulars we proposed to speak of; it remains that we next consider from what causes and how alterations in government arise, and of what nature they are, and to what the destruction of each state is owing; and also to what form any form of polity is most likely to shift into, and what are the means to be used for the general preservation of governments, as well as what are applicable to any particular state; and also of the remedies which are to be applied either to all in general, or to any one considered separately, when they are in a state of corruption: and here we ought first to lay down this principle, that there are many governments, all of which approve of what is just and what is analogically equal; and yet have failed from attaining thereunto, as we have already mentioned; thus democracies have arisen from supposing that those who are equal in one thing are so in every other circumstance; as, because they are equal in liberty, they are equal in everything else; and oligarchies, from supposing that those who are unequal in one thing are unequal in all; that when men are so in point of fortune, that inequality extends to everything else. Hence it follows, that those who in some respects are equal with others think it right to endeavour to partake of an equality with them in everything; and those who are superior to others endeavour to get still more; and it is this more which is the inequality: thus most states, though they have some notion of what is just, yet are almost totally wrong; and, upon this account, when either party has not that share in the administration which answers to his expectations, he becomes seditious: but those who of all others have the greatest right to be so are the last that are; namely, those who excel in virtue; for they alone can be called generally superior. There are, too, some persons of distinguished families who, because they are so, disdain to be on an equality with others, for those esteem themselves noble who boast of their ancestors' merit and fortune: these, to speak truth, are the origin and fountain from whence seditions arise. The alterations which men may propose to make in governments are two; for either they may change the state already established into some other, as when they propose to erect an oligarchy where there is a democracy; or a democracy, or free state, where there is an oligarchy, or an aristocracy from these, or those from that; or else, when they have no objection to the established government, which they like very well, but choose to have the sole management in it themselves; either in the hands of a few or one only. They will also raise commotions concerning the degree in which they would have the established power; as if, for instance, the government is an oligarchy, to have it more purely so, and in the same manner if it is a democracy, or else to have it less so; and, in like manner, whatever may be the nature of the government, either to extend or contract its powers; or else to make some alterations in some parts of it; as to establish or abolish a particular magistracy, as some persons say Lysander endeavoured to abolish the kingly power in Sparta; and Pausanias that of the ephori. Thus in Epidamnus there was an alteration in one part of the constitution, for instead of the philarchi they established a senate. It is also necessary for all the magistrates at Athens; to attend in the court of the Helisea when any new magistrate is created: the power of the archon also in that state partakes of the nature of an oligarchy: inequality is always the occasion of sedition, but not when those who are unequal are treated in a different manner correspondent to that inequality. Thus kingly power is unequal when exercised over equals. Upon the whole, those who aim after an equality are the cause of seditions. Equality is twofold, either in number or value. Equality in number is when two things contain the same parts or the same quantity; equality in value is by proportion as two exceeds one, and three two by the same number-thus by proportion four exceeds two, and two one in the same degree, for two is the same part of four that one is of two; that is to say, half. Now, all agree in what is absolutely and simply just; but, as we have already said they dispute concerning proportionate value; for some persons, if they are equal in one respect, think themselves equal in all; others, if they are superior in one thing, think they may claim the superiority in all; from whence chiefly arise two sorts of governments, a democracy and an oligarchy; for nobility and virtue are to be found only amongst a few; the contrary amongst the many; there being in no place a hundred of the first to be met with, but enough of the last everywhere. But to establish a government entirely upon either of these equalities is wrong, and this the example of those so established makes evident, for none of them have been stable; and for this reason, that it is impossible that whatever is wrong at the first and in its principles should not at last meet with a bad end: for which reason in some things an equality of numbers ought to take place, in others an equality in value. However, a democracy is safer and less liable to sedition than an oligarchy; for in this latter it may arise from two causes, for either the few in power may conspire against each other or against the people; but in a democracy only one; namely, against the few who aim at exclusive power; but there is no instance worth speaking of, of a sedition of the people against themselves. Moreover, a government composed of men of moderate fortunes comes much nearer to a democracy than an oligarchy, and is the safest of all such states.

CHAPTER II

Since we are inquiring into the causes of seditions and revolutions in governments, we must begin entirely with the first principles from whence they arise. Now these, so to speak, are nearly three in number; which we must first distinguish in general from each other, and endeavour to show in what situation people are who begin a sedition; and for what causes; and thirdly, what are the beginnings of political troubles and mutual quarrels with each other. Now that cause which of all others most universally inclines men to desire to bring about a change in government is that which I have already mentioned; for those who aim at equality will be ever ready for sedition, if they see those whom they esteem their equals possess more than they do, as well as those also who are not content with equality but aim at superiority, if they think that while they deserve more than, they have only equal with, or less than, their inferiors. Now, what they aim at may be either just or unjust; just, when those who are inferior are seditious, that they may be equal; unjust, when those who are equal are so, that they may be superior. These, then, are the situations in which men will be seditious: the causes for which they will be so are profit and honour; and their contrary: for, to avoid dishonour or loss of fortune by mulcts, either on their own account or their friends, they will raise a commotion in the state. The original causes which dispose men to the things which I have mentioned are, taken in one manner, seven in number, in another they are more; two of which are the same with those that have been already mentioned: but influencing in a different manner; for profit and honour sharpen men against each other; not to get the possession of them for themselves (which was what I just now supposed), but when they see others, some justly, others unjustly, engrossing them. The other causes are haughtiness, fear, eminence, contempt, disproportionate increase in some part of the state. There are also other things which in a different manner will occasion revolutions in governments; as election intrigues, neglect, want of numbers, a too great dissimilarity of circumstances.

CHAPTER III

What influence ill-treatment and profit have for this purpose, and how they may be the causes of sedition, is almost self-evident; for when the magistrates are haughty and endeavour to make greater profits than their office gives them, they not only occasion seditions amongst each other, but against the state also who gave them their power; and this their avarice has two objects, either private property or the property of the state. What influence honours have, and how they may occasion sedition, is evident enough; for those who are themselves unhonoured while they see others honoured, will be ready for any disturbance: and these things are done unjustly when any one is either honoured or discarded contrary to their deserts, justly when they are according to them. Excessive honours are also a cause of sedition when one person or more are greater than the state and the power of the government can permit; for then a monarchy or a dynasty is usually established: on which account the ostracism was introduced in some places, as at Argos and Athens: though it is better to guard against such excesses in the founding of a state, than when they have been permitted to take place, to correct them afterward. Those who have been guilty of crimes will be the cause of sedition, through fear of punishment; as will those also who expect an injury, that they may prevent it; as was the case at Rhodes, when the nobles conspired against the people on account of the decrees they expected would pass against them. Contempt also is a cause of sedition and conspiracies; as in oligarchies, where there are many who have no share in the administration. The rich also even in democracies, despising the disorder and anarchy which will arise, hope to better themselves by the same means which happened at Thebes after the battle of Oenophyta, where, in consequence of bad administration, the democracy was destroyed; as it was at Megara, where the power of the people was lost through anarchy and disorder; the same thing happened at Syracuse before the tyranny of Gelon; and at Rhodes there was the same sedition before the popular government was overthrown. Revolutions in state will also arise from a disproportionate increase; for as the body consists of many parts, it ought to increase proportion-ably to preserve its symmetry, which would otherwise be destroyed; as if the foot was to be four cubits long, and the rest of the body but two palms; it might otherwise be changed into an animal of a different form, if it increase beyond proportion not only in quantity, but also in disposition of parts; so also a city consists of parts, some of which may often increase without notice, as the number of poor in democracies and free states. They will also sometimes happen by accident, as at Tarentum, a little after the Median war, where so many of the nobles were killed in a battle by the Iapygi, that from a free state the government was turned into a democracy; and at Argos, where so many of the citizens were killed by Cleomenes the Spartan, that they were obliged to admit several husbandmen to the freedom of the state: and at Athens, through the unfortunate event of the infantry battles, the number of the nobles was reduced by the soldiers being chosen from the list of citizens in the Lacedaemonian wars. Revolutions also sometimes take place in a democracy, though seldomer; for where the rich grow numerous or properties increase, they become oligarchies or dynasties. Governments also sometimes alter without seditions by a combination of the meaner people; as at Hersea: for which purpose they changed the mode of election from votes to lots, and thus got themselves chosen: and by negligence, as when the citizens admit those who are not friends to the constitution into the chief offices of the state, which happened at Orus, when the oligarchy of the archons was put an end to at the election of Heracleodorus, who changed that form of government into a democratic free state. By little and little, I mean by this, that very often great alterations silently take place in the form of government from people's overlooking small matters; as at Ambracia, where the census was originally small, but at last became nothing at all, as if a little and nothing at all were nearly or entirely alike. That state also is liable to seditions which is composed of different nations, till their differences are blended together and undistinguishable; for as a city cannot be composed of every multitude, so neither can it in every given time; for which reason all those republics which have hitherto been originally composed of different people or afterwards admitted their neighbours to the freedom of their city, have been most liable to revolutions; as when the Achaeans joined with the Traezenians in founding Sybaris; for soon after, growing more powerful than the Traezenians, they expelled them from the city; from whence came the proverb of Sybarite wickedness: and again, disputes from a like cause happened at Thurium between the Sybarites and those who had joined with them in building the city; for they assuming upon these, on account of the country being their own, were driven out. And at Byzantium the new citizens, being detected in plots against the state, were driven out of the city by force of arms. The Antisseans also, having taken in those who were banished from Chios, afterwards did the same thing; and also the Zancleans, after having taken in the people of Samos. The Appolloniats, in the Euxine Sea, having admitted their sojourners to the freedom of their city, were troubled with seditions: and the Syracusians, after the expulsion of their tyrants, having enrolled strangers and mercenaries amongst their citizens, quarrelled with each other and came to an open rupture: and the people of Amphipolis, having taken in a colony of Chalcidians, were the greater part of them driven out of the city by them. Many persons occasion seditions in oligarchies because they think themselves ill-used in not sharing the honours of the state with their equals, as I have already mentioned; but in democracies the principal people do the same because they have not more than an equal share with others who are not equal to them. The situation of the place will also sometimes occasion disturbances in the state when the ground is not well adapted for one city; as at Clazomene, where the people who lived in that part of the town called Chytrum quarrelled with them who lived in the island, and the Colophonians with the Notians. At Athens too the disposition of the citizens is not the same, for those who live in the Piraeus are more attached to a popular government than those who live in the city properly so called; for as the interposition of a rivulet, however small, will occasion the line of the phalanx to fluctuate, so any trifling disagreement will be the cause of seditions; but they will not so soon flow from anything else as from the disagreement between virtue and vice, and next to that between poverty and richès, and so on in order, one cause having more influence than another; one of which that I last mentioned.

CHAPTER IV

But seditions in government do not arise for little things, but from them; for their immediate cause is something of moment. Now, trifling quarrels are attended with the greatest consequences when they arise between persons of the first distinction in the state, as was the case with the Syracusians in a remote period; for a revolution in the government was brought about by a quarrel between two young men who were in office, upon a love affair; for one of them being absent, the other seduced his mistress; he in his turn, offended with this, persuaded his friend's wife to come and live with him; and upon this the whole city took part either with the one or the other, and the government was overturned: therefore every one at the beginning of such disputes ought to take care to avoid the consequences; and to smother up all quarrels which may happen to arise amongst those in power, for the mischief lies in the beginning; for the beginning is said to be half of the business, so that what was then but a little fault will be found afterwards to bear its full proportion to what follows. Moreover, disputes between men of note involve the whole city in their consequences; in Hestiaea, after the Median war: two brothers having a dispute about their paternal estate; he who was the poorer, from the other's having concealed part of the effects, and some money which his father had found, engaged the popular party on his side, while the other, who was rich, the men of fashion. And at Delphos, a quarrel about a wedding was the beginning of all the seditions that afterwards arose amongst them; for the bridegroom, being terrified by some unlucky omen upon waiting upon the bride, went away without marrying her; which her relations resenting, contrived secretly to convey some sacred money into his pocket while he was sacrificing, and then killed him as an impious person. At Mitylene also, a dispute, which arose concerning a right of heritage, was the beginning of great evils, and a war with the Athenians, in which Paches took their city, for Timophanes, a man of fortune, leaving two daughters, Doxander, who was circumvented in procuring them in marriage for his two sons, began a sedition, and excited the Athenians to attack them, being the host of that state. There was also a dispute at Phocea, concerning a right of inheritance, between Mnasis, the father of Mnasis, and Euthucrates, the father of Onomarchus, which brought on the Phoceans the sacred war. The government too of Epidamnus was changed from a quarrel that arose from an intended marriage; for a certain man having contracted his daughter in marriage, the father of the young person to whom she was contracted, being archon, punishes him, upon which account he, resenting the affront, associated himself with those who were excluded from any share in the government, and brought about a revolution. A government may be changed either into an oligarchy, democracy, or a free state; when the magistrates, or any part of the city acquire great credit, or are increased in power, as the court of Areopagus at Athens, having procured great credit during the Median war, added firmness to their administration; and, on the other hand, the maritime force, composed of the commonalty, having gained the victory at Salamis, by their power at sea, got the lead in the state, and strengthened the popular party: and at Argos, the nobles, having gained great credit by the battle of Mantinea against the Lacedaemonians, endeavoured to dissolve the democracy. And at Syracuse, the victory in their war with the Athenians being owing to the common people, they changed their free state into a democracy: and at Chalcis, the people having taken off the tyrant Phocis, together with the nobles, immediately seized the government: and at Ambracia also the people, having expelled the tyrant Periander, with his party, placed the supreme power in themselves. And this in general ought to be known, that whosoever has been the occasion of a state being powerful, whether private persons, or magistrates, a certain tribe, or any particular part of the citizens, or the multitude, be they who they will, will be the cause of disputes in the state. For either some persons, who envy them the honours they have acquired, will begin to be seditious, or they, on account of the dignity they have acquired, will not be content with their former equality. A state is also liable to commotions when those parts of it which seem to be opposite to each other approach to an equality, as the rich and the common people; so that the part which is between them both is either nothing at all, or too little to be noticed; for if one party is so much more powerful than the other, as to be evidently stronger, that other will not be willing to hazard the danger: for which reason those who are superior in excellence and virtue will never be the cause of seditions; for they will be too few for that purpose when compared to the many. In general, the beginning and the causes of seditions in all states are such as I have now described, and revolutions therein are brought about in two ways, either by violence or fraud: if by violence, either at first by compelling them to submit to the change when it is made. It may also be brought about by fraud in two different ways, either when the people, being at first deceived, willingly consent to an alteration in their government, and are afterwards obliged by force to abide by it: as, for instance, when the four hundred imposed upon the people by telling them that the king of Persia would supply them with money for the war against the Lacedaemonians; and after they had been guilty of this falsity, they endeavoured to keep possession of the supreme power; or when they are at first persuaded and afterwards consent to be governed: and by one of these methods which I have mentioned are all revolutions in governments brought about.

CHAPTER V

We ought now to inquire into those events which will arise from these causes in every species of government. Democracies will be most subject to revolutions from the dishonesty of their demagogues; for partly, by informing against men of property, they induce them to join together through self-defence, for a common fear will make the greatest enemies unite; and partly by setting the common people against them: and this is what any one may continually see practised in many states. In the island of Cos, for instance, the democracy was subverted by the wickedness of the demagogues, for the nobles entered into a combination with each other. And at Rhodes the demagogues, by distributing of bribes, prevented the people from paying the trierarchs what was owing to them, who were obliged by the number of actions they were harassed with to conspire together and destroy the popular state. The same thing was brought about at Heraclea, soon after the settlement of the city, by the same persons; for the citizens of note, being ill treated by them, quitted the city, but afterwards joining together they returned and overthrew the popular state. Just in the same manner the democracy was destroyed in Megara; for there the demagogues, to procure money by confiscations, drove out the nobles, till the number of those who were banished was considerable, who, returning, got the better of the people in a battle, and established an oligarchy. The like happened at Cume, during the time of the democracy, which Thrasymachus destroyed; and whoever considers what has happened in other states may perceive the same revolutions to have arisen from the same causes. The demagogues, to curry favour with the people, drive the nobles to conspire together, either by dividing their estates, or obliging them to spend them on public services, or by banishing them, that they may confiscate the fortunes of the wealthy. In former times, when the same person was both demagogue and general, the democracies were changed into tyrannies; and indeed most of the ancient tyrannies arose from those states: a reason for which then subsisted, but not now; for at that time the demagogues were of the soldiery; for they were not then powerful by their eloquence; but, now the art of oratory is cultivated, the able speakers are at present the demagogues; but, as they are unqualified to act in a military capacity, they cannot impose themselves on the people as tyrants, if we except in one or two trifling instances. Formerly, too, tyrannies were more common than now, on account of the very extensive powers with which some magistrates were entrusted: as the prytanes at Miletus; for they were supreme in many things of the last consequence; and also because at that time the cities were not of that very great extent, the people in general living in the country, and being employed in husbandry, which gave them, who took the lead in public affairs, an opportunity, if they had a turn for war, to make themselves tyrants; which they all did when they had gained the confidence of the people; and this confidence was their hatred to the rich. This was the case of Pisistratus at Athens, when he opposed the Pediaci: and of Theagenes in Megara, who slaughtered the cattle belonging to the rich, after he had seized those who kept them by the riverside. Dionysius also, for accusing Daphnseus and the rich, was thought worthy of being raised to a tyranny, from the confidence which the people had of his being a popular man in consequence of these enmities. A government shall also alter from its ancient and approved democratic form into one entirely new, if there is no census to regulate the election of magistrates; for, as the election is with the people, the demagogues who are desirous of being in office, to flatter them, will endeavour with all their power to make the people superior even to the laws. To prevent this entirely, or at least in a great measure, the magistrates should be elected by the tribes, and not by the people at large. These are nearly the revolutions to which democracies are liable, and also the causes from whence they arise.

CHAPTER VI

There are two things which of all others most evidently occasion a revolution in an oligarchy; one is, when the people are ill used, for then every individual is ripe for sedition; more particularly if one of the oligarchy should happen to be their leader; as Lygdamis, at Naxus, who was afterwards tyrant of that island. Seditions also which arise from different causes will differ from each other; for sometimes a revolution is brought about by the rich who have no share in the administration, which is in the hands of a very few indeed: and this happened at Massilia, Ister, Heraclea, and other cities; for those who had no share in the government ceased not to raise disputes till they were admitted to it: first the elder brothers, and then the younger also: for in some places the father and son are never in office at the same time; in others the elder and younger brother: and where this is observed the oligarchy partakes something of a free state. At Ister it was changed into a democracy; in Heraclea, instead of being in the hands of a few, it consisted of six hundred. At Cnidus the oligarchy was destroyed by the nobles quarrelling with each other, because the government was in the hands of so few: for there, as we have just mentioned, if the father was in office, the son could not; or, if there were many brothers, the eldest only; for the people, taking advantage of their disputes, elected one of the nobles for their general, and got the victory: for where there are seditions government is weak. And formerly at Erithria, during the oligarchy of the Basilides, although the state flourished greatly under their excellent management, yet because the people were displeased that the power should be in the hands of so few, they changed the government. Oligarchies also are subject to revolutions, from those who are in office therein, from the quarrels of the demagogues with each other. The demagogues are of two sorts; one who flatter the few when they are in power: for even these have their demagogues; such was Charicles at Athens, who had great influence over the thirty; and, in the same manner, Phrynichus over the four hundred. The others are those demagogues who have a share in the oligarchy, and flatter the people: such were the state-guardians at Larissa, who flattered the people because they were elected by them. And this will always happen in every oligarchy where the magistrates do not elect themselves, but are chosen out of men either of great fortune or certain ranks, by the soldiers or by the people; as was the custom at Abydos. And when the judicial department is not in the hands of the supreme power, the demagogues, favouring the people in their causes, overturn the government; which happened at Heraclea in Pontus: and also when some desire to contract the power of the oligarchy into fewer hands; for those who endeavour to support an equality are obliged to apply to the people for assistance. An oligarchy is also subject to revolutions when the nobility spend their fortunes by luxury; for such persons are desirous of innovations, and either endeavour to be tyrants themselves or to support others in being so, as Hypparinus supported Dionysius of Syracuse. And at Amphipolis one Cleotimus collected a colony of Chalcidians, and when they came set them to quarrel with the rich: and at AEgina a certain person who brought an action against Chares attempted on that account to alter the government. Sometimes they will try to raise commotions, sometimes they will rob the public, and then quarrel with each other, or else fight with those who endeavour to detect them; which was the case at Apollonia in Pontus. But if the members of an oligarchy agree among themselves the state is not very easily destroyed without some external force. Pharsalus is a proof of this, where, though the place is small, yet the citizens have great power, from the prudent use they make of it. An oligarchy also will be destroyed when they create another oligarchy under it; that is, when the management of public affairs is in the hands of a few, and not equally, but when all of them do not partake of the supreme power, as happened once at Elis, where the supreme power in general was in the hands of a very few out of whom a senate was chosen, consisting but of ninety, who held their places for life; and their mode of election was calculated to preserve the power amongst each other's families, like the senators at Lacedaemon. An oligarchy is liable to a revolution both in time of war and peace; in war, because through a distrust in the citizens the government is obliged to employ mercenary troops, and he to whom they give the command of the army will very often assume the tyranny, as Timophanes did at Corinth; and if they appoint more than one general, they will very probably establish a dynasty: and sometimes, through fear of this, they are forced to let the people in general have some share in the government, because they are obliged to employ them. In peace, from their want of confidence in each other, they will entrust the guardianship of the state to mercenaries and their general, who will be an arbiter between them, and sometimes become master of both, which happened at Larissa, when Simos and the Aleuadae had the chief power. The same thing happened at Abydos, during the time of the political clubs, of which Iphiades' was one. Commotions also will happen in an oligarchy from one party's overbearing and insulting another, or from their quarrelling about their law-suits or marriages. How their marriages, for instance, will have that effect has been already shown: and in Eretria, Diagoras destroyed the oligarchy of the knights upon the same account. A sedition also arose at Heraclea, from a certain person being condemned by the court; and at Thebes, in consequence of a man's being guilty of adultery; the punishment indeed which Eurytion suffered at Heraclea was just, yet it was illegally executed: as was that at Thebes upon Archias; for their enemies endeavoured to have them publicly bound in the pillory. Many revolutions also have been brought about in oligarchies by those who could not brook the despotism which those persons assumed who were in power, as at Cnidus and Chios. Changes also may happen by accident in what we call a free state and in an oligarchy; wheresoever the senators, judges, and magistrates are chosen according to a certain census; for it often happens that the highest census is fixed at first; so that a few only could have a share in the government, in an oligarchy, or in a free state those of moderate fortunes only; when the city grows rich, through peace or some other happy cause, it becomes so little that every one's fortune is equal to the census, so that the whole community may partake of all the honours of government; and this change sometimes happens by little and little, and insensible approaches, sometimes quicker. These are the revolutions and seditions that arise in oligarchies, and the causes to which they are owing: and indeed both democracies and oligarchies sometimes alter, not into governments of a contrary form, but into those of the same government; as, for instance, from having the supreme power in the law to vest it in the ruling party, or the contrariwise.

CHAPTER VII

Commotions also arise in aristocracies, from there being so few persons in power (as we have already observed they do in oligarchies, for in this particular an aristocracy is most near an oligarchy, for in both these states the administration of public affairs is in the hands of a few; not that this arises from the same cause in both, though herein they chiefly seem alike): and these will necessarily be most likely to happen when the generality of the people are high-spirited and think themselves equal to each other in merit; such were those at Lacedasmon, called the Partheniae (for these were, as well as others, descendants of citizens), who being detected in a conspiracy against the state, were sent to found Tarentum. They will happen also when some great men are disgraced by those who have received higher honours than themselves, to whom they are no ways inferior in abilities, as Lysander by the kings: or when an ambitious man cannot get into power, as Cinadon, who, in the reign of Agesilaus, was chief in a conspiracy against the Spartans: and also when some are too poor and others too rich, which will most frequently happen in time of war; as at Lacedaemon during the Messenian war, which is proved by a poem of Tyrtaeus, called "Eunomia;" for some persons being reduced thereby, desired that the lands might be divided: and also when some person of very high rank might still be higher if he could rule alone, which seemed to be Pausanias's intention at Lacedaemon, when he was their general in the Median war, and Anno's at Carthage. But free states and aristocracies are mostly destroyed from want of a fixed administration of public affairs; the cause of which evil arises at first from want of a due mixture of the democratic and the oligarchic parts in a free state; and in an aristocracy from the same causes, and also from virtue not being properly joined to power; but chiefly from the two first, I mean the undue mixture of the democratic and oligarchic parts; for these two are what all free states endeavour to blend together, and many of those which we call aristocracies, in this particular these states differ from each other, and on this account the one of them is less stable than the other, for that state which inclines most to an oligarchy is called an aristocracy, and that which inclines most to a democracy is called a free state; on which account this latter is more secure than the former, for the wider the foundation the securer the building, and it is ever best to live where equality prevails. But the rich, if the community gives them rank, very often endeavour to insult and tyrannise over others. On the whole, whichever way a government inclines, in that it will settle, each party supporting their own. Thus a free state will become a democracy; an aristocracy an oligarchy; or the contrary, an aristocracy may change into a democracy (for the poor, if they think themselves injured, directly take part with the contrary side) and a free state into an oligarchy. The only firm state is that where every one enjoys that equality he has a right to and fully possesses what is his own. And what I have been speaking of happened to the Thurians; for the magistrates being elected according to a very high census, it was altered to a lower, and they were subdivided into more courts, but in consequence of the nobles possessing all the land, contrary to law; the state was too much of an oligarchy, which gave them an opportunity of encroaching greatly on the rest of the people; but these, after they had been well inured to war, so far got the better of their guards as to expel every one out of the country who possessed more than he ought. Moreover, as all aristocracies are free oligarchies, the nobles therein endeavour to have rather too much power, as at Lacedaemon, where property is now in the hands of a few, and the nobles have too much liberty to do as they please and make such alliances as they please. Thus the city of the Locrians was ruined from an alliance with Dionysius; which state was neither a democracy nor well-tempered aristocracy. But an aristocracy chiefly approaches to a secret change by its being destroyed by degrees, as we have already said of all governments in general; and this happens from the cause of the alteration being trifling; for whenever anything which in the least regards the state is treated with contempt, after that something else, and this of a little more consequence, will be more easily altered, until the whole fabric of government is entirely subverted, which happened in the government of Thurium; for the law being that they should continue soldiers for five years, some young men of a martial disposition, who were in great esteem amongst their officers, despising those who had the management of public affairs, and imagining they could easily accomplish their intention, first endeavoured to abolish this law, with a view of having it lawful to continue the same person perpetually in the military, perceiving that the people would readily appoint them. Upon this, the magistrates who are called counselors first joined together with an intention to oppose it but were afterwards induced to agree to it, from a belief that if that law was not repealed they would permit the management of all other public affairs to remain in their hands; but afterwards, when they endeavoured to restrain some fresh alterations that were making, they found that they could do nothing, for the whole form of government was altered into a dynasty of those who first introduced the innovations. In short, all governments are liable to be destroyed either from within or from without; from without when they have for their neighbour a state whose policy is contrary to theirs, and indeed if it has great power the same thing will happen if it is not their neighbour; of which both the Athenians and the Lacedaemonians are a proof; for the one, when conquerors everywhere destroyed the oligarchies; the other the democracies. These are the chief causes of revolutions and dissensions in governments.

CHAPTER VIII

We are now to consider upon what the preservation of governments in general and of each state in particular depends; and, in the first place, it is evident that if we are right in the causes we have assigned for their destruction, we know also the means of their preservation; for things contrary produce contraries: but destruction and preservation are contrary to each other. In well-tempered governments it requires as much care as anything whatsoever, that nothing be done contrary to law: and this ought chiefly to be attended to in matters of small consequence; for an illegality that approaches insensibly, approaches secretly, as in a family small expenses continually repeated consume a man's income; for the understanding is deceived thereby, as by this false argument; if every part is little, then the whole is little: now, this in one sense is true, in another is false, for the whole and all the parts together are large, though made up of small parts. The first therefore of anything is what the state ought to guard against. In the next place, no credit ought to be given to those who endeavour to deceive the people with false pretences; for they will be confuted by facts. The different ways in which they will attempt to do this have been already mentioned. You may often perceive both aristocracies and oligarchies continuing firm, not from the stability of their forms of government, but from the wise conduct of the magistrates, both towards those who have a part in the management of public affairs, and those also who have not: towards those who have not, by never injuring them; and also introducing those who are of most consequence amongst them into office; nor disgracing those who are desirous of honour; or encroaching on the property of individuals; towards those who have, by behaving to each other upon an equality; for that equality which the favourers of a democracy desire to have established in the state is not only just, but convenient also, amongst those who are of the same rank: for which reason, if the administration is in the hands of many, those rules which are established in democracies will be very useful; as to let no one continue in office longer than six months: that all those who are of the same rank may have their turn; for between these there is a sort of democracy: for which reason demagogues are most likely to arise up amongst them, as we have already mentioned: besides, by this means both aristocracies and democracies will be the less liable to be corrupted into dynasties, because it will not be so easy for those who are magistrates for a little to do as much mischief as they could in a long time: for it is from hence that tyrannies arise in democracies and oligarchies; for either those who are most powerful in each state establish a tyranny, as the demagogues in the one, the dynasties in the other, or the chief magistrates who have been long in power. Governments are sometimes preserved not only by having the means of their corruption at a great distance, but also by its being very near them; for those who are alarmed at some impending evil keep a stricter hand over the state; for which reason it is necessary for those who have the guardianship of the constitution to be able to awaken the fears of the people, that they may preserve it, and not like a night-guard to be remiss in protecting the state, but to make the distant danger appear at hand. Great care ought also to be used to endeavour to restrain the quarrels and disputes of the nobles by laws, as well as to prevent those who are not already engaged in them from taking a part therein; for to perceive an evil at its very first approach is not the lot of every one, but of the politician. To prevent any alteration taking place in an oligarchy or free state on account of the census, if that happens to continue the same while the quantity of money is increased, it will be useful to take a general account of the whole amount of it in former times, to compare it with the present, and to do this every year in those cities where the census is yearly, in larger communities once in three or five years; and if the whole should be found much larger or much less than it was at the time when the census was first established in the state, let there be a law either to extend or contract it, doing both these according to its increase or decrease; if it increases making the census larger, and if it decreases smaller: and if this latter is not done in oligarchies and free states, you will have a dynasty arise in the one, an oligarchy in the other: if the former is not, free states will be changed into democracies, and oligarchies into free states or democracies. It is a general maxim in democracies, oligarchies, monarchies, and indeed in all governments, not to let any one acquire a rank far superior to the rest of the community, but rather to endeavour to confer moderate honours for a continuance than great ones for a short time; for these latter spoil men, for it is not every one who can bear prosperity: but if this rule is not observed, let not those honours which were conferred all at once be all at once taken away, but rather by degrees. But, above all things, let this regulation be made by the law, that no one shall have too much power, either by means of his fortune or friends; but if he has, for his excess therein, let it be contrived that he shall quit the country. Now, as many persons promote innovations, that they may enjoy their own particular manner of living, there ought to be a particular officer to inspect the manners of every one, and see that these are not contrary to the genius of the state in which he lives, whether it may be an oligarchy, a democracy, or any other form of government; and, for the same reason, those should be guarded against who are most prosperous in the city: the means of doing which is by appointing those who are otherwise to the business and the offices of the state. I mean, to oppose men of account to the common people, the poor to the rich, and to blend both these into one body, and to increase the numbers of those who are in the middle rank; and this will prevent those seditions which arise from an inequality of condition. But above all, in every state it is necessary, both by the laws and every other method possible, to prevent those who are employed by the public from being venal, and this particularly in an oligarchy; for then the people will not be so much displeased from seeing themselves excluded from a share in the government (nay, they will rather be glad to have leisure to attend their private affairs) as at suspecting that the officers of the state steal the public money, then indeed they are afflicted with double concern, both because they are deprived of the honours of the state, and pillaged by those who enjoy them. There is one method of blending together a democracy and an aristocracy, if office brought no profit; by which means both the rich and the poor will enjoy what they desire; for to admit all to a share in the government is democratical; that the rich should be in office is aristocratical. This must be done by letting no public employment whatsoever be attended with any emolument; for the poor will not desire to be in office when they can get nothing by it, but had rather attend to their own affairs: but the rich will choose it, as they want nothing of the community. Thus the poor will increase their fortunes by being wholly employed in their own concerns; and the principal part of the people will not be governed by the lower sort. To prevent the exchequer from being defrauded, let all public money be delivered out openly in the face of the whole city, and let copies of the accounts be deposited in the different wards tribes, and divisions. But, as the magistrates are to execute their offices without any advantages, the law ought to provide proper honours for those who execute them well. In democracies also it is necessary that the rich should be protected, by not permitting their lands to be divided, nor even the produce of them, which in some states is done unperceivably. It would be also better if the people would prevent them when they offer to exhibit a number of unnecessary and yet expensive public entertainments of plays, music, processions, and the like. In an oligarchy it is necessary to take great care of the poor, and allot them public employments which are gainful; and, if any of the rich insult them, to let their punishment be severer than if they insulted one of their own rank; and to let estates pass by affinity, and not gift: nor to permit any person to have more than one; for by this means property will be more equally divided, and the greater part of the poor get into better circumstances. It is also serviceable in a democracy and an oligarchy to allot those who take no part in public affairs an equality or a preference in other things; the rich in a democracy, to the poor in an oligarchy: but still all the principal offices in the state to be filled only by those who are best qualified to discharge them.

CHAPTER IX

There are three qualifications necessary for those who fill the first departments in government; first of all, an affection for the established constitution; second place, abilities every way completely equal to the business of their office; in the third, virtue and justice correspondent to the nature of that particular state they are placed in; for if justice is not the same in all states, it is evident that there must be different species thereof. There may be some doubt, when all these qualifications do not in the same persons, in what manner the choice shall be made; as for instance, suppose that one person is an accomplished general, but a bad man and no friend to the constitution; another is just and a friend to it, which shall we prefer? we should then consider of two qualities, which of them the generality possess in a greater degree, which in a less; for which reason in the choice of a general we should regard his courage more than his virtue as the more uncommon quality; as there are fewer capable of conducting an army than there are good men: but, to protect the state or manage the finances, the contrary rule should be followed; for these require greater virtue than the generality are possessed of, but only that knowledge which is common to all. It may be asked, if a man has abilities equal to his appointment in the state, and is affectionate to the constitution, what occasion is there for being virtuous, since these two things alone are sufficient to enable him to be useful to the public? it is, because those who possess those qualities are often deficient in prudence; for, as they often neglect their own affairs, though they know them and love themselves, so nothing will prevent their serving the public in the same manner. In short, whatsoever the laws contain which we allow to be useful to the state contributes to its preservation: but its first and principal support is (as has been often insisted upon) to have the number of those who desire to preserve it greater than those who wish to destroy it. Above all things that ought not to be forgotten which many governments now corrupted neglect; namely, to preserve a mean. For many things seemingly favourable to a democracy destroy a democracy, and many things seemingly favourable to an oligarchy destroy an oligarchy. Those who think this the only virtue extend it to excess, not considering that as a nose which varies a little from perfect straightness, either towards a hook nose or a flat one, may yet be beautiful and agreeable to look at; but if this particularity is extended beyond measure, first of all the properties of the part is lost, but at last it can hardly be admitted to be a nose at all, on account of the excess of the rise or sinking: thus it is with other parts of the human body; so also the same thing is true with respect to states; for both an oligarchy and a democracy may something vary from their most perfect form and yet be well constituted; but if any one endeavours to extend either of them too far, at first he will make the government the worse for it, but at last there will be no government at all remaining. The lawgiver and the politician therefore should know well what preserves and what destroys a democracy or an oligarchy, for neither the one nor the other can possibly continue without rich and poor: but that whenever an entire equality of circumstances prevails, the state must necessarily become of another form; so that those who destroy these laws, which authorise an inequality in property, destroy the government. It is also an error in democracies for the demagogues to endeavour to make the common people superior to the laws; and thus by setting them at variance with the rich, dividing one city into two; whereas they ought rather to speak in favour of the rich. In oligarchies, on the contrary, it is wrong to support those who are in administration against the people. The oaths also which they take in an oligarchy ought to be contrary to what they now are; for, at present, in some places they swear, "I will be adverse to the common people, and contrive all I can against them;" whereas they ought rather to suppose and pretend the contrary; expressing in their oaths, that they will not injure the people. But of all things which I have mentioned, that which contributes most to preserve the state is, what is now most despised, to educate your children for the state; for the most useful laws, and most approved by every statesman, will be of no service if the citizens are not accustomed to and brought up in the principles of the constitution; of a democracy, if that is by law established; of an oligarchy, if that is; for if there are bad morals in one man, there are in the city. But to educate a child fit for the state, it must not be done in the manner which would please either those who have the power in an oligarchy or those who desire a democracy, but so as they may be able to conduct either of these forms of governments. But now the children of the magistrates in an oligarchy are brought up too delicately, and the children of the poor hardy with exercise and labour; so that they are both desirous of and able to promote innovations. In democracies of the purest form they pursue a method which is contrary to their welfare; the reason of which is, that they define liberty wrong: now, there are two things which seem to be the objects of a democracy, that the people in general should possess the supreme power, and all enjoy freedom; for that which is just seems to be equal, and what the people think equal, that is a law: now, their freedom and equality consists in every one's doing what they please: that is in such a democracy every one may live as he likes; "as his inclination guides," in the words of Euripides: but this is wrong, for no one ought to think it slavery to live in subjection to government, but protection. Thus I have mentioned the causes of corruption in different states, and the means of their preservation.

CHAPTER X

It now remains that we speak of monarchies, their causes of corruption, and means of preservation; and indeed almost the same things which have been said of other governments happen to kingdoms and tyrannies; for a kingdom partakes of an aristocracy, a tyranny of the worst species of an oligarchy and democracy; for which reason it is the worst that man can submit to, as being composed of two, both of which are bad, and collectively retains all the corruptions and all the defects of both these states. These two species of monarchies arise from principles contrary to each other: a kingdom is formed to protect the better sort of people against the multitude, and kings are appointed out of those, who are chosen either for their superior virtue and actions flowing from virtuous principles, or else from their noble descent; but a tyrant is chosen out of the meanest populace; an enemy to the better sort, that the common people may not be oppressed by them. That this is true experience convinces us; for the generality of tyrants were indeed mere demagogues, who gained credit with the people by oppressing the nobles. Some tyrannies were established in this manner after the cities were considerably enlarged-- others before that time, by kings who exceeded the power which their country allowed them, from a desire of governing despotically: others were founded by those who were elected to the superior offices in the state; for formerly the people appointed officers for life, who came to be at the head of civil and religious affairs, and these chose one out of their body in whom the supreme power over all the magistrates was placed. By all these means it was easy to establish a tyranny, if they chose it; for their power was ready at hand, either by their being kings, or else by enjoying the honours of the state; thus Phidon at Argos and other tyrants enjoyed originally the kingly power; Phalaris and others in Ionia, the honours of the state. Pansetius at Leontium, Cypselus at Corinth, Pisistratus at Athens, Dionysius at Syracuse, and others, acquired theirs by having been demagogues. A kingdom, as we have said, partakes much of the nature of an aristocracy, and is bestowed according to worth, as either virtue, family, beneficent actions, or these joined with power; for those who have been benefactors to cities and states, or have it in their powers to be so, have acquired this honour, and those who have prevented a people from falling into slavery by war, as Codrus, or those who have freed them from it, as Cyrus, or the founders of cities, or settlers of colonies, as the kings of Sparta, Macedon, and Molossus. A king desires to be the guardian of his people, that those who have property may be secure in the possession of it, and that the people in general meet with no injury; but a tyrant, as has been often said, has no regard to the common good, except for his own advantage; his only object is pleasure, but a king's is virtue: what a tyrant therefore is ambitious of engrossing is wealth, but a king rather honour. The guards too of a king are citizens, a tyrant's foreigners.

That a tyranny contains all that is bad both in a democracy and an oligarchy is evident; with an oligarchy it has for its end gain, as the only means of providing the tyrant with guards and the luxuries of life; like that it places no confidence in the people; and therefore deprives them of the use of arms: it is also common to them both to persecute the populace, to drive them out of the city and their own habitations. With a democracy it quarrels with the nobles, and destroys them both publicly and privately, or drives them into banishment, as rivals and an impediment to the government; hence naturally arise conspiracies both amongst those who desire to govern and those who desire not to be slaves; hence arose Periander's advice to Thrasybulus to take off the tallest stalks, hinting thereby, that it was necessary to make away with the eminent citizens. We ought then in reason, as has been already said, to account for the changes which arise in a monarchy from the same causes which produce them in other states: for, through injustice received, fear, and contempt, many of those who are under a monarchical government conspire against it; but of all species of injustice, injurious contempt has most influence on them for that purpose: sometimes it is owing to their being deprived of their private fortunes. The dissolution too of a kingdom and a tyranny are generally the same; for monarchs abound in wealth and honour, which all are desirous to obtain. Of plots: some aim at the life of those who govern, others at their government; the first arises from hatred to their persons; which hatred may be owing to many causes, either of which will be sufficient to excite their anger, and the generality of those who are under the influence of that passion will join in a conspiracy, not for the sake of their own advancement, but for revenge. Thus the plot against the children of Pisistratus arose from their injurious treatment of Harmodius's sister, and insulting him also; for Harmodius resenting the injury done to his sister, and Aristogiton the injury done to Harmodius. Periander the tyrant of Ambracia also lost his life by a conspiracy, for some improper liberties he took with a boy in his cups: and Philip was slain by Pausanias for neglecting to revenge him of the affront he had received from Attains; as was Amintas the Little by Darda, for insulting him on account of his age; and the eunuch by Evagoras the Cyprian in revenge for having taken his son's wife away from him....

Many also who have had their bodies scourged with stripes have, through resentment, either killed those who caused them to be inflicted or conspired against them, even when they had kingly power, as at Mitylene Megacles, joining with his friends, killed the Penthelidee, who used to go about striking those they met with clubs. Thus, in later times, Smendes killed Penthilus for whipping him and dragging him away from his wife. Decamnichus also was the chief cause of the conspiracy against Archelaus, for he urged others on: the occasion of his resentment was his having delivered him to Euripides the poet to be scourged; for Euripides was greatly offended with him for having said something of the foulness of his breath. And many others have been killed or conspired against on the same account. Fear too is a cause which produces the same effects, as well in monarchies as in other states: thus Artabanes conspired against Xerxes through fear of punishment for having hanged Darius according to his orders, whom he supposed he intended to pardon, as the order was given at supper-time. Some kings also have been dethroned and killed in consequence of the contempt they were held in by the people; as some one conspired against Sardanapalus, having seen him spinning with his wife, if what is related of him is true, or if not of him, it may very probably be true of some one else. Dion also conspired against Dionysius the Younger, seeing his subjects desirous of a conspiracy, and that he himself was always drunk: and even a man's friends will do this if they despise him; for from the confidence he places in them, they think that they shall not be found out. Those also who think they shall gain his throne will conspire against a king through contempt; for as they are powerful themselves, and despise the danger, on account of their own strength, they will readily attempt it. Thus a general at the head of his army will endeavour to dethrone the monarch, as Cyrus did Astyages, despising both his manner of life and his forces; his forces for want of action, his life for its effeminacy: thus Suthes, the Thracian, who was general to Amadocus, conspired against him. Sometimes more than one of these causes will excite men to enter into conspiracies, as contempt and desire of gain; as in the instance of Mithridates against Ariobarzanes. Those also who are of a bold disposition, and have gained military honours amongst kings, will of all others be most like to engage in sedition; for strength and courage united inspire great bravery: whenever, therefore, these join in one person, he will be very ready for conspiracies, as he will easily conquer. Those who conspire against a tyrant through love of glory and honour have a different motive in view from what I have already mentioned; for, like all others who embrace danger, they have only glory and honour in view, and think, not as some do, of the wealth and pomp they may acquire, but engage in this as they would in any other noble action, that they may be illustrious and distinguished, and destroy a tyrant, not to succeed in his tyranny, but to acquire renown. No doubt but the number of those who act upon this principle is small, for we must suppose they regard their own safety as nothing in case they should not succeed, and must embrace the opinion of Dion (which few can do) when he made war upon Dionysius with a very few troops; for he said, that let the advantage he made be ever so little it would satisfy him to have gained it; and that, should it be his lot to die the moment he had gained footing in his country, he should think his death sufficiently glorious. A tyranny also is exposed to the same destruction as all other states are, from too powerful neighbours: for it is evident, that an opposition of principles will make them desirous of subverting it; and what they desire, all who can, do: and there is a principle of opposition in one state to another, as a democracy against a tyranny, as says Hesiod, "a potter against a potter;" for the extreme of a democracy is a tyranny; a kingly power against an aristocracy, from their different forms of government--for which reason the Lacedaemonians destroyed many tyrannies; as did the Syracusians during the prosperity of their state. Nor are they only destroyed from without, but also from within, when those who have no share in the power bring about a revolution, as happened to Gelon, and lately to Dionysius; to the first, by means of Thrasybulus, the brother of Hiero, who nattered Gelon's son, and induced him to lead a life of pleasure, that he himself might govern; but the family joined together and endeavoured to support the tyranny and expel Thrasybulus; but those whom they made of their party seized the opportunity and expelled the whole family. Dion made war against his relation Dionysius, and being assisted by the people, first expelled and then killed him. As there are two causes which chiefly induce men to conspire against tyrants, hatred and contempt, one of these, namely hatred, seems inseparable from them. Contempt also is often the cause of their destruction: for though, for instance, those who raised themselves to the supreme power generally preserved it; but those who received it from them have, to speak truth, almost immediately all of them lost it; for, falling into an effeminate way of life, they soon grew despicable, and generally fell victims to conspiracies. Part of their hatred may be very fitly ascribed to anger; for in some cases this is their motive to action: for it is often a cause which impels them to act more powerfully than hatred, and they proceed with greater obstinacy against those whom they attack, as this passion is not under the direction of reason. Many persons also indulge this passion through contempt; which occasioned the fall of the Pisistratidae and many others. But hatred is more powerful than anger; for anger is accompanied with grief, which prevents the entrance of reason; but hatred is free from it. In short, whatever causes may be assigned as the destruction of a pure oligarchy unmixed with any other government and an extreme democracy, the same may be applied to a tyranny; for these are divided tyrannies.

Kingdoms are seldom destroyed by any outward attack; for which reason they are generally very stable; but they have many causes of subversion within; of which two are the principal; one is when those who are in power excite a sedition, the other when they endeavour to establish a tyranny by assuming greater power than the law gives them. A kingdom, indeed, is not what we ever see erected in our times, but rather monarchies and tyrannies; for a kingly government is one that is voluntarily submitted to, and its supreme power admitted upon great occasions: but where many are equal, and there are none in any respect so much better than another as to be qualified for the greatness and dignity of government over them, then these equals will not willingly submit to be commanded; but if any one assumes the government, either by force or fraud, this is a tyranny. To what we have already said we shall add, the causes of revolutions in an hereditary kingdom. One of these is, that many of those who enjoy it are naturally proper objects of contempt only: another is, that they are insolent while their power is not despotic; but they possess kingly honours only. Such a state is soon destroyed; for a king exists but while the people are willing to obey, as their submission to him is voluntary, but to a tyrant involuntary. These and such-like are the causes of the destruction of monarchies.

CHAPTER XI

Monarchies, in a word, are preserved by means contrary to what I have already mentioned as the cause of their destruction; but to speak to each separately: the stability of a kingdom will depend upon the power of the king's being kept within moderate bounds; for by how much the less extensive his power is, by so much the longer will his government continue; for he will be less despotic and more upon an equality of condition with those he governs; who, on that account, will envy him the less.

It was on this account that the kingdom of the Molossi continued so long; and the Lacedaemonians from their government's being from the beginning divided into two parts, and also by the moderation introduced into the other parts of it by Theopompus, and his establishment of the ephori; for by taking something from the power he increased the duration of the kingdom, so that in some measure he made it not less, but bigger; as they say he replied to his wife, who asked him if he was not ashamed to deliver down his kingdom to his children reduced from what he received it from his ancestors? No, says he, I give it him more lasting. Tyrannies are preserved two ways most opposite to each other, one of which is when the power is delegated from one to the other, and in this manner many tyrants govern in their states. Report says that Periander founded many of these. There are also many of them to be met with amongst the Persians. What has been already mentioned is as conducive as anything can be to preserve a tyranny; namely, to keep down those who are of an aspiring disposition, to take off those who will not submit, to allow no public meals, no clubs, no education, nothing at all, but to guard against everything that gives rise to high spirits or mutual confidence; nor to suffer the learned meetings of those who are at leisure to hold conversation with each other; and to endeavour by every means possible to keep all the people strangers to each other; for knowledge increases mutual confidence; and to oblige all strangers to appear in public, and to live near the city-gate, that all their actions may be sufficiently seen; for those who are kept like slaves seldom entertain any noble thoughts: in short, to imitate everything which the Persians and barbarians do, for they all contribute to support slavery; and to endeavour to know what every one who is under their power does and says; and for this purpose to employ spies: such were those women whom the Syracusians called potagogides Hiero also used to send out listeners wherever there was any meeting or conversation; for the people dare not speak with freedom for fear of such persons; and if any one does, there is the less chance of its being concealed; and to endeavour that the whole community should mutually accuse and come to blows with each other, friend with friend, the commons with the nobles, and the rich with each other. It is also advantageous for a tyranny that all those who are under it should be oppressed with poverty, that they may not be able to compose a guard; and that, being employed in procuring their daily bread, they may have no leisure to conspire against their tyrants. The Pyramids of Egypt are a proof of this, and the votive edifices of the Cyposelidse, and the temple of Jupiter Olympus, built by the Pisistratidae, and the works of Polycrates at Samos; for all these produced one end, the keeping the people poor. It is necessary also to multiply taxes, as at Syracuse; where Dionysius in the space of five years collected all the private property of his subjects into his own coffers. A tyrant also should endeavour to engage his subjects in a war, that they may have employment and continually depend upon their general. A king is preserved by his friends, but a tyrant is of all persons the man who can place no confidence in friends, as every one has it in his desire and these chiefly in their power to destroy him. All these things also which are done in an extreme democracy should be done in a tyranny, as permitting great licentiousness to the women in the house, that they may reveal their husbands' secrets; and showing great indulgence to slaves also for the same reason; for slaves and women conspire not against tyrants: but when they are treated with kindness, both of them are abettors of tyrants, and extreme democracies also; and the people too in such a state desire to be despotic. For which reason flatterers are in repute in both these: the demagogue in the democracy, for he is the proper flatterer of the people; among tyrants, he who will servilely adapt himself to their humours; for this is the business of flatterers. And for this reason tyrants always love the worst of wretches, for they rejoice in being flattered, which no man of a liberal spirit will submit to; for they love the virtuous, but flatter none. Bad men too are fit for bad purposes; "like to like," as the proverb says. A tyrant also should show no favour to a man of worth or a freeman; for he should think, that no one deserved to be thought these but himself; for he who supports his dignity, and is a friend to freedom, encroaches upon the superiority and the despotism of the tyrant: such men, therefore, they naturally hate, as destructive to their government. A tyrant also should rather admit strangers to his table and familiarity than citizens, as these are his enemies, but the others have no design against him. These and such-like are the supports of a tyranny, for it comprehends whatsoever is wicked. But all these things may be comprehended in three divisions, for there are three objects which a tyranny has in view; one of which is, that the citizens should be of poor abject dispositions; for such men never propose to conspire against any one. The second is, that they should have no confidence in each other; for while they have not this, the tyrant is safe enough from destruction. For which reason they are always at enmity with those of merit, as hurtful to their government; not only as they scorn to be governed despotically, but also because they can rely upon each other's fidelity, and others can rely upon theirs, and because they will not inform against their associates, nor any one else. The third is, that they shall be totally without the means of doing anything; for no one undertakes what is impossible for him to perform: so that without power a tyranny can never be destroyed. These, then, are the three objects which the inclinations of tyrants desire to see accomplished; for all their tyrannical plans tend to promote one of these three ends, that their people may neither have mutual confidence, power, nor spirit. This, then, is one of the two methods of preserving tyrannies: the other proceeds in a way quite contrary to what has been already described, and which may be discerned from considering to what the destruction of a kingdom is owing; for as one cause of that is, making the government approach near to a tyranny, so the safety of a tyranny consists in making the government nearly kingly; preserving only one thing, namely power, that not only the willing, but the unwilling also, must be obliged to submit; for if this is once lost, the tyranny is at an end. This, then, as the foundation, must be preserved: in other particulars carefully do and affect to seem like a king; first, appear to pay a great attention to what belongs to the public; nor make such profuse presents as will offend the people; while they are to supply the money out of the hard labour of their own hands, and see it given in profusion to mistresses, foreigners, and fiddlers; keeping an exact account both of what you receive and pay; which is a practice some tyrants do actually follow, by which means they seem rather fathers of families than tyrants: nor need you ever fear the want of money while you have the supreme power of the state in your own hands. It is also much better for those tyrants who quit their kingdom to do this than to leave behind them money they have hoarded up; for their regents will be much less desirous of making innovations, and they are more to be dreaded by absent tyrants than the citizens; for such of them as he suspects he takes with him, but these regents must be left behind. He should also endeavour to appear to collect such taxes and require such services as the exigencies of the state demand, that whenever they are wanted they may be ready in time of war; and particularly to take care that he appear to collect and keep them not as his own property, but the public's. His appearance also should not be severe, but respectable, so that he should inspire those who approach him with veneration and not fear; but this will not be easily accomplished if he is despised. If, therefore, he will not take the pains to acquire any other, he ought to endeavour to be a man of political abilities, and to fix that opinion of himself in the judgment of his subjects. He should also take care not to appear to be guilty of the least offence against modesty, nor to suffer it in those under him: nor to permit the women of his family to treat others haughtily; for the haughtiness of women has been the ruin of many tyrants. With respect to the pleasures of sense, he ought to do directly contrary to the practice of some tyrants at present; for they do not only continually indulge themselves in them for many days together, but they seem also to desire to have other witnesses of it, that they may wonder at their happiness; whereas he ought really to be moderate in these, and, if not, to appear to others to avoid them-for it is not the sober man who is exposed either to plots or contempt, but the drunkard; not the early riser, but the sluggard. His conduct in general should also be contrary to what is reported of former tyrants; for he ought to improve and adorn his city, so as to seem a guardian and not a tyrant; and, moreover., always to seem particularly attentive to the worship of the gods; for from persons of such a character men entertain less fears of suffering anything illegal while they suppose that he who governs them is religious and reverences the gods; and they will be less inclined to raise insinuations against such a one, as being peculiarly under their protection: but this must be so done as to give no occasion for any suspicion of hypocrisy. He should also take care to show such respect to men of merit in every particular, that they should not think they could be treated with greater distinction by their fellow-citizens in a free state. He should also let all honours flow immediately from himself, but every censure from his subordinate officers and judges. It is also a common protection of all monarchies not to make one person too great, or, certainly, not many; for they will support each other: but, if it is necessary to entrust any large powers to one person, to take care that it is not one of an ardent spirit; for this disposition is upon every opportunity most ready for a revolution: and, if it should seem necessary to deprive any one of his power, to do it by degrees, and not reduce him all at once. It is also necessary to abstain from all kinds of insolence; more particularly from corporal punishment; which you must be most cautious never to exercise over those who have a delicate sense of honour; for, as those who love money are touched to the quick when anything affects their property, so are men of honour and principle when they receive any disgrace: therefore, either never employ personal punishment, or, if you do, let it be only in the manner in which a father would correct his son, and not with contempt; and, upon the whole, make amends for any seeming disgrace by bestowing greater honours. But of all persons who are most likely to entertain designs against the person of a tyrant, those are chiefly to be feared and guarded against who regard as nothing the loss of their own lives, so that they can but accomplish their purpose: be very careful therefore of those who either think themselves affronted, or those who are dear to them; for those who are excited by anger to revenge regard as nothing their own persons: for, as Heraclitus says, it is dangerous to fight with an angry man who will purchase with his life the thing he aims at. As all cities are composed of two sorts of persons, the rich and the poor, it is necessary that both these should find equal protection from him who governs them, and that the one party should not have it in their power to injure the other; but that the tyrant should attach to himself that party which is the most powerful; which, if he does, he will have no occasion either to make his slaves free, or to deprive citizens of their arms; for the strength of either of the parties added to his own forces will render him superior to any conspiracy. It would be superfluous to go through all particulars; for the rule of conduct which the tyrant ought to pursue is evident enough, and that is, to affect to appear not the tyrant, but the king; the guardian of those he governs, not their plunderer, but their protector, and to affect the middle rank in life, not one superior to all others: he should, therefore, associate his nobles with him and soothe his people; for his government will not only be necessarily more honourable and worthy of imitation, as it will be over men of worth, and not abject wretches who perpetually both hate and fear him; but it will be also more durable. Let him also frame his life so that his manners may be consentaneous to virtue, or at least let half of them be so, that he may not be altogether wicked, but only so in part.

CHAPTER XII

Indeed an oligarchy and a tyranny are of all governments of the shortest duration. The tyranny of Orthagoras and his family at Sicyon, it is true, continued longer than any other: the reason for which was, that they used their power with moderation, and were in many particulars obedient to the laws; and, as Clisthenes was an able general, he never fell into contempt, and by the care he took that in many particulars his government should be popular. He is reported also to have presented a person with a crown who adjudged the victory to another; and some say that it is the statue of that judge which is placed in the forum.

They say also, that Pisistratus submitted to be summoned into the court of the Areopagites. The second that we shall mention is the tyranny of the Cypselidæ, at Corinth, which continued seventy-seven years and six months; for Cypselus was tyrant there thirty years, Periander forty-four, and Psammetichus, the son of Georgias, three years; the reason for which was, that Cypselus was a popular man, and governed without guards. Periander indeed ruled like a tyrant, but then he was an able general. The third was that of the Pisistradidæ at Athens; but it was not continual: for Pisistratus himself was twice expelled; so that out of thirty-three years he was only fifteen in power, and his son eighteen; so that the whole time was thirty-three years. Of the rest we shall mention that of Hiero, and Gelo at

Syracuse; and this did not continue long, for both their reigns were only eighteen years; for Gelo died in the eighth year of his tyranny, and Hiero in his tenth. Thrasybulus fell in his eleventh month, and many other tyrannies have continued a very short time. We have now gone through the general cases of corruption and means of preservation both in free states and monarchies. In Plato's Republic, Socrates is introduced treating upon the changes which different governments are liable to: but his discourse is faulty; for he does not particularly mention what changes the best and first governments are liable to; for he only assigns the general cause, of nothing being immutable, but that in time everything will alter [***tr.: text is unintelligible here***] he conceives that nature will then produce bad men, who will not submit to education, and in this, probably, he is not wrong; for it is certain that there are some persons whom it is impossible by any education to make good men; but why should this change be more peculiar to what he calls the best-formed government, than to all other forms, and indeed to all other things that exist? and in respect to his assigned time, as the cause of the alteration of all things, we find that those which did not begin to exist at the same time cease to be at the same time; so that, if anything came into beginning the day before the solstice, it must alter at the same time. Besides, why should such a form of government be changed into the Lacedaemonian? for, in general, when governments alter, they alter into the contrary species to what they before were, and not into one like their former. And this reasoning holds true of other changes; for he says, that from the Lacedaemonian form it changes into an oligarchy, and from thence into a democracy, and from a democracy into a tyranny: and sometimes a contrary change takes place, as from a democracy into an oligarchy, rather than into a monarchy. With respect to a tyranny he neither says whether there will be any change in it; or if not, to what cause it will be owing; or if there is, into what other state it will alter: but the reason of this is, that a tyranny is an indeterminate government; and, according to him, every state ought to alter into the first, and most perfect, thus the continuity and circle would be preserved. But one tyranny often changed into another; as at Syria, from Myron's to Clisthenes'; or into an oligarchy, as was Antileo's at Chalcas; or into a democracy, as was Gelo's at Syracuse; or into an aristocracy, as was Charilaus's at Lacedaemon, and at Carthage. An oligarchy is also changed into a tyranny; such was the rise of most of the ancient tyrannies in Sicily; at Leontini, into the tyranny of Panaetius; at Gela, into that of Cleander; at Rhegium into that of Anaxilaus; and the like in many other cities. It is absurd also to suppose, that a state is changed into an oligarchy because those who are in power are avaricious and greedy of money, and not because those who are by far richer than their fellow citizens think it unfair that those who have nothing should have an equal share in the rule of the state with themselves, who possess so much-for in many oligarchies it is not allowable to be employed in money-getting, and there are many laws to prevent it. But in Carthage, which is a democracy, money-getting is creditable, and yet their form of government remains unaltered. It is also absurd to say, that in an oligarchy there are two cities, one of the poor and another of the rich; for why should this happen to them more than to the Lacedaemonians, or any other state where all possess not equal property, or where all are not equally good? for though no one member of the community should be poorer than he was before, yet a democracy might nevertheless change into an oligarchy; if the rich should be more powerful than the poor, and the one too negligent, and the other attentive: and though these changes are owing to many causes, yet he mentions but one only, that the citizens become poor by luxury, and paying interest-money; as if at first they were all rich, or the greater part of them: but this is not so, but when some of those who have the principal management of public affairs lose their fortunes, they will endeavour to bring about a revolution; but when others do, nothing of consequence will follow, nor when such states do alter is there any more reason for their altering into a democracy than any other. Besides, though some of the members of the community may not have spent their fortunes, yet if they share not in the honours of the state, or if they are ill-used and insulted, they will endeavour to raise seditions, and bring about a revolution, that they may be allowed to do as they like; which, Plato says, arises from too much liberty. Although there are many oligarchies and democracies, yet Socrates, when he is treating of the changes they may undergo, speaks of them as if there was but one of each sort.

BOOK VI

CHAPTER I

We have already shown what is the nature of the supreme council in the state, and wherein one may differ from another, and how the different magistrates should be regulated; and also the judicial department, and what is best suited to what state; and also to what causes both the destruction and preservation of governments are owing.

As there are very many species of democracies, as well as of other states, it will not be amiss to consider at the same time anything which we may have omitted to mention concerning either of them, and to allot to each that mode of conduct which is peculiar to and advantageous for them; and also to inquire into the combinations of all these different modes of government which we have mentioned; for as these are blended together the government is altered, as from an aristocracy to be an oligarchy, and from a free state to be a democracy. Now, I mean by those combinations of government (which I ought to examine into, but have not yet done), namely, whether the deliberative department and the election of magistrates is regulated in a manner correspondent to an oligarchy, or the judicial to an aristocracy, or the deliberative part only to an oligarchy, and the election of magistrates to an aristocracy, or whether, in any other manner, everything is not regulated according to the nature of the government. But we will first consider what particular sort of democracy is fitted to a particular city, and also what particular oligarchy to a particular people; and of other states, what is advantageous to what. It is also necessary to show clearly, not only which of these governments is best for a state, but also how it ought to be established there, and other things we will treat of briefly.

And first, we will speak of a democracy; and this will at the same time show clearly the nature of its opposite which some persons call an oligarchy; and in doing this we must examine into all the parts of a democracy, and everything that is connected therewith; for from the manner in which these are compounded together different species of democracies arise: and hence it is that they are more than one, and of various natures. Now, there are two causes which occasion there being so many democracies; one of which is that which we have already mentioned; namely, there being different sorts of people; for in one country the majority are husbandmen, in another mechanics, and hired servants; if the first of these is added to the second, and the third to both of them, the democracy will not only differ in the particular of better or worse, but in this, that it will be no longer the same government; the other is that which we will now speak of. The different things which are connected with democracies and seem to make part of these states, do, from their being joined to them, render them different from others: this attending a few, that more, and another all. It is necessary that he who would found any state which he may happen to approve of, or correct one, should be acquainted with all these particulars. All founders of states endeavour to comprehend within their own plan everything of nearly the same kind with it; but in doing this they err, in the manner I have already described in treating of the preservation and destruction of governments. I will now speak of these first principles and manners, and whatever else a democratical state requires.

CHAPTER II

Now the foundation of a democratical state is liberty, and people have been accustomed to say this as if here only liberty was to be found; for they affirm that this is the end proposed by every democracy. But one part of liberty is to govern and be governed alternately; for, according to democratical justice, equality is measured by numbers, and not by worth: and this being just, it is necessary that the supreme power should be vested in the people at large; and that what the majority determine should be final: so that in a democracy the poor ought to have more power than the rich, as being the greater number; for this is one mark of liberty which all framers of a democracy lay down as a criterion of that state; another is, to live as every one likes; for this, they say, is a right which liberty gives, since he is a slave who must live as he likes not. This, then, is another criterion of a democracy. Hence arises the claim to be under no command whatsoever to any one, upon any account, any otherwise than by rotation, and that just as far only as that person is, in his turn, under his also. This also is conducive to that equality which liberty demands. These things being premised, and such being the government, it follows that such rules as the following should be observed in it, that all the magistrates should be chosen out of all the people, and all to command each, and each in his turn all: that all the magistrates should be chosen by lot, except to those offices only which required some particular knowledge and skill: that no census, or a very small one, should be required to qualify a man for any office: that none should be in the same employment twice, or very few, and very seldom, except in the army: that all their appointments should be limited to a very short time, or at least as many as possible: that the whole community should be qualified to judge in all causes whatsoever, let the object be ever so extensive, ever so interesting, or of ever so high a nature; as at Athens, where the people at large judge the magistrates when they come out of office, and decide concerning public affairs as well as private contracts: that the supreme power should be in the public assembly; and that no magistrate should be allowed any discretionary power but in a few instances, and of no consequence to public business. Of all magistrates a senate is best suited to a democracy, where the whole community is not paid for giving their attendance; for in that case it loses its power; for then the people will bring all causes before them, by appeal, as we have already mentioned in a former book. In the next place, there should, if possible, be a fund to pay all the citizens--who have any share in the management of public affairs, either as members of the assembly, judges, and magistrates; but if this cannot be done, at least the magistrates, the judges the senators, and members of the supreme assembly, and also those officers who are obliged to eat at a common table ought to be paid. Moreover, as an oligarchy is said to be a government of men of family, fortune, and education; so, on the contrary, a democracy is a government in the hands of men of no birth, indigent circumstances, and mechanical employments. In this state also no office should be for life; and, if any such should remain after the government has been long changed into a democracy, they should endeavour by degrees to diminish the power; and also elect by lot instead of vote. These things, then, appertain to all democracies; namely, to be established on that principle of justice which is homogeneous to those governments; that is, that all the members of the state, by number, should enjoy an equality, which seems chiefly to constitute a democracy, or government of the people: for it seems perfectly equal that the rich should have no more share in the government than the poor, nor be alone in power; but that all should be equal, according to number; for thus, they think, the equality and liberty of the state best preserved.

CHAPTER III

In the next place we must inquire how this equality is to be procured. Shall the qualifications be divided so that five hundred rich should be equal to a thousand poor, or shall the thousand have equal power with the five hundred? or shall we not establish our equality in this manner? but divide indeed thus, and afterwards taking an equal number both out of the five hundred and the thousand, invest them with the power of creating the magistrates and judges. Is this state then established according to perfect democratical justice, or rather that which is guided by numbers only? For the defenders of a democracy say, that that is just which the majority approve of: but the favourers of an oligarchy say, that that is just which those who have most approve of; and that we ought to be directed by the value of property. Both the propositions are unjust; for if we agree with what the few propose we erect a tyranny: for if it should happen that an individual should have more than the rest who are rich, according to oligarchical justice, this man alone has a right to the supreme power; but if superiority of numbers is to prevail, injustice will then be done by confiscating the property of the rich, who are few, as we have already said. What then that equality is, which both parties will admit, must be collected from the definition of right which is common to them both; for they both say that what the majority of the state approves of ought to be established. Be it so; but not entirely: but since a city happens to be made up of two different ranks of people, the rich and the poor, let that be established which is approved of by both these, or the greater part: but should there be opposite sentiments, let that be established which shall be approved of by the greater part: but let this be according to the census; for instance, if there should be ten of the rich and twenty of the poor, and six of the first and fifteen of the last should agree upon any measure, and the remaining four of the rich should join with the remaining five of the poor in opposing it, that party whose census when added together should determine which opinion should be law, and should these happen to be equal, it should be regarded as a case similar to an assembly or court of justice dividing equally upon any question that comes before them, who either determine it by lot or some such method. But although, with respect to what is equal and just, it may be very difficult to establish the truth, yet it is much easier to do than to persuade those who have it in their power to encroach upon others to be guided thereby; for the weak always desire what is equal and just, but the powerful pay no regard thereunto.

CHAPTER IV

There are four kinds of democracies. The best is that which is composed of those first in order, as we have already said, and this also is the most ancient of any. I call that the first which every one would place so, was he to divide the people; for the best part of these are the husbandmen. We see, then, that a democracy may be framed where the majority live by tillage or pasturage; for, as their property is but small, they will not be at leisure perpetually to hold public assemblies, but will be continually employed in following their own business, not having otherwise the means of living; nor will they be desirous of what another enjoys, but will rather like to follow their own business than meddle with state affairs and accept the offices of government, which will be attended with no great profit; for the major part of mankind are rather desirous of riches than honour (a proof of this is, that they submitted to the tyrannies in ancient times, and do now submit to the oligarchies, if no one hinders them in their usual occupations, or deprives them of their property; for some of them soon get rich, others are removed from poverty); besides, their having the right of election and calling their magistrates to account for their conduct when they come out of office, will satisfy their desire of honours, if any of them entertain that passion: for in some states, though the commonalty have not the right of electing the magistrates, yet it is vested in part of that body chosen to represent them: and it is sufficient for the people at large to possess the deliberative power: and this ought to be considered as a species of democracy; such was that formerly at Mantinsea: for which reason it is proper for the democracy we have been now treating of to have a power (and it has been usual for them to have it) of censuring their magistrates when out of office, and sitting in judgment upon all causes: but that the chief magistrates should be elected, and according to a certain census, which should vary with the rank of their office, or else not by a census, but according to their abilities for their respective appointments. A state thus constituted must be well constituted; for the magistracies will be always filled with the best men with the approbation of the people; who will not envy their superiors: and these and the nobles should be content with this part in the administration; for they will not be governed by their inferiors. They will be also careful to use their power with moderation, as there are others to whom full power is delegated to censure their conduct; for it is very serviceable to the state to have them dependent upon others, and not to be permitted to do whatsoever they choose; for with such a liberty there would be no check to that evil particle there is in every one: therefore it is necessary and most for the benefit of the state that the offices thereof should be filled by the principal persons in it, whose characters are unblemished, and that the people are not oppressed. It is now evident that this is the best species of democracy, and on what account; because the people are such and have such powers as they ought to have. To establish a democracy of husbandmen some of those laws which were observed in many ancient states are universally useful; as, for instance, on no account to permit any one to possess more than a certain quantity of land, or within a certain distance from the city. Formerly also, in some states, no one was allowed to sell their original lot of land. They also mention a law of one Oxylus, which forbade any one to add to their patrimony by usury. We ought also to follow the law of the Aphutaeans, as useful to direct us in this particular we are now speaking of; for they having but very little ground, while they were a numerous people, and at the same time were all husbandmen, did not include all their lands within the census, but divided them in such a manner that, according to the census, the poor had more power than the rich. Next to the commonalty of husbandmen is one of shepherds and herdsmen; for they have many things in common with them, and, by their way of life, are excellently qualified to make good soldiers, stout in body, and able to continue in the open air all night. The generality of the people of whom other democracies are composed are much worse than these; for their lives are wretched nor have they any business with virtue in anything they do; these are your mechanics, your exchange-men, and hired servants; as all these sorts of men frequent the exchange and the citadel, they can readily attend the public assembly; whereas the husbandmen, being more dispersed in the country, cannot so easily meet together; nor are they equally desirous of doing it with these others! When a country happens to be so situated that a great part of the land lies at a distance from the city, there it is easy to establish a good democracy or a free state for the people in general will be obliged to live in the country; so that it will be necessary in such a democracy, though there may be an exchange-mob at hand, never to allow a legal assembly without the inhabitants of the country attend. We have shown in what manner the first and best democracy ought to be established, and it will be equally evident as to the rest, for from these we should proceed as a guide, and always separate the meanest of the people from the rest. But the last and worst, which gives to every citizen without distinction a share in every part of the administration, is what few citizens can bear, nor is it easy to preserve for any long time, unless well supported by laws and manners. We have already noticed almost every cause that can destroy either this or any other state. Those who have taken the lead in such a democracy have endeavoured to support it, and make the people powerful by collecting together as many persons as they could and giving them their freedom, not only legitimately but naturally born, and also if either of their parents were citizens, that is to say, if either their father or mother; and this method is better suited to this state than any other: and thus the demagogues have usually managed. They ought, however, to take care, and do this no longer than the common people are superior to the nobles and those of the middle rank, and then stop; for, if they proceed still further, they will make the state disorderly, and the nobles will ill brook the power of the common people, and be full of resentment against it; which was the cause of an insurrection at Cyrene: for a little evil is overlooked, but when it becomes a great one it strikes the eye. It is, moreover, very-useful in such a state to do as Clisthenes did at Athens, when he was desirous of increasing the power of the people, and as those did who established the democracy in Cyrene; that is, to institute many tribes and fraternities, and to make the religious rites of private persons few, and those common; and every means is to be contrived to associate and blend the people together as much as possible; and that all former customs be broken through. Moreover, whatsoever is practised in a tyranny seems adapted to a democracy of this species; as, for instance, the licentiousness of the slaves, the women, and the children; for this to a certain degree is useful in such a state; and also to overlook every one's living as they choose; for many will support such a government: for it is more agreeable to many to live without any control than as prudence would direct.

CHAPTER V

It is also the business of the legislator and all those who would support a government of this sort not to make it too great a work, or too perfect; but to aim only to render it stable: for, let a state be constituted ever so badly, there is no difficulty in its continuing a few days: they should therefore endeavour to procure its safety by all those ways which we have described in assigning the causes of the preservation and destruction of governments; avoiding what is hurtful, and by framing such laws, written and unwritten, as contain those things which chiefly tend to the preservation of the state; nor to suppose that that is useful either for a democratic or an oligarchic form of government which contributes to make them more purely so, but what will contribute to their duration: but our demagogues at present, to flatter the people, occasion frequent confiscations in the courts; for which reason those who have the welfare of the state really at heart should act directly opposite to what they do, and enact a law to prevent forfeitures from being divided amongst the people or paid into the treasury, but to have them set apart for sacred uses: for those who are of a bad disposition would not then be the less cautious, as their punishment would be the same; and the community would not be so ready to condemn those whom they sat in judgment on when they were to get nothing by it: they should also take care that the causes which are brought before the public should be as few as possible, and punish with the utmost severity those who rashly brought an action against any one; for it is not the commons but the nobles who are generally prosecuted: for in all things the citizens of the same state ought to be affectionate to each other, at least not to treat those who have the chief power in it as their enemies. Now, as the democracies which have been lately established are very numerous, and it is difficult to get the common people to attend the public assemblies without they are paid for it, this, when there is not a sufficient public revenue, is fatal to the nobles; for the deficiencies therein must be necessarily made up by taxes, confiscations, and fines imposed by corrupt courts of justice: which things have already destroyed many democracies. Whenever, then, the revenues of the state are small, there should be but few public assemblies and but few courts of justice: these, however, should have very extensive jurisdictions, but should continue sitting a few days only, for by this means the rich would not fear the expense, although they should receive nothing for their attendance, though the poor did; and judgment also would be given much better; for the rich will not choose to be long absent from their own affairs, but will willingly be so for a short time: and, when there are sufficient revenues, a different conduct ought to be pursued from what the demagogues at present follow; for now they divide the surplus of the public money amongst the poor; these receive it and again want the same supply, while the giving it is like pouring water into a sieve: but the true patriot in a democracy ought to take care that the majority of the community are not too poor, for this is the cause of rapacity in that government; he therefore should endeavour that they may enjoy perpetual plenty; and as this also is advantageous to the rich, what can be saved out of the public money should be put by, and then divided at once amongst the poor, if possible, in such a quantity as may enable every one of them to purchase a little field, and, if that cannot be done, at least to give each of them enough to procure the implements of trade and husbandry; and if there is not enough for all to receive so much at once, then to divide it according to tribes or any other allotment. In the meantime let the rich pay them for necessary services, but not be obliged to find them in useless amusements. And something like this was the manner in which they managed at Carthage, and preserved the affections of the people; for by continually sending some of their community into colonies they procured plenty. It is also worthy of a sensible and generous nobility to divide the poor amongst them, and supplying them with what is necessary, induce them to work; or to imitate the conduct of the people at Tarentum: for they, permitting the poor to partake in common of everything which is needful for them, gain the affections of the commonalty. They have also two different ways of electing their magistrates; for some are chosen by vote, others by lot; by the last, that the people at large may have some share in the administration; by the former, that the state may be well governed: the same may be accomplished if of the same magistrates you choose some by vote, others by lot. And thus much for the manner in which democracies ought to be established.

CHAPTER VI

What has been already said will almost of itself sufficiently show how an oligarchy ought to be founded; for he who would frame such a state should have in his view a democracy to oppose it; for every species of oligarchy should be founded on principles diametrically opposite to some species of democracy.

The first and best-framed oligarchy is that which approaches near to what we call a free state; in which there ought to be two different census, the one high, the other low: from those who are within the latter the ordinary officers of the state ought to be chosen; from the former the supreme magistrates: nor should any one be excluded from a part of the administration who was within the census; which should be so regulated that the commonalty who are included in it should by means thereof be superior to those who have no share in the government; for those who are to have the management of public affairs ought always to be chosen out of the better sort of the people. Much in the same manner ought that oligarchy to be established which is next in order: but as to that which is most opposite to a pure democracy, and approaches nearest to a dynasty and a tyranny, as it is of all others the worst, so it requires the greatest care and caution to preserve it: for as bodies of sound and healthy constitutions and ships which are well manned and well found for sailing can bear many injuries without perishing, while a diseased body or a leaky ship with an indifferent crew cannot support the least shock; so the worst-established governments want most looking after. A number of citizens is the preservation of a democracy; for these are opposed to those rights which are founded in rank: on the contrary, the preservation of an oligarchy depends upon the due regulation of the different orders in the society.

CHAPTER VII

As the greater part of the community are divided into four sorts of people; husbandmen, mechanics, traders, and hired servants; and as those who are employed in war may likewise be divided into four; the horsemen, the heavy-armed soldier, the light-armed, and the sailor, where the nature of the country can admit a great number of horse; there a powerful oligarchy may be easily established: for the safety of the inhabitants depends upon a force of that sort; but those who can support the expense of horsemen must be persons of some considerable fortune. Where the troops are chiefly heavy-armed, there an oligarchy, inferior in power to the other, may be established; for the heavy-armed are rather made up of men of substance than the poor: but the light-armed and the sailors always contribute to support a democracy: but where the number of these is very great and a sedition arises, the other parts of the community fight at a disadvantage; but a remedy for this evil is to be learned from skilful generals, who always mix a proper number of light-armed soldiers with their horse and heavy-armed: for it is with those that the populace get the better of the men of fortune in an insurrection; for these being lighter are easily a match for the horse and the heavy-armed: so that for an oligarchy to form a body of troops from these is to form it against itself: but as a city is composed of persons of different ages, some young and some old, the fathers should teach their sons, while they were very young, a light and easy exercise; but, when they are grown up, they should be perfect in every warlike exercise. Now, the admission of the people to any share in the government should either be (as I said before) regulated by a census, or else, as at Thebes, allowed to those who for a certain time have ceased from any mechanic employment, or as at Massalia, where they are chosen according to their worth, whether citizens or foreigners. With respect to the magistrates of the highest rank which it may be necessary to have in a state, the services they are bound to do the public should be expressly laid down, to prevent the common people from being desirous of accepting their employments, and also to induce them to regard their magistrates with favour when they know what a price they pay for their honours. It is also necessary that the magistrates, upon entering into their offices, should make magnificent sacrifices and erect some public structure, that the people partaking of the entertainment, and seeing the city ornamented with votive gifts in their temples and public structures, may see with pleasure the stability of the government: add to this also, that the nobles will have their generosity recorded: but now this is not the conduct which those who are at present at the head of an oligarchy pursue, but the contrary; for they are not more desirous of honour than of gain; for which reason such oligarchies may more properly be called little democracies. Thus we have explained on what principles a democracy and an oligarchy ought to be established.

CHAPTER VIII

After what has been said I proceed next to treat particularly of the magistrates; of what nature they should be, how many, and for what purpose, as I have already mentioned: for without necessary magistrates no state can exist, nor without those which contribute to its dignity and good order can exist happily: now it is necessary that in small states the magistrates should be few; in a large one, many: also to know well what offices may be joined together, and what ought to be separated. The first thing necessary is to establish proper regulators in the markets; for which purpose a certain magistrate should be appointed to inspect their contracts and preserve good order; for of necessity, in almost every city there must be both buyers and sellers to supply each other's mutual wants: and this is what is most productive of the comforts of life; for the sake of which men seem to have joined together in one community. A second care, and nearly related to the first, is to have an eye both to the public and private edifices in the city, that they may be an ornament; and also to take care of all buildings which are likely to fall: and to see that the highways are kept in proper repair; and also that the landmarks between different estates are preserved, that there may be no disputes on that account; and all other business of the same nature. Now, this business may be divided into several branches, over each of which in populous cities they appoint a separate person; one to inspect the buildings, another the fountains, another the harbours; and they are called the inspectors of the city. A third, which is very like the last, and conversant nearly about the same objects, only in the country, is to take care of what is done out of the city. The officers who have this employment we call inspectors of the lands, or inspectors of the woods; but the business of all three of them is the same. There must also be other officers appointed to receive the public revenue and to deliver it out to those who are in the different departments of the state: these are called receivers or quaestors. There must also be another, before whom all private contracts and sentences of courts should be enrolled, as well as proceedings and declarations. Sometimes this employment is divided amongst many, but there is one supreme over the rest; these are called proctors, notaries, and the like. Next to these is an officer whose business is of all others the most necessary, and yet most difficult; namely, to take care that sentence is executed upon those who are condemned; and that every one pays the fines laid on him; and also to have the charge of those who are in prison. This office is very disagreeable on account of the odium attending it, so that no one will engage therein without it is made very profitable, or, if they do, will they be willing to execute it according to law; but it is most necessary, as it is of no service to pass judgment in any cause without that judgment is carried into execution: for without this human society could not subsist: for which reason it is best that this office should not be executed by one person, but by some of the magistrates of the other courts. In like manner, the taking care that those fines which are ordered by the judges are levied should be divided amongst different persons. And as different magistrates judge different causes, let the causes of the young be heard by the young: and as to those which are already brought to a hearing, let one person pass sentence, and another see it executed: as, for instance, let the magistrates who have the care of the public buildings execute the sentence which the inspectors of the markets have passed, and the like in other cases: for by so much the less odium attends those who carry the laws into execution, by so much the easier will they be properly put in force: therefore for the same persons to pass the sentence and to execute it will subject them to general hatred; and if they pass it upon all, they will be considered as the enemies of all. Thus one person has often the custody of the prisoner's body, while another sees the sentence against him executed, as the eleven did at Athens: for which reason it is prudent to separate these offices, and to give great attention thereunto as equally necessary with anything we have already mentioned; for it will certainly happen that men of character will decline accepting this office, and worthless persons cannot properly be entrusted with it, as having themselves rather an occasion for a guard than being qualified to guard others. This, therefore, ought by no means to be a separate office from others; nor should it be continually allotted to any individuals, but the young men; where there is a city-guard, the youths ought in turns to take these offices upon them. These, then, as the most necessary magistrates, ought to be first mentioned: next to these are others no less necessary, but of much higher rank, for they ought to be men of great skill and fidelity. These are they who have the guard of the city, and provide everything that is necessary for war; whose business it is, both in war and peace, to defend the walls and the gates, and to take care to muster and marshal the citizens. Over all these there are sometimes more officers, sometimes fewer: thus in little cities there is only one whom they call either general or polemarch; but where there are horse and light-armed troops, and bowmen, and sailors, they sometimes put distinct commanders over each of these; who again have others under them, according to their different divisions; all of which join together to make one military body: and thus much for this department. Since some of the magistrates, if not all, have business with the public money, it is necessary that there should be other officers, whose employment should be nothing else than to take an account of what they have, and correct any mismanagement therein. But besides all these magistrates there is one who is supreme over them all, who very often has in his own power the disposal of the public revenue and taxes; who presides over the people when the supreme power is in them; for there must be some magistrate who has a power to summon them together, and to preside as head of the state. These are sometimes called preadvisers; but where there are many, more properly a council. These are nearly the civil magistrates which are requisite to a government: but there are other persons whose business is confined to religion; as the priests, and those who are to take care of the temples, that they are kept in proper repair, or, if they fall down, that they may be rebuilt; and whatever else belongs to public worship. This charge is sometimes entrusted to one person, as in very small cities: in others it is delegated to many, and these distinct from the priesthood, as the builders or keepers of holy places, and officers of the sacred revenue. Next to these are those who are appointed to have the general care of all those public sacrifices to the tutelar god of the state, which the laws do not entrust to the priests: and these in different states have different appellations. To enumerate in few words the different departments of all those magistrates who are necessary: these are either religion, war, taxes, expenditures, markets, public buildings, harbours, highways. Belonging to the courts of justice there are scribes to enroll private contracts; and there must also be guards set over the prisoners, others to see the law is executed, council on either side, and also others to watch over the conduct of those who are to decide the causes. Amongst the magistrates also may finally be reckoned those who are to give their advice in public affairs. But separate states, who are peculiarly happy and have leisure to attend to more minute particulars, and are very attentive to good order, require particular magistrates for themselves; such as those who have the government of the women; who are to see the laws are executed; who take care of the boys and preside over their education. To these may be added those who have the care of their gymnastic exercises, their theatres, and every other public spectacle which there may happen to be. Some of these, however, are not of general use; as the governors of the women: for the poor are obliged to employ their wives and children in servile offices for want of slaves. As there are three magistrates to whom some states entrust the supreme power; namely, guardians of the laws, preadvisers, and senators; guardians of the laws suit best to an aristocracy, preadvisers to an oligarchy, and a senate to a democracy. And thus much briefly concerning all magistrates.

BOOK VII

CHAPTER I

He who proposes to make that inquiry which is necessary concerning what government is best, ought first to determine what manner of living is most eligible; for while this remains uncertain it will also be equally uncertain what government is best: for, provided no unexpected accidents interfere, it is highly probable, that those who enjoy the best government will live the most happily according to their circumstances; he ought, therefore, first to know what manner of life is most desirable for all; and afterwards whether this life is the same to the man and the citizen, or different. As I imagine that I have already sufficiently shown what sort of life is best in my popular discourses on that subject, I think I may very properly repeat the same here; as most certainly no one ever called in question the propriety of one of the divisions; namely, that as what is good, relative to man, may be divided into three sorts, what is external, what appertains to the body, and what to the soul, it is evident that all these must conspire to make a man happy: for no one would say that a man was happy who had no fortitude, no temperance, no justice, no prudence; but was afraid of the flies that flew round him: nor would abstain from the meanest theft if he was either hungry or dry, or would murder his dearest friend for a farthing; and also was in every particular as wanting in his understanding as an infant or an idiot. These truths are so evident that all must agree to them; though some may dispute about the quantity and the degree: for they may think, that a very little virtue is sufficient for happiness; but for riches, property, power, honour, and all such things, they endeavour to increase them without bounds: but to such we reply, that it is easy to prove from what experience teaches us in these cases, that these external goods produce not virtue, but virtue them. As to a happy life, whether it is to be found in pleasure or virtue or both, certain it is, that those whose morals are most pure, and whose understandings are best cultivated, will enjoy more of it, although their fortune is but moderate than those do who own an exuberance of wealth, are deficient in those; and this utility any one who reflects may easily convince himself of; for whatsoever is external has its boundary, as a machine, and whatsoever is useful in its excess is either necessarily hurtful, or at best useless to the possessor; but every good quality of the soul the higher it is in degree, so much the more useful it is, if it is permitted on this subject to use the word useful as well as noble. It is also very evident, that the accidents of each subject take place of each other, as the subjects themselves, of which we allow they are accidents, differ from each other in value; so that if the soul is more noble than any outward possession, as the body, both in itself and with respect to us, it must be admitted of course that the best accidents of each must follow the same analogy. Besides, it is for the sake of the soul that these things are desirable; and it is on this account that wise men should desire them, not the soul for them. Let us therefore be well assured, that every one enjoys as much happiness as he possesses virtue and wisdom, and acts according to their dictates; since for this we have the example of GOD Himself, who is completely happy, not from any external good, but in Himself, and because such is His nature. For good fortune is something different from happiness, as every good which depends not on the mind is owing to chance or fortune; but it is not from fortune that any one is wise and just: hence it follows, that that city is happiest which is the best and acts best: for no one can do well who acts not well; nor can the deeds either of man or city be praiseworthy without virtue and wisdom; for whatsoever is just, or wise, or prudent in a man, the same things are just, wise, and prudent in a city.

Thus much by way of introduction; for I could not but just touch upon this subject, though I could not go through a complete investigation of it, as it properly belongs to another question: let us at present suppose so much, that a man's happiest life, both as an individual and as a citizen, is a life of virtue, accompanied with those enjoyments which virtue usually procures. If there are any who are not convinced by what I have said, their doubts shall be answered hereafter, at present we shall proceed according to our intended method.

CHAPTER II

It now remains for us to say whether the happiness of any individual man and the city is the same or different: but this also is evident; for whosoever supposes that riches will make a person happy, must place the happiness of the city in riches if it possesses them; those who prefer a life which enjoys a tyrannic power over others will also think, that the city which has many others under its command is most happy: thus also if any one approves a man for his virtue, he will think the most worthy city the happiest: but here there are two particulars which require consideration, one of which is, whether it is the most eligible life to be a member of the community and enjoy the rights of a citizen, or whether to live as a stranger, without interfering in public affairs; and also what form of government is to be preferred, and what disposition of the state is best; whether the whole community should be eligible to a share in the administration, or only the greater part, and some only: as this, therefore, is a subject of political examination and speculation, and not what concerns the individual, and the first of these is what we are at present engaged in, the one of these I am not obliged to speak to, the other is the proper business of my present design. It is evident that government must be the best which is so established, that every one therein may have it in his power to act virtuously and live happily: but some, who admit that a life of virtue is most eligible, still doubt which is preferable a public life of active virtue, or one entirely disengaged from what is without and spent in contemplation; which some say is the only one worthy of a philosopher; and one of these two different modes of life both now and formerly seem to have been chosen by all those who were the most virtuous men; I mean the public or philosophic. And yet it is of no little consequence on which side the truth lies; for a man of sense must naturally incline to the better choice; both as an individual and a citizen. Some think that a tyrannic government over those near us is the greatest injustice; but that a political one is not unjust: but that still is a restraint on the pleasures and tranquillity of life. Others hold the quite contrary opinion, and think that a public and active life is the only life for man: for that private persons have no opportunity of practising any one virtue, more than they have who are engaged in public life the management of the state. These are their sentiments; others say, that a tyrannical and despotical mode of government is the only happy one; for even amongst some free states the object of their laws seems to be to tyrannise over their neighbours: so that the generality of political institutions, wheresoever dispersed, if they have any one common object in view, have all of them this, to conquer and govern. It is evident, both from the laws of the Lacedaemonians and Cretans, as well as by the manner in which they educated their children, that all which they had in view was to make them soldiers: besides, among all nations, those who have power enough and reduce others to servitude are honoured on that account; as were the Scythians, Persians, Thracians, and Gauls: with some there are laws to heighten the virtue of courage; thus they tell us that at Carthage they allowed every person to wear as many rings for distinction as he had served campaigns. There was also a law in Macedonia, that a man who had not himself killed an enemy should be obliged to wear a halter; among the Scythians, at a festival, none were permitted to drink out of the cup was carried about who had not done the same thing. Among the Iberians, a warlike nation, they fixed as many columns upon a man's tomb as he had slain enemies: and among different nations different things of this sort prevail, some of them established by law, others by custom. Probably it may seem too absurd to those who are willing to take this subject into their consideration to inquire whether it is the business of a legislator to be able to point out by what means a state may govern and tyrannise over its neighbours, whether they will, or will not: for how can that belong either to the politician or legislator which is unlawful? for that cannot be lawful which is done not only justly, but unjustly also: for a conquest may be unjustly made. But we see nothing of this in the arts: for it is the business neither of the physician nor the pilot to use either persuasion or force, the one to his patients, the other to his passengers: and yet many seem to think a despotic government is a political one, and what they would not allow to be just or proper, if exercised over themselves, they will not blush to exercise over others; for they endeavour to be wisely governed themselves, but think it of no consequence whether others are so or not: but a despotic power is absurd, except only where nature has framed the one party for dominion, the other for subordination; and therefore no one ought to assume it over all in general, but those only which are the proper objects thereof: thus no one should hunt men either for food or sacrifice, but what is fit for those purposes, and these are wild animals which are eatable.

Now a city which is well governed might be very happy in itself while it enjoyed a good system of laws, although it should happen to be so situated as to have no connection with any other state, though its constitution should not be framed for war or conquest; for it would then have no occasion for these. It is evident therefore that the business of war is to be considered as commendable, not as a final end, but as the means of procuring it. It is the duty of a good legislator to examine carefully into his state; and the nature of the people, and how they may partake of every intercourse, of a good life, and of the happiness which results from it: and in this respect some laws and customs differ from others. It is also the duty of a legislator, if he has any neighbouring states to consider in what manner he shall oppose each of them, or what good offices he shall show them. But what should be the final end of the best governments will be considered hereafter.

CHAPTER III

We will now speak to those who, while they agree that a life of virtue is most eligible, yet differ in the use of it addressing ourselves to both these parties; for there are some who disapprove of all political governments, and think that the life of one who is really free is different from the life of a citizen, and of all others most eligible: others again think that the citizen is the best; and that it is impossible for him who does nothing to be well employed; but that virtuous activity and happiness are the same thing. Now both parties in some particulars say what is right, in others what is wrong, thus, that the life of a freeman is better than the life of a slave is true, for a slave, as a slave, is employed in nothing honourable; for the common servile employments which he is commanded to perform have nothing virtuous in them; but, on the other hand, it is not true that a submission to all sorts of governments is slavery; for the government of freemen differs not more from the government of slaves than slavery and freedom differ from each other in their nature; and how they do has been already mentioned. To prefer doing of nothing to virtuous activity is also wrong, for happiness consists in action, and many noble ends are produced by the actions of the just and wise. From what we have already determined on this subject, some one probably may think, that supreme power is of all things best, as that will enable a man to command very many useful services from others; so that he who can obtain this ought not to give it up to another, but rather to seize it: and, for this purpose, the father should have no attention or regard for the son, or the son for the father, or friend for friend; for what is best is most eligible: but to be a member of the community and be in felicity is best. What these persons advance might probably be true, if the supreme good was certainly theirs who plunder and use violence to others: but it is most unlikely that it should be so; for it is a mere supposition: for it does not follow that their actions are honourable who thus assume the supreme power over others, without they were by nature as superior to them as a man to a woman, a father to a child, a master to a slave: so that he who so far forsakes the paths of virtue can never return back from whence he departed from them: for amongst equals whatever is fair and just ought to be reciprocal; for this is equal and right; but that equals should not partake of what is equal, or like to like, is contrary to nature: but whatever is contrary to nature is not right; therefore, if there is any one superior to the rest of the community in virtue and abilities for active life, him it is proper to follow, him it is right to obey, but the one alone will not do, but must be joined to the other also: and, if we are right in what we have now said, it follows that happiness consists in virtuous activity, and that both with respect to the community as well as the individual an active life is the happiest: not that an active life must necessarily refer to other persons, as some think, or that those studies alone are practical which are pursued to teach others what to do; for those are much more so whose final object is in themselves, and to improve the judgment and understanding of the man; for virtuous activity has an end, therefore is something practical; nay, those who contrive the plan which others follow are more particularly said to act, and are superior to the workmen who execute their designs. But it is not necessary that states which choose to have no intercourse with others should remain inactive; for the several members thereof may have mutual intercourse with each other; for there are many opportunities for this among the different citizens; the same thing is true of every individual: for, was it otherwise, neither could the Deity nor the universe be perfect; to neither of whom can anything external separately exist. Hence it is evident that that very same life which is happy for each individual is happy also for the state and every member of it.

CHAPTER IV

As I have now finished what was introductory to this subject, and considered at large the nature of other states, it now remains that I should first say what ought to be the establishment of a city which one should form according to one's wish; for no good state can exist without a moderate proportion of what is necessary. Many things therefore ought to be forethought of as desirable, but none of them such as are impossible: I mean relative to the number of citizens and the extent of the territory: for as other artificers, such as the weaver and the shipwright, ought to have such materials as are fit for their work, since so much the better they are, by so much superior will the work itself necessarily be; so also ought the legislator and politician endeavour to procure proper materials for the business they have in hand. Now the first and principal instrument of the politician is the number of the people; he should therefore know how many, and what they naturally ought to be: in like manner the country, how large, and what it is. Most persons think that it is necessary for a city to be large to be happy: but, should this be true, they cannot tell what is a large one and what a small one; for according to the multitude of the inhabitants they estimate the greatness of it; but they ought rather to consider its strength than its numbers; for a state has a certain object in view, and from the power which it has in itself of accomplishing it, its greatness ought to be estimated; as a person might say, that Hippocrates was a greater physician, though not a greater man, than one that exceeded him in the size of his body: but if it was proper to determine the strength of the city from the number of the inhabitants, it should never be collected from the multitude in general who may happen to be in it; for in a city there must necessarily be many slaves, sojourners, and foreigners; but from those who are really part of the city and properly constitute its members; a multitude of these is indeed a proof of a large city, but in a state where a large number of mechanics inhabit, and but few soldiers, such a state cannot be great; for the greatness of the city, and the number of men in it, are not the same thing. This too is evident from fact, that it is very difficult, if not impossible, to govern properly a very numerous body of men; for of all the states which appear well governed we find not one where the rights of a citizen are open to an indiscriminate multitude. And this is also evident from the nature of the thing; for as law is a certain order, so good law is of course a certain good order: but too large a multitude are incapable of this, unless under the government of that DIVINE POWER which comprehends the universe. Not but that, as quantity and variety are usually essential to beauty, the perfection of a city consists in the largeness of it as far as that largeness is consistent with that order already mentioned: but still there is a determinate size to all cities, as well as everything else, whether animals, plants, or machines, for each of these, if they are neither too little nor too big, have their proper powers; but when they have not their due growth, or are badly constructed, as a ship a span long is not properly a ship, nor one of two furlongs length, but when it is of a fit size; for either from its smallness or from its largeness it may be quite useless: so is it with a city; one that is too small has not in itself the power of self-defence, but this is essential to a city: one that is too large is capable of self-defence in what is necessary; but then it is a nation and not a city: for it will be very difficult to accommodate a form of government to it: for who would choose to be the general of such an unwieldy multitude, or who could be their herald but a stentor? The first thing therefore necessary is, that a city should consist of such numbers as will be sufficient to enable the inhabitants to live happily in their political community: and it follows, that the more the inhabitants exceed that necessary number the greater will the city be: but this must not be, as we have already said, without bounds; but what is its proper limit experience will easily show, and this experience is to be collected from the actions both of the governors and the governed. Now, as it belongs to the first to direct the inferior magistrates and to act as judges, it follows that they can neither determine causes with justice nor issue their orders with propriety without they know the characters of their fellow-citizens: so that whenever this happens not to be done in these two particulars, the state must of necessity be badly managed; for in both of them it is not right to determine too hastily and without proper knowledge, which must evidently be the case where the number of the citizens is too many: besides, it is more easy for strangers and sojourners to assume the rights of citizens, as they will easily escape detection in so great a multitude. It is evident, then, that the best boundary for a city is that wherein the numbers are the greatest possible, that they may be the better able to be sufficient in themselves, while at the same time they are not too large to be under the eye and government of the magistrates. And thus let us determine the extent of a city.

CHAPTER V

What we have said concerning a city may nearly be applied to a country; for as to what soil it should be, every one evidently will commend it if it is such as is sufficient in itself to furnish what will make the inhabitants happy; for which purpose it must be able to supply them with all the necessaries of life; for it is the having these in plenty, without any want, which makes them content. As to its extent, it should be such as may enable the inhabitants to live at their ease with freedom and temperance. Whether we have done right or wrong in fixing this limit to the territory shall be considered more minutely hereafter, when we come particularly to inquire into property, and what fortune is requisite for a man to live on, and how and in what manner they ought to employ it; for there are many doubts upon this question, while each party insists upon their own plan of life being carried to an excess, the one of severity, the other of indulgence. What the situation of the country should be it is not difficult to determine, in some particulars respecting that we ought to be advised by those who are skilful in military affairs. It should be difficult of access to an enemy, but easy to the inhabitants: and as we said, that the number of inhabitants ought to be such as can come under the eye of the magistrate, so should it be with the country; for then it is easily defended. As to the position of the city, if one could place it to one's wish, it is convenient to fix it on the seaside: with respect to the country, one situation which it ought to have has been already mentioned, namely, that it should be so placed as easily to give assistance to all places, and also to receive the necessaries of life from all parts, and also wood, or any other materials which may happen to be in the country.

CHAPTER VI

But with respect to placing a city in the neighbourhood of the sea, there are some who have many doubts whether it is serviceable or hurtful to a well-regulated state; for they say, that the resort of persons brought up under a different system of government is disserviceable to the state, as well by impeding the laws as by their numbers; for a multitude of merchants must necessarily arise from their trafficking backward and forward upon the seas, which will hinder the well-governing of the city: but if this inconvenience should not arise, it is evident that it is better, both on account of safety and also for the easier acquisition of the necessaries of life, that both the city and the country should be near the sea; for it is necessary that those who are to sustain the attack of the enemy should be ready with their assistance both by land and by sea, and to oppose any inroad, both ways if possible but if not, at least where they are most powerful, which they may do while they possess both. A maritime situation is also useful for receiving from others what your own country will not produce, and exporting those necessaries of your own growth which are more than you have occasion for; but a city ought to traffic to supply its own wants, and not the wants of others; for those who themselves furnish an open market for every one, do it for the sake of gain; which it is not proper for a well-established state to do, neither should they encourage such a commerce. Now, as we see that many places and cities have docks and harbours lying very convenient for the city, while those who frequent them have no communication with the citadel, and yet they are not too far off, but are surrounded by walls and such-like fortifications, it is evident, that if any good arises from such an intercourse the city will receive it, but if anything hurtful, it will be easy to restrain it by a law declaring and deputing whom the state will allow to have an intercourse with each other, and whom not. As to a naval power, it is by no means doubtful that it is necessary to have one to a certain degree; and this not only for the sake of the city itself, but also because it may be necessary to appear formidable to some of the neighbouring states, or to be able to assist them as well by sea as by land; but to know how great that force should be, the health of the state should be inquired into, and if that appears vigorous and enables her to take the lead of other communities, it is necessary that her force should correspond with her actions. As for that multitude of people which a maritime power creates, they are by no means necessary to a state, nor ought they to make a part of the citizens; for the mariners and infantry, who have the command, are freemen, and upon these depends a naval engagement: but when there are many servants and husbandmen, there they will always have a number of sailors, as we now see happens to some states, as in Heraclea, where they man many triremes, though the extent of their city is much inferior to some others. And thus we determine concerning the country, the port, the city, the sea, and a maritime power: as to the number of the citizens, what that ought to be we have already said.

CHAPTER VII

We now proceed to point out what natural disposition the members of the community ought to be of: but this any one will easily perceive who will cast his eye over the states of Greece, of all others the most celebrated, and also the other different nations of this habitable world. Those who live in cold countries, as the north of Europe, are full of courage, but wanting in understanding and the arts: therefore they are very tenacious of their liberty; but, not being politicians, they cannot reduce their neighbours under their power: but the Asiatics, whose understandings are quick, and who are conversant in the arts, are deficient in courage; and therefore are always conquered and the slaves of others: but the Grecians, placed as it were between these two boundaries, so partake of them both as to be at the same time both courageous and sensible; for which reason Greece continues free, and governed in the best manner possible, and capable of commanding the whole world, could they agree upon one system of policy. Now this is the difference between the Grecians and other nations, that the latter have but one of these qualities, whereas in the former they are both happily blended together. Hence it is evident, that those persons ought to be both sensible and courageous who will readily obey a legislator, the object of whose laws is virtue. As to what some persons say, that the military must be mild and tender to those they know, but severe and cruel to those they know not, it is courage which makes any one lovely; for that is the faculty of the soul which we most admire: as a proof of this, our resentment rises higher against our friends and acquaintance than against those we know not: for which reason Archilaus accusing his friends says very properly to himself, Shall my friends insult me? The spirit of freedom and command also is what all inherit who are of this disposition for courage is commanding and invincible. It also is not right for any one to say, that you should be severe to those you know not; for this behaviour is proper for no one: nor are those who are of a noble disposition harsh in their manners, excepting only to the wicked; and when they are particularly so, it is, as has been already said, against their friends, when they think they have injured them; which is agreeable to reason: for when those who think they ought to receive a favour from any one do not receive it, beside the injury done them, they consider what they are deprived of: hence the saying, "Cruel are the wars of brothers;" and this, "Those who have greatly loved do greatly hate." And thus we have nearly determined how many the inhabitants of a city ought to be, and what their natural disposition, and also the country how large, and of what sort is necessary; I say nearly, because it is needless to endeavour at as great accuracy in those things which are the objects of the senses as in those which are inquired into by the understanding only.

CHAPTER VIII

As in natural bodies those things are not admitted to be parts of them without which the whole would not exist, so also it is evident that in a political state everything that is necessary thereunto is not to be considered as a part of it, nor any other community from whence one whole is made; for one thing ought to be common and the same to the community, whether they partake of it equally or unequally, as, for instance, food, land, or the like; but when one thing is for the benefit of one person, and another for the benefit of another, in this there is nothing like a community, excepting that one makes it and the other uses it; as, for instance, between any instrument employed in making any work, and the workmen, as there is nothing common between the house and the builder, but the art of the builder is employed on the house. Thus property is necessary for states, but property is no part of the state, though many species of it have life; but a city is a community of equals, for the purpose of enjoying the best life possible: but the happiest life is the best which consists in the perfect practice of virtuous energies: as therefore some persons have great, others little or no opportunity of being employed in these, it is evident that this is the cause of the difference there is between the different cities and communities there are to be found; for while each of these endeavour to acquire what is best by various and different means, they give rise to different modes of living and different forms of government. We are now to consider what those things are without which a city cannot possibly exist; for what we call parts of the city must of necessity inhere in it: and this we shall plainly understand, if we know the number of things necessary to a city: first, the inhabitants must have food: secondly, arts, for many instruments are necessary in life: thirdly, arms, for it is necessary that the community should have an armed force within themselves, both to support their government against those of their own body who might refuse obedience to it, and also to defend it from those who might attempt to attack it from without: fourthly, a certain revenue, as well for the internal necessities of the state as for the business of war: fifthly, which is indeed the chief concern, a religious establishment: sixthly in order, but first of all in necessity, a court to determine both criminal and civil causes. These things are absolutely necessary, so to speak, in every state; for a city is a number of people not accidentally met together, but with a purpose of ensuring to themselves sufficient independency and self-protection; and if anything necessary for these purposes is wanting, it is impossible that in such a situation these ends can be obtained. It is necessary therefore that a city should be capable of acquiring all these things: for this purpose a proper number of husbandmen are necessary to procure food, also artificers and soldiers, and rich men, and priests and judges, to determine what is right and proper.

CHAPTER IX

Having determined thus far, it remains that we consider whether all these different employments shall be open to all; for it is possible to continue the same persons always husbandmen, artificers, judges, or counsellors; or shall we appoint different persons to each of those employments which we have already mentioned; or shall some of them be appropriated to particulars, and others of course common to all? but this does not take place in every state, for, as we have already said, it is possible that all may be common to all, or not, but only common to some; and this is the difference between one government and another: for in democracies the whole community partakes of everything, but in oligarchies it is different.

Since we are inquiring what is the best government possible, and it is admitted to be that in which the citizens are happy; and that, as we have already said, it is impossible to obtain happiness without virtue; it follows, that in the best-governed states, where the citizens are really men of intrinsic and not relative goodness, none of them should be permitted to exercise any mechanic employment or follow merchandise, as being ignoble and destructive to virtue; neither should they be husband-men, that they may be at leisure to improve in virtue and perform the duty they owe to the state. With respect to the employments of a soldier, a senator, and a judge, which are evidently necessary to the community, shall they be allotted to different persons, or shall the same person execute both? This question, too, is easily answered: for in some cases the same persons may execute them, in others they should be different, where the different employments require different abilities, as when courage is wanting for one, judgment for the other, there they should be allotted to different persons; but when it is evident, that it is impossible to oblige those who have arms in their hands, and can insist on their own terms, to be always under command; there these different employments should be trusted to one person; for those who have arms in their hands have it in their option whether they will or will not assume the supreme power: to these two (namely, those who have courage and judgment) the government must be entrusted; but not in the same manner, but as nature directs; what requires courage to the young, what requires judgment to the old; for with the young is courage, with the old is wisdom: thus each will be allotted the part they are fit for according to their different merits. It is also necessary that the landed property should belong to these men; for it is necessary that the citizens should be rich, and these are the men proper for citizens; for no mechanic ought to be admitted to the rights of a citizen, nor any other sort of people whose employment is not entirely noble, honourable, and virtuous; this is evident from the principle we at first set out with; for to be happy it is necessary to be virtuous; and no one should say that a city is happy while he considers only one part of its citizens, but for that purpose he ought to examine into all of them. It is evident, therefore, that the landed property should belong to these, though it may be necessary for them to have husbandmen, either slaves, barbarians, or servants. There remains of the different classes of the people whom we have enumerated, the priests, for these evidently compose a rank by themselves; for neither are they to be reckoned amongst the husbandmen nor the mechanics; for reverence to the gods is highly becoming every state: and since the citizens have been divided into orders, the military and the council, and it is proper to offer due worship to the gods, and since it is necessary that those who are employed in their service should have nothing else to do, let the business of the priesthood be allotted to those who are in years. We have now shown what is necessary to the existence of a city, and of what parts it consists, and that husbandmen, mechanic, and mercenary servants are necessary to a city; but that the parts of it are soldiers and sailors, and that these are always different from those, but from each other only occasionally.

CHAPTER X

It seems neither now nor very lately to have been known to those philosophers who have made politics their study, that a city ought to be divided by families into different orders of men; and that the husbandmen and soldiers should be kept separate from each other; which custom is even to this day preserved in Egypt and in Crete; also Sesostris having founded it in Egypt, Minos in Crete. Common meals seem also to have been an ancient regulation, and to have been established in Crete during the reign of Minos, and in a still more remote period in Italy; for those who are the best judges in that country say that one Italus being king of AEnotria., from whom the people, changing their names, were called Italians instead of AEnotrians, and that part of Europe was called Italy which is bounded by the Scylletic Gulf on the one side and the Lametic on the other, the distance between which is about half a day's journey. This Italus, they relate, made the AEnotrians, who were formerly shepherds, husbandmen, and gave them different laws from what they had before, and to have been the first who established common meals, for which reason some of his descendants still use them, and observe some of his laws. The Opici inhabit that part which lies towards the Tyrrhenian Sea, who both now are and formerly were called Ausonians. The Chones inhabited the part toward Iapigia and the Ionian Sea which is called Syrtis. These Chones were descended from the AEnotrians. Hence arose the custom of common meals, but the separation of the citizens into different families from Egypt: for the reign of Sesostris is of much higher antiquity than that of Minos. As we ought to think that most other things were found out in a long, nay, even in a boundless time (reason teaching us that want would make us first invent that which was necessary, and, when that was obtained, then those things which were requisite for the conveniences and ornament of life), so should we conclude the same with respect to a political state; now everything in Egypt bears the marks of the most remote antiquity, for these people seem to be the most ancient of all others, and to have acquired laws and political order; we should therefore make a proper use of what is told us of them, and endeavour to find out what they have omitted. We have already said, that the landed property ought to belong to the military and those who partake of the government of the state; and that therefore the husbandmen should be a separate order of people; and how large and of what nature the country ought to be: we will first treat of the division of the land, and of the husbandmen, how many and of what sort they ought to be; since we by no means hold that property ought to be common, as some persons have said, only thus far, in friendship, it should be their custom to let no citizen want subsistence. As to common meals, it is in general agreed that they are proper in well-regulated cities; my reasons for approving of them shall be mentioned hereafter: they are what all the citizens ought to partake of; but it will not be easy for the poor, out of what is their own, to furnish as much as they are ordered to do, and supply their own house besides. The expense also of religious worship should be defrayed by the whole state. Of necessity therefore the land ought to be divided into two parts, one of which should belong to the community in general, the other to the individuals separately; and each of these parts should again be subdivided into two: half of that which belongs to the public should be appropriated to maintain the worship of the gods, the other half to support the common meals. Half of that which belongs to the individuals should be at the extremity of the country, the other half near the city, so that these two portions being allotted to each person, all would partake of land in both places, which would be both equal and right; and induce them to act in concert with greater harmony in any war with their neighbours: for when the land is not divided in this manner, one party neglects the inroads of the enemy on the borders, the other makes it a matter of too much consequence and more than is necessary; for which reason in some places there is a law which forbids the inhabitants of the borders to have any vote in the council when they are debating upon a war which is made against them as their private interest might prevent their voting impartially. Thus therefore the country ought to be divided and for the reasons before mentioned. Could one have one's choice, the husbandmen should by all means be slaves, not of the same nation, or men of any spirit; for thus they would be laborious in their business, and safe from attempting any novelties: next to these barbarian servants are to be preferred, similar in natural disposition to these we have already mentioned. Of these, let those who are to cultivate the private property of the individual belong to that individual, and those who are to cultivate the public territory belong to the public. In what manner these slaves ought to be used, and for what reason it is very proper that they should have the promise of their liberty made them, as a reward for their services, shall be mentioned hereafter.

CHAPTER XI

We have already mentioned, that both the city and all the country should communicate both with the sea and the continent as much as possible. There are these four things which we should be particularly desirous of in the position of the city with respect to itself: in the first place, health is to be consulted as the first thing necessary: now a city which fronts the east and receives the winds which blow from thence is esteemed most healthful; next to this that which has a northern position is to be preferred, as best in winter. It should next be contrived that it may have a proper situation for the business of government and for defence in war: that in war the citizens may have easy access to it; but that it may be difficult of access to, and hardly to be taken by, the enemy. In the next place particularly, that there may be plenty of water, and rivers near at hand: but if those cannot be found, very large cisterns must be prepared to save rain-water, so that there may be no want of it in case they should be driven into the town in time of war. And as great care should be taken of the health of the inhabitants, the first thing to be attended to is, that the city should have a good situation and a good position; the second is, that they may have good water to drink; and this not be negligently taken care of; for what we chiefly and most frequently use for the support of the body must principally influence the health of it; and this influence is what the air and water naturally have: for which reason in all wise governments the waters ought to be appropriated to different purposes, and if they are not equally good, and if there is not a plenty of necessary water, that which is to drink should be separated from that which is for other uses. As to fortified places, what is proper for some governments is not proper for all; as, for instance, a lofty citadel is proper for a monarchy and an oligarchy; a city built upon a plain suits a democracy; neither of these for an aristocracy, but rather many strong places. As to the form of private houses, those are thought to be best and most useful for their different purposes which are distinct and separate from each other, and built in the modern manner, after the plan of Hippodamus: but for safety in time of war, on the contrary, they should be built as they formerly were; for they were such that strangers could not easily find their way out of them, and the method of access to them such as an enemy could with difficulty find out if he proposed to besiege them. A city therefore should have both these sorts of buildings, which may easily be contrived if any one will so regulate them as the planters do their rows of vines; not that the buildings throughout the city should be detached from each other, only in some parts of it; thus elegance and safety will be equally consulted. With respect to walls, those who say that a courageous people ought not to have any, pay too much respect to obsolete notions; particularly as we may see those who pride themselves therein continually confuted by facts. It is indeed disreputable for those who are equal, or nearly so, to the enemy, to endeavour to take refuge within their walls--but since it very often happens, that those who make the attack are too powerful for the bravery and courage of those few who oppose them to resist, if you would not suffer the calamities of war and the insolence of the enemy, it must be thought the part of a good soldier to seek for safety under the shelter and protection of walls more especially since so many missile weapons and machines have been most ingeniously invented to besiege cities with. Indeed to neglect surrounding a city with a wall would be similar to choosing a country which is easy of access to an enemy, or levelling the eminences of it; or as if an individual should not have a wall to his house lest it should be thought that the owner of it was a coward: nor should this be left unconsidered, that those who have a city surrounded with walls may act both ways, either as if it had or as if it had not; but where it has not they cannot do this. If this is true, it is not only necessary to have walls, but care must be taken that they may be a proper ornament to the city, as well as a defence in time of war; not only according to the old methods, but the modern improvements also: for as those who make offensive war endeavour by every way possible to gain advantages over their adversaries, so should those who are upon the defensive employ all the means already known, and such new ones as philosophy can invent, to defend themselves: for those who are well prepared are seldom first attacked.

CHAPTER XII

As the citizens in general are to eat at public tables in certain companies, and it is necessary that the walls should have bulwarks and towers in proper places and at proper distances, it is evident that it will be very necessary to have some of these in the towers; let the buildings for this purpose be made the ornaments of the walls. As to temples for public worship, and the hall for the public tables of the chief magistrates, they ought to be built in proper places, and contiguous to each other, except those temples which the law or the oracle orders to be separate from all other buildings; and let these be in such a conspicuous eminence, that they may have every advantage of situation, and in the neighbourhood of that part of the city which is best fortified. Adjoining to this place there ought to be a large square, like that which they call in Thessaly The Square of Freedom, in which nothing is permitted to be bought or sold; into which no mechanic nor husbandman, nor any such person, should be permitted to enter, unless commanded by the magistrates. It will also be an ornament to this place if the gymnastic exercises of the elders are performed in it. It is also proper, that for performing these exercises the citizens should be divided into distinct classes, according to their ages, and that the young persons should have proper officers to be with them, and that the seniors should be with the magistrates; for having them before their eyes would greatly inspire true modesty and ingenuous fear. There ought to be another square separate from this for buying and selling, which should be so situated as to be commodious for the reception of goods both by sea and land. As the citizens may be divided into magistrates and priests, it is proper that the public tables of the priests should be in buildings near the temples. Those of the magistrates who preside over contracts, indictments, and such-like, and also over the markets, and the public streets near the square, or some public way, I mean the square where things are bought and sold; for I intended the other for those who are at leisure, and this for necessary business. The same order which I have directed here should be observed also in the country; for there also their magistrates such as the surveyors of the woods and overseers of the grounds, must necessarily have their common tables and their towers, for the purpose of protection against an enemy. There ought also to be temples erected at proper places, both to the gods and the heroes; but it is unnecessary to dwell longer and most minutely on these particulars--for it is by no means difficult to plan these things, it is rather so to carry them into execution; for the theory is the child of our wishes, but the practical part must depend upon fortune; for which reason we shall decline saying anything farther upon these subjects.

CHAPTER XIII

We will now show of what numbers and of what sort of people a government ought to consist, that the state may be happy and well administered. As there are two particulars on which the excellence and perfection of everything depend, one of these is, that the object and end proposed should be proper; the other, that the means to accomplish it should be adapted to that purpose; for it may happen that these may either agree or disagree with each other; for the end we propose may be good, but in taking the means to obtain it we may err; at other times we may have the right and proper means in our power, but the end may be bad, and sometimes we may mistake in both; as in the art of medicine the physician does not sometimes know in what situation the body ought to be, to be healthy; nor what to do to procure the end he aims at. In every art and science, therefore, we should be master of this knowledge, namely, the proper end, and the means to obtain it. Now it is evident that all persons are desirous to live well and be happy; but that some have the means thereof in their own power, others not; and this either through nature or fortune; for many ingredients are necessary to a happy life; but fewer to those who are of a good than to those who are of a bad disposition. There are others who continually have the means of happiness in their own power, but do not rightly apply them. Since we propose to inquire what government is best, namely, that by which a state may be best administered, and that state is best administered where the people are the happiest, it is evident that happiness is a thing we should not be unacquainted with. Now, I have already said in my treatise on Morals (if I may here make any use of what I have there shown), that happiness consists in the energy and perfect practice of virtue; and this not relatively, but simply; I mean by relatively, what is necessary in some certain circumstances; by simply, what is good and fair in itself: of the first sort are just punishments, and restraints in a just cause; for they arise from virtue and are necessary, and on that account are virtuous; though it is more desirable that neither any state nor any individual should stand in need of them; but those actions which are intended either to procure honour or wealth are simply good; the others eligible only to remove an evil; these, on the contrary, are the foundation and means of relative good. A worthy man indeed will bear poverty, disease, and other unfortunate accidents with a noble mind; but happiness consists in the contrary to these (now we have already determined in our treatise on Morals, that he is a man of worth who considers what is good because it is virtuous as what is simply good; it is evident, therefore, that all the actions of such a one must be worthy and simply good): this has led some persons to conclude, that the cause of happiness was external goods; which would be as if any one should suppose that the playing well upon the lyre was owing to the instrument, and not to the art. It necessarily follows from what has been said, that some things should be ready at hand and others procured by the legislator; for which reason in founding a city we earnestly wish that there may be plenty of those things which are supposed to be under the dominion of fortune (for some things we admit her to be mistress over); but for a state to be worthy and great is not only the work of fortune but of knowledge and judgment also. But for a state to be worthy it is necessary that those citizens which are in the administration should be worthy also; but as in our city every citizen is to be so, we must consider how this may be accomplished; for if this is what every one could be, and not some individuals only, it would be more desirable; for then it would follow, that what might be done by one might be done by all. Men are worthy and good three ways; by nature, by custom, by reason. In the first place, a man ought to be born a man, and not any other animal; that is to say, he ought to have both a body and soul; but it avails not to be only born with some things, for custom makes great alterations; for there are some things in nature capable of alteration either way which are fixed by custom, either for the better or the worse. Now, other animals live chiefly a life of nature; and in very few things according to custom; but man lives according to reason also, which he alone is endowed with; wherefore he ought to make all these accord with each other; for if men followed reason, and were persuaded that it was best to obey her, they would act in many respects contrary to nature and custom. What men ought naturally to be, to make good members of a community, I have already determined; the rest of this discourse therefore shall be upon education; for some things are acquired by habit, others by hearing them.

CHAPTER XIV

As every political community consists of those who govern and of those who are governed, let us consider whether during the continuance of their lives they ought to be the same persons or different; for it is evident that the mode of education should be adapted to this distinction. Now, if one man differed from another as much, as we believe, the gods and heroes differ from men: in the first place, being far their superiors in body; and, secondly, in the soul: so that the superiority of the governors over the governed might be evident beyond a doubt, it is certain that it would be better for the one always to govern, the other always to be governed: but, as this is not easy to obtain, and kings are not so superior to those they govern as Scylax informs us they are in India, it is evident that for many reasons it is necessary that all in their turns should both govern and be governed: for it is just that those who are equal should have everything alike; and it is difficult for a state to continue which is founded in injustice; for all those in the country who are desirous of innovation will apply themselves to those who are under the government of the rest, and such will be their numbers in the state, that it will be impossible for the magistrates to get the better of them. But that the governors ought to excel the governed is beyond a doubt; the legislator therefore ought to consider how this shall be, and how it may be contrived that all shall have their equal share in the administration. Now, with respect to this it will be first said, that nature herself has directed us in our choice, laying down the selfsame thing when she has made some young, others old: the first of whom it becomes to obey, the latter to command; for no one when he is young is offended at his being under government, or thinks himself too good for it; more especially when he considers that he himself shall receive the same honours which he pays when he shall arrive at a proper age. In some respects it must be acknowledged that the governors and the governed are the same, in others they are different; it is therefore necessary that their education should be in some respect the same, in others different: as they say, that he will be a good governor who has first learnt to obey. Now of governments, as we have already said, some are instituted for the sake of him who commands; others for him who obeys: of the first sort is that of the master over the servant; of the latter, that of freemen over each other. Now some things which are commanded differ from others; not in the business, but in the end proposed thereby: for which reason many works, even of a servile nature, are not disgraceful for young freemen to perform; for many things which are ordered to be done are not honourable or dishonourable so much in their own nature as in the end which is proposed, and the reason for which they are undertaken. Since then we have determined, that the virtue of a good citizen and good governor is the same as of a good man; and that every one before he commands should have first obeyed, it is the business of the legislator to consider how his citizens may be good men, what education is necessary to that purpose, and what is the final object of a good life. The soul of man may be divided into two parts; that which has reason in itself, and that which hath not, but is capable of obeying its dictates: and according to the virtues of these two parts a man is said to be good: but of those virtues which are the ends, it will not be difficult for those to determine who adopt the division I have already given; for the inferior is always for the sake of the superior; and this is equally evident both in the works of art as well as in those of nature; but that is superior which has reason. Reason itself also is divided into two parts, in the manner we usually divide it; the theoretic and the practical; which division therefore seems necessary for this part also: the same analogy holds good with respect to actions; of which those which are of a superior nature ought always to be chosen by those who have it in their power; for that is always most eligible to every one which will procure the best ends. Now life is divided into labour and rest, war and peace; and of what we do the objects are partly necessary and useful, partly noble: and we should give the same preference to these that we do to the different parts of the soul and its actions, as war to procure peace; labour, rest; and the useful, the noble. The politician, therefore, who composes a body of laws ought to extend his views to everything; the different parts of the soul and their actions; more particularly to those things which are of a superior nature and ends; and, in the same manner, to the lives of men and their different actions.

They ought to be fitted both for labour and war, but rather for rest and peace; and also to do what is necessary and useful, but rather what is fair and noble. It is to those objects that the education of the children ought to tend, and of all the youths who want instruction. All the Grecian states which now seem best governed, and the legislators who founded those states, appear not to have framed their polity with a view to the best end, or to every virtue, in their laws and education; but eagerly to have attended to what is useful and productive of gain: and nearly of the same opinion with these are some persons who have written lately, who, by praising the Lacedaemonian state, show they approve of the intention of the legislator in making war and victory the end of his government. But how contrary to reason this is, is easily proved by argument, and has already been proved by facts (but as the generality of men desire to have an extensive command, that they may have everything desirable in the greater abundance; so Thibron and others who have written on that state seem to approve of their legislator for having procured them an extensive command by continually enuring them to all sorts of dangers and hardships): for it is evident, since the Lacedemonians have now no hope that the supreme power will be in their own hand, that neither are they happy nor was their legislator wise. This also is ridiculous, that while they preserved an obedience to their laws, and no one opposed their being governed by them, they lost the means of being honourable: but these people understand not rightly what sort of government it is which ought to reflect honour on the legislator; for a government of freemen is nobler than despotic power, and more consonant to virtue. Moreover, neither should a city be thought happy, nor should a legislator be commended, because he has so trained the people as to conquer their neighbours; for in this there is a great inconvenience: since it is evident that upon this principle every citizen who can will endeavour to procure the supreme power in his own city; which crime the Lacedaemonians accuse Pausanias of, though he enjoyed such great honours.

Such reasoning and such laws are neither political, useful nor true: but a legislator ought to instil those laws on the minds of men which are most useful for them, both in their public and private capacities. The rendering a people fit for war, that they may enslave their inferiors ought not to be the care of the legislator; but that they may not themselves be reduced to slavery by others. In the next place, he should take care that the object of his government is the safety of those who are under it, and not a despotism over all: in the third place, that those only are slaves who are fit to be only so. Reason indeed concurs with experience in showing that all the attention which the legislator pays to the business of war, and all other rules which he lays down, should have for their object rest and peace; since most of those states (which we usually see) are preserved by war; but, after they have acquired a supreme power over those around them, are ruined; for during peace, like a sword, they lose their brightness: the fault of which lies in the legislator, who never taught them how to be at rest.

CHAPTER XV

As there is one end common to a man both as an individual and a citizen, it is evident that a good man and a good citizen must have the same object in view; it is evident that all the virtues which lead to rest are necessary; for, as we have often said, the end of war is peace, of labour, rest; but those virtues whose object is rest, and those also whose object is labour, are necessary for a liberal life and rest; for we want a supply of many necessary things that we may be at rest. A city therefore ought to be temperate, brave, and patient; for, according to the proverb, "Rest is not for slaves;" but those who cannot bravely face danger are the slaves of those who attack them. Bravery, therefore, and patience are necessary for labour, philosophy for rest, and temperance and justice in both; but these chiefly in time of peace and rest; for war obliges men to be just and temperate; but the enjoyment of pleasure, with the rest of peace, is more apt to produce insolence; those indeed who are easy in their circumstances, and enjoy everything that can make them happy, have great occasion for the virtues of temperance and justice. Thus if there are, as the poets tell us, any inhabitants in the happy isles, to these a higher degree of philosophy, temperance, and justice will be necessary, as they live at their ease in the full plenty of every sensual pleasure. It is evident, therefore, that these virtues are necessary in every state that would be happy or worthy; for he who is worthless can never enjoy real good, much less is he qualified to be at rest; but can appear good only by labour and being at war, but in peace and at rest the meanest of creatures. For which reason virtue should not be cultivated as the Lacedaemonians did; for they did not differ from others in their opinion concerning the supreme good, but in imagining this good was to be procured by a particular virtue; but since there are greater goods than those of war, it is evident that the enjoyment of those which are valuable in themselves should be desired, rather than those virtues which are useful in war; but how and by what means this is to be acquired is now to be considered. We have already assigned three causes on which it will depend; nature, custom, and reason, arid shown what sort of men nature must produce for this purpose; it remains then that we determine which we shall first begin by in education, reason or custom, for these ought always to preserve the most entire harmony with each other; for it may happen that reason may err from the end proposed, and be corrected by custom. In the first place, it is evident that in this as in other things, its beginning or production arises from some principle, and its end also arises from another principle, which is itself an end. Now, with us, reason and intelligence are the end of nature; our production, therefore, and our manners ought to be accommodated to both these. In the next place, as the soul and the body are two distinct things, so also we see that the soul is divided into two parts, the reasoning and not-reasoning, with their habits which are two in number, one belonging to each, namely appetite and intelligence; and as the body is in production before the soul, so is the not-reasoning part of the soul before the reasoning; and this is evident; for anger, will and desire are to be seen in children nearly as soon as they are born; but reason and intelligence spring up as they grow to maturity. The body, therefore, necessarily demands our care before the soul; next the appetites for the sake of the mind; the body for the sake of the soul.

CHAPTER XVI

If then the legislator ought to take care that the bodies of the children are as perfect as possible, his first attention ought to be given to matrimony; at what time and in what situation it is proper that the citizens should engage in the nuptial contract. Now, with respect to this alliance, the legislator ought both to consider the parties and their time of life, that they may grow old at the same part of time, and that their bodily powers may not be different; that is to say, the man being able to have children, but the woman too old to bear them; or, on the contrary, the woman be young enough to produce children, but the man too old to be a father; for from such a situation discords and disputes continually arise. In the next place, with respect to the succession of children, there ought not to be too great an interval of time between them and their parents; for when there is, the parent can receive no benefit from his child's affection, or the child any advantage from his father's protection; neither should the difference in years be too little, as great inconveniences may arise from it; as it prevents that proper reverence being shown to a father by a boy who considers him as nearly his equal in age, and also from the disputes it occasions in the economy of the family. But, to return from this digression, care ought to be taken that the bodies of the children may be such as will answer the expectations of the legislator; this also will be affected by the same means. Since season for the production of children is determined (not exactly, but to speak in general), namely, for the man till seventy years, and the woman till fifty, the entering into the marriage state, as far as time is concerned, should be regulated by these periods. It is extremely bad for the children when the father is too young; for in all animals whatsoever the parts of the young are imperfect, and are more likely to be productive of females than males, and diminutive also in size; the same thing of course necessarily holds true in men; as a proof of this you may see in those cities where the men and women usually marry very young, the people in general are very small and ill framed; in child-birth also the women suffer more, and many of them die. And thus some persons tell us the oracle of Traezenium should be explained, as if it referred to the many women who were destroyed by too early marriages, and not their gathering their fruits too soon. It is also conducive to temperance not to marry too soon; for women who do so are apt to be intemperate. It also prevents the bodies of men from acquiring their full size if they marry before their growth is completed; for this is the determinate period, which prevents any further increase; for which reason the proper time for a woman to marry is eighteen, for a man thirty-seven, a little more or less; for when they marry at that time their bodies are in perfection, and they will also cease to have children at a proper time; and moreover with respect to the succession of the children, if they have them at the time which may reasonably be expected, they will be just arriving into perfection when their parents are sinking down under the load of seventy years. And thus much for the time which is proper for marriage; but moreover a proper season of the year should be observed, as many persons do now, and appropriate the winter for this business. The married couple ought also to regard the precepts of physicians and naturalists, each of whom have treated on these subjects. What is the fit disposition of the body will be better mentioned when we come to speak of the education of the child; we will just slightly mention a few particulars. Now, there is no occasion that any one should have the habit of body of a wrestler to be either a good citizen, or to enjoy a good constitution, or to be the father of healthy children; neither should he be infirm or too much dispirited by misfortunes, but between both these. He ought to have a habit of labour, but not of too violent labour; nor should that be confined to one object only, as the wrestler's is; but to such things as are proper for freemen. These things are equally necessary both for men and women. Women with child should also take care that their diet is not too sparing, and that they use sufficient exercise; which it will be easy for the legislator to effect if he commands them once every day to repair to the worship of the gods who are supposed to preside over matrimony. But, contrary to what is proper for the body, the mind ought to be kept as tranquil as possible; for as plants partake of the nature of the soil, so does the child receive much of the disposition of the mother. With respect to the exposing or bringing up of children, let it be a law, that nothing imperfect or maimed shall be brought up,.......... As the proper time has been pointed out for a man and a woman to enter into the marriage state, so also let us determine how long it is advantageous for the community that they should have children; for as the children of those who are too young are imperfect both in body and mind, so also those whose parents are too old are weak in both: while therefore the body continues in perfection, which (as some poets say, who reckon the different periods of life by sevens) is till fifty years, or four or five more, the children may be equally perfect; but when the parents are past that age it is better they should have no more. With respect to any connection between a man and a woman, or a woman and a man, when either of the parties are betrothed, let it be held in utter detestation on any pretext whatsoever; but should any one be guilty of such a thing after the marriage is consummated, let his infamy be as great as his guilt deserves.

CHAPTER XVII

When a child is born it must be supposed that the strength of its body will depend greatly upon the quality of its food. Now whoever will examine into the nature of animals, and also observe those people who are very desirous their children should acquire a warlike habit, will find that they feed them chiefly with milk, as being best accommodated to their bodies, but without wine, to prevent any distempers: those motions also which are natural to their age are very serviceable; and to prevent any of their limbs from being crooked, on account of their extreme ductility, some people even now use particular machines that their bodies may not be distorted. It is also useful to enure them to the cold when they are very little; for this is very serviceable for their health; and also to enure them to the business of war; for which reason it is customary with many of the barbarians to dip their children in rivers when the water is cold; with others to clothe them very slightly, as among the Celts; for whatever it is possible to accustom children to, it is best to accustom them to it at first, but to do it by degrees: besides, boys have naturally a habit of loving the cold, on account of the heat. These, then, and such-like things ought to be the first object of our attention: the next age to this continues till the child is five years old; during which time it is best to teach him nothing at all, not even necessary labour, lest it should hinder his growth; but he should be accustomed to use so much motion as not to acquire a lazy habit of body; which he will get by various means and by play also: his play also ought to be neither illiberal nor too laborious nor lazy. Their governors and preceptors also should take care what sort of tales and stories it may be proper for them to hear; for all these ought to pave the way for their future instruction: for which reason the generality of their play should be imitations of what they are afterwards to do seriously. They too do wrong who forbid by laws the disputes between boys and their quarrels, for they contribute to increase their growth--as they are a sort of exercise to the body: for the struggles of the heart and the compression of the spirits give strength to those who labour, which happens to boys in their disputes. The preceptors also ought to have an eye upon their manner of life, and those with whom they converse; and to take care that they are never in the company of slaves. At this time and till they are seven years old it is necessary that they should be educated at home. It is also very proper to banish, both from their hearing and sight, everything which is illiberal and the like. Indeed it is as much the business of the legislator as anything else, to banish every indecent expression out of the state: for from a permission to speak whatever is shameful, very quickly arises the doing it, and this particularly with young people: for which reason let them never speak nor hear any such thing: but if it appears that any freeman has done or said anything that is forbidden before he is of age to be thought fit to partake of the common meals, let him be punished by disgrace and stripes; but if a person above that age does so, let him be treated as you would a slave, on account of his being infamous. Since we forbid his speaking everything which is forbidden, it is necessary that he neither sees obscene stories nor pictures; the magistrates therefore are to take care that there are no statues or pictures of anything of this nature, except only to those gods to whom the law permits them, and to which the law allows persons of a certain age to pay their devotions, for themselves, their wives, and children. It should also be illegal for young persons to be present either at iambics or comedies before they are arrived at that age when they are allowed to partake of the pleasures of the table: indeed a good education will preserve them from all the evils which attend on these things. We have at present just touched upon this subject; it will be our business hereafter, when we properly come to it, to determine whether this care of children is unnecessary, or, if necessary, in what manner it must be done; at present we have only mentioned it as necessary. Probably the saying of Theodoras, the tragic actor, was not a bad one: That he would permit no one, not even the meanest actor, to go upon the stage before him, that he might first engage the ear of the audience. The same thing happens both in our connections with men and things: what we meet with first pleases best; for which reason children should be kept strangers to everything which is bad, more particularly whatsoever is loose and offensive to good manners. When five years are accomplished, the two next may be very properly employed in being spectators of those exercises they will afterwards have to learn. There are two periods into which education ought to be divided, according to the age of the child; the one is from his being seven years of age to the time of puberty; the other from thence till he is one-and-twenty: for those who divide ages by the number seven are in general wrong: it is much better to follow the division of nature; for every art and every instruction is intended to complete what nature has left defective: we must first consider if any regulation whatsoever is requisite for children; in the next place, if it is advantageous to make it a common care, or that every one should act therein as he pleases, which is the general practice in most cities; in the third place, what it ought to be.

BOOK VIII

CHAPTER I

No one can doubt that the magistrate ought greatly to interest himself in the care of youth; for where it is neglected it is hurtful to the city, for every state ought to be governed according to its particular nature; for the form and manners of each government are peculiar to itself; and these, as they originally established it, so they usually still preserve it. For instance, democratic forms and manners a democracy; oligarchic, an oligarchy: but, universally, the best manners produce the best government. Besides, as in every business and art there are some things which men are to learn first and be made accustomed to, which are necessary to perform their several works; so it is evident that the same thing is necessary in the practice of virtue. As there is one end in view in every city, it is evident that education ought to be one and the same in each; and that this should be a common care, and not the individual's, as it now is, when every one takes care of his own children separately; and their instructions are particular also, each person teaching them as they please; but what ought to be engaged in ought to be common to all. Besides, no one ought to think that any citizen belongs to him in particular, but to the state in general; for each one is a part of the state, and it is the natural duty of each part to regard the good of the whole: and for this the Lacedaemonians may be praised; for they give the greatest attention to education, and make it public. It is evident, then, that there should be laws concerning education, and that it should be public.

CHAPTER II

What education is, and how children ought to be instructed, is what should be well known; for there are doubts concerning the business of it, as all people do not agree in those things they would have a child taught, both with respect to their improvement in virtue and a happy life: nor is it clear whether the object of it should be to improve the reason or rectify the morals. From the present mode of education we cannot determine with certainty to which men incline, whether to instruct a child in what will be useful to him in life; or what tends to virtue, and what is excellent: for all these things have their separate defenders. As to virtue, there is no particular in which they all agree: for as all do not equally esteem all virtues, it reasonably follows that they will not cultivate the same. It is evident that what is necessary ought to be taught to all: but that which is necessary for one is not necessary for all; for there ought to be a distinction between the employment of a freeman and a slave. The first of these should be taught everything useful which will not make those who know it mean. Every work is to be esteemed mean, and every art and every discipline which renders the body, the mind, or the understanding of freemen unfit for the habit and practice of virtue: for which reason all those arts which tend to deform the body are called mean, and all those employments which are exercised for gain; for they take off from the freedom of the mind and render it sordid. There are also some liberal arts which are not improper for freemen to apply to in a certain degree; but to endeavour to acquire a perfect skill in them is exposed to the faults I have just mentioned; for there is a great deal of difference in the reason for which any one does or learns anything: for it is not illiberal to engage in it for one's self, one's friend, or in the cause of virtue; while, at the same time, to do it for the sake of another may seem to be acting the part of a servant and a slave. The mode of instruction which now prevails seems to partake of both parts.

CHAPTER III

There are four things which it is usual to teach children--reading, gymnastic exercises, and music, to which (in the fourth place) some add painting. Reading and painting are both of them of singular use in life, and gymnastic exercises, as productive of courage. As to music, some persons may doubt, as most persons now use it for the sake of pleasure: but those who originally made it part of education did it because, as has been already said, nature requires that we should not only be properly employed, but to be able to enjoy leisure honourably: for this (to repeat what I have already said) is of all things the principal. But, though both labour and rest are necessary, yet the latter is preferable to the first; and by all means we ought to learn what we should do when at rest: for we ought not to employ that time at play; for then play would be the necessary business of our lives. But if this cannot be, play is more necessary for those who labour than those who are at rest: for he who labours requires relaxation; which play will supply: for as labour is attended with pain and continued exertion, it is necessary that play should be introduced, under proper regulations, as a medicine: for such an employment of the mind is a relaxation to it, and eases with pleasure. Now rest itself seems to partake of pleasure, of happiness, and an agreeable life: but this cannot be theirs who labour, but theirs who are at rest; for he who labours, labours for the sake of some end which he has not: but happiness is an end which all persons think is attended with pleasure and not with pain: but all persons do not agree in making this pleasure consist in the same thing; for each one has his particular standard, correspondent to his own habits; but the best man proposes the best pleasure, and that which arises from the noblest actions. But it is evident, that to live a life of rest there are some things which a man must learn and be instructed in; and that the object of this learning and this instruction centres in their acquisition: but the learning and instruction which is given for labour has for its object other things; for which reason the ancients made music a part of education; not as a thing necessary, for it is not of that nature, nor as a thing useful, as reading, in the common course of life, or for managing of a family, or for learning anything as useful in public life. Painting also seems useful to enable a man to judge more accurately of the productions of the finer arts: nor is it like the gymnastic exercises, which contribute to health and strength; for neither of these things do we see produced by music; there remains for it then to be the employment of our rest, which they had in view who introduced it; and, thinking it a proper employment for freemen, to them they allotted it; as Homer sings:

"How right to call Thalia to the feast:"

and of some others he says:

"The bard was call'd, to ravish every ear:"

and, in another place, he makes Ulysses say the happiest part of man's life is

"When at the festal board, in order plac'd, They hear the song."

It is evident, then, that there is a certain education in which a child may be instructed, not as useful nor as necessary, but as noble and liberal: but whether this is one or more than one, and of what sort they are, and how to be taught, shall be considered hereafter: we are now got so far on our way as to show that we have the testimony of the ancients in our favour, by what they have delivered down upon education--for music makes this plain. Moreover, it is necessary to instruct children in what is useful, not only on account of its being useful in itself, as, for instance, to learn to read, but also as the means of acquiring other different sorts of instruction: thus they should be instructed in painting, not only to prevent their being mistaken in purchasing pictures, or in buying or selling of vases, but rather as it makes them judges of the beauties of the human form; for to be always hunting after the profitable ill agrees with great and freeborn souls. As it is evident whether a boy should be first taught morals or reasoning, and whether his body or his understanding should be first cultivated, it is plain that boys should be first put under the care of the different masters of the gymnastic arts, both to form their bodies and teach them their exercises.

CHAPTER IV

Now those states which seem to take the greatest care of their children's education, bestow their chief attention on wrestling, though it both prevents the increase of the body and hurts the form of it. This fault the Lacedaemonians did not fall into, for they made their children fierce by painful labour, as chiefly useful to inspire them with courage: though, as we have already often said, this is neither the only thing nor the principal thing necessary to attend to; and even with respect to this they may not thus attain their end; for we do not find either in other animals, or other nations, that courage necessarily attends the most cruel, but rather the milder, and those who have the dispositions of lions: for there are many people who are eager both to kill men and to devour human flesh, as the Achaeans and Heniochi in Pontus, and many others in Asia, some of whom are as bad, others worse than these, who indeed live by tyranny, but are men of no courage. Nay, we know that the Lacedaemonians themselves, while they continued those painful labours, and were superior to all others (though now they are inferior to many, both in war and gymnastic exercises), did not acquire their superiority by training their youth to these exercises, but because those who were disciplined opposed those who were not disciplined at all. What is fair and honourable ought then to take place in education of what is fierce and cruel: for it is not a wolf, nor any other wild beast, which will brave any noble danger, but rather a good man. So that those who permit boys to engage too earnestly in these exercises, while they do not take care to instruct them in what is necessary to do, to speak the real truth, render them mean and vile, accomplished only in one duty of a citizen, and in every other respect, as reason evinces, good for nothing. Nor should we form our judgments from past events, but from what we see at present: for now they have rivals in their mode of education, whereas formerly they had not. That gymnastic exercises are useful, and in what manner, is admitted; for during youth it is very proper to go through a course of those which are most gentle, omitting that violent diet and those painful exercises which are prescribed as necessary; that they may not prevent the growth of the body: and it is no small proof that they have this effect, that amongst the Olympic candidates we can scarce find two or three who have gained a victory both when boys and men: because the necessary exercises they went through when young deprived them of their strength. When they have allotted three years from the time of puberty to other parts of education, they are then of a proper age to submit to labour and a regulated diet; for it is impossible for the mind and body both to labour at the same time, as they are productive of contrary evils to each other; the labour of the body preventing the progress of the mind, and the mind of the body.

CHAPTER V

With respect to music we have already spoken a little in a doubtful manner upon this subject. It will be proper to go over again more particularly what we then said, which may serve as an introduction to what any other person may choose to offer thereon; for it is no easy matter to distinctly point out what power it has, nor on what accounts one should apply it, whether as an amusement and refreshment, as sleep or wine; as these are nothing serious, but pleasing, and the killers of care, as Euripides says; for which reason they class in the same order and use for the same purpose all these, namely, sleep, wine, and music, to which some add dancing; or shall we rather suppose that music tends to be productive of virtue, having a power, as the gymnastic exercises have to form the body in a certain way, to influence the manners so as to accustom its professors to rejoice rightly? or shall we say, that it is of any service in the conduct of life, and an assistant to prudence? for this also is a third property which has been attributed to it. Now that boys are not to be instructed in it as play is evident; for those who learn don't play, for to learn is rather troublesome; neither is it proper to permit boys at their age to enjoy perfect leisure; for to cease to improve is by no means fit for what is as yet imperfect; but it may be thought that the earnest attention of boys in this art is for the sake of that amusement they will enjoy when they come to be men and completely formed; but, if this is the case, why are they themselves to learn it, and not follow the practice of the kings of the Medes and Persians, who enjoy the pleasure of music by hearing others play, and being shown its beauties by them; for of necessity those must be better skilled therein who make this science their particular study and business, than those who have only spent so much time at it as was sufficient just to learn the principles of it. But if this is a reason for a child's being taught anything, they ought also to learn the art of cookery, but this is absurd. The same doubt occurs if music has a power of improving the manners; for why should they on this account themselves learn it, and not reap every advantage of regulating the passions or forming a judgment on the merits of the performance by hearing others, as the Lacedaemonians; for they, without having ever learnt music, are yet able to judge accurately what is good and what is bad; the same reasoning may be applied if music is supposed to be the amusement of those who live an elegant and easy life, why should they learn themselves, and not rather enjoy the benefit of others' skill. Let us here consider what is our belief of the immortal gods in this particular. Now we find the poets never represent Jupiter himself as singing and playing; nay, we ourselves treat the professors of these arts as mean people, and say that no one would practise them but a drunkard or a buffoon. But probably we may consider this subject more at large hereafter. The first question is, whether music is or is not to make a part of education? and of those three things which have been assigned as its proper employment, which is the right? Is it to instruct, to amuse, or to employ the vacant hours of those who live at rest? or may not all three be properly allotted to it? for it appears to partake of them all; for play is necessary for relaxation, and relaxation pleasant, as it is a medicine for that uneasiness which arises from labour. It is admitted also that a happy life must be an honourable one, and a pleasant one too, since happiness consists in both these; and we all agree that music is one of the most pleasing things, whether alone or accompanied with a voice; as Musseus says, "Music's the sweetest joy of man;" for which reason it is justly admitted into every company and every happy life, as having the power of inspiring joy. So that from this any one may suppose that it is necessary to instruct young persons in it; for all those pleasures which are harmless are not only conducive to the final end of life, but serve also as relaxations; and, as men are but rarely in the attainment of that final end, they often cease from their labour and apply to amusement, with no further view than to acquire the pleasure attending it. It is therefore useful to enjoy such pleasures as these. There are some persons who make play and amusement their end, and probably that end has some pleasure annexed to it, but not what should be; but while men seek the one they accept the other for it; because there is some likeness in human actions to the end; for the end is pursued for the sake of nothing else that attends it; but for itself only; and pleasures like these are sought for, not on account of what follows them, but on account of what has gone before them, as labour and grief; for which reason they seek for happiness in these sort of pleasures; and that this is the reason any one may easily perceive. That music should be pursued, not on this account only, but also as it is very serviceable during the hours of relaxation from labour, probably no one doubts; we should also inquire whether besides this use it may not also have another of nobler nature--and we ought not only to partake of the common pleasure arising from it (which all have the sensation of, for music naturally gives pleasure, therefore the use of it is agreeable to all ages and all dispositions); but also to examine if it tends anything to improve our manners and our souls. And this will be easily known if we feel our dispositions any way influenced thereby; and that they are so is evident from many other instances, as well as the music at the Olympic games; and this confessedly fills the soul with enthusiasm; but enthusiasm is an affection of the soul which strongly agitates the disposition. Besides, all those who hear any imitations sympathise therewith; and this when they are conveyed even without rhythm or verse. Moreover, as music is one of those things which are pleasant, and as virtue itself consists in rightly enjoying, loving, and hating, it is evident that we ought not to learn or accustom ourselves to anything so much as to judge right and rejoice in honourable manners and noble actions. But anger and mildness, courage and modesty, and their contraries, as well as all other dispositions of the mind, are most naturally imitated by music and poetry; which is plain by experience, for when we hear these our very soul is altered; and he who is affected either with joy or grief by the imitation of any objects, is in very nearly the same situation as if he was affected by the objects themselves; thus, if any person is pleased with seeing a statue of any one on no other account but its beauty, it is evident that the sight of the original from whence it was taken would also be pleasing; now it happens in the other senses there is no imitation of manners; that is to say, in the touch and the taste; in the objects of sight, a very little; for these are merely representations of things, and the perceptions which they excite are in a manner common to all. Besides, statues and paintings are not properly imitations of manners, but rather signs and marks which show the body is affected by some passion. However, the difference is not great, yet young men ought not to view the paintings of Pauso, but of Polygnotus, or any other painter or statuary who expresses manners. But in poetry and music there are imitations of manners; and this is evident, for different harmonies differ from each other so much by nature, that those who hear them are differently affected, and are not in the same disposition of mind when one is performed as when another is; the one, for instance, occasions grief and contracts the soul, as the mixed Lydian: others soften the mind, and as it were dissolve the heart: others fix it in a firm and settled state, such is the power of the Doric music only; while the Phrygian fills the soul with enthusiasm, as has been well described by those who have written philosophically upon this part of education; for they bring examples of what they advance from the things themselves. The same holds true with respect to rhythm; some fix the disposition, others occasion a change in it; some act more violently, others more liberally. From what has been said it is evident what an influence music has over the disposition of the mind, and how variously it can fascinate it: and if it can do this, most certainly it is what youth ought to be instructed in. And indeed the learning of music is particularly adapted to their disposition; for at their time of life they do not willingly attend to anything which is not agreeable; but music is naturally one of the most agreeable things; and there seems to be a certain connection between harmony and rhythm; for which reason some wise men held the soul itself to be harmony; others, that it contains it.

CHAPTER VI

We will now determine whether it is proper that children should be taught to sing, and play upon any instrument, which we have before made a matter of doubt. Now, it is well known that it makes a great deal of difference when you would qualify any one in any art, for the person himself to learn the practical part of it; for it is a thing very difficult, if not impossible, for a man to be a good judge of what he himself cannot do. It is also very necessary that children should have some employment which will amuse them; for which reason the rattle of Archytas seems well contrived, which they give children to play with, to prevent their breaking those things which are about the house; for at their age they cannot sit still: this therefore is well adapted to infants, as instruction ought to be their rattle as they grow up; hence it is evident that they should be so taught music as to be able to practise it. Nor is it difficult to say what is becoming or unbecoming of their age, or to answer the objections which some make to this employment as mean and low. In the first place, it is necessary for them to practise, that they may be judges of the art: for which reason this should be done when they are young; but when they are grown older the practical part may be dropped; while they will still continue judges of what is excellent in the art, and take a proper pleasure therein, from the knowledge they acquired of it in their youth. As to the censure which some persons throw upon music, as something mean and low, it is not difficult to answer that, if we will but consider how far we propose those who are to be educated so as to become good citizens should be instructed in this art, and what music and what rhythms they should be acquainted with; and also what instruments they should play upon; for in these there is probably a difference. Such then is the proper answer to that censure: for it must be admitted, that in some cases nothing can prevent music being attended, to a certain degree, with the bad effects which are ascribed to it; it is therefore clear that the learning of it should never prevent the business of riper years; nor render the body effeminate, and unfit for the business of war or the state; but it should be practised by the young, judged of by the old. That children may learn music properly, it is necessary that they should not be employed in those parts of it which are the objects of dispute between the masters in that science; nor should they perform such pieces as are wondered at from the difficulty of their execution; and which, from being first exhibited in the public games, are now become a part of education; but let them learn so much of it as to be able to receive proper pleasure from excellent music and rhythms; and not that only which music must make all animals feel, and also slaves and boys, but more. It is therefore plain what instruments they should use; thus, they should never be taught to play upon the flute, or any other instrument which requires great skill, as the harp or the like, but on such as will make them good judges of music, or any other instruction: besides, the flute is not a moral instrument, but rather one that will inflame the passions, and is therefore rather to be used when the soul is to be animated than when instruction is intended. Let me add also, that there is something therein which is quite contrary to what education requires; as the player on the flute is prevented from speaking: for which reason our forefathers very properly forbade the use of it to youth and freemen, though they themselves at first used it; for when their riches procured them greater leisure, they grew more animated in the cause of virtue; and both before and after the Median war their noble actions so exalted their minds that they attended to every part of education; selecting no one in particular, but endeavouring to collect the whole: for which reason they introduced the flute also, as one of the instruments they were to learn to play on. At Lacedaemon the choregus himself played on the flute; and it was so common at Athens that almost every freeman understood it, as is evident from the tablet which Thrasippus dedicated when he was choregus; but afterwards they rejected it as dangerous; having become better judges of what tended to promote virtue and what did not. For the same reason many of the ancient instruments were thrown aside, as the dulcimer and the lyre; as also those which were to inspire those who played on them with pleasure, and which required a nice finger and great skill to play well on. What the ancients tell us, by way of fable, of the flute is indeed very rational; namely, that after Minerva had found it, she threw it away: nor are they wrong who say that the goddess disliked it for deforming the face of him who played thereon: not but that it is more probable that she rejected it as the knowledge thereof contributed nothing to the improvement of the mind. Now, we regard Minerva as the inventress of arts and sciences. As we disapprove of a child's being taught to understand instruments, and to play like a master (which we would have confined to those who are candidates for the prize in that science; for they play not to improve themselves in virtue, but to please those who hear them, and gratify their importunity); therefore we think the practice of it unfit for freemen; but then it should be confined to those who are paid for doing it; for it usually gives people sordid notions, for the end they have in view is bad: for the impertinent spectator is accustomed to make them change their music; so that the artists who attend to him regulate their bodies according to his motions.

CHAPTER VII

We are now to enter into an inquiry concerning harmony and rhythm; whether all sorts of these are to be employed in education, or whether some peculiar ones are to be selected; and also whether we should give the same directions to those who are engaged in music as part of education, or whether there is something different from these two. Now, as all music consists in melody and rhythm, we ought not to be unacquainted with the power which each of these has in education; and whether we should rather choose music in which melody prevails, or rhythm: but when I consider how many things have been well written upon these subjects, not only by some musicians of the present age, but also by some philosophers who are perfectly skilled in that part of music which belongs to education; we will refer those who desire a very particular knowledge therein to those writers, and shall only treat of it in general terms, without descending to particulars. Melody is divided by some philosophers, whose notions we approve of, into moral, practical, and that which fills the mind with enthusiasm: they also allot to each of these a particular kind of harmony which naturally corresponds therewith: and we say that music should not be applied to one purpose only, but many; both for instruction and purifying the soul (now I use the word purifying at present without any explanation, but shall speak more at large of it in my Poetics); and, in the third place, as an agreeable manner of spending the time and a relaxation from the uneasiness of the mind. It is evident that all harmonies are to be used; but not for all purposes; but the most moral in education: but to please the ear, when others play, the most active and enthusiastic; for that passion which is to be found very strong in some souls is to be met with also in all; but the difference in different persons consists in its being in a less or greater degree, as pity, fear, and enthusiasm also; which latter is so powerful in some as to overpower the soul: and yet we see those persons, by the application of sacred music to soothe their mind, rendered as sedate and composed as if they had employed the art of the physician: and this must necessarily happen to the compassionate, the fearful, and all those who are subdued by their passions: nay, all persons, as far as they are affected with those passions, admit of the same cure, and are restored to tranquillity with pleasure. In the same manner, all music which has the power of purifying the soul affords a harmless pleasure to man. Such, therefore, should be the harmony and such the music which those who contend with each other in the theatre should exhibit: but as the audience is composed of two sorts of people, the free and the well-instructed, the rude the mean mechanics, and hired servants, and a long collection of the like, there must be some music and some spectacles to please and soothe them; for as their minds are as it were perverted from their natural habits, so also is there an unnatural harmony, and overcharged music which is accommodated to their taste: but what is according to nature gives pleasure to every one, therefore those who are to contend upon the theatre should be allowed to use this species of music. But in education ethic melody and ethic harmony should be used, which is the Doric, as we have already said, or any other which those philosophers who are skilful in that music which is to be employed in education shall approve of. But Socrates, in Plato's Republic, is very wrong when he permits only the Phrygian music to be used as well as the Doric, particularly as amongst other instruments he banishes the flute; for the Phrygian music has the same power in harmony as the flute has amongst the instruments; for they are both pathetic and raise the mind: and this the practice of the poets proves; for in their bacchanal songs, or whenever they describe any violent emotions of the mind, the flute is the instrument they chiefly use: and the Phrygian harmony is most suitable to these subjects. Now, that the dithyrambic measure is Phrygian is allowed by general consent; and those who are conversant in studies of this sort bring many proofs of it; as, for instance, when Philoxenus endeavoured to compose dithyrambic music for Doric harmony, he naturally fell back again into Phrygian, as being fittest for that purpose; as every one indeed agrees, that the Doric music is most serious, and fittest to inspire courage: and, as we always commend the middle as being between the two extremes, and the Doric has this relation with respect to other harmonies, it is evident that is what the youth ought to be instructed in. There are two things to be taken into consideration, both what is possible and what is proper; every one then should chiefly endeavour to attain those things which contain both these qualities: but this is to be regulated by different times of life; for instance, it is not easy for those who are advanced in years to sing such pieces of music as require very high notes, for nature points out to them those which are gentle and require little strength of voice (for which reason some who are skilful in music justly find fault with Socrates for forbidding the youth to be instructed in gentle harmony; as if, like wine, it would make them drunk, whereas the effect of that is to render men bacchanals, and not make them languid): these therefore are what should employ those who are grown old. Moreover, if there is any harmony which is proper for a child's age, as being at the same time elegant and instructive, as the Lydian of all others seems chiefly to be-These then are as it were the three boundaries of education, moderation, possibility, and decorum.

www.ingramcontent.com/pod-product-compliance
Lightning Source LLC
Chambersburg PA
CBHW031809190326
41518CB00006B/261